1001 LETTERS FOR ALL OCCASIONS

1001 LETTERS FOR ALL OCCASIONS

The Best Models for Every Business and Personal Need

COREY SANDLER AND JANICE KEEFE

Adams Media
Avon, Massachusetts

Published by
Adams Media, a division of F+W Media, Inc.
57 Littlefield Street, Avon, MA 02322. U.S.A.
www.adamsmedia.com

ISBN 10: 1-58062-890-7
ISBN 13: 978-1-58062-890-7
Printed in the United States of America.

J I H

Library of Congress Cataloging-in-Publication Data
Sandler, Corey
1,001 letters for all occasions / Corey Sandler and Janice Keefe.
p. cm.
ISBN 1-58062-890-7
1. Letter writing. 2. English language—Rhetoric. 3. Form letters.
I. Title: One thousand and one letters for all occasions. II. Title: One
thousand one letters for all occasions. III. Keefe, Janice. IV. Title.
PE1483.S215 2004
395.4—dc21
2003004467

Dedication

To our children William and Tessa, in college.
Would you send us a letter sometime?

—*The Authors*

Contents

Acknowledgments

Dear Reader:

A letter is pretty unique as a form of communication—one person can conceive of its message, put pen to paper (or fingers to keyboard) to produce it, and even hand-deliver it to its intended recipient.

Not so with a book. Though this book bears just two names on the cover, in truth there were dozens of capable and creative people involved in its conceptualization, design, production, and distribution.

We'd like to thank Bob Adams and his capable editors and production staff, including Gary Krebs, Kate Epstein, and Kate Petrella. Thanks, too, to Gene Brissie, godfather of this and many other books we have written over the years.

And most of all, thanks to you, dear reader, for buying this book. We wish you great success in all of your communications.

Best regards,
Corey Sandler and Janice Keefe

About This Book

Dear Reader:

Put it in writing. For some people these are threatening words.

Yet we all need to prepare letters throughout our lives: letters to employers, to schools, to doctors, to insurance companies, to friends, to strangers. Sometimes the letters are formal, sometimes breezily casual, sometimes printed, sometimes handwritten, and sometimes dispatched with the click of a mouse as an e-mail.

Every situation may seem one-of-a-kind, but in fact nearly all of our letters are based on common underpinnings: a request or a complaint or a compliment. In *1001 Letters for All Occasions,* you'll find examples to help you get started.

These letters are yours for the copying, adapting, rewriting, and inspiration. You may find one letter that exactly matches your needs; more likely, you'll find bits and pieces from several letters that you can put together—with your own specifics—into a written communication of your own.

Sincerely,
The Authors

About the Authors

Dear Reader:

We expect you are wondering what gives Corey Sandler and Janice Keefe the right stuff to write this book.

We'd like to think our combined backgrounds give an encouraging answer.

Corey Sandler is the author of more than 150 books on business, travel, and entertainment topics. He has worked more than thirty-five years in communications: as a newspaper and wire service reporter for Gannett Newspapers and the Associated Press, as director of public information for an agency of the New York State government, and as editor-in-chief of two national business publications. For the past decade he has worked full-time as an author of nonfiction books and packaging of other titles through his company Word Association, Inc.

Among his current bestselling books are *Fix Your Own PC,* Seventh Edition, from Wiley Press, and the Econoguide Travel Book Series from Globe-Pequot Press. You can see his current titles on the Internet, at *www.econoguide.com.*

Janice Keefe worked for Hearst Newspapers and an agency of the New York State government before joining Word Association, Inc., as manager.

If you'd like to write to the authors, please see the final letter in this book for our particulars.

Sincerely,
Corey Sandler and Janice Keefe

1 The Basics

Dear Reader:

Ready?
Fire!
Aim.

How often have you thought that was your game plan when it came to communicating your needs, wants, and wishes? You're ready to express yourself. Boom—you fire your best shot. And then . . . you wish you had been a bit more prepared, organized, and clear.

That's one of the great advantages of writing a letter. It's an exercise that requires planning and clarity of thought, and it allows the luxury of editing your words before they are dispatched.

The end result of a letter is a logically organized, carefully stated announcement, request, demand, or complaint.

Not all that many years ago, letters were the primary means of formal and business communication. To invite someone to a dinner, you sent a note. To buy something from afar, you dispatched a written order. To register a complaint or make a request, you crafted a letter.

Today, letters are still a fine way to communicate with precision, and in this book you'll find 1,001 examples to serve as models. But these days we are also just as likely—probably more likely—to communicate by telephone or e-mail or in person.

Our view is this: The act of creating a letter—whether you end up sending it by mail or using it as the preparation for a phone call, e-mail, or face-to-face conversation—is a tremendously valuable exercise in establishing clear and unambiguous communication.

This book presents hundreds of classic and ultramodern situations in which we are called upon to communicate. The letters in this book range from formal announcements and invitations to casual notes to teachers and friends. We'll give examples of letters you might write in search of a job, in complaint about a noisy neighbor, or in support of a friend in need. There are examples of letters that ask for a refund for shoddy merchandise or praise the extra effort of a salesperson or a public servant.

Although the purpose of this book is to help you get started on writing your own letters, we hope you'll enjoy reading all of the examples in this book. Think of this book as an epistolary novel—a story told in the form of letters.

Our universe of examples is centered around the wondrously diverse (and totally fictitious) world of Smalltown, Ohio, a place that has a little bit of just about everything: schools, churches, charities, small businesses, insurance companies, a hospital, police and fire departments, and a local government. The events referred to in the letters take place over a period of a few years. You'll meet a cast of characters who are not afraid to put pen to paper, or fingers to keyboard, in pursuit of their rights and interests.

We concentrate on letters from individuals and community organizations, but you'll also find a selection of basic letters from small businesses.

Please note that none of the names of people, companies, or organizations are meant to represent actual people or groups, and any similarity to real entities is purely coincidental.

You are welcome to adapt any of the letters in this book to your own needs. You also can mix and match elements of the letters if that helps you to communicate with clarity.

Remember your goal: ready, ***aim,*** fire.

Sincerely,
Corey Sandler and Janice Keefe

Why Write a Letter?

Dear Reader:

Why write a letter?

How many times in your life have you regretted something you said in an off-the-cuff phone call or a direct conversation with a friend or business acquaintance? And how often do you wish you had a copy of what you said to someone to refer to later?

A phone call is quick, and it is an excellent way to convey a bit of information: I'll be home soon, something has happened, your order has shipped.

But a letter is the best way to convey feelings, or to communicate with authority: I'm so sorry, I'm so happy, I need to formally advise you of something.

A letter gives you the opportunity to craft your message and to review it for clarity, accuracy, and the proper tone. (One of the advantages of the computer age is the ease of creating a large number of drafts of letters before committing the final version to print. Even if you're writing your letter by hand, you still have control over its final form.)

And there are some very important human qualities that come in the envelope with a letter.

For most people, the act of writing a letter is the gateway to introspection. In personal letters, the act of putting something down in writing helps you think about yourself and the person to whom you are writing.

For a business letter, the process gives the writer the time to carefully consider goals and means.

And the recipient of a letter knows that someone was thinking of them, and willing to devote the time to put words in print.

With great care,
The Authors

Sometimes, the First Thing We Do Is Send in the Lawyers

Dear Reader:

A letter puts you on record. The recipient can keep your words forever, and refer to it many times. As the sender, you can keep a copy of your letter as evidence of any statements or promises you made.

Of course, it is this near-permanency that makes for legal evidence. In some circumstances a lawyer will insist that communications be made in writing in order to preserve a record of promises or threats; at other times, a lawyer may advise that nothing be put down in writing to protect against a permanent, indisputable record.

If you have any concerns that your communication may expose you to legal risk, you should consult a lawyer or other professional adviser. Most state bar associations and many local legal organizations offer free or low-cost consultations, allowing you to ask for advice or assistance on legal issues before they become court cases.

If you are writing a letter from a business and there are any legal issues involved, consider consulting the corporate attorney, your company's human resources department, or a public company's investor relations manager.

With all due consideration,
The Authors

How to Write a Letter

Dear Reader:

Writing a clear and concise letter is a combination of art and science.

The art lies in choosing the right words and using them in a way that clearly communicates your intent.

The science involves the proper form for a letter: the return address, the addressee, the salutation, and the closing. This book is not intended to teach—or even to observe—every last one of the ages-old rules of etiquette and the modern conception of political correctness. Each of the letters is acceptable and appropriate to the occasion and its formality.

Our theory of letter writing begins with a step you need to take before you even begin to write a letter. First you must imagine that the person with whom you are hoping to communicate is seated across the table from you. Then consider that you have just one moment to convey your message, make your complaint, or ask your favor. What would you say?

The value of this exercise is to come up with what Hollywood screenwriters call the "high concept." It's the idea that a thousand-page novel or a two-hour movie or a complex six-page letter can be distilled into a single sentence that sums up its point.

If William Shakespeare were pitching a movie based on Romeo and Juliet, he might be forced to say, "A great love, split by a family feud and destroyed in a tragic misunderstanding."

The bottom line of the movie Titanic could be: "Boy meets girl, ship hits iceberg, girl loses boy, girl keeps pendant."

And if you were to sum up your detailed letter of complaint to the mayor, the high concept might be: "I am very unhappy with the condition of the road in front of my house and I want you to do something about it immediately."

You may note one significant difference between the summation of the play and movie, and the recap of the letter: this letter—and nearly every example you'll find in this book—makes use of the active voice.

Examples of the *active voice* follow:

> I feel unhappy. I announce something. I want you to do something. I invite you to attend an event. I object to your policy. I want a refund.

Compare them to the soporific tone of the *passive voice:*

> It would be appreciated if you would assist. An invitation is enclosed. We are registering an objection to your policy. A refund is due us.

Remember to aim before you fire. Stop to consider the intent of your letter.

In this book, we'll give you 1,001 examples of letters in which the high concept is evident and the message is clear.

Sincerely,
The Authors

The Elements of a Letter

Dear Reader:

Writing a letter without making a plan is like setting out to bake a cake without consulting a recipe and gathering the ingredients.

And so, before we say a word about writing a productive letter, let's explore the three basic ingredients:

- An unambiguous declaration of your goal.
- A clear and accurate statement of the facts.
- A courteous but firm tone.

As we go through this book, we'll help you concoct a recipe for each type of letter:

- If you're writing to complain, sum up your problem in a simple sentence—the product didn't work, the repair was inadequate, the food was bad, the hotel room was dirty.
- If you are writing to express sympathy, say so, in words from your heart.
- If you are asking for a favor, lay out your reasons clearly.
- If you are writing to apply for a job, make it clear why you should stand out from the crowd.

All of these points sound very obvious. But we wish we had a dollar for every letter we've received that begins with the written equivalent of a "how's the weather" conversation starter in the course of our careers.

Write your letter as if you had only one chance to gain the attention of its intended reader. That may well be the case.

Sincerely,
The Authors

What Is a Letter?

Dear Reader:

A letter is a "messenger of sympathy and love, servant of parted friends, consoler of the lonely, bond of the scattered family, enlarger of the common life." So wrote Charles W. Eliot, a famed educator who was president of Harvard University from 1869 to 1909.

In the twenty-first century, letters are just one form of communication. We live in a time when people walk the streets, drive the roads, and fly from place to place with a cell phone at their ear and an e-mail device on their hip.

A letter is a *simplex* communication, going in one direction only. Compare it to a *duplex* communication, like a phone call or face-to-face conversation, in which each side jockeys for position at the podium.

As a simplex communication, letters provide the opportunity to present your case uninterrupted. However, you also have the responsibility to consider the other person's point of view and sensibilities; to ignore them is to risk having your message rejected or ignored.

Before you begin to write, devote a few moments to thought. Ask yourself some essential questions, including:

- **Is this a personal letter or a business letter?** A personal letter is less formal, and you can more or less make your own rules. A letter to a business or government agency, though, is more formal and requires you to include specific information and documentation. A letter from a business or agency is generally the most carefully limited form of written communication; in many cases your words amount to a commitment by a legal entity.

- **Who is the letter sent to?** If at all possible, you should address a letter to a specific person. If necessary, make a phone call and ask for the proper person. What do you know about that person? Is there some way to find out a bit more information about him or her?

And take it from one of the authors whose name can be applied to either sex: There is no quicker way to turn someone off—or at least alert them that the letter writer does not know them or did not bother to do a tiny bit of investigation—than to send a letter with an incorrect salutation. If you have any doubt about the sex of the person you are writing to, the spelling of his or her name, their job title, or other essential details, make a telephone call to their office. You don't have to identify yourself; it is perfectly acceptable to say, "I just wanted to check a few details before I send a letter."

In some cases, you will not be able to obtain a specific name. For example, if you are writing to the customer service department at a large store, or to a government agency, your letter will likely be dealt with by whichever clerk or bureaucrat opens it. Here you can use a nonspecific greeting such as "Dear Customer Service," "Dear Board of Public Health," or "Dear Advisory Committee."

It is no longer considered proper to begin untargeted letters with "Dear Sir." You can instead use "Dear Sir or Madam" or, more simply, "Dear People."

The purposely vague "To Whom It May Concern" is a bright red flag to the reader that you have no idea to whom you are writing. We would avoid it except in a few instances such as a general letter of reference.

- **What is my relationship to the person to whom I am writing?** Am I a customer? A job applicant? An employer? A supplier? A friend? A casual acquaintance? A parishioner? A citizen and voter?
- **Is this the best time to send the letter?** Businesses and individuals have seasons. We know better than to send a casual note or make a nonessential telephone call to a tax accountant in early April; his or her attention is likely to be focused on the income tax filing deadline. Similarly, a teacher may be especially busy around the end of a term but more available earlier or later.
- **Why am I writing this letter? What do I hope to accomplish?** As we will show in the letters that follow, your letter must be clearly stated, and you should use an active voice to directly ask for a particular response. And your request should be reasonable and legal.
- **How would I react if I were the recipient of this letter?** Consider whether you would be offended by the letter you are writing; decide, too, how you would respond to any request or demand in the letter.

Be honest here. If you're in the right and the issue is important, go ahead and send the letter. But do so with some realistic sense of a likely response.

Best regards,
The Authors

How to Make a Personal Letter More Personal

Dear Reader:

The difference between a business letter and a personal letter is obvious: the latter is *personal.* Open with something that sets the tone.

Go beyond the recounting of news, and express your feelings. Say why you've written the letter, or why you were thinking of the person it is addressed to. Connect the news at the heart of the letter to the person you are writing to, or to someone you both know.

Be truthful. That doesn't mean abandon all attempts at tactfulness. A proper level of courtesy—not too much and certainly not too little—makes it more likely that your sentiments will be accepted or your request granted.

Think about the voice you use in your letter. This means the use of "I" and "you." Telling the reader that "I want to work with you" or "I have a problem that you can help solve" draws you both into the process. Then look for a way to join your interests and those of the recipient with "we" and "us."

Don't overdo the first-person singular, though. A letter dotted with I, me, and mine doesn't make the reader feel included.

Warm regards,
The Authors

Getting It Right

Dear Reader:

We know that not all of us are blessed with a great vocabulary or excellent spelling and grammar skills. A decade or so ago, we could *almost* excuse a few errors in letters written to us. But for most of us there is no longer an excuse for mistakes. Every current computer word-processing program includes a spelling and grammar checker that will highlight suspicious words or phrases and suggest corrections. Don't skip proofreading your letter before you send it, though, because a basic spellchecker in a computer can't tell you whether you've used the wrong word in a sentence. If you type "I'd like to see you next weak," the computer won't raise an objection!

If you are planning to handwrite a letter, create your draft on a computer and then transcribe it in your own hand. (If you don't have a computer in your home, you should be able to use one at a public library or an Internet café, or borrow a friend's machine.)

If all else fails, invest in a good dictionary and style book, and use them.

If the letter is not too personal, consider showing it to a friend or acquaintance for a final reading before it is dispatched. None of us, including professional authors, should attempt to be their own final editor. We know perfectly well what we meant to say, and sometimes we cannot see the errors that lie right in front of our eyes.

Sincerely,
The Authors

How to Write Well

Dear Reader:

Writing is an art. If writing was a mathematical equation, there would have been thousands or millions of the likes of William Shakespeare or Mark Twain or James Joyce.

What makes good letter writing, then? It's a lot easier to describe what makes a good letter go bad:

- An opening that does not grab your attention and clearly state its purpose.
- A jumble of irrelevant or inconsequential detail that muddies your case.
- Florid, obscure, emotionally charged, or inappropriate language.
- Too much of a demand on the reader's time.
- A closing statement that doesn't sum up your point or call the reader to action.

Unless you are presenting a legal notice or a contract or a set of detailed instructions—beyond the scope of this book—the purpose of a letter is to convey information or ask questions. The shorter and simpler the statement of a problem or the delivery of news, the more likely it is to be read and understood.

By the way, did you notice how effectively a bit of formatting—indentations, bullets, asterisks, and other devices—makes key elements of a letter stand out on the page? This is a very effective way to highlight your key points. Take care not to overdo special formatting, though. If everything is highlighted, nothing will stand out.

Yours truly,
The Authors

The Mechanics of Writing a Letter

Corey Sandler and Janice Keefe
Word Association, Inc.
P.O. Box 2779
Nantucket, MA 02584

Mrs. Esteem D. Reader
123 Your Street
Yourtown, State 98765

April 5, 2004

Dear Mrs. Reader:

The basic structure of a formal or business letter is designed to sandwich the purpose of the communication within essential information to help you identify the sender and, in some instances, confirm any commitments made by the writer.

Although there are a number of different formats that can be used for a letter, all of them are variations of the style used in the example you are reading right now. The components, from top to bottom, are as follows:

Return address. This information tells you the name and address of the sender. Some styles include the name of the sender and his or her title, while others give only the mailing address of the sender. The name of the sender is repeated in the signature block at the end of the letter. Modern communicants often add their e-mail address and sometimes an Internet Web site to the address block.

Inside address. Here you list the name and address of the intended recipient. This section includes the most formal and full exposition of the addressee's name and title. For example, for an individual, the inside address might read "Mrs. Esteem D. Reader" as above.

For an officeholder, the inside address might read "The Honorable William Keefe, Speaker of the House of Representatives."

The inside address confirms the identity of the intended recipient and serves as an element of the implied or explicit contract for any promises made in the letter.

You can put the recipient's name and title on the same line, or separate them on individual lines.

Date. The date is important to establish the currency of the letter, and is an ordinary element of a contract. The date can refer to when the letter was dispatched, or can indicate the day when the bid, proposal, or promise was made.

Salutation. Here the sender connects directly to the recipient. In an informal letter, you can use just their first name or their nickname if you know the person well. For example, Mrs. Esteem D. Reader may be known to her friends as Esty, and the salutation can use that name.

In a business letter, and especially a letter to an officeholder or member of the clergy, the military, or royalty, the salutation should use the proper form of address. For example, a letter to a U.S. Senator might be introduced as "Dear Senator Smith." A letter to an Episcopal bishop might bear a salutation of "The Right Reverend Arlo Seeger, Bishop of Fall River."

One other thing: If you do not know the sex of the addressee (and cannot unobtrusively determine it with a phone call or other inquiry) you can drop the formal title, as in "Dear Esteem D. Reader," although this is an indication to the recipient that you do not know them well.

Modern culture frowns on "Dear Sir," since it makes an assumption that the unknown recipient will be male. You're better off addressing the letter to the recipient's office, such as "Dear Board of Elections" or "Dear Customer Service." Do not use "To whom it may concern" except in a nonspecific letter of reference.

Body. The space between the salutation and the closing is home to the letter itself.

The entire letter should be as clear and direct as possible, but you should pay special attention to the first paragraph—what a newspaper writer would call the "lead." Use that first paragraph to present the purpose of the letter, and then use subsequent paragraphs to provide the details and to clearly outline what you would like the recipient to do in response.

Closing. We sum up our state of mind or our purpose in writing with the closing. We are sincerely yours, or thankful, or obedient. This summation serves no real purpose, but it is an expected courtesy; a letter without a polite closing seems more like a summons than a respectful communication.

Signature block. Your signature seals the deal. On a typed or computer-printed letter, the signature shows (at least in theory) that the sender actually handled the letter. An authenticated signature is an element of a binding contract.

Proper style calls for your name to be printed or typed below the closing to make it easy for the recipient to read your signature.

Enclosure reference or CC. If your letter includes an enclosed form or a copy of previous correspondence or other documentation, you can indicate its inclusion in the letter by ending the letter with a line that starts with *Enclosure:* and specifies the nature of the attached material. You can also make reference in your letter to any attached material.

The bottom of the letter is also the place to indicate whether the letter has also been sent to others. The traditional way to indicate this is to add *cc:* and list the names of other recipients. (If you're not of a certain age, you might not know that *cc* used to mean a "carbon copy" was created and sent.)

Design of the letter. Use a standard typeface for your letter. The most common style is Courier, a version of the traditional typewriter font. Avoid "art" typefaces and unusual styles for business and formal letters. They may be acceptable in informal correspondence, although some recipients may find them hard to read.

A letter looks more personalized when it is not justified. This means that the left margin is even, but the right margin varies slightly based on the length of each sentence.

Lines of type should be single-spaced, and margins should be used to balance the letter on the page. One design rule calls for equal margins on the top and sides, with a slightly larger bottom margin.

Each paragraph can be indented about five spaces, or every paragraph can be set flush left without an indent but with an additional line of space at the end of each paragraph. The address and signature blocks can be set flush with the left or right margins.

Sincerely,

Corey Sandler and Janice Keefe

Corey Sandler and Janice Keefe

Enclosure: 1,000 other letters

2 Congratulations

Dear Reader:

To congratulate someone is to join in an expression of pleasure at the happiness, good fortune, or achievement of another.

A letter of congratulations is one of the more gracious communications for any of us. We are sharing in someone's joy without asking for anything in return.

The best letters of congratulation include a bit of yourself in the message. Tell the recipient why you are happy for them, or why their achievement has particular meaning to you. Extend an offer for a celebration if appropriate, or offer a bit of lighthearted advice.

Your letter should make it clear that you enjoy the opportunity to join in a moment of joy.

It is never too late to send congratulations, but you should try to send your best wishes as soon as possible, while the glow is strong. If your letter is belated, explain the reason.

Sincerely,
The Authors

Congratulations to couple on their marriage

Dear Cynthia and David:

We just heard the wonderful news that two of our favorite people have become a couple. Harold and I add our best wishes to the many you will receive.

When you newlyweds feel like having company, let us take you to dinner to celebrate.

Fondly,
Monica Diamond

Congratulations to friend on birth of a baby

Dear Janet:

I just heard the wonderful news about your beautiful baby boy.

Congratulations to you and John and baby Francis. I am so happy for the three of you.

Fondly,
Morgan

Congratulations on new position

Roger Hamilton, Director of Physical Therapy
Smalltown General Hospital
Smalltown, OH

Dear Roger:

I wanted to express my personal congratulations to you on your appointment as director of physical therapy here at the hospital. We are very fortunate to have someone of your obvious abilities and background associated with SGH, and we look forward to a long relationship with you.

Sincerely,
Cornelius Floy, President
Smalltown General Hospital

Congratulations on friend's promotion

Dear Ben:

Way to go, Ben! I just heard about your appointment as the new accounts manager at Tri-County Investment.

I knew you when we were both struggling college students in Basic Finance—struggling to stay awake, that is.

Congratulations, you deserve it.

Best regards,
Morgan Diamond

Congratulations on friend's retirement

Dear Jerry:

I just heard through the grapevine that after many long and productive years the senior counsel at Smith, Conroy, and Fisher has decided it's time to hang up his briefcase.

I'm sure you will be greatly missed. I'm also sure you're going to thrive in retirement.

If retirement agrees with you as much as it has with me, you will find there are not enough hours in the day to do everything you want or are asked to do. Maybe I can put in a request for a bit of that time for a round of golf and a leisurely lunch at the club.

Call me when you have a spare moment.

Sincerely,
Harold Diamond

Congratulations on selling house and moving to apartment

Ron and Emma Miller
Smalltown, OH

Dear Ron and Emma:

We just heard the news that you two are simplifying life and have moved into an apartment.

Lucky you: no more snow shoveling, lawn mowing, and furnace repairs. Enjoy your free time. Let's get together for dinner soon.

Sincerely,
Mick and Sylvia

Congratulations on retirement of business associate

Phil Armani
Ten Strings Guitar Company
Smalltown, OH

Dear Phil:

I just heard the news that Ten Strings Guitar Company will have to get along without their best salesman. We will certainly miss you. Everyone you dealt with appreciated your expertise and good humor.

Good luck in your retirement. Please come by and see us sometime.

Sincerely,
John Diamond
Diamond Music Hall

Congratulations on friend's new job

Don Meachy
Nearby, OH

Dear Don:

I've just heard that you are now one of the gainfully employed. Congratulations! One of us had to lead the way into corporate America, and the logical choice was you.

I hear you landed a great job; I know you'll do well!

Sincerely,
Josh

Congratulations to performers in show

John Dallas, Artistic Director
Smalltown Community Theatre
Smalltown, OH

Dear John:

John and I were thrilled with yesterday's opening night of The Music Man at the Smalltown Community Theatre. The cast was superb, the sets and costumes lovely, and the music was perfect.

We are very proud to be among the Golden Circle patrons of the SCT and look forward to many more successful seasons.

Sincerely,
Monica Diamond

Congratulations to grandson on entering law school

Dear Josh:

We just heard the wonderful news that you've been accepted at the School of Law at Smalltown University.

It is hard to believe that our grandson is now a mature and thoughtful man who has definite ideas about his future. We wish you much success in this new phase of your life; you will always have our love.

Love,
Your Grandparents

Congratulations to granddaughter on college acceptance

Dear Heather:

We can't believe it: The last of our grandchildren is off to college.

You have always made us so proud of you over the years. You can count on our love and support as you tackle your next exciting challenge.

With all our love,
Your Grandparents

Congratulations on volunteering

Dear Grandma:

I just heard that you will be volunteering in the gift shop at Smalltown General Hospital. Good for you, grandma!

The Diamond/Hamilton family is well represented at SGH, with you, me, and Roger being there. Now we can get together for lunch; I can help you find the best offerings in the cafeteria.

Love,
Morgan

Congratulations to grandchild on graduation from college

Dear Josh:

Congratulations! It's hard for us to believe that our youngest grandson has graduated from college and been accepted to law school. We are so proud of you.

Your grandmother and I would like to make a little contribution to help you with the costs of your own apartment and law school.

Love,
Grandma and Grandpa Miller

Congratulations on election to club office

Hank Billings
Smalltown Senior Center
Smalltown, OH

Dear Hank:

Congratulations on your election as president of the senior center. I think you're going to be a great success at the job, and you can count me in for any committees you think appropriate.

Sincerely,
Walter Ballou

Congratulations on election to club office from losing candidate

Hank Billings
Smalltown Senior Center
Smalltown, OH

Dear Hank:

Congratulations. We both ran a good race, and you won. As I prepare to turn over the gavel to you, I want you to know that I would be happy to assist you in any way I can to help the senior center in the year to come.

Sincerely,
Harold Diamond

Congratulations on winning major prize

George Tashlick
Smalltown, OH

Dear George:

Congratulations on winning the Rotary Club benefit drawing. Your contribution helped the club raise more than $10,000 for our charitable activities here in Smalltown.

We hope you have a great time on your all-expenses-paid weekend in Cincinnati. Please contact Harry Gould at Go Away Travel Agency to make arrangements for your trip.

Sincerely,
Jonathan Baker, President
Smalltown Rotary Club

Congratulations to friend on winning major prize

George Tashlick
Smalltown, OH

Dear George:

Way to go, George! You had the golden ticket at the Rotary Club. The next time I buy a lottery ticket, I intend to have you pick the numbers for me.

I hope you and Claudia have a great time on your trip.

Sincerely,
Ron Miller

Congratulations to friend for charity work

Lena Whalen
Smalltown, OH

Dear Lena:

You did a superb job organizing this year's clothing drive. I have worked on many but this was the smoothest and best run, by far. Bravo for a job well done!

Fondly,
Monica

Welcome to wife of new pastor

Jean Evans
Smalltown Congregational Church
Smalltown, OH

Dear Mrs. Evans:

As president of the ladies auxiliary of Smalltown Congregational Church I wish to extend a warm welcome to you and Reverend Evans. We have been eagerly awaiting your arrival and will do all we can to help you and your family comfortably settle into life in Smalltown.

Please feel free to call on me. I would consider it an honor to be of assistance.

Sincerely,
Monica Diamond

Compliments to pastor about Christmas decorations

The Reverend Dr. Bartley Evans
Smalltown Congregational Church
Smalltown, OH

Dear Dr. Evans:

The church looked more beautiful than ever for the Christmas Eve service. The flowers, decorations, and the formal robes of the choir were marvelous, and your inspirational message made this blessed night very special.

Sincerely,
Monica Diamond

Belated congratulations on new job

Andrea Benedict
Smalltown, OH

Dear Andrea:

Shame on me. I was so preoccupied with my own personal wedding extravaganza that I forgot to send you a note telling you how happy I am to hear of your wonderful new job. Tate, Coffey, and Miller have got themselves one super general counsel.

Congratulations!

Sincerely,
Morgan Hamilton

Congratulations to newly married couple

Dear Morgan and Roger:

Living in London certainly has its advantages. The downside is being so far from friends and family. I'm so sorry I couldn't be at your wedding on Saturday, but I certainly was there in spirit.

Congratulations, good friends, and have a wonderful life together!

Love,
Mark

Congratulations on marriage from employer

Morgan and Roger Hamilton
Smalltown, OH

Dear Morgan and Roger:

On behalf of Smalltown General Hospital, I want to congratulate you on your marriage.

We are all very happy for you, and proud of the fact that you met here at the hospital. Please accept our best wishes.

Sincerely,
Jennings Bergen, Human Resources Department
Smalltown General Hospital
Smalltown, OH

Congratulations to grandchild on receiving driver's license

Dear Heather:

We just heard the news: another Diamond behind the wheel.

Congratulations! Getting your driver's license is an important milestone in this journey of life. You are a mature and sensible young woman and we know you will make an excellent driver.

We are both proud of you. Drop by sometime and let us see you driving; we'll pay for the gas.

Love,
Grandma and Grandpa Diamond

Congratulations on winning golf championship

Dear Stan:

I hear that Tiger Woods is looking over his shoulder these days. Congratulations, Stan, it's always nice to see someone of a certain age beat the younger guys at golf. But, this championship was won by simply being the best.

When do you turn pro?

Regards,
Harold Diamond

3 Thanks

Dear Reader:

Most of us are happy to perform a favor for a friend or a family member. In business, we are usually quite willing to offer a special service or consideration to a customer.

A true favor requires no payment or obligation. But common courtesy does call for thanks.

Special consideration in business transactions should be politely acknowledged. A favor by a friend deserves a heartfelt and personalized expression of thanks.

As is true for many of the letters in this book, the act of writing a personal note of thanks is a way to give a bit of yourself in return.

Thanks again for buying this book.

Sincerely,
The Authors

Thanking neighbor for picking up sick child at school

Dear Pam:

You saved the day for Brian and us!

Thank you so much for picking up Brian at school yesterday while I was at work. His stomachache was nothing serious—probably too much syrup on his pancakes at breakfast.

I was so relieved to be able to rely on a good neighbor.

Please remember that we are available any time you need us.

Sincerely,
Karen Diamond

Thanks for dinner party

Dear Ann:

Thank you so much for including us at your lovely dinner last Friday. Everything was exquisite—the food, the atmosphere, and the company. It was an unforgettable evening.

Warm regards,
Laura

Thanks to roommate's parents for weekend visit

Walter and Helen Rogers
Big Mountain, ME

Dear Mr. and Mrs. Rogers:

Thank you so much for inviting me to come home with Amy to Maine for a week of skiing during winter break.

The mountain was great, and I've never seen so much snow! (And I've never skied so well or so much.)

You were very gracious hosts. I really enjoyed meeting you and your family.

Sincerely,
Heather Diamond

Thanks to nurses and hospital personnel

Fourth Floor Nurses Station
Smalltown General Hospital
Smalltown, OH

Dear Nursing Staff:

I was recently a patient at Smalltown General Hospital, undergoing a disc operation and recovery.

The entire staff of doctors, nurses, aides, and support personnel could not have done more to make this difficult time less stressful for me and my family. The medical care and consideration I received was excellent.

Although I do not hope for a repeat visit anytime soon, I have no reservations about the quality of service at Smalltown General.

Sincerely,
Harold Diamond
cc: Dr. Timothy Todd, chief of medical services

Thanking friend for support during illness of husband

Dear Hazel:

Harold is home from the hospital now and doing well. I know he must be close to normal because he has begun criticizing my treatment of his beloved hydrangeas.

Thank you for all you did for us while Harold was hospitalized. I really appreciated your help in getting me to and from the hospital, as well as the delicious meals that miraculously appeared in my refrigerator and the emotional support you provided.

You are a true friend.

When we are out and about again, please let us take you to lunch. We will have much to talk about.

Fondly,
Monica

Thanking EMTs after accident

Chief Bill Macy
Smalltown Fire Department
Smalltown, OH

Dear Chief Macy:

Our son Joshua was involved in the very serious accident at the Crosstown Shopping Center on the night of January 6. Fortunately, his injuries were relatively minor and he will fully recover.

I wanted to thank you and the fire department's emergency medical technicians for their professional assistance to Joshua.

Your EMTs had the scene organized within minutes, and got right down to the critical job of helping those who were hurt. Their quick action enabled our son to get the timely medical treatment he needed. I am sure they saved some lives that night.

I realize that the EMTs are professionals and this is their job, but I hope you will pass along our thanks and appreciation for a job well done.

Thank you,
Laura Diamond

Thanks for expression of sympathy

Dear Laura and John:

Thank you for your kind words of support. Martha was indeed a special person and our loss is very great. The entire family gains strength from the many expressions of sympathy we have received from those who knew her.

Sincerely,
Ron Taylor

Thanks for advice about son's career

Dear Walt:

Thanks for meeting with Josh and giving him the benefit of your advice about the legal profession. As I am sure you could tell, he is very enthusiastic about law school and eager to begin.

He got a lot out of your talk and I can't think of a better example for him to follow than yours.

Sincerely,
John Diamond

Thanks for dog-sitting

Dear Carol and Jim:

Thanks again for taking care of our Jackson last weekend. He enjoyed your hospitality so much he seemed a little unhappy to leave your house when we picked him up.

We will be more than happy to reciprocate anytime you need us. We'd love to entertain Taffy.

Sincerely,
Laura Diamond

Thanks for financial advice

Pedro Peterson
Peterson and Associates, Accounting
Smalltown, OH

Dear Mr. Peterson:

Thank you for your time on the phone yesterday. I know you have worked on my father's books for many years and I hope someday to have a business for which I can engage your expertise as an accountant.

As I explained, my fiancé and I are in the midst of merging our assets and liabilities as we prepare for our married life. Your expertise and advice was much appreciated, and I do plan to take you up on your offer to discuss our net worth statement soon.

Sincerely,
Morgan Diamond

Thanks to acquaintance for helping set up job interview

Marsha Collins, Administrator
Smalltown Historical Foundation
Smalltown, OH

Dear Marsha:

Thank you for setting up the interview with Paul Smith, the director of the SHF, for my granddaughter Heather. She met with him last week and yesterday was offered the summer internship she sought. Heather is thrilled to be working at the Historical Foundation this summer. I know she will be a fine representative and a most enthusiastic worker.

Sincerely,
Monica Diamond

Thanks from new intern for interview

Marsha Collins, Administrator
Smalltown Historical Foundation
Smalltown, OH

Dear Mrs. Collins:

Thank you for setting up the interview with Mr. Smith at the Historical Foundation. I was hired for the job and begin next week.

I am very excited about this opportunity and appreciate your help.

Sincerely,
Heather Diamond

Thanks to friend of family for graduation check

Dear Mr. & Mrs. Sanders:

Thank you so much for remembering me on my graduation. I start college in the fall and I will invest your check wisely in books and school supplies.

Thank you again for your kindness.

Sincerely,
Heather Diamond

Thanks to volunteers at open house

Dear Volunteer:

Thank you for giving so generously of your time last Sunday at our open house.

The celebration of the opening of the new addition to the Smalltown Senior Center was a huge success. Now it is up to all of us to use the library, conference room, and performance space well.

Sincerely,
Monica Diamond
Honorary Fundraising Chairperson, Smalltown Senior Center

Thanks for donation made in couple's name

Dear Laura:

Thank you again for being part of our special evening to celebrate the renewal of our wedding vows. I must say I enjoyed everything better the second time around: less stress, no jitters, and we had the grandchildren to enjoy.

Thank you also for the donation you made in our name to the Conservation Foundation. It is a favorite cause of ours.

Sincerely,
Sharon Peters

Thanks for baby shower cash gift

Dear Morgan:

Thank you for coming to my baby shower, and for your generous gift. We have decided to make it the first contribution to May-Li's college fund.

We hope you'll come back soon for a quieter lunch, if such a thing is still possible. Our life is suddenly so much more hectic, but so much more joyful.

Fondly,
Lynn

Thanks for baby shower clothing gift

Dear Julia:

Thank you for coming to my baby shower, and for your lovely gift. May-Li was wearing her cute new outfit by the end of the day; she's making quite a fashion statement.

We hope you'll come back soon for a quieter lunch, if such a thing is still possible. Our life is suddenly so much more hectic, but so much more joyful.

Fondly,
Lynn

Thanks for wedding gift to couple who attended wedding

Dear Mark and Lisa:

Thank you for your very thoughtful wedding gift. When Roger and I had dinner at your house last spring and admired your fine Haskins knives, we really weren't hinting that we'd like some of our own. But we certainly were thrilled to receive a set.

It was wonderful seeing you at the wedding; it meant a lot that you were able to be with us on our special day.

Sincerely,
Morgan and Roger Hamilton

Thanks for wedding gift to couple who did not attend wedding

Dear Jean and Stan:

Roger and I want to thank you for your wedding gift of silver from our wedding registry. At some point in the near future we will have enough to entertain our special friends, and we hope to see you then.

Thanks again for your thoughtfulness.

Sincerely,
Morgan and Roger Hamilton

Thanks for surprise party

To all of my coworkers at Smalltown Community College:

I want to thank everyone for making this past semester one of the best experiences of my life. I couldn't wait to come to work each day, not just because I knew I would be learning something new, but because I was working with the most intelligent, funny, and warm people I have ever known.

Thank you for my party—it truly was a surprise—and for the lovely piece of luggage. I will take it with me to London for my semester abroad; I won't need anything, though, to remind me of how gracious and supportive you've been. I will miss you all.

Fondly,
Jessica Nolan

Thanks for senior day at museum

Dr. Thomas Q. Fleming, Director
Smalltown Art Museum
Smalltown, OH

Dear Dr. Fleming:

On behalf of all of us at the Senior Center, I want to extend sincere thanks to the Smalltown Art Museum for designating October 16 as Senior Appreciation Day, offering free admission to seniors.

You can count on a large turnout at the museum on that day.

Sincerely,
Harold Diamond, President
Smalltown Senior Center

Thanks for senior discount at club

Jack Jones, Owner
Stay Fit Health Club
Smalltown, OH

Dear Mr. Jones:

I want to thank you for the offer of a 50 percent discount on health club membership to seniors at the Smalltown Senior Center.

We will publicize the offer in our newsletter, to be published next week.

Sincerely,
Harold Diamond, President
Smalltown Senior Center

Thanks for senior discount at store

Federico Friendly, General Manager
Value-Mart Department Store
Smalltown, OH

Dear Mr. Friendly:

We are pleased to share with our members your offer of "Senior Tuesdays" at Value-Mart. The 15 percent discount you offer is very generous, and we have already made plans to organize day trips to the store on Tuesdays.

Sincerely,
Harold Diamond, President
Smalltown Senior Center

Thanks to bus company for senior shopping bus

Harold Allen, Manager
Smalltown Transit Authority
Smalltown, OH

Dear Mr. Allen:

On behalf of the Smalltown Senior Center, I want to thank you for setting up the special holiday shopping bus service.

In next week's newsletter, we will tell our members about the free bus service to downtown on Tuesdays during December, sponsored by the Smalltown Merchants Association.

Sincerely,
Harold Diamond, President
Smalltown Senior Center

Thanks for offer of help from losing candidate

Harold Diamond, President
Smalltown Senior Center
Smalltown, OH

Dear Harold:

Thank you for your most gracious letter of congratulations about the election. I wish we both could have won.

In a way, we both can; I intend to accept your offer of assistance and call on you to work with me on club business in the coming year.

Sincerely,
Hank Billings

Thanks for friend's advice

Steve Barton
Smalltown, OH

Dear Steve:

Thank you for coming through for me again. Just hearing your words of support and guidance about Emma's medical problems were a tremendous help. I know Emma and I will handle this minor obstacle as we have handled so many others in our almost sixty years of marriage.

Let's get together soon with the ladies.

Sincerely,
Ron Miller

Thanks for watching house while on vacation

Monica and Harold Diamond
Smalltown, OH

Dear Monica and Harold:

Thank you so much for watching the house while we circled the globe by cruise ship. We had a marvelous time and look forward to showing you our pictures and the treasures we collected—including something very special we found in Venice that we brought back just for you.

I'll call you soon to find a time to get together.

Sincerely,
Marge Clinton

Thanks for job congratulations

Morgan Hamilton
Smalltown, OH

Dear Morgan:

Thanks for your best wishes on my new job. It's a little scary being referred to as general counsel, but I'm looking forward to getting used to it. I didn't even notice that your congratulations were late; as I recall, you were semi-famous in college for your tardy arrival to class!

My best to you and your new husband. Let's get together for lunch sometime soon.

Sincerely,
Andrea

Thanks to seller of winning ticket for prize

John Diamond
Smalltown, OH

Dear John:

I just wanted to thank you for selling me what turned out to be the winning ticket for the Rotary Club fundraising lottery. I was glad to contribute, and Claudia and I will raise a toast to you as we enjoy our weekend in Cincinnati.

Sincerely,
George Tashlick

Thanks for expression of sympathy

Laura Diamond
Smalltown, OH

Dear Laura:

Thank you for your expression of support after Jim lost his job. As always, you knew exactly what to say.

We're counting our blessings and going on with our lives. We have a few encouraging possibilities, and I will let you know when something positive works out.

Sincerely,
Joyce Fleming

Thanks to professor for special efforts

Professor Sheila Davenport
Media Studies
Smalltown University
Smalltown, OH

Dear Professor Davenport:

I want to thank you for working with me to help me raise my grade in Media Studies. Adjusting to life in college was a little overwhelming for me but I think I'm on the right track now, thanks to caring and supportive teachers like you.

Sincerely,
Amy Rogers

Thanks to minister for ceremony

The Reverend Peter Hall
Smalltown Congregational Church
Smalltown, OH

Dear Mr. Hall:

Morgan and I want to thank you for the lovely wedding service. Your words, especially the passage from Corinthians 13:4–7, have stayed with us:

"Love is patient; love is kind and envies no one. Love is never boastful, nor conceited, nor rude; never selfish, not quick to take offense. Love keeps no score of wrongs.

There is nothing love cannot face; there is no limit to its faith, its hope, and its endurance."

We hope to live by that for the rest of our lives.

Sincerely,
Roger Hamilton

Thanks to teacher for special opportunity

Professor Fran Brownback
Political Science Department
Smalltown University
Smalltown, OH

Dear Professor Brownback:

Thank you so much for nominating me to represent the freshman class at the mock United Nations session in Columbus. I am happy to accept, and look forward to learning more about the U.N. and my assigned nation of Kiribati.

As you suggested, I will prepare a presentation on the session and submit it for extra credit when I return.

Sincerely,
Amy Rogers

Thanks to supporter of theater group

Milton Boyle
Smalltown, OH

Dear Mr. Boyle:

Thank you for adding your name to the list of those interested in establishing a repertory theater here in Smalltown. The response—from actors, technicians, and patrons—was overwhelming.

We will be holding an informational meeting this Friday, May 16, at 7 P.M. in the media room at the Smalltown Public Library. We hope you will bring your ideas and your creativity, and most important, bring yourself.

Sincerely,
Laura Diamond

4 Apologies

Dear Reader:

I'm sorry. I did something wrong, or someone who works for me or lives in my household made a mistake, and I want you to know that I offer an apology. And if appropriate, I want to tell you what I plan to do to make things right.

A letter of apology should be very specific and personal. Be direct and use an active voice. Take a lesson from—and do not follow—the mealy-mouthed politician who is only able to say, "mistakes were made."

Sincerely,
Corey Sandler

Apology to someone left off invitation list

Audrey Morgan
Smalltown, OH

Dear Audrey:

I just received the list of invitees to the thank-you luncheon for those who helped at the Garden Club's annual meeting.

Audrey, I was horrified to find that your name had been omitted from the list, and from the program. What a terrible mistake!

You did so much to make this meeting a success. Please accept my personal invitation to attend the luncheon on Tuesday, May 23, at The Castle at noon. I intend to recognize you in my speech.

Sincerely,
Laura Diamond, president
Smalltown Garden Club

Apology for misunderstanding

Brad Bell
Smalltown, OH

Dear Brad:

You and I should know better than to discuss politics at a dinner party. I value your friendship too much to allow our disagreement about the coming election to come between us.

Next time, let's stick to baseball.

Sincerely,
Harold Diamond

Apology for child's behavior

Mary Ann Hayes
Fairview, PA

Dear Mary Ann:

I wanted to apologize—mother to mother—for Hannah's behavior at your daughter's birthday party the other night. She obviously had too much (soda) to drink.

We've spoken to her, and she'll be making her own apology to Christie soon.

Best regards,
Karen Diamond

Apology for missing appointment

Al Catel
Smalltown, OH

Dear Al:

I'm so sorry I missed our appointment for this morning; I got held up in a faculty meeting and could not break away.

Please call me to reschedule. I am available any weekday except Friday from 2 to 4 P.M., and because I missed our meeting I also am willing to drop by the office any time Saturday if that works better for you.

My apologies.

Sincerely,
Prof. Laura Diamond
Smalltown Community College

Apology for breaking item at party

Ellen Gates
Smalltown, OH

Dear Ellen:

I want to thank you again for the lovely lunch the other day; I enjoyed catching up on old times with you and Marilu.

Although you were very gracious about it, I feel terrible about breaking one of your favorite coffee cups—I never knew there were so many varieties of cow spots. I was shopping the next day and I saw another cup with pictures of cows all over it, and I thought of you again.

Please add this cup to your collection.

Sincerely,
Monica Diamond

Apology for missing dinner party

Dear Beth:

I hope you know us well enough to realize that we would never have missed your dinner party without a very good reason. As we were leaving for your house we got a call informing us that our son was involved in an automobile accident. He was taken to the emergency room, and our only thought at the time was to be with him.

The very good news is that he was not badly hurt and will fully recover.

We would much rather have been at your dinner party; I'm sure it was a lovely evening.

We hope to see you again sometime soon.

Sincerely,
Laura Diamond

Apology for missing birthday

Dear Florence:

I never thought I would let something as important to me as your birthday slip by. Unlike you, I must be getting old.

My only consolation is that I will have many more opportunities in the future to get it right.

Fondly,
Monica Diamond

Apology for damaged dress

Dear Morgan:

I am so sorry that you found a stain on the dress I borrowed from you. I should have noticed the damage. Please believe me when I tell you I had no idea it was there.

I hope you will allow me to take you out to lunch, and to your favorite store to buy a replacement.

Sincerely,
Judy

5 Get Well

Dear Reader:

We all get sick, and we all know that even the cheeriest among us can get down in the dumps when our health is less than perfect. Get-well letters are a way to cheer up someone and let them know you are thinking of them.

If you know the person well, match the tone to their personality. Some people take no offense (and may prefer) a lighthearted comment or joke. Others can use a spiritual boost—tell them they are in your prayers. A sick child might appreciate a little gift (check with the parents for advice).

And we all can use an expression of love.

Warm regards,
The Authors

Friend hospitalized for serious illness

Dear Helen:

I am so sorry to hear that you are back in the hospital. Your lovely daughter, Jennifer, has been very gracious in keeping us current. She tells us that in spite of a setback your wonderful spirit continues to shine and that your main concerns are for your family and friends.

Harold's and my thoughts and prayers are with you. When you feel like having a bit of company, please pass the word. We'd love to come and spend time with you.

Fondly,
Monica

Humorous note about minor accident

Dear Cathy:

Sorry to hear about your mishap. I guess this will delay your comeback for the Summer Olympics, eh?

Seriously, I hope the arm heals fast. Maybe next time you should try out for the debating team instead of the gymnastics club.

Love,
Morgan

About friend's health

Dear Joan, Jane, and Beth:

It is with some difficulty that I write this letter, but I think it is important. I saw Harriet and her husband Hank in the grocery store yesterday.

We all know that she has been ailing for some time, but it is now obvious that she is seriously ill. Hank confirms it, but says her spirits are good and in most every way she is the Harriet we have known and loved for so long.

I think this is the time to demonstrate how strong our friendship is.

I would like to gather a small group of friends to visit her at home. We can arrange with Hank for the right time, and bring some treats.

I hope we can try to put something together for next week. I will be in touch soon.

Sincerely,
Monica

Follow-up letter to sick friend

Dear Harriet:

It was so good to spend some time with you Tuesday. I must admit that even after all these years, the four of us make quite a handsome group. And, it has been a lot of years. You are one of my oldest and dearest friends.

Let's try to have these little get-togethers more often. It helps all of us appreciate the value of a true friendship.

Fondly,
Monica

To grandchild home after tonsillectomy

Dear Brian:

Grandma and I are glad you are home from the hospital.

Do you weigh any less without those tonsils?

Your mom and dad said you were really brave and will be playing with your friends and back in school soon. In the meantime, enjoy the ice cream, pudding, and Popsicles. That doesn't sound like a diet worth complaining about.

Love,
Grandma and Grandpa Miller

To friend out with the flu

Dear Myra:

We just heard that you were down with the flu; we hope you recover soon.

Please let us know if there is anything we can do. Would you like us to make a trip to the grocery for you?

Please give us a call.

Fondly,
Emma Miller

Best wishes

Florence Eddy
Smalltown, OH

Dear Flo:

I just wanted to take this time to tell you how lovely you looked at the Senior Center dinner last Saturday; I barely had time to speak with you there.

I know it has been a hard winter for you, but I understand the news is encouraging and we are all wishing the best for you.

You've been a source of comfort and strength to me over the years, and I hope you know how appreciative I've been of that.

Fondly,
Monica

Support to ill associate

Diana Rollings
Smalltown, OH

Dear Diana:

I just heard that you would be out of the office for a while. I hope everything is fine and that you will be able to return soon. We miss you.

In the meantime, don't worry about anything here at the office. We will make sure your work is covered.

Sincerely,
Morgan Hamilton

6 Condolences

Dear Reader:

When we write to express sympathy, we are reaching out with compassion to someone who has experienced a loss or a trauma.

Before you write, consider what you know about the person who suffered the loss, or about the person who died. More so than with many other letters, your communication may be kept as part of the family history.

A letter of sympathy need not be lengthy, but anything you can add to personalize the note adds to its value.

With our best wishes,
The Authors

Dear Reader:

It never hurts to send a simple letter expressing your condolences to someone who has lost a family member.

If you knew the departed person well, or know the person you are writing to, it is appropriate to add a short remembrance.

The less well you knew the person who died, or his or her family, the more formal your note should be.

Where you can easily get into trouble is an effort to go beyond your personal knowledge. If you didn't know the person who died, don't fabricate a comment about his sense of humor, or her love of family. Be very careful not to insert a specific religious reference if you're not certain of how it will be received.

Don't take on a role you don't deserve. If you are not a minister or a psychologist or a family counselor, don't offer advice on how to deal with the loss. It is more than sufficient to express your sorrow and wish the family well.

If you know the family and want to offer some personal assistance, it's okay to do so, but don't make the offer unless you're prepared to follow through.

And in this day of computers and executive assistants, one way to quickly convey your personal involvement in the letter of condolence is to handwrite the letter on personal stationery. At the very least, you can add a handwritten note at the end of a printed letter.

Sincerely,
The Authors

Death of friend's wife

Dear Gene:

John and I were deeply saddened to hear of Martha's passing. We have our own warm remembrances of a lovely and gracious person.

Martha was courageous to the end, always thinking of family and friends ahead of herself. We were privileged to have her as a friend.

Please accept our sympathies. Our thoughts go with you and the rest of your family.

Sincerely,
Laura Diamond

Death of friend's husband

Dear Carolyn:

Harold and I were deeply saddened to hear of George's passing. He was a devoted husband to you and a dear friend to all of us.

We will cherish his memory. We know your sorrows are very great at this time, and our thoughts and prayers are with you.

When the time is right, please call us. We would like to spend time with you.

Sincerely,
Monica

Death of friend's mother

Dear Paula:

I was so sorry to learn of your mother's passing. She was a warm and gracious lady who will be missed not just by her family but by all who knew her.

Please extend my condolences to your entire family.

With my deepest sympathy,
Laura Diamond

Belated condolence

Margaret Sweeney
Smalltown, OH

Dear Margaret:

Ron and I have just returned after being out of the country for several weeks. We were deeply saddened to hear that Graham passed away while we were gone.

Please accept our belated condolences; we will miss him very much.

Sincerely,
Emma and Ron Miller

Sympathy over breakup of marriage

Dear Pam:

I was so sorry to hear that you and Tom have separated. Roger and I care deeply for both of you and wish there was something we could do to ease the pain you must be feeling.

When you want to see a friend, please call me.

Fondly,
Morgan

Sympathy on miscarriage

Dear Rachel:

I was so saddened to hear of your loss.

When you feel like having company, please call me; I'm a good listener.

Fondly,
Morgan

Death of pet

Dear Jean:

I was so sorry to hear of the death of your beloved cat Sobaka. She was a beautiful little soul and had a long and happy life in your home. She gave love to us all.

Sincerely,
Monica Diamond

Sorrow over house fire

Dear Tina and Steve:

John and I were shocked and saddened to learn of the devastating fire that destroyed your house. I'm sure you are upset about the loss of your possessions, but we are so thankful that you all escaped without injury.

Please let us know how we can help. We are here for you.

Sincerely,
Laura Diamond

7 Engagements, Weddings, and Births

continued

continued

Dear Reader:

Love, marriage, and a baby carriage are a joyous part of life for most adults, and we enjoy sharing our happiness with family and friends. Letters about engagements, weddings, and births can be very formal or they can be chatty, personal notes. The purpose is to proclaim the news and welcome others to share in the joy.

Similarly, invitations to engagement parties, wedding ceremonies, baby showers, and other events can be formal or informal. The essential details—who, what, when, and where—need to be spelled out precisely. The reason for the celebration is self-evident!

Yours truly,
The Authors

Dear Reader:

It is considered socially acceptable to send printed invitations and announcements for many of life's milepost events. You can order formal announcements from a print shop or a Web site. Keep in mind, though, that etiquette experts still advise hand-addressing the envelopes.

These days, when our mailboxes are filled with all sorts of nonpersonal correspondence, you also should consider the impact you can make with a handwritten or at least personally drafted letter to inform a friend or acquaintance of important news.

Sincerely,
The Authors

Formal announcement of engagement

Laura and John Diamond
announce the engagement
of Morgan Miller Diamond
to
Roger Hamilton
of Smalltown, Ohio

Informal announcement of engagement

Dear Friends:

I am thrilled to announce that our daughter Morgan is engaged to marry Roger Hamilton. They will marry this summer.

Morgan works in the medical laboratory at Smalltown General Hospital and plans to attend graduate school this fall to study hospital administration.

Roger is a physical therapist at the hospital.

We're very happy with Morgan's choice; Roger will be a great addition to the family and we know that our friends will enjoy meeting him.

Best regards,
Laura and John Diamond

Engagement notice to newspaper

Style Editor
Smalltown Banner
Smalltown, OH

Dear Editor:

Enclosed is the information about Morgan Diamond's engagement. I have written the announcement in the form recommended by the paper and I am also enclosing a black-and-white picture. If anything else is required, please call me.

Sincerely,
Laura Diamond

Informal save the date for wedding

Leslie Davis
New York, NY

Dear Leslie:

Saturday, May 20: mark it with a big heart on your calendar! Roger and I have set that date for our wedding, and you absolutely have to be here. I just couldn't think of starting the rest of my life without my oldest and dearest friend on hand.

As they say on TV, details to follow.

Love,
Morgan

Formal save the date for wedding

Please save the date of
Saturday, the twentieth of May
for the wedding of
Morgan Miller Diamond
to
Roger Hamilton

From friend to parents of engaged daughter

Dear Laura and John:

Thank you for sharing the wonderful news of Morgan's engagement. Knowing Morgan as we do, we are sure Roger is aware of what a fantastic partner he is getting.

If the kids seek a role model of a good marriage, they need only look to yours.

Sincerely,
Ken and Grace

To mother of bride on announcement of engagement

Dear Laura:

It is hard to believe that our little girls are grown. Rob and I will be thinking of you and your entire family in the very busy months ahead.

Please send our best wishes to Morgan and her future husband, Roger.

Sincerely,
Helen O'Brien

From acquaintance to engaged friend

Dear Morgan:

I am so happy to hear of your engagement to Roger.

One of the benefits of working at the hospital is meeting people like the both of you.

Separately you are great individuals; together you make a super couple.

Sincerely,
Lisa Hanson

Engagement of friend

Dear Morgan:

I am so happy to hear of your engagement to Roger. I must confess, though, it is not a surprise. When I had lunch with both of you recently, I could see that you made a wonderful couple.

Please keep me up-to-date on all your plans and pass on my regards to Roger; I know he realizes how fortunate he is.

Sincerely,
Dawn

From friend of fiancé to newly engaged woman

Dear Morgan:

I am sure Roger has spoken about me quite a bit; I trust you don't believe any of it. Roger and I have been friends for a long time, since grade school in fact, and I'm the keeper of all the embarrassing secrets. I'll be glad to share.

Seriously, Morgan, let me say how thrilled I am that the two of you are engaged. I do feel I know you already because he has told me so much about you, and how lucky he feels to have found you. I can't wait 'til we meet.

Did he ever tell you his nickname in third grade was the kissing bandit?

Sincerely,
Kevin George

From sister of fiancé welcoming to family

Dear Morgan:

We're all so thrilled that the two of you have made it official.

That allows me to formally welcome you to the Hamilton family. Like most brothers and sisters, Roger and I don't see eye-to-eye on everything, but this time I couldn't agree with him more.

Roger will be getting a wonderful partner for life, and I pick up a great friend and sister-in-law in the bargain.

Fondly,
Anna

Requesting restaurant information and menus for wedding

Banquet Manager
Sebastian's on the Lake
Smalltown, OH

Dear Manager:

My daughter and her fiancé are to be married on Saturday, May 20. We have had many delightful meals at your restaurant and have been guests at various functions there.

We would like to have the wedding reception at Sebastian's. Please let me know if that date is open, and send us menus and price lists.

Sincerely,
Laura Diamond

Turning down a restaurant as a possible reception location

Stephanie Nolan, Banquet Manager
Sebastian's on the Lake
Smalltown, OH

Dear Stephanie:

Thank you for the information on Sebastian's. We have, however, made other arrangements for our daughter's wedding. We will certainly keep you in mind for future gatherings.

Thank you.

Laura Diamond

Ordering wedding cake

Flora Lalique
Pain du Jour
Smalltown, OH

Dear Flora:

Roger and I enjoyed meeting with you last Thursday to discuss the plans for our wedding cake. I had to push Roger out the door before he ate too many samples and outgrew his tux.

We would love for you to bake our wedding cake. We especially liked your suggestion of a croquembouche, the traditional French wedding cake of cream-filled choux puffs decorated in spun sugar.

I will be in later next week (minus Roger) to go over details and make the deposit.

Sincerely,
Morgan Diamond

Inquiring about availability of church for wedding

Office Manager
Nearby Central Church
Nearby, OH

Dear Office Manager:

We are planning our daughter's wedding and want to know about the availability of the church for the ceremony. Our daughter and her fiancé have chosen Saturday, May 20, for their wedding.

We expect a gathering of about 200 people. The reception will be held after the ceremony at a restaurant or catering hall.

If the church is available, would you please let us know what sort of arrangements we would need to make, and the typical donation from families.

Sincerely,
Laura Diamond

Inquiring about availability of wedding hall

Sharon Leonard
Leonard's Wedding Hall
Smalltown, OH

Dear Ms. Leonard:

My daughter and her fiancé are to be married on Saturday, May 20. We have attended a number of events at Leonard's and we are considering having the wedding reception at your hall.

Please let me know if that date is open for an afternoon reception and dinner, and send us menus and price lists.

Sincerely,
Laura Diamond

Requesting special-needs accommodation at reception

Sharon Leonard
Leonard's Wedding Hall
Smalltown, OH

Dear Ms. Leonard:

Thank you for your time when we visited last week. We are considering having our wedding reception at your facility.

We have one other concern that I hope you can help us with: My grandmother uses a wheelchair and requires the use of an oxygen bottle. I would like to know the details of your accommodations for visitors with special needs such as hers.

Will she be able to make her way through all of the rooms for the affair? Where are the handicapped parking spaces?

Sincerely,
Morgan Diamond

Booking site for wedding

Sandra Morgan, Events Coordinator
Smalltown Art Museum
Smalltown, OH

Dear Ms. Morgan:

Thank you for meeting with us yesterday to discuss our wedding plans. We have always considered the Smalltown Art Museum to be a treasure, and we are thrilled at the prospect of having our wedding reception and ceremony there.

Please reserve Saturday, May 20 for our wedding.

We are available at your convenience to go over details and make a deposit. Please call to arrange a time.

We both feel that starting our life together at such a special place is a good omen.

Sincerely,
Morgan Diamond and Roger Hamilton

Formal wedding invitation

Mr. and Mrs. John Diamond
request the honor of your presence
at the marriage of their daughter
Morgan Miller Diamond
to
Roger Hamilton

On Saturday, the twentieth of May
Two thousand and four
at half past two o'clock

Wedding Pavilion
Smalltown Art Museum
Smalltown, OH

Alternate formal wedding invitation

The parents of
Jill Kiefer and Larry Van Dyke
invite you to join them at a reception
celebrating their children's marriage
Saturday, August 19, from 2 until 6 o'clock
100 Southbury Road

RSVP xxx-xxx-xxxx.

Reception at wedding site

Reception
Immediately following the ceremony

Wedding Pavilion
Smalltown Art Museum
Smalltown, OH

Reception at different location

Reception
Following the ceremony

Sebastian's on the Lake
Lakeview Road
Smalltown, OH

Map enclosed

Request for an RSVP

The favor of a reply
is requested by the
Fifteenth of April

M________
❒ will attend
❒ declines with regret

Formal acceptance of invitation to wedding

Mr. and Mrs. Samuel Bebe accept with pleasure your invitation to the marriage of your daughter, Heather Diamond, to Roger Hamilton, son of Helen and George Hamilton, on Saturday, the twentieth of May, at half past two o'clock at the Wedding Pavilion of the Smalltown Art Museum, Smalltown, Ohio.

Partial acceptance of invitation to wedding

Mr. and Mrs. Jasper Ray are honored to accept your kind invitation to the wedding of your daughter, Morgan Diamond, to Roger Hamilton, son of Helen and George

Hamilton, on Saturday, the twentieth of May at half past two o'clock at the Wedding Pavilion of the Smalltown Art Museum, Smalltown, Ohio.

We regret that due to a prior engagement, we will be unable to attend the reception following the wedding.

Alternate partial acceptance of invitation to wedding

Mr. Sanford Thomas gratefully accepts your kind invitation to the wedding of your daughter, Morgan Diamond to Roger Hamilton, son of Helen and George Hamilton, on Saturday, the twentieth of May at half past two o'clock at the Wedding Pavilion of the Smalltown Art Museum, Smalltown, Ohio.

I regret, though, that Mrs. Gretchen Thomas will not be in attendance.

Asking minister to perform wedding

The Reverend Peter Hall
Smalltown Congregational Church
Smalltown, OH

Dear Mr. Hall:

Twenty-five years ago you baptized our baby Morgan; this May, John will walk Morgan down the aisle at her wedding. It would be an honor to have you officiate at this very special occasion.

Morgan is to be married on Saturday, May 20, at 2:30 P.M. on the grounds of the Smalltown Art Museum.

Please let us know if you are available to officiate and, if so, a time when we can come to meet with you to discuss the details.

Sincerely,
Laura Diamond

Seeking information about floral pieces for wedding

Rose Ragosa
Bright Seeds and Bulbs Florist
Smalltown, OH

Dear Ms. Ragosa:

Our family has visited your florist shop many times in the past when we needed just the right touch with flowers. We have never been disappointed.

Our daughter is to be married this spring and we are looking for someone who can help us express the beauty of this day.

Please call me to set a time when my daughter and I can come in to discuss our ideas and get some expert advice from you.

Sincerely,
Laura Diamond

Seeking information from caterer

Emeril Gassé
Midnight Buffet Caterers
Smalltown, OH

Dear Mr. Gassé:

My daughter and her fiancé are to be married on Saturday, May 20, with a ceremony and reception on the grounds of the Smalltown Art Museum.

Your company was recommended to us by several prominent Smalltown residents.

Can we arrange a time to meet? We have a lot of ideas but also many questions. Please call at your convenience.

Sincerely,
Laura Diamond

Ordering tent for ceremony

Smalltown Rental Center
Smalltown, OH

Dear People:

My daughter and her fiancé are to be married on May 20 on the grounds of the Smalltown Art Museum. We would like to make arrangements to rent a tent and seating for 200 guests for the ceremony.

Sandra Morgan, events coordinator at the museum, suggested we consider renting equipment from your company. Please send us information about available tents, seating, and other items we might need.

Sincerely,
John Diamond

Requesting special hotel rate for wedding guests

Gerald Spiller, General Manager
Serenity Now Hotel
Smalltown, OH

Dear Mr. Spiller:

My daughter and her fiancé will be married on May 20. The Smalltown Art Museum grounds will be the site of both the ceremony and reception.

We anticipate that between the two families, about fifty couples will need accommodations for the night of May 20. We would like to be able to recommend a quality hotel like Serenity Now to our guests.

Would you be able to accommodate our guests for that night? Can you offer them a significant discount? What deadline would be necessary for reservations?

We would appreciate a response by February 20, as we will be printing and mailing invitations soon thereafter.

Sincerely,
Laura Diamond

Inquiry about photographer for wedding

John Ernest Weinberg
Weinberg Photography
Smalltown, OH

Dear Mr. Weinberg:

I admire the work you did at the weddings of several of my friends in recent years, and I'm considering hiring you to document my own special day.

I will be married on May 20 at the Smalltown Art Museum. Would you please give me a call soon to set an appointment to discuss photography for the wedding?

Thank you.

Sincerely,
Morgan Diamond

Engaging musician for wedding

Catherine Gibson
Classical Harpist
Smalltown, OH

Dear Ms. Gibson:

I had the pleasure of hearing you play at a wedding I attended last winter. I am getting married this spring and hope that my fiancé and I can engage your services for our wedding.

We are getting married on Saturday, May 20, and the ceremony and reception will be on the grounds of the Smalltown Art Museum.

We would like to have you play for about an hour as guests arrive, and then again after the ceremony for about two hours while we have cocktails and dinner.

Please let me know if you are available. If you are, my fiancé and I will arrange to meet with you to discuss your fee and the selection of music.

Sincerely,
Morgan Diamond

Engaging band for reception

Rick Jackson
Jackson and the Shelties
Smalltown, OH

Dear Mr. Jackson:

I have been a fan of your music for some time. I am getting married this spring and would like to have your group play at our reception. The date is May 20, and the reception will take place on the grounds of the Smalltown Art Museum.

We would like to have music and dancing from 4 to 6 P.M. Please contact me as soon as possible so that my fiancée and I can arrange to meet with you to discuss your fee and the music.

Sincerely,
Roger Hamilton

Hiring caterer for wedding

Emeril Gassé
Midnight Buffet Caterers
Smalltown, OH

Dear Emeril:

Thank you for meeting with us last week, and for the delicious samples you brought for us to taste. I told Roger to enjoy our wedding dinner, because he won't get such fine dining from me for some time, if ever.

We would love for you to handle all the food preparation and service for our reception.

At your convenience, let's get together again to go over menus, times, and details.

Sincerely,
Morgan Diamond

Limousine service for wedding

Willie's Limousine Service
Smalltown, OH

Dear Willie:

My daughter will be getting married on Saturday, May 20. We would like to arrange for a limousine to take her from our home, at the address on this letter, to the Smalltown Art Museum, where the ceremony and reception will take place.

Would you please call soon to tell us about availability and charges?

Sincerely
John Diamond

Invitation to rehearsal dinner

George and Helen Hamilton
request the pleasure of your company
at a rehearsal dinner
in honor of
Morgan Miller Diamond
and
Roger Hamilton
on Friday, the nineteenth of May
at seven o'clock
Sebastian's on the Lake
Smalltown, OH

RSVP xxx-xxx-xxxx

Welcoming granddaughter's fiancé to family

Roger Hamilton
Smalltown, OH

Dear Roger:

As the elder statesman (or just the oldest member) of the Diamond/Miller clan, I want to officially welcome you to our family. You have chosen a true gem, and we could not be more pleased.

Morgan's grandmother and I will get much pleasure watching the two of you (from a non-interfering distance, of course) as you go through the joys and struggles of married life. We know you have a strong enough bond that your love will grow as the years pass.

We hope some day you will have the joy of writing a letter like this to your own first grandchild when he or she contemplates marriage.

Fondly,
Ron and Emma

Offering thank-you gift to reception site

Sandra Morgan, Events Coordinator
Smalltown Art Museum
Smalltown, OH

Dear Sandra:

As you know, my fiancé, Roger Hamilton, and I will be married on the grounds of the Smalltown Art Museum on Saturday, May 20. We are both thrilled to be able to begin our married life in such a beautiful and magical place.

We would like to make a small gift to the museum to commemorate this date—perhaps a tree or a bench for the garden, or some other meaningful addition. We'd appreciate any suggestions you might have.

Sincerely,
Morgan Diamond

Thanks to sister for being in wedding

Heather Diamond
Smalltown, OH

Dear Heather:

I hope your future includes a day as wonderful as the one Roger and I had on Saturday. We are so happy to be beginning our lives together, and it was very special to me to have my little sister as maid of honor.

Thank you for all you did for me and with me . . . and to me. You were my obnoxious little sister and I was your snooty older sibling; now you're a bright and genuinely interesting young woman . . . and Roger's favorite sister-in-law.

Even though you'll never have a little sister in your wedding, I guess you will have to settle for an older one who will always love you and treasure you as a friend.

Love,
Morgan

To child member of the wedding

Hannah Diamond
Smalltown, OH

Dear Hannah:

What a wonderful job you did in the wedding! You looked so pretty and knew just where to throw the rose petals. Uncle Roger and I were proud of you.

I hope you like this locket. You can put a picture in it of someone who is most important to you now (maybe your stuffed bear, Molly) and change it as you grow bigger and bigger.

When I was just about your age, a long time ago, I was in your great-aunt Liz's wedding, and I was given a locket just like this one. Guess whose picture I have in it now? Uncle Roger's.

Love,
Aunt Morgan

Thanks to caterer

Emeril Gassé
Midnight Buffet Caterers
Smalltown, OH

Dear Emeril:

The meal you prepared for our wedding was très magnifique! Much better than my French.

Thank you for doing such a fine job with all the food. The vegetarian and low-sodium dishes you so worried about were wonderful. I tried them—in fact, I tried just about everything.

Please feel free to use us as references (and taste-testers) for future weddings.

Sincerely,
Morgan Hamilton

Cancellation of an engagement

Mr. and Mrs. George Ford announce that
the engagement of their daughter
Barbara Allan and Mr. Dan Seeger
has been ended by mutual consent

Cancellation of a scheduled wedding

Mr. and Mrs. George Ford announce
that the marriage of their daughter
Barbara Allan
to
Mr. Dan Seeger
will not occur

Cancellation of wedding ceremony and reception because of unforeseen event

Mr. and Mrs. George Ford
regret they are obliged to recall
the invitations to the marriage of their daughter
Barbara Allan to Mr. Dan Seeger
Due to the death of Mr. Seeger's father
Paul E. Seeger
The ceremony will be held privately
In the presence of the immediate family

Postponement of a scheduled wedding

Mr. and Mrs. George Ford announce
that the marriage of their daughter
Barbara Allan
to
Mr. Dan Seeger
will be postponed until September

A new invitation will be forthcoming

Informal letter about cancellation of wedding

Dear Morgan:

I wish this were a happier letter but I must write it anyway. Dan and I have decided to cancel our wedding plans. It was a mutual decision and we part as friends.

We will be returning all of the beautiful gifts everyone so generously gave us.

Thanks for your understanding and support. I do believe that things work out for the best.

Sincerely,
Barbara

Return of gifts

Dear Friends:

As you know, Dan and I have decided to cancel our wedding. As painful as it was to call off our plans, we decided it would be better to do so now rather than enter into a marriage without a full commitment.

With this letter I am returning your wedding gift. We truly appreciate your expression of best wishes to us both.

Sincerely,
Barbara Allan Ford

Announcing adoption of baby

Dear Friends:

Kevin and I are thrilled to tell you that we have completed the adoption proceedings of our daughter May-Li. The three of us returned from China last week—a family at last!

She was born on March 13, and her older brother Scott thinks she is just the greatest.

Sincerely,
Lynn

Welcoming party for adopted baby

Dear Friends:

We would be honored if you would join us at our home on Sunday, May 6, for an informal party to welcome our new daughter, May-Li.

She's only six months old, but she already has made it clear she loves to be the center of attention.

Sincerely,
Lynn

8 Invitations and Requests

continued

Dear Reader:

An invitation is not an order; it is a courteous request to attend an event or to do something.

Your invitation should include all of the necessary details, and it should demonstrate formal or informal good manners: we would love to have you attend; we request the honor of your presence; we seek the pleasure of your company.

Whether or not an invitation specifically asks for an RSVP, or regrets, good manners calls for a reply: we will be honored to attend; we will be happy to be present; we deeply regret we will be unable to attend; because of a previous commitment we must decline.

With our deepest regards,
The Authors

Asking neighbor to be emergency contact for school

Pam Nicklaus
Fairview, PA

Dear Pam:

We have been asked by the elementary school to list an emergency contact for Brian in case he needs to come home because of illness. Would you be willing to be that contact?

As you know, I work from home most of the time but occasionally have to go into the office.

I would be happy to do the same for you, picking up Shelly when needed.

Sincerely,
Karen Diamond

Invitation to graduation party

Dear Jean and Bob:

On Saturday, June 26, our daughter Heather will be graduating from high school. We hope you'll join us as we commemorate this special day with family and friends.

We'll have an open house from 5 to 9 P.M. and hope you can drop by during that time.

Sincerely,
Laura Diamond

Declining invitation

Dear Betty:

Thank you so much for including us in the group that will be celebrating your anniversary. Forty years! What a wonderful milestone for such a wonderful couple.

Unfortunately, we will not be able to attend the party. Our daughter Heather graduates from high school that day and we'll be spending our time with her.

I will call you soon, though, to see if we can get together for dinner to celebrate your anniversary and raise a toast to our new college student.

Sincerely,
Laura Diamond

Invitation to dinner party

Dear Dot:

On Saturday, July 16, we will be hosting a small dinner party, and we would love to have you join us.

John's brother Ed and his lovely wife Marilyn will be visiting us for a few weeks, and we would like to introduce them to some of our special friends.

Please join us at our house for cocktails at 7 P.M. We look forward to seeing you both again.

Fondly,
Laura

Formal invitation to cocktail party

The pleasure of your company is requested by
Mr. and Mrs. Walter Undershot
for cocktails
to meet
Miss Cleona Puccini
international opera star
Thursday, September 19
at 7:00 P.M.
in the Regal Suite
Smalltown Tilton Hotel

Invitation to international dinner party

Jane Simon
Smalltown, OH

Dear Jane:

Get out your passports: our dinner group is going around the world.

On Saturday, September 18, at 7 P.M., we will be hosting an international dinner at our house. We're asking each couple to prepare one entrée and one appetizer or dessert to share with five other couples. We're hoping for a completely illogical mix of wonderful food from around the world.

I hope you and Sam can make it; you're among our most imaginative cooks.

Please call to RSVP and to register your dish with me so that we can avoid duplication.

Sincerely,
Laura Diamond

Invitation to beer tasting party

Leo and Cathy Burns
Smalltown, OH

Dear Leo and Cathy:

So you think you really know your beer? We're calling your bluff.

Please join us at our house on Sunday, October 14, at 6 P.M. for dinner and a beer tasting party. We're going to offer six different brews—hidden within plain brown wrappers—and give you the chance to voice your opinions on each and see if you really can tell the difference between Cheap Suds and Golden Hops.

Please let us know if you're going to come.

Sincerely,
John Diamond

Invitation to adult costume party

Dear Friends:

Why should we let the kids have all the fun at Halloween?

Please join us on Saturday, October 29, at 7 P.M. in the recreation room at the Lakeview Senior Apartment Complex for an adult costume party. We'll have food, music, and (we hope) some most unusual attendees.

We're looking forward to your frightful appearance.

Sincerely,
Ron Miller

Invitation to New Year's Party

Carl and Debbie Gradstein
Smalltown, OH

Dear Carl and Debbie:

We hope you'll join us on New Year's Eve for a special party—our first as a married couple.

We'll serve dinner and drinks starting at 8 P.M., and toast the new year at midnight.

Please let us know if you can attend.

Sincerely,
Morgan and Roger Hamilton

Invitation to World Series party

Dear Friends:

Go Red Sox!

Yes, I know Boston didn't make it to the World Series. Again.

But that doesn't mean we can't have a party to watch the opening game of the series Friday night (October 8). I'll be rooting against the Yankees, which is not quite the same as rooting for the Braves. You can choose your own side.

The game and the party start at 7 P.M., and we'll be serving stadium haute cuisine: hot dogs, pizza, popcorn, and beer. Please leave your cleats at home.

Sincerely,
Josh Diamond

Invitation to friends for a reunion

Dear Alumni:

Can you believe it's been five years since we graduated from Smalltown University?

Our little group has more or less kept in touch, and for that we are very fortunate. To commemorate this special occasion, though, we are going to go one step further. We are actually going to try to see each other, in person, face-to-face.

Nancy, Brad, and I are trying to pick a Saturday in June when we can meet for dinner, go over old times, and fill in everybody on what's happening to such fabulous and interesting people.

Please get in touch with one of us and give us some dates when you are available.

Best regards,
Morgan

Accepting invitation to reunion

Dear Morgan:

Count me in. I just checked my very heavy social calendar for June and guess what, I'm free every Saturday!

Things aren't that dismal, but even if Prince Charming finally arrived to whisk me off on some romantic getaway, I'd tell him to return in July.

Seriously, great idea, just give me the date and time. I can't wait.

Best regards,
Lisa

Formal acceptance of invitation

Mr. John Diamond gratefully accepts your kind invitation to dinner at the Smalltown University Club on Friday, November twenty-second, at six-thirty P.M.

More cordial formal acceptance of invitation

Mr. and Mrs. John Diamond are pleased to accept your gracious invitation to a reception in honor of your daughter, Ruth, on Friday evening, the eleventh of April, at seven o'clock at the Smalltown Library.

Declining reunion invitation

Dear Morgan:

The reunion is a great idea, but I'm afraid I can't make it in June. I'm working now for Philips Technology and they're sending me to Seattle for some training.

Please keep me posted on plans and addresses; I hope I can get together with you guys on a less formal basis sometime later in the year.

Sincerely,
Tom

Invitation to renewal of wedding vows

Dear Laura and John:

After thirty-five years of living together, Jim and I are getting married . . . again, that is. We have decided to renew our vows, this time with family, friends, and children.

Please join us on Saturday, March 25, at 7 P.M. at the Crystal House. The Reverend Michael Smith will perform the service, as he did so many years ago, and a reception will follow our ceremony.

No presents, please; this time around we have everything we need.

Sincerely,
Sharon Peters

Formal invitation to renewal of wedding vows

Together with their children and grandchildren
Jim and Sharon Peters
invite you to join with them
as they renew their wedding vows
on Saturday, the nineteenth of August
two thousand and four
at eleven A.M.
Smalltown Congregational Church

Reception following
RSVP xxx-xxx-xxxx No gifts, please

Acceptance of wedding vows invitation

Dear Sharon:

I cannot think of anywhere we would rather be than with you and Jim as you renew your vows.

If any couple can make the next thirty-five years even better than the first time through, it is the two of you. We accept with pleasure.

Sincerely,
Laura Diamond

Acceptance with regrets about leaving early

Mr. and Mrs. William O'Brien are delighted to accept your gracious invitation to brunch at Sebastian's on the Lake on Saturday, the nineteenth of April, at 10:30 A.M.

Unfortunately, we will have to leave early, at 11:30 A.M., due to a prior engagement.

Acceptance with regrets

Gladys Adams is delighted to accept your gracious invitation to a reception for Benjamin Channing on Sunday, July 3, at Oysters Grille.

Unfortunately, Stephen Adams regrets that he will be unable to attend because of a prior commitment.

Asking about interest in class reunion

Barbara Randolph
Smalltown, OH

Dear Barbara:

Can you believe that this June will mark thirty-five years since we graduated from Smalltown High School? Where did the years go? I certainly haven't gotten older, have you?

We had a great class with some really special people, and I'd like to see (almost) every one of them again. I've run this by a few of our former classmates who still live in Smalltown: Bob Gucci, Hillary Adams Smith, and Mary Barker Lewis. They're pumped.

Barbara, you are the most organized person I know—you've been like that all the way back to when you were class secretary. Would you like to help get this going?

Sincerely,
John Diamond
President, Class of 1969

Letter from classmate expressing interest in reunion

John Diamond
Smalltown, OH

Dear Mr. President:

John, you must have read my mind. Just the other day I found myself telling my kids a cleaned-up version of the story of Ken Roth's magic act at the senior talent show.

Actually, I keep in touch with quite a few of our old classmates in and out of Smalltown. I am sure we would have enough for some kind of get-together.

I'll contact the school to get a list of the most recent addresses they have for our class. There are also places to go on the Internet to find people.

We can write to everyone and start appointing committees. Just like the Junior Prom.

Sincerely,
Barbara Randolph
Secretary, Class of 1969

Suggesting draft of invitation letter for reunion

John Diamond
Smalltown, OH

Dear John:

I received the address list for the school, and I'm flooded with memories.

Attached is a draft of the letter announcing the reunion. Would you please add your usual sparkle to it?

We also need to set a date. I was trying to think of a time when most people would be free to come to Smalltown from other places; I was thinking of mid-July. Perhaps we should ask people to choose from a set of possible dates and settle on the one that will bring us the most possible attendees.

Sincerely,
Barbara

Announcement of reunion

Dear members of Smalltown High School Class of 1969:

I bet you haven't been referred to that way in a long time; thirty-five years, as a matter of fact.

But we—class president John Diamond and class secretary Barbara Benjamin Randolph—are back, and we're asking for your help in organizing a reunion. We would like to get together for dinner, dancing, bad jokes, and a joyful recounting of our most embarrassing moments in Smalltown.

Before we get too far into the details of where and what, we want to try to pick a date when as many people as possible can come home to Smalltown. Please fill out the attached form to indicate if you are interested in coming to a reunion, and indicate which of the suggested dates are good for you. Number them from 1 (your preferred date) to your least preferred date. Mark any date you cannot make with a "no."

I'm looking forward to seeing everybody again . . . I think!

Sincerely,
Barbara Benjamin Randolph
Secretary, Class of 1969

Report on response to initial reunion letter

John Diamond
Smalltown, OH

Dear John:

The Class of 1969 seems eager to get back together; of the 83 letters I sent out, I have already received 50 responses, and 41 of our classmates are interested in coming.

(Would you believe Simon Ross is chief of psychiatry at a big hospital in New York?)

I've gone ahead and made some committee appointments. Emily Baker Potter, who still lives in Smalltown, will work on finding a restaurant. Don Johns (crazy Don, with the Mustang, is a car dealer, of course) will look into finding a band.

Once we get a handle on the costs, we can send a letter specifying the date and amount.

Sincerely,
Barbara

Details for reunion

John Diamond
Smalltown, OH

Dear John:

The details for the reunion are falling into place nicely. Emily got a great price for dinner at Rodeo Steak House. And Don has hired a band called Jackson and the Shelties. Should I be afraid?

We have a near-final count of 115 attendees, including 75 grads plus 40 wives, husbands, and assorted significant others.

Marsha Ryan is coming early all the way from Portland, Maine, to do the decorations. She's an interior decorator. Mike Davis is working on the history and is doing a funny, clever job.

It looks like the winner of the longest-trip prize will be Sam Morrison, who is coming all the way from Juneau, Alaska.

Sincerely,
Barbara

Announcement of reunion date

Dear members of Smalltown High School Class of 1969:

Dry-clean your minis, bring out your love beads, and mark your calendars. We've chosen Saturday, July 16, as the date for the thirty-fifth anniversary reunion.

We tried to pick a date when the most people could attend. If we've managed to choose one that is impossible for you—if you're dining with the Queen of England or picking up a Nobel Prize that day—please drop me a note so that we can extend your regrets (with an explanation) to the class.

We will be sending out a formal invitation soon, with all the details.

Sincerely,
Barbara Benjamin Randolph
Secretary, Class of 1969

Invitation to class reunion

Dear members of Smalltown High School Class of 1969:

Thirty-five years ago we gathered on the stage of the Smalltown High School auditorium. Principal Whalen gave us our diplomas, a handshake, and permission to conquer the world.

We have, of course, done exactly that.

Please join your classmates for a reunion on Saturday, July 16. We'll gather at 7 P.M. at Rodeo Steak House, 19 Pleasant Street, in Smalltown. We will begin with an informal cocktail party, and then move on to dinner, speeches, and dancing.

Class historian Michael Davis (British Studies teacher at Greenland High School in Vermont) will read the fractured tales of SHS graduates, and we will hand out some long-overdue awards.

Of course, spouses and significant others are invited. Please fill out the enclosed RSVP card and include your check for dinner.

For those of you coming from out of town, Charley Fossum of Sleepy Town Motel has volunteered discount rooms to classmates.

Hope to see you back in Smalltown.

Sincerely,
John Diamond
President, Class of 1969

Thanks to reunion co-chair

Barbara Randolph
Smalltown, OH

Dear Barbara:

Once again, congratulations. You did a terrific job organizing the reunion. I don't think I had such a good time at any point in all four years of high school.

A few of us are getting together at my house for dinner on Wednesday evening, July 27, to go over all the final details, expenses, and thank-yous. Please join us at 6:30 P.M.

Sincerely,
John

Request to watch house while on vacation

Monica Diamond
Smalltown, OH

Dear Monica:

Our round-the-world trip is approaching quickly and we're getting a bit anxious about the grand adventure—we've never done anything this extravagant before.

As we discussed a few weeks back, we would really appreciate you and Harold keeping an eye on our house while we travel. The post office will hold the mail, and we've canceled the newspaper, but please look for any packages or fliers that might still be delivered while we are away.

You have a key to the house. Thanks for your offer to water the plants—they only need attention every few days.

I have attached a copy of our complete itinerary, including the emergency phone number on the cruise ship and our e-mail address; we expect to be checking for e-mails every few days at Internet cafés in port.

Thanks again. We promise an invitation to our gala slide show when we return.

Sincerely,
Marge Clinton

Arranging anniversary party at senior center

Social Director
Lakeview Apartments
Smalltown, OH

Dear Director:

My parents, Ron and Emma Miller, will be celebrating their sixtieth wedding anniversary in a few weeks.

The family has decided that the best place to celebrate this amazing milestone would be among friends and family at their retirement home at Lakeview Apartments.

We would like to have a reception for all residents and our family in the lounge on Thursday, April 23, from 3 to 5 P.M.

Please let me know if this would be possible. We would arrange for light refreshments and a band.

Most important: We would like to keep this a surprise to mom and dad for as long as possible. We are going to ask Jack Ryan of the senior activities group to quietly spread the word.

I look forward to hearing from you soon.

Sincerely,
Laura Diamond

Arranging anniversary party details

Jack Ryan, President
Senior Activities Center
Lakeview Apartments
Smalltown, OH

Dear Jack:

My parents, Ron and Emma Miller, will be celebrating their sixtieth wedding anniversary on April 23, and I am arranging for a surprise reception for them in the lounge at the complex on April 23 between 3 and 5 P.M.

They speak so highly of the friends they have made at Lakeview that we thought it would be wonderful for my parents to share some part of this special day with all of you.

We will arrange for refreshments and a band. We do not expect guests to bring gifts.

If possible, we would like the party to be a surprise for them. Is there some way we can notify everyone but my parents of this little reception?

I look forward to hearing from you.

Sincerely,
Laura Diamond

Response on anniversary party details

Laura Diamond
Smalltown, OH

Dear Laura:

I remember meeting you when your parents moved in.

Ron and Emma have very quickly become an important part of our little community, and we thank you for letting us all be part of their special day.

I will circulate an invitation and try as hard as humanly possible to see that the party is kept a surprise. Please let us know how you'd like the invitation to read.

Also let us know what sort of volunteer help you could use in setup and decorations for the party.

Sincerely,
Jack Ryan

Informal anniversary invitation

Jack Ryan, President
Senior Activities Center
Lakeview Apartments
Smalltown, OH

Dear Jack:

Thank you for your kind note. We could use a few extra hands on April 23 to bring in the food and hang some decorations. I'll be in touch when we have details.

Here is some suggested language for the invitation:

To all residents of Lakeview Apartments:

Sixty years ago, a very young Emma Coffin and a dashing and handsome Ron Miller promised to love and cherish each other for the rest of their lives. Now, with a different generation of their family and new but dear friends, we will celebrate that commitment once more.

Please join us in a SURPRISE reception for Emma and Ron in the lounge on April 23 from 3 to 5 P.M.

No gifts, please, just the pleasure of your company.

And please, don't spoil the surprise.

Jack Ryan, President

Formal invitation to anniversary celebration

You are cordially invited to share
in a celebration of
George and Jean Strong's 50th Anniversary
Cocktails, hors d'oeuvres, and lunch
Saturday, July 3, 1 P.M.–5 P.M.
Smalltown Lakeside Hotel
Smalltown, OH

Given by their children and grandchildren

Thank you for surprise anniversary party

Dear residents:

We would like to thank all of the dear friends who made our anniversary so special. We truly were surprised—at first we were a bit miffed that no one seemed to want to talk to us about our upcoming anniversary, and then we found out that all of you were conspiring behind our backs for this wonderful party.

Our daughter Laura was right when she told you there was not another place we would have rather been on that day.

Sincerely,
Ron and Emma Miller

Invitation to child's birthday party at home

Brittany Kelly
Smalltown, OH

Dear Brittany:

Please come to my party!
It's my fourth birthday. I'm going to have a huge cake and we'll play games.
Please have one of your parents call my mom to let us know if you can come.

The date: Saturday, May 22 from 1 to 3 P.M.
My phone: (xxx) xxx-xxxx

Hannah

P.S. Please tell your parents that there will be a barbecue for the grownups, too.

Invitation to child's birthday at museum

Louise Herman
Fairview, PA

Dear Louise:

Brian is inviting some of his friends to a birthday celebration, which will take place in the recreation room at the Fairview Children's Museum on Saturday, November 13, from 2 to 5 P.M.

We will meet in the lobby at 2 P.M. and be given a private tour of the museum and a session with a professional (temporary) tattoo artist and face painter. After that we will proceed to the recreation room for burgers, fries, and a cake.

Brian will be distributing the invitations at school.

Feel free to leave Christopher at the museum during the hours of the party. Please let us know if you will be picking him up at 5 P.M. or if he will need a ride home.

Sincerely,
Karen Diamond

Invitation to adult birthday party

Jim and Cindy Sullivan
Smalltown, OH

Dear Jim and Cindy:

Morgan's birthday is August 19 (she'd kill me if I told you the exact details). I am planning what I hope will be a surprise party for her on that day.

I'd love it if you would be one of the guests.

Here's the plan: Please arrive at Caruso's Italian Restaurant at 7 P.M. on August 19. Tell Enrico you're there for Morgan's party and he'll take you to the private room at the back. I'll bring Morgan to Caruso's at 7:30 P.M.

Please let me know if you can make it. We'd love to have you there.

Sincerely,
Roger Hamilton

Letter to college asking for birthday cake for daughter

Dining Services
Smalltown University
Smalltown, OH

Dear People:

My daughter Heather Diamond is a freshman at Smalltown University, living in Maple Hall, Room 560.

I notice in the information packet we received from the college that it is possible to arrange for the delivery of a birthday cake.

I would like to have a cake sent to her room on September 28. The inscription should say: "Happy Birthday Heather. Love, Mom and Dad."

Please let me know about the charges.

Sincerely,
Laura Diamond

Invitation to tenth wedding anniversary party

Louise and Greg Herman
Fairview, PA

Dear Louise and Greg:

We hope you'll join us at an informal party on Friday, November 30, at 8 P.M. to celebrate our tenth wedding anniversary.

We'll provide the champagne and cake; we're asking our friends to bring the noisemakers and the confetti. No gifts, please.

Please let us know if you're available.

Sincerely,
Karen and Michael Diamond

Informal invitation to twenty-fifth wedding anniversary party

Mort and Shelley Gorman
Smalltown, OH

Dear Mort and Shelley:

We would very much like the pleasure of your company at a Silver Wedding Anniversary Party for our dear friends Diana and David Windsor, to be held at our house on June 19 from 7 to 11 P.M.

Entertainment will be provided by Jackson and the Shelties, and dinner will be served in a gala tent.

Please reply to me with acceptances or regrets by June 1.

Laura Diamond
Smalltown, OH

Informal invitation to fiftieth wedding anniversary/family reunion

To the extended Diamond clan and friends:

My younger sister Jean and her husband, George Strong, will reach the fifty-year marker in their happily married life on July 3.

To celebrate this momentous occasion, we have decided to have a gala Golden Anniversary and Diamond Family Reunion on that day.

We would be honored if you could join us in the Grand Ballroom of the Smalltown Lakeside Hotel on Saturday, July 3, from 1 to 5 P.M. for lunch. Dress is informal.

I will be putting together a family history video to show at the party; if you have any treasured family pictures or other artifacts, please contact me. I promise to quickly return whatever you send me.

Please RSVP to me by June 15.

Sincerely,
Harold Diamond

Invitation to memorial service

Carol Turner
Smalltown, OH

Dear Carol:

I am writing to let you know that there will be a memorial service for Lisa Decker on Saturday, March 16, at 10 A.M. in the chapel at the Smalltown Congregational Church.

It is hard to believe that she has been gone a whole year. Afterward a small group of us will go out for breakfast and share our special "Lisa" stories. I hope you can join us.

Sincerely,
Laura Diamond

Informal invitation to bridal shower

Tiffany Davis
Smalltown, OH

Dear Tiffany:

Please join us on Tuesday, March 3, at 7 P.M. for a bridal shower for Morgan. We will be meeting at my friend Sharon's house at 876 Jackson Street in Smalltown.

I hope you can make it. Please give me a call to tell us if you're coming; my phone number is (xxx) xxx-xxxx.

Sincerely,
Heather Diamond

Formal invitation to bridal shower

Please join us
for a
bridal shower
in honor of
Morgan Diamond
Friday, April 12
123 Main Street
Smalltown, OH
6:30 P.M.
Given by:
Heather Diamond

RSVP: xxx-xxx-xxxx

Invitation to memorial tree planting ceremony

Monica Diamond
Smalltown, OH

Dear Monica:

Please join us on Veterans Day, Monday, November 11, at 10 A.M. for a ceremony to celebrate the heroic efforts of those veterans who fought and died in our wars.

We will be planting a weeping willow on the grounds of the library. Eventually the tree will shade the benches used by many of our visitors.

The ceremony will include an honor guard from the Smalltown VFW, and the Smalltown High School choir. We look forward to seeing you there.

Sincerely,
Lillian Arnold, Librarian

Invitation to birthday party for oldest resident

Dear Neighbors:

On Monday, December 16, Agatha Cooney will be ninety-eight years young—the reigning champion here at Lakeview Senior Apartment Complex.

Please join us in the Reception Lounge at 3 P.M. on that day to celebrate the birthday of this grand lady in appropriate fashion.

We will be wishing her many happy returns and feasting on some of Agatha's favorites, including carrot cake and mint tea. We hope to see you there.

Sincerely,
Emma Miller, Reception Committee

Invitation to retirement dinner

Laura Diamond, Chairperson
Political Science Department
Smalltown Community College
Smalltown, OH

Dear Laura:

After twenty-five years of extraordinary service, Dr. Ursula Keller will be retiring from active teaching to write full time.

She will be greatly missed by her colleagues and the thousands of students she has inspired through the years.

Please join us for a gala dinner on Thursday, June 1, at 7 P.M. at Le Petite Fleur. Among speakers will be President Marlene Francis and a panel of mystery guests who studied with Dr. Keller over the years and went on to great distinction.

An RSVP card is enclosed. Please send your check for the dinner, made payable to Smalltown Community College Entertainment Fund, to my office before May 20.

I hope to see you as we pay tribute to this most outstanding educator.

Sincerely,
Walter Damon, Chairman
Mathematics Department

Invitation to election night party

Maureen Goshen
Smalltown, OH

Dear Maureen:

Read 'em and weep . . . or cheer. We'll have fun either way.

I hope you'll join a group of friends—of all political persuasions—at our quadrennial presidential election vote count party. This year we'll have four televisions tuned to different networks, a computer with a live Internet link, and enough munchies and libations to last until the final concession speech.

The counting starts at 7 P.M.

Please let us know if you're going to be able to attend.

Sincerely,
Emma and Ron Miller

Invitation to armchair theater

Dear neighbors:

It's a long, long way to Broadway, but that doesn't mean we can't enjoy a bit of theater right here in Fairview.

You're invited to attend—and participate in—an evening of armchair theater at our home on Saturday, April 5, at 7 P.M. We're going to put on a performance of Michael Frayn's hilarious <u>Noises Off</u>.

In case you've never been to an armchair theater, here's what we do: Each participant is given a copy of the script for a play and is assigned a part by the casting director (that would be me). We pull up our armchairs (and dining room chairs and lawn chairs) into a circle and work our way through the play for our own enjoyment.

It's a lot of fun, and we hope you'll join us. Please give me a call to let me know if you're going to attend.

Sincerely,
Karen Diamond

Declining request to make a presentation

Jack Lewis, President
Sounds Hearing Aid Company
Smalltown, OH

Dear Mr. Lewis:

Thank you for your offer to make a presentation to our group about new technologies in hearing aids. We must, however, decline your offer at this time.

We do not permit presentations by commercial organizations unless our members request it and the invitation is extended by the board.

Sincerely,
Harold Diamond, President
Smalltown Senior Center

Declining request for extra guest at dinner

Helen Grower
Smalltown, OH

Dear Helen:

Thank you for responding to my invitation to the Bon Voyage party for the Franks.

Any other time I would love to welcome Peter's brother, his wife, and her mother to our home. However, for this particular dinner we have limited space at the table. I have hired a professional caterer to serve a Tuscan menu to celebrate the Franks' upcoming trip, and my caterer would abandon me if I increased the guest list.

We will certainly get together another time.

Sincerely,
Laura Diamond

9 Friendship and Support

Dear Reader:

Here's a how-d'ye-do: Close friends don't need to send formal letters to communicate feelings or ask simple favors. But a heartfelt note from a buddy can become a treasured token of friendship.

By its nature, a friendship note is informal and breezy. The best of these letters sometimes seem to pick up in midsentence from the last conversation between the two friends.

Yours,
The Authors

Friend's birthday

Dear Jim:

Happy birthday to you! Happy birthday to you! Since I can't be there to serenade you, this will just have to do. Let this be the start of a really great year.

Best regards,
Morgan

Friend's anniversary

Dear Marge and Bill:

John and I want to add our heartiest best wishes to the many you will undoubtedly receive today.

Congratulations on your loving and successful marriage.

Fondly,
Laura Diamond

Best wishes on new house

Dear Bertha and Tom:

We want to be among the first to wish you much happiness in your new house. May you enjoy many years of joy and pleasure there.

Sincerely,
Laura Diamond

Bon voyage for travelers

Langley and Marjorie Clinton
Smalltown, OH

Dear Lang and Gloria:

Best wishes to you on your trip—three months at sea sailing around the world sounds just about perfect. We look forward to seeing your pictures and hearing your stories when you return.

We'll keep an eye on your house, water the plants, and check for any packages and newspapers that are delivered in error.

Bon voyage!
Monica and Harold Diamond

To out-of-touch friend

Dear Sue:

I was preparing one of my favorite dishes today—Mediterranean Chicken—and I remembered that you were the author of this masterpiece.

Thank you for sharing this with me, but more important, thanks for being a friend all these years. We've been out of touch too long. Let's get together soon.

Fondly,
Monica

Asking for recipe

Dear Sonya:

Just a note to thank you for inviting me for tea on Saturday. It was a lovely time and so pleasant to see old friends again.

If it is not a family secret could you share the recipe of that delicious chocolate cake we devoured? I have never tasted any as good.

Fondly,
Laura

Response to request for recipe

Dear Laura:

I am so pleased you enjoyed the chocolate cake, but I'm afraid I can't divulge the recipe. It's not a family secret—I must confess that I didn't bake it.

There is a small bakery at Fourth and Smith Streets called La Croûte Supérieure. Everything is so irresistible there; my car somehow seems to drive there all by itself.

I guess if I can't give you a recipe, I can at least recommend an excellent bakery.

Keep in touch.
Sonya

Declining request for recipe

Laura Diamond
Smalltown, OH

Dear Mrs. Diamond:

Thank you for your kind words. Sebastian's on the Lake is fortunate to have such enthusiastic patrons as you and your husband.

I am also flattered by your appreciation of my preparation of Steak au Poivre. I must decline, though, to go into details about our recipe except to say that we use bourbon instead of red wine. After all, if everyone prepared it as I do, we may lose the pleasure of your company at our restaurant.

The next time you and your husband are dining at Sebastian's, show this letter to Jules, the maitre d', and I would be happy to send a bottle of wine to your table with my compliments.

Bon Appetite!
Jacques Parent

Passing along information requested

Dear Fran:

I just remembered the name of that book we were both trying to recall: it was Following the Equator by Mark Twain. I have a copy if you want to borrow it, or you can order your own.

It was great seeing you at lunch; let's do it again soon.

Susan

Thanks for recommending store

Dear Sonya:

Thank you for recommending La Croûte Supérieure. We are having Morgan's future in-laws over for dinner next week and I will make it a point to serve that wonderful cake.

Fondly,
Laura

P.S. I'll keep your little secret to myself. All of us at the table were convinced that you were the best baker in town.

Offering to stay with child

Dear Lynn and Kevin:

Thank you for sharing the wonderful news about the adoption of May-Li. Roger and I are very happy for all of you.

Roger and I would like to offer our services as amateur baby sitters. We would love to stay with May-Li and Scott and let the two of you go out and celebrate.

It would be good training for us.

Love,
Morgan

Offering baby clothes to new mother

Dear Janet:

I just heard from my sister-in-law, Morgan, of the birth of your new baby. I am thrilled for you and John.

We have just moved to Fairview, and in the process brought along a few boxes of very carefully cleaned and washed baby clothes. We have no expectations of needing them for ourselves—trust me—and hope you would accept them as a gift.

If you are interested call me, and I will send them along.

Sincerely,
Karen Diamond

Follow-up on offer of baby clothes to new mother

Dear Janet:

Thank you for the lovely note about the baby clothing.

You will be amazed at how quickly your baby will grow out of clothing . . . and how expensive it is. I hope you will pass along the clothes to another mother when you are through with them.

Sincerely,
Karen Diamond

Personal problem of friend

Dear Joan:

Our lunch group will not be the same until you are here again. We hope that everything will work out for the best soon and we can welcome you back.

We miss you.

Sincerely,
Laura

Thanks for Christmas newsletter

Dear Neil and Catherine:

The only thing we enjoy more than receiving your annual Christmas newsletter is the holiday itself. Your letters have become a family tradition around here; we save them all year.

We're thrilled to hear about Connie's success in her first job.

We're not nearly so organized with a newsletter. The Diamond/Miller family had a good year, and we're all healthy, which is the most important news. I'll give you a call soon to let you know the details.

We wish you all the best in the new year.

Sincerely,
Laura and John

To colleague who lost job

Sam Ingway
Smalltown, OH

Dear Sam:

I just got word of the downsizing of the economics department. I was shocked to hear that the university did not renew your contract.

This is a tremendous loss to the school, your students, and your colleagues, who have come to rely on your perspectives on so many areas.

I know it is just a matter of time before you are in front of a classroom again. Please count on me for any help you may need.

Sincerely,
Laura Diamond

Support to friend who lost job

Craig Firth
Smalltown, OH

Dear Craig:

I just heard about the layoffs at Amalgamated Industries, and I was very sorry to hear that you lost your job. As you may know, I lost my job a year ago when the home office reorganized the sales division at Integrated Outsourcing. It was announced as a "downsizing" but as far as I'm concerned, getting laid off means getting laid off.

In any case, out of adversity comes strength. I took the opportunity (and six weeks of unemployment checks) to reassess my goals and embark on a new career path.

I'm sure you'll land on your feet soon. If you'd like to brainstorm a bit, please give me a call at any time.

Sincerely,
Al Miller

Notifying friends of change in mailing address

Dear friends:

We're still at the same old place, but the post office has changed our mailing address. Please update your little black books as follows:

Wallis and Grommet Silver
123 Old Fort Street
Smalltown, OH 45601

Now, how about sending us a card?

Sincerely,
Grommet

Support to business associate in financial difficulty

Gordon Cushman
Gordon's Variety Store
Smalltown, OH

Dear Gordon:

It saddened me greatly to hear of the imminent closing of Gordon's Variety Store.

Just like you, I know the terrific challenge of maintaining a retail store in downtown. You and I were the "old men" of Main Street.

I wish you success and happiness in whatever you choose to do next.

Sincerely,
John Diamond

Support to friend in financial difficulty

Joyce Fleming
Smalltown, OH

Dear Joyce:

I was so sorry to hear that Jim lost his job. These are difficult and trying times for many of us, and we are being tested in many ways.

I wanted you to know that you and Jim and your family are in our thoughts and prayers. I know all of you will come out of this stronger.

Sincerely,
Laura Diamond

Asking for friend's advice

Steve Barton
Smalltown, OH

Dear Steve:

Every time I pick up the Smalltown Banner or (forgive me!) watch the news on television, I long for the days when you and I were responsible for putting out a darn good newspaper. We made a formidable pair.

I'm writing to ask you for help with something more personal, though.

As you may know, Emma's condition has recently reached the stage where she must use a wheelchair all the time. We count our blessings and try to continue our life as close to normal as possible, but Emma does sometimes get upset about her lot in life.

I know you and Nora went through a similar experience after her accident. If you could share with me some of your strategies on dealing with such a change in lifestyle, I would certainly appreciate it. I have always taken your advice in the past and I can use it again.

Sincerely,
Ron Miller

Offering assistance to job seeker

Kevin Duffy
Waterford, NY

Dear Kevin:

I just heard from our mutual friend, Kathy Davis, that you are applying for a job at a law firm in the Smalltown area. Roger and I would like to offer the comforts of our humble but convenient apartment if you are in need of a place to stay. We'd also be happy to show you around town.

Let us know if we can be of assistance.

Sincerely,
Morgan Diamond

10 Entertainment

Dear Reader:

Let them entertain you . . . at dinner, at the theater, at the ballpark, and most anywhere else. Entertainment is big business, and proprietors are quite prepared to deal with consumers seeking special arrangements, such as buying a block of seats, renting a facility for a private party, or requesting a special menu.

Be specific in your requests. Remember that you are putting forth the elements of what will become a contract between you and a supplier.

We wish you a grand time.

Sincerely yours,
The Authors

Buying block of seats at a sports stadium

Toledo Mudhens
Group Ticket Sales
Fifth Third Field
Toledo, OH

Dear People:

I would like to receive a price on a block of 100 tickets for Saturday, June 5, for the Toledo Mudhens against the Columbus Clippers.

We are planning to bring a group of elementary school T-ball players from Fairview, Pennsylvania. Our group would consist of about 70 children and 30 adult chaperones. We would like to be seated together in the nondrinking section.

Please also advise us about other opportunities, including meeting the players and coaches.

Sincerely,
Michael Diamond, Coach
Fairview Boys and Girls Club T-ball Team

Asking for group discount at amusement park

Group Sales
Fun World Amusement Park
Smalltown, OH

Dear People:

We would like to receive a price for a group visit to Fun World on Saturday, May 29. We plan to bring 26 guests—20 high school seniors and 6 chaperones—from the Smalltown High School Yearbook Committee.

Can you also advise about the availability of the picnic area at the park, and a schedule of shows planned for that day?

Sincerely,
Laura Diamond

Asking about price to rent skating rink for event

Melissa Horton, General Manager
Fairview Skating Rink
Fairview, PA

Dear Ms. Horton:

We would like a price quote for the rental of the Jackson Municipal Skating Rink for a party for parents and children of Fairview Elementary School. We're looking for a weeknight in January or February, from about 5 P.M. to 8 P.M.

We'd like a price that includes use of the facilities and a discounted rate for skate rental. We estimate that about 100 to 150 youngsters and 100 adults will attend.

I look forward to hearing from you soon to discuss possibilities.

Sincerely,
Fran Murphy, Principal
Fairview Elementary School

Call for tryouts

Milton Boyle
Smalltown, OH

Dear Milt:

Thanks for attending the organizational meeting for the Smalltown Repertory Theater. We are very excited about the prospects for our group. Which brings us to this: you are invited to attend auditions for our first show: Our Town, by Thornton Wilder.

We're looking for a cast of fifteen principals to play members of the Gibbs and Webb families plus minor characters, and we'll also need about a dozen stagehands, lighting and sound technicians, makeup artists, and dressers. We'd suggest you familiarize yourself with Thornton Wilder's wonderful play; you can also rent the 1940 movie version, which is close but not identical to the original.

The audition will be held in the auditorium of Smalltown High School on Tuesday, September 6, at 7 P.M. Callbacks will be made very soon after, with rehearsals beginning September 13. We expect to present our first performance in early November.

Please feel free to call me with any questions.

Sincerely,
Laura Diamond

To restaurant asking for recipe

Vitale Capizzo
Capizzo's Ristorante
Smalltown, OH

Dear Mr. Capizzo:

I recently was the guest of honor at my birthday celebration at your restaurant. We had a marvelous evening.

I was particularly fond of an appetizer we ordered: Pasta al forno con ripieno di carne e spinaci (oven baked pasta with meat and spinach).

Would it be possible to get the recipe? I don't often try to duplicate something I enjoy at a restaurant, but this was an extraordinary dish. I promise not to open my own restaurant, and to make regular visits to Capizzo's in search of other favorites.

Sincerely,
Laura Diamond

Thanking chef for recipe

Vitale Capizzo
Capizzo's Ristorante
Smalltown, OH

Dear Mr. Capizzo:

Thank you for graciously sending me the recipe for Pasta al forno con ripieno di carne e spinaci.

I plan to serve it at a dinner party soon, and pass along the word about the marvelous menus at Capizzo's.

Sincerely,
Laura Diamond

Asking caterer to create special menu for party

Dmitri Florian
Splendid Feast Caterers
Smalltown, OH

Dear Mr. Florian:

Very dear friends of ours will be leaving in a few weeks for a trip to Tuscany. As a surprise, I would like to arrange a small dinner party with a Tuscan menu for Saturday, August 19.

Could you propose a Tuscan menu and give us a price for a party of eight at our home? Two of my personal favorite appetizers include bruschetta with grilled eggplant, and prosciutto and figs. Entrees I enjoy include saltimboca ala Romana, and swordfish with orange sauce and gremolata.

I look forward to hearing from you.

Sincerely,
Laura Diamond

11 Borrowing

Dear Reader:

"Neither a borrower nor a lender be." That's probably good advice, but not necessarily a rule that all of us can always follow.

A friend or a neighbor may have a tool or a device that's not readily available, or a specialized piece of equipment that could help you solve a problem. It is not unreasonable to ask to borrow something impersonal like a tool or a book; depending on your relationship, it may be less reasonable to ask for the use of something personal and possibly irreplaceable, such as jewelry or certain articles of clothing.

In any case, remember that you are entering into a contract. When you borrow something, you are taking temporary custody with the intention of returning the item. Implied in that transaction is that the item will be undamaged, and that you will make good for any damage or loss.

You also need to graciously accept the possibility that your request to borrow an item will be turned down.

Wishing you the best of luck, we are,

Sincerely yours,
The Authors

Asking for loan of tools

Dear Fred:

I guess I've been envious of your garden too long. This year I decided to get back to nature (more or less) and exercise my green thumb. I have earmarked a patch of the backyard and will attempt to plant some vegetables.

I tried turning the soil over myself, but that didn't work. I know you have a tiller that you use for your garden, and I would appreciate it if you would allow me to borrow it for a day.

I promise to treat it well and fill up the gas tank.

Sincerely,
John Diamond

Thanks for loan of tools

Dear Fred:

Many thanks for allowing me to borrow your tiller. If it's convenient, I'd like to pick it up this coming Saturday, May 13. Please let me know if that is okay with you.

Sincerely,
John

Return of borrowed tool

Dear Fred:

My garden is fully tilled, and the plants spent their first night in my backyard. Thanks so much for the loan of the tiller.

I took the liberty of checking with your wife to see what a successful gardener like you would like. Please use these gardening gloves in good health.

Sincerely,
John

Declining to loan item

Dear Bob:

I hope you will forgive me, but I really don't feel comfortable lending out my video camera. It is very expensive, and more to the point, very fragile. I would be very concerned about the possibility that it might become damaged, and I don't want to burden you with that sort of responsibility.

Do you know that Portman's Camera Store in Smalltown has a few cameras they rent by the week?

Sincerely,
Jack

Asking for return of borrowed item

Dear Ben:

When I lent you my hedge clippers a couple of weeks ago I was happy to do so.

I'd appreciate the return of the clippers soon. Monica says we are living in a jungle and I need to get to work.

Best regards,
Harold

Friend returns damaged dress

Dear Judy:

I just received the package with the dress you borrowed last month. I appreciate the thank-you note and the fact that you had a great time in the Caribbean.

However, I can't believe that you were not aware of the condition of the dress. There is a big red stain on the front. I took it to the cleaners and they said it was probably wine. They could not guarantee that even with cleaning it will be fit to wear.

I am upset about the dress, but even more that you didn't mention it. Our friendship is too important to me to let this put a strain on our relationship. I look forward to hearing from you.

Sincerely,
Morgan

Asking for payment of repairs

Dear Harry:

I'm sorry to have to tell you that I found a serious problem with the lawnmower you borrowed last week. The mulching blade apparently struck a rock or other obstruction and was bent out of shape. The mower was inoperable in that condition.

As you remember, I demonstrated the mower to you when you came to pick it up, and it performed properly at that time.

I took it to Green Point Garden Center and they replaced the blade, straightened the rotor, and tuned up the engine. I'll pay for the tune-up, but the cost of the repair was $79.45 and I'd like to discuss who should pay for this.

Thank you.

Sincerely,
Tom

Offering to share purchase cost of equipment

Dear Arthur:

Winter is coming, and I can't stop thinking about clearing the snow from the driveway.

You and I spoke last spring about the possibility of sharing the purchase of a snowblower. I think it's great idea.

I checked around town and found that we could get a 25-horsepower Abominable Snowblower from Green Point Garden Center for about $600. We could store the machine in my garden shed, and both have access to it when snowflakes fall.

Ralph

Request to borrow vehicle

Chuck Van
Smalltown, OH

Dear Chuck:

I have a favor to ask but before I do, please understand that in no way will my feelings be hurt if you can't oblige.

Mary and I have a lot of household stuff we need to take to our summer place at Mirror Lake—nothing huge, but a lot of boxes of small things like dishes, lamps, and blankets. Everything would just fit in one trip with a van like the one in your driveway.

If it would be possible, we would appreciate the use of your van to make one round trip to the lake. We are very flexible on date and time, and whatever conditions you have are fine. We'd be happy to pay a mileage charge to reimburse you for the use of the vehicle; can I suggest 25 cents per mile?

And we'd also be happy to invite you and Sue to use the place some weekend. The fishing is great and the sunsets are beautiful!

Sincerely,
Bob Stevens

Conditions for borrowing vehicle

Dear Bob:

I've been thinking about your request to borrow our van to drive to your summer home for the week. I'd be happy to help you out.

I checked with our insurance agent and she told me I can give you written permission to drive the car, and that our insurance would remain in force as long as we did not charge you a fee for its use. So, we must decline your offer of 25 cents per mile. When you return the car, though, perhaps we could discuss some other arrangement.

I have attached a legal letter suggested by my insurance agent in which you agree to carry your own liability insurance and also to reimburse us for any losses to the vehicle not covered by our own policy.

Sincerely,
Chuck

12 Travel Arrangements

Dear Reader:

If you're the sort of person who accepts whatever you come across, however you find it, Godspeed. If you're like us, though, you're pretty particular about how you travel, where you stay, and what you'll do when you get there. If that's the case, it makes a lot of sense to get your arrangements down in writing.

The letters in the section that follows can be sent by mail, by fax, or by e-mail. Be sure to keep copies of all responses, and carry them with you during the journey. On one of our recent trips, an e-mail confirmation saved the day when we arrived at an ungodly hour in Reykjavik. We didn't speak Icelandic and the clerk knew little English, but the e-mail included a confirmation number that translated our needs into a room for the night.

Bon voyage,
The Authors

Requesting brochure

Seaside Resort
Seaside, FL

Dear People:

My husband and I plan to visit Seaside, Florida, this coming March. We will be bringing our two small children, ages four and six.

Please send a brochure with prices, descriptions of facilities, and any children's activities offered. I also am interested in receiving notice of any special offers and last-minute discounts.

Thank you,
Karen Diamond

Requesting brochure in Spanish

El Balneario Soleado
Cancún, México

Estimados señores:

Mi esposo y yo estamos preparando a visitar el Balneario Soleado este marzo. Llegaremos con nuestros dos pequeños hijos, cuatro y seis años de edad.

Por favor, mándennos un folleto con los precios, descripciones de los servicios, e información sobre las actividades para niños. Además, me gustaría recibir noticias de ofertas especiales y descuentos de última hora.

Muchas gracias,
Karen Diamond

Questions before reservation

Reservations Department
Seaside Resort
Seaside, FL

Dear Reservations Department:

Thank you for sending me the information I requested. We are planning a visit in March 2005.

I have a few questions:

Do the two-bedroom housekeeping units face the ocean or the pool?

Is there an in-room babysitting service available in the evenings? Are the baby sitters certified by the resort?

Is there an age restriction for young children in the dining room?

Is there a supermarket nearby if we decide to do any cooking on our own?

Are there any other restaurants in the immediate area that young children would enjoy?

I look forward to your response.

Sincerely,
Karen Diamond

Special need at hotel

Reservations Department
Seaside Resort
Seaside, FL

Dear Reservations Department:

I am prepared to make a reservation for an ocean-view two-bedroom housekeeping unit from March 13 through 21, 2005.

I do, though, need confirmation that the hotel will be able to guarantee that we can stay in a nonsmoking unit.

My six-year-old son is allergic to smoke and its residue. If you can assure me that we will be able to reserve a nonsmoking room, we will be happy to make our reservation.

Please advise me in writing of the availability of such a room, and we will respond with a deposit.

Sincerely,
Karen Diamond

Confirming special reservation

John Parker, General Manager
Seaside Resort
Seaside, FL

Dear Mr. Parker:

Thank you for responding to my inquiries regarding our plans to stay at Seaside Resort in March 2005.

Per your assurances, we want to reserve a two-bedroom nonsmoking housekeeping unit with an ocean view. In your letter you guaranteed availability of a nonsmoking room in this class, or an upgrade to a nonsmoking suite or cottage.

Enclosed is a check in the amount of $250 as a deposit for the week's stay; the nightly room rate is $250 plus tax. Your published policy allows us to cancel the reservation and receive a full refund of our deposit with forty-eight hours' advance notice.

We will arrive at Seaside on Saturday, March 13, in the early afternoon and will depart on Sunday, March 21, in the morning.

After check-in, we will sign up our two children, ages four and six, for some of the appropriate activities listed in your current brochure. We also want to arrange for an in-room baby sitter for Monday, March 15, from 6 P.M. to midnight.

I look forward to receiving confirmation of our reservation, and to our visit.

Sincerely,
Karen Diamond

Praising trip

John Parker, General Manager
Seaside Resort
Seaside, FL

Dear Mr. Parker:

We have just returned from our visit to Seaside Resort, and I wanted to thank you for a wonderful time and for your special consideration for our family. We were very concerned that we be booked into a nonsmoking room because of our son's allergies; not only were we upgraded into a nonsmoking suite, but we also found a complete set of new linens and towels in our room—along with your note of welcome.

We took advantage of everything from horseback riding to swimming and sailing. Our children were enrolled in your excellent child care facilities and we enjoyed the adult amenities, including the health club and the fine dining.

Next year I am going to suggest to my extended family that we have a family reunion at Seaside.

Please keep us on your mailing list, and let us know about any special deals and promotions you offer to devoted customers . . . like us.

Sincerely,
Karen Diamond

Requesting return of deposit

Dream Vacation House Rentals
Nantucket, MA

Dear Reservations Department:

On February 16, we sent a deposit to reserve a house on Nantucket for the week of July 20 to 27, 2005. Our confirmation number is 6SJ7-00-JUL20.

Unfortunately, a family problem has arisen and we will be unable to go on vacation at that time. Please cancel our reservation and return our deposit.

Under the terms of the rental agreement, we are due a full refund of the deposit because the cancellation comes more than sixty days before the date of arrival.

Please send a check to me at the above address.

We hope to be able to visit next year.

Sincerely,
Laura Diamond

Requesting return of deposit in Spanish

Casas Monterrey
Quepos, Costa Rica

Estimado agente de reservas:

En 16 febrero, yo le mandé un depósito para alquiler una casa en Casas Monterrey para la semana en julio, desde el 20 a 27. El número de confirmación es 6SJ7-00-JUL20.

Desafortunadamente, un inesperado problema familial nos impide tomar vacaciones. Por favor, anule la reserva y nos devuelva el depósito.

En acordancia con las condiciones del contrato de alquiler, tenemos derecho de recibir el reembolso de la suma total, porque la anulación es hecha mas que 60 días antes de la fecha de llegar.

Por favor, mánde el cheque a la dirección escrita arriba.

Espero que mi familia podrá visitar a Casas Monterrey por el próximo año.

Atentamente,
Laura Diamond

Requesting return of deposit in French

Provence, France

Cher Département de Réservation:

Le 16 février, nous avons envoyé un dépôt pour réserver une maison sur Provence pour la semaine du 20 à 27 juillet, 2005. Notre numéro de confirmation est 6SJ7-00-JUL20.

Malheureusement, un problème de famille a surgi et nous serons incapables de partir en vacances à ce moment-là. S'il vous plaît annulez notre réservation et retournez notre dépôt. Sous les termes de l'accord de loyer, nous sommes dûs un remboursement plein du dépôt parce que l'annulation vient plus de 60 jours avant la date de l'arrivée. S'il vous plaît envoyez un chèque à l'adresse ci-dessus mentionnée. Nous espérons pouvoir visiter l'année prochaine.

Sincèrement,
Laura Diamond

Requesting return of deposit in Italian

Appartamenti in Affito per la Vacanza
Siena, Italy

Sezione della Prenotazione:

Il 16 febbraio, abbiamo mandato un acconto per la prenotazione della casa a Siena per la settimana 20-27 luglio, 2005. Il nostro numero è 6SJ7-00-JUL20.

Purtroppo, c'era una situazione con la nostra famiglia, e allora, non possiamo andare a Siena per la vacanza durante quella settimana. Per favore, potrebbe cancellare la nostra prenotazione e potrebbe rinviare il nostro acconto.

Come ha scritto nel contratto, riceviamo il rimborso completo, perché abbiamo cancellato più di 60 giorni prima del giorno d'arrivo.

Per favore, potrebbe mandare i soldi al indirizzo sopra.
Vorremmo venire a Siena l'anno prossimo.

Grazie,
Laura Diamond

Letter to travel agency canceling trip

Marilu Sunshine
Go Away Travel Agency
Smalltown, OH

Dear Ms. Sunshine:

My husband, Harold, and I booked a cruise through your agency. We have reservations on a Windbourne Cruise from Fort Lauderdale, November 16 through 25, 2005.

Unfortunately, my husband will be having minor surgery and we will be unable to go on the trip. Per your advice, we had purchased the optional No Worries Travel Insurance Policy.

According to the terms of that policy, we are able to cancel the cruise and receive a full refund of our advance payment because of a medical condition. I have attached a copy of a letter from our physician, Dr. Martin Todd, confirming the surgery.

Please send a check to me at the above address. After my husband gets back on his feet, we plan to call you to schedule a new cruise on Windbourne or another cruise line.

Sincerely,
Monica Diamond

To hotel about item left behind

Housekeeping Supervisor
Seaside Resort
Seaside, FL

Dear Housekeeping Supervisor:

In March of this year our family spent a wonderful vacation at your resort. We have been home for two weeks, and my four-year-old son just discovered that he left his favorite pillow behind. It was a small handmade creation with pictures of cows all over it.

I realize it could have been easily overlooked and thrown out, but if you have a lost-and-found, perhaps it is languishing there. I don't think you will have any trouble identifying it.

Thank you for any assistance you can give.

Sincerely,
Karen Diamond

Thanks for special effort at hotel

Maria Milagro, Housekeeping Supervisor
Seaside Resort
Seaside, FL

Dear Ms. Milagro:

You are truly incredible. I wrote asking about the pillow my son left behind with little hope that it actually would be found. When the package from Seaside came last week it was like Christmas morning all over again. You have made a little boy very happy, and his parents appreciative of a first-class operation.

Thank you,
Karen Diamond
cc: John Parker, General Manager

To tour operator requesting return of item

Sea It All Tours
Soggy Bottom, FL

Dear People:

On March 15 my family was on one of your Glass Bottom Boat Tours. When we returned to our hotel, we discovered that my son left behind a black plastic CD case. The case must have fallen off his lap and onto the floor. It has his name and address on the inside cover.

If the case has been found, I would appreciate it if you would ship it to us at the address on this letter. We will be happy to pay the cost of postage.

Sincerely,
Karen Diamond

Requesting information on tours for handicapped

Stay Away Travel Agency
Nearby, OH

Dear People:

My parents—both in their eighties—are interested in taking a cruise to the Caribbean this coming winter.

My mother uses a walker and sometimes requires a wheelchair. Could you please advise us about cruise lines that are able to accommodate handicapped travelers, and also suggest itineraries that might be best suited to their needs?

They are flexible on itinerary and dates, preferring to travel for about two weeks in February or March.

Sincerely,
Laura Diamond

To visitors bureau

Nantucket Visitors Bureau
Nantucket, MA

Dear People:

We are considering a trip to your area next summer. Please send information on accommodations and recreation, as well as a schedule of activities.

Thank you.

Sincerely,
Laura Diamond

To visitors bureau about activities

Maine Convention and Visitors Bureau
Bangor, ME

Dear People:

My family is planning a ski vacation in Maine this winter. Most of us are eager to hit the slopes, but some in the group prefer other distractions, namely shopping.

Please send me information about the best place to stay to take advantage of the best skiing as well as outlet shopping.

Sincerely,
Karen Diamond

Seeking parking information at bus terminal

Station Manager
Greydog Bus Lines
Smalltown, OH

Dear Manager:

My wife and I plan to take a charter bus trip from your station on September 30. This is our first time using bus transportation, and I would like to know where we can safely park our car for several nights.

Sincerely,
Ron Miller

Seeking ferry schedules

Woods Hole, Martha's Vineyard & Nantucket Steamship Authority
Woods Hole, MA

Dear People:

Please send me a ferry schedule for a trip from Cape Cod to Nantucket in mid-July. Do you offer senior citizen discounts on tickets?

Sincerely,
Monica Diamond

Thanks for advice on trip

Dear Ron:

Thanks for your note about GoldenSeas Cruise Line. Their ships and itineraries sound terrific.

I've asked our travel agent to look into their policy about guests bringing oxygen tanks on board, because Louise occasionally needs oxygen. I don't think we will be the first ones making this request.

We'll study the brochures and guidebooks you gave us and be in contact soon to book a trip.

Sincerely,
Bill

To cruise line about medical needs

Customer Service
GoldenSeas Cruise Line
Fort Lauderdale, FL

Dear People:

We are considering taking a cruise on one of your ships but want to make sure you can accommodate us.

My wife has a nonacute respiratory condition and occasionally needs to use oxygen. We have portable containers at home and they suffice for her needs. Would this present a problem?

Sincerely,
William Hower

Request frequent flier miles

Customer Service
Ferguson Airlines
Midwest, IL

Re: Frequent flier account FA30003

Dear People:

On November 16, 2004, I flew Ferguson Airlines flight #148 from Toledo to Seattle, returning on November 24 on flight #153. I have enclosed a copy of the boarding passes for these flights.

My most recent frequent flier statement does not reflect these flights. Please credit my account with the appropriate miles.

Sincerely,
Roger Hamilton

Asking credit for unused frequent flier miles

Customer Service
Ferguson Airlines
Midwest, IL

Re: Frequent flier account FA30003

Dear People:

In January of this year I used 30,000 frequent flier miles to obtain a round-trip ticket from Pittsburgh to Aspen, departing February 16 and returning February 23.

Because of a family emergency, I was forced to cancel that trip. My most recent statement from Ferguson Airlines does not reflect the cancellation of the trip or the credit of those miles back to the account.

Please update my account accordingly.

Sincerely,
Roger Hamilton

Praising flight attendant

Customer Service
Ferguson Airlines
Midwest, IL

Dear People:

My wife and I recently flew from Toledo to Boston on Ferguson Airlines.

My wife has some difficulty walking, and must use a walker and occasionally a wheelchair to get around. Before the trip, we were very concerned about her comfort on the flight.

The flight attendant on this trip, Brenda Wilton, could not have been more gracious or considerate. She went out of her way to help us from the moment we came on board until we were met at Boston by a porter with a wheelchair.

I hope you will pass along our appreciation.

Sincerely,
Ron Miller

Complaint about flight

Customer Service
Ferguson Airlines
Midwest, IL

Dear People:

We have been satisfied customers of Ferguson Airlines for many years, flying frequently from Ohio to all points around the nation. We have always found your personnel to be very considerate of customers.

It is with that history that I write to you to complain about the cabin crew we flew with on flight #532 from Austin to Boston on June 19. Something must have gone wrong between the two cabin attendants before the flight, because the two of them were all but fighting in the aisle.

Food and drink was served about an hour late, and my wife's request for a lemon to put in her soda was met with, "You'll have to ask the other flight attendant." I heard another couple's request for pillows and blankets turned down flat: "Can't you see I'm busy?"

I didn't write down the names of the attendants; I'm sure you can determine them from your own records.

I hope this was a one-time problem. We will probably give Ferguson Airlines one more chance on our next trip, but another unpleasant flight will be the last one for us with your company.

Sincerely,
Ron Miller

To automobile association asking for trip planning

Member Services
National Automobile Association
Smalltown, OH

Re: Membership No. xxxx-xxxx

Dear People:

Please design a trip route for me from Smalltown, Ohio, to Waterford, New York.

I would like to have a route that takes us directly to Waterford, and then returns by way of Niagara Falls, Toronto, and Chicago. Please also provide us with current guides to New York State, Ontario, and Illinois.

Sincerely,
Harold Diamond

Requesting travel information for international trip

L'Agence Touristique Départementale d'Haute-Savoie
Albertville
France

Dear People:

I will be in Albertville in May on a class trip, staying with a local family. Could you please send me maps and other information about Albertville so that we can plan our trip? We will also be visiting other areas in the Haute-Savoie region.

Can you also provide information about the availability of Internet cafés and telephone offices in the area?

Thank you.

Heather Diamond

Requesting travel information for international trip in Spanish

La agencia turística de Andalucía
Seville, España

Estimados señores:

Este mayo, nuestro clase va a hacer un viaje estudiantil a Sevilla, donde quedaremos con las familias locales. Si es posible, por favor mándennos mapas y otra información sobre la ciudad para que podamos planear los detalles de nuestro viaje. Además, visitaremos otras locales de Andalucía.

También, esperamos que nos puedan facilitar información sobre la disponibilidad de los cibercafés y oficinas de teléfono en el vecindario.

Muchas gracias,
Heather Diamond

Requesting travel information for international trip in French

L'Agence Touristique Départamentale d'Haute-Savoie
Albertville, France

Chères Personnes:

Je serai à Albertville en mai en voyage de classe, restant avec une famille locale. Pourriez-vous m'envoyer des cartes et d'autres informations sur Albertville de sorte que nous puissions projeter notre voyage? Nous visiterons aussi d'autres secteurs dans la région d'Haute-Savoie. Pouvez-vous aussi fournir des informations au sujet de la disponibilité des cafés d'Internet et des bureaux de téléphone dans le secteur?

Merci.
Heather Diamond

Requesting travel information for international trip in Italian

L'Ufficio Turistico per la città di Firenze
Firenze, Italia

Cari Signori,

Sarò a Firenze con la mia scuola in maggio, e abiterò con una famiglia del posto. Per favore, potrebbe mandare una pianta e anche l'informazione della città? Così, possiamo fare una programma per il nostro viaggio. Inoltre, vorremmo vedere le altre città in Toscana.

Potrebbe mandare anche l'informazione con la disponibilità della posta elettronica e i telefoni a Firenze?

Grazie,
Heather Diamond

Requesting travel arrangements for group trip

Erica Redecker
Go Away Travel Company
Smalltown, OH

Dear Erica:

As we discussed, I would like to receive a bid from your company for airline travel for the Smalltown High School French Club, departing Smalltown for Paris on May 15.

There will be sixteen students plus three chaperones on the trip. We would like you to investigate group rates from major airlines as well as consolidator and charter airline fares. In addition, we would expect a discount on the ticket prices as a partial rebate of your travel agent's commission.

We will be seeking competitive bids from two other travel agents, including one out-of-town agency recommended to us by the Alliance Française.

Thank you.

Laura Diamond

To cell phone company inquiring about service overseas

Customer Service
Lastel Communications
Boulder, CO

Concerning: account xxxxxxxx

Dear Customer Service:

I am writing to inquire about the availability of cell phone service in France for the above account. Our daughter will be in Paris and Albertville in May of this year and will be using our phone.

We currently use a Zokia Worldspan phone, which we were told could be used in Europe with proper programming.

Please also advise us of the per-minute charges for use of the phone from France.

Sincerely,
Laura Diamond

To credit card company notifying of travel

Customer Service
American Express

Account: xxxx-xxxx-xxxx-xxxx

Dear Customer Service:

I am writing to inform you that my daughter Heather Diamond will be traveling in Europe, visiting France and Switzerland from May 15 through June 1. We authorize use of the card in those countries during that period.

Sincerely,
Laura Diamond

13 Local Travel Concerns

Dear Reader:

Around the block isn't as far as around the globe, but the same principles apply: The more specific your needs, the more you need to get it in writing. State your requirements, and ask for confirmation that they will be met.

We wish you the best of luck in all your travels.

Sincerely,
The Authors

Inquiring about taxi charges to airport

ABC Taxi Company
Smalltown, OH

Dear People:

On September 13, my wife and I will need to get to Smalltown Airport from my office at Diamond Music Hall, 123 Main Street, Smalltown.

We would like to be picked up at 2 P.M. and will need one of your large vans. We have a large amount of luggage, including a pair of tubas.

Please inform us of the cost of the taxi service and your availability.

Sincerely,
John Diamond

Requesting quote for scheduled weekly taxi service

ABC Taxi Company
Smalltown, OH

Dear People:

My daughter is a student at Smalltown University. For the next month she is going to be involved in an allergy study at Smalltown General Hospital. I do not want her taking public transportation at night.

She needs transportation to the hospital from the Student Union at Smalltown University on November 1, 8, 15, 22, 29, and December 6.

She would need to be picked up at 7 P.M. at the University and taken to the hospital, and then picked up at the hospital at 9 P.M. for the return to Smalltown University.

Could you give me a flat price for these six roundtrips?

Sincerely,
Laura Diamond

Accepting bid for scheduled weekly taxi service

John Olds, Dispatcher
ABC Taxi Company
Smalltown, OH

Dear Mr. Olds:

Thank you for your bid to transport our daughter from Smalltown University to the hospital for six trips in November and December. We would like to arrange for the service as you have proposed:

From Smalltown University Student Union to Smalltown General Hospital at 7 P.M., on November 1, 8, 15, 22, 29, and December 6.

From Smalltown General Hospital to Smalltown University Student Union on the same days at 9 P.M.

You will bill us a flat fee of $60 for the six roundtrips.

Thank you.

Sincerely,
Laura Diamond

Suggesting bus route change

General Manager
Smalltown Transit Authority
Smalltown, OH

Dear General Manager:

My wife and I are residents of the Lakeview Senior Apartment Complex. We have been asked by some of the residents here to see if we can help improve their ability to get around town independently.

The closest bus stop is half a mile below the apartment complex, down a steep hill. Very few of the residents here feel comfortable walking all the way to (and especially from) the bus stop.

We are asking if the route for Bus 16 could be altered slightly to come up the hill to the complex.

I can promise you several very grateful riders each day in each direction.

I look forward to hearing from you soon.

Sincerely,
Ron Miller

Follow-up to bus company about route change

Harold Allen, Manager
Smalltown Transit Authority
Smalltown, OH

Dear Mr. Allen:

Thank you for your response to my suggestion of a change in the routing of Bus 16 to include a stop at the Lakeview Senior Apartment Complex.

You wrote that your survey did not indicate there would be sufficient ridership to justify a stop here.

I am enclosing a petition signed by fifty-two members of our community asking for bus service. If each of the signers were to ride the bus just once a week, by my calculations that would be the equivalent of filling a bus.

May I make a suggestion? Since most of the residents here would want to use the bus during off-peak hours, from about 10 A.M. to 4 P.M., perhaps the route could be altered for just that period of time. This would avoid delays during the morning and evening rush hours.

Please advise.

Sincerely,
Ron Miller

Thanks for bus route change

Harold Allen, Manager
Smalltown Transit Authority
Smalltown, OH

Dear Mr. Allen:

Thank you for listening to the voice of the residents of the Lakeview Senior Apartment Complex.

We understand that the bus company will institute a three-month test of service to the front door of our complex every day between 10 A.M. and 3 P.M. heading into town, and from 11 A.M. to 4 P.M. returning from Smalltown.

This coming Tuesday at 10 A.M., you will find a contingent of people ready and eager to make the ride into town for shopping for the day.

We appreciate this service very much.

Sincerely,
Ron Miller

Open letter about bus route change

The Editor
Smalltown Banner
Smalltown, OH

To the Editor:

On behalf of the Lakeview Senior Apartment Complex, I want to thank the Smalltown Transit Authority for adding a stop on Route 16 to serve the residents.

The bus company will institute a three-month test of service to the front door of our complex every day between 10 A.M. and 3 P.M. heading into town, and from 11 A.M. to 4 P.M. returning from Smalltown.

We very much appreciate the chance to travel independently to town for shopping and entertainment, and plan to support the bus service as best we can.

Sincerely,
Ron Miller

14 Shopping

Dear Reader:

In these modern times, there is not much that you cannot purchase from a catalog or from an Internet retailer. The buying process is simple—click here or circle this number, and provide your credit card number. But when it comes time to return an item or make a claim for damage, we're back to ink on paper.

When writing to a retailer, be specific about the product you are writing about and make a clear and direct statement of what you want the retailer to do: send me one; take this back and return an undamaged item; take this back and issue a credit (and specify the manner); correct the billing as follows. Be specific in your reference to dates of purchase and other appropriate time references.

Good shopping!

Sincerely,
Janice Keefe

Requesting catalog

Customer Service
J. Hutton Catalog Merchants
Ruraltown, MN

Dear Customer Service:

Please put me on your mailing list to receive all catalogs. I also would be interested in learning about any special offers or sales. Please send all material to the address in this letter.

Sincerely,
Laura Diamond

Placing an order

Customer Service
J. Hutton Catalog Merchants
Ruraltown, MN

Dear People:

Please process my order for merchandise from your current spring sale catalog.

I have attached the order form from the catalog, which includes item numbers, sizes, and colors.

Please note the following special instructions: I would like the shirt (item #xxx-xxxxx) to be monogrammed with block initials JKD. I understand there is a $5 additional charge for monogramming.

I would like all items to be sent to my son at college: Joshua Diamond
Smalltown University
Box 1214
Smalltown, OH

My credit card information and billing address are listed on the order form.

Sincerely,
Laura Diamond

Checking on order

Customer Service
J. Hutton Catalog Merchants
Ruraltown, MN

Dear Customer Service:

I recently placed an order by mail for items to be sent to my son at college. I am enclosing a copy of that order. It has been three weeks and as yet he has not received the items, and we have not received confirmation of the order.

Please check on the shipping status and notify me. My daytime phone number is (xxx) xxx-xxxx.

Sincerely,
Laura Diamond

Exchange of item

Customer Service
J. Hutton Catalog Merchants
Ruraltown, MN

Dear People:

Enclosed please find a pair of linen trousers that I recently received as part of a larger order.

The pants as received were 40 waist, 34 length. I would like to exchange them for the same pants, 36 waist, 32 length.

I am enclosing a copy of the invoice and order number.

I understand there is no additional shipping charge for an exchange.

Please send the merchandise to my Smalltown University address, as follows:

Joshua Diamond
Smalltown University
Box 1214
Smalltown, OH

Sincerely,
Joshua Diamond

Error on bill

Customer Service
J. Hutton Catalog Merchants
Ruraltown, MN

Dear Customer Service:

I recently placed an order by mail to be sent to my son in college. The merchandise reached him satisfactorily, but when I received my current credit card bill I noticed a discrepancy in the amount quoted in your catalog and the amount I was billed. I am sending a copy of my original order.

The sport coat, item #xxx-xxxxx, is listed on page 23 of your spring sale catalog as being on sale for $145. The original price of the sport coat was $165, and according to my credit card bill, I was charged that amount rather than the sale price.

Please adjust my credit card for the $20 overcharge.

Sincerely,
Laura Diamond

Inquiring about bulk purchase of product

Consumer Affairs
Fishbone Foods
Farmtown, IA

Dear People:

I have been a fan of your salad dressings for quite some time. As I now have to watch my cholesterol levels, I select from the nonfat choices. My favorite is the Tru-Flavor Nonfat Low-Calorie Blue Cheese Dressing.

In my family, we use several bottles per week.

Do you sell directly to the retail consumer? I would be willing to buy by the case and have it sent directly to my home. Please advise.

Sincerely,
Ron Miller

Seeking larger packages of product

Customer Service
Great Champions Dog Food
Gravy Boat, OK

Dear People:

We have ordered bags of your Great Champions food from your catalog (and most recently, from your Web site) for several years.

Jackson, our Shetland sheepdog, subsists almost entirely on your food. We have been purchasing 10-pound bags once or twice a month.

Do you offer larger bags, say 25-pounders? Do you offer a volume discount if we were to buy 100 pounds at a time?

Please advise.

Sincerely,
John Diamond

Notifying credit card company of overcharge

Customer Service
VISA
Norfolk, VA

Concerning: VISA #xxxx-xxxx-xxx-xxxx
Laura Diamond
Main Street
Smalltown, OH

Dear People:

On my current Visa bill there is an error in the amount I was billed and the amount quoted in a catalog purchase.

The transaction dated March 14, 20xx, from J. Hutton Catalog Merchants is listed at $259.22. That is $20 higher than the sale price quoted in the catalog. The correct amount I should have been billed is $239.22.

I have notified J. Hutton directly of this discrepancy and hope that it will be taken care of by them. In the meantime, please note that I dispute this charge.

Sincerely,
Laura Diamond

Requesting pickup of merchandise

Customer Service
Value-Mart Department Store
Smalltown, OH

Dear Customer Service:

On November 24, 20xx, my husband and I purchased a Panatronic 24-inch model 6SJ7-4444 television set from your store. I am enclosing a copy of the sales receipt.

My husband and I are both in our seventies, and we appreciated the help we received loading the TV into our car. We imposed on a neighbor to assist us in bringing it into the house.

As soon as we plugged it in, we realized that the set was defective.

I am writing to find out if someone from Value-Mart can pick up the set from our home to return it to the store.

We are frequent customers at Value-Mart and have been for many years. We appreciate the extras Value-Mart extends to senior citizens, and hope you can accommodate us.

Please advise.

Sincerely,
Monica Diamond

Praise for salesperson

Federico Friendly, General Manager
Value-Mart Department Store
Smalltown, OH

Dear Mr. Friendly:

I am writing to bring to your attention the extra effort extended by Mark Richards, who works in the electronics department of your store.

My husband and I recently purchased a 24-inch Panatronic television set which had to be replaced. We are senior citizens, and could not easily get the TV back to the store.

We conveyed that information to Value-Mart, and Mr. Richards called us within a day. Not only did he personally come to our house to pick up the TV, but he brought a replacement model and set it up for us.

We have always appreciated Value-Mart for its prices. Now we can also praise your customer service.

Sincerely,
Monica Diamond

Complaint about salesperson

Manager
Stephanie's Boutique
Smalltown, OH

Dear Manager:

I have been a frequent customer of Stephanie's over the years, and I purchase all of my special-occasion outfits from your store. Until this past week, all of my visits have been pleasant.

Last week I was in the store shopping with my daughter-in law for outfits for an upcoming wedding. She brought along her two children, ages four and six.

From the moment we entered the store we were made to feel as if we should have checked the children at the door, or better yet, left them outside to play in traffic.

Your salesperson, Tracy, was rude and condescending to us, and downright unpleasant to the children.

I can't see how I could ever return to your store after such treatment.

Sincerely,
Laura Diamond

Response from store about incident

Laura Diamond
Smalltown, OH

Dear Ms. Diamond:

Please accept my sincere apologies for the unpleasant experience you had in our store last week. I am embarrassed by the whole situation. This is not what shopping at Stephanie's is all about.

I have spoken with Tracy about the incident and made it clear to her that in no way do we want our customers—or their children—to feel unwelcome in our shop.

And I have decided to spruce up a small storage room at the back of the store to serve as a play area stocked with toys and art supplies for young children while their parents are shopping. By the next time you come in, we hope to have the room ready to show you.

We do hope you will give us another chance. If you will call me before you come in, I would be most honored to personally help you with your purchases for the wedding, and to offer a 25 percent discount to both of you for those purchases.

Sincerely,
Stephanie Miller
Stephanie's Boutique

Complaint about mail-order policies

Mail Order Department
Rocky Mountain Associates
Denver, CO

Dear People:

I am an avid mail-order shopper. In fact, I do most of my buying from catalogs and over the Internet.

In recent years I have made many purchases from Rocky Mountain Associates, both in the store and by mail order. And while I have no problem with the service and quality of your merchandise, I do find one recent change in your charges unacceptable.

I strongly object to the $4.50 service charge you now add to all mail orders. This fee is in addition to your shipping charges, which I already find to be higher than those of your competitors.

I'd like to know if your company plans to continue adding this charge in the future. I am considering taking my business elsewhere.

Sincerely,
Laura Diamond

Complaint about price discrepancy

Mail Order Department
J.W. Smith Clothing
Bigtown, NY

Dear People:

I am writing to complain of a discrepancy I encountered between the price of an item in your catalog and in one of your retail outlets.

I recently ordered a dress from your catalog, item #xxx-xxxxx. The price was $108, which I paid by credit card. I have attached a copy of the invoice I received from your shipping department.

Two days later I visited my local mall and stopped in at the J.W. Smith store there. I found the same dress, priced at $79.

I would like to receive a refund of the difference ($29). I assume that would be a better solution than packaging up the dress and shipping it back to you for a full refund.

Please advise.

Sincerely,
Morgan Diamond

Complaint about quality of product received

Customer Service
J.W. Smith Clothing
Bigtown, NY

Dear People:

I am returning a leather jacket I recently purchased through your catalog. I am enclosing the necessary paperwork for a refund.

I am a frequent customer of J.W. Smith Clothing, both in your retail stores and by mail, because I appreciate the value, selection, and service. I must, though, comment on the inferior quality of this jacket. I was appalled at the poor grade of the leather and the cheap zipper, especially considering the price of the jacket.

Overall, it is not worthy of being a J.W. Smith product.

Sincerely,
Morgan Diamond

Complaint to Better Business Bureau about product

Better Business Bureau
Smalltown, OH

Dear Better Business Bureau:

I am writing to register a complaint about a local retail business, Jay's Movies and Video Games at 18 Main Street, Smalltown.

In April I purchased a videotape of a Japanese animated film, a particular interest of mine. The movie I purchased specifically stated on the sealed box that it was dubbed in English, but when I played it on my VCR it was all in the original Japanese.

I took the tape back to the store the next day, and at first they gave me a hard time because I opened the box. They then took back the tape and promised to order an English-language version for me. I waited more than five weeks and then was told that the store was unable to obtain an English version.

I asked for a refund, but they refused to give me cash. They offered only a store credit, because the original purchase was made more than thirty days ago.

I consider this an unacceptable business practice and want others in Smalltown to be aware of such problems. And I would also appreciate the assistance of the BBB in obtaining a refund, in the amount of $32.59.

Sincerely,
Joshua Diamond

Follow-up on complaint to Better Business Bureau about product

Brigitte Gardini, Consumer Advocate
Better Business Bureau
Smalltown, OH

Dear Ms. Gardini:

Thank you for your assistance in dealing with Jay's Movies and Video Games.

Today I received a full refund of my purchase, along with a $10 gift certificate for a future purchase.

I do hope that Jay's will treat me—and all other customers—better in the future.

Thanks to you and the Better Business Bureau for your help.

Sincerely,
Joshua Diamond

Complaint to Better Business Bureau about practice of camera store

Consumer Advocate
Smalltown Better Business Bureau
Smalltown, OH

Dear People:

I am writing to inform you of a shady—and possibly illegal—business practice at a local retail store.

In the Sunday, April 16, 2005 edition of the Smalltown Banner, Bill's Photo Emporium on Main Street advertised a Penkon AE-1 SLR camera for $199, an extremely good price. I immediately went to the store to purchase the camera, arriving just as the door was opened at noon.

I was waited on by Bill himself, and when I asked to buy the Penkon camera he told me they were sold out, but he did have a much better model for $50 more.

I produced the ad, and told Bill that I wanted the one that he had advertised. I pointed out that I was the first customer through the door since the ad ran.

The bottom line: Bill said he didn't think he could obtain a Penkon AE-1 to sell at the advertised price. He kept pushing the more expensive model.

I consider this an example of bait-and-switch advertising. I have no intention of making any further purchases from this store, and will recommend to my friends that they also stay away.

I'd like the Better Business Bureau to investigate this situation.

Sincerely,
Ron Miller

Complaint about business cards

Better Quality Printing
Smalltown, OH

Dear People:

Today I received my order of new business cards. I am very dissatisfied with the quality.

Although the text is correct, it appears as if the entire batch of cards was trimmed on an angle, resulting in downward-sloping text.

These cards do not present a professional appearance, and I do not intend to use them. Please advise.

Sincerely,
Laura Diamond

Follow-up to complaint about business cards

Al Manutius
Better Quality Printing
Smalltown, OH

Dear Mr. Manutius:

Thank you for your prompt attention to the problem with my business cards. I was very impressed when a courier arrived this morning with the reprinted set of cards, just one day after my letter arrived at your shop.

You have restored my appreciation for your company's customer service.

Sincerely,
Laura Diamond

Returning defective article of clothing

Customer Service
American Chicken Clothing
East Overshoe, ME

Dear People:

I am a big fan of your store, buying a great deal of clothing for my two children from your Web site and retail stores.

About a year ago, I purchased a light jacket (AE77 Performance Jacket) for my son to take to college. He wore it only a few times, since it is appropriate only for the fall and spring, not the winter.

When he returned from school I found that the main zipper was broken; it will not close.

On your Web site you advertise "Hassle-free returns. Any Time. No Problems."

Unfortunately, I cannot locate a copy of the purchase receipt. I assume, though, that since the jacket was purchased from your Web site you will be able to locate the record of the sale.

Please advise me on how to take advantage of your guarantee.

Sincerely,
Laura Diamond

Asking for assistance in collecting rebate

Customer Service
Morgan's Department Store
Smalltown, OH

Dear Customer Service:

Two weeks ago, I purchased a set of Franklin cookware at your store. One of the reasons I purchased this particular brand was the rebate offered by the company.

I was ready to send the necessary paperwork to Franklin to get the money back when I saw that I need a store rebate form, which was to have been given to me by the seller at the time of purchase.

I am enclosing a photocopy of my receipt; please send me the necessary rebate form.

Sincerely,
Monica Diamond

Requesting status of rebate

Customer Service
Franklin Cookware
Rubbertown, OH

Dear Customer Service:

I sent in the forms and receipts for a $50 rebate from Franklin Cookware on December 2, 2004. According to the paperwork, I should have received a check from your company within six weeks.

As of February 15, 2005, I have not received the rebate.

Attached is a photocopy of the receipt and rebate coupon form I sent to your company.

Please advise me when I will receive the rebate check.

Sincerely,
Monica Diamond

Follow-up on rebate not received

Customer Service
PC-USA
Smalltown, OH

Dear Customer Service:

This is my second request asking for the status of a $50 rebate on the purchase of a computer monitor. I mailed the original rebate request more than eight weeks ago; as of today, March 15, 2005, the payment has not been received.

I am attaching copies of all paperwork required for this reimbursement.

I have made many purchases at your store for business and personal needs. I expect to receive the rebate before I make further purchases there or make any recommendations to my friends to shop at PC-USA.

Please advise.

Sincerely,
John Diamond

15 Quality and Warranties

Dear Reader:

Take it back. Fix it right. Cancel my subscription.

In almost every transaction, the buyer has a right to hold a reasonable expectation that a product will perform as promised and that it will remain in working condition for at least the period guaranteed at the time of sale.

State and federal laws set basic levels of merchantability, and most stores add their own promises, ranging from a ten-day exchange period to a no-questions-asked lifetime money-back guarantee. Your job as a buyer is to know a retailer's policy *before* you make a purchase, and then be ready to politely but firmly pursue the delivery of those promises. Be specific in your mention of date of purchase and other related time references.

Caveat emptor.

Sincerely,
The Authors

Complaint about quality of product

Consumer Affairs
Edson Cereal Company
Oatmeal, MN

Dear People:

I am a frequent buyer of your Krispy Krunch cereal.

When I was about halfway through my latest box, I noticed a small piece of white plastic in the package.

I am enclosing the object as well as the box top, which includes the manufacturing lot number.

Before I purchase another box of Krispy Krunch, I would like to know the source of the contamination of the product.

Sincerely,
Harold Diamond

Praising product

Consumer Affairs
Fishbone Foods
Farmtown, IA

Dear People:

I don't ordinarily write fan mail to salad dressing companies. But I feel compelled to praise the "new and improved" Tru-Flavor Nonfat Low-Calorie Blue Cheese Dressing with Flavor Chunks.

This salad dressing tastes so good it's almost a bonus that it doesn't have the fat and the calories of the real thing.

Thank you for making it available.

Sincerely,
Harold Diamond

Inquiry about problems with product

Customer Service
Smith Gas Grill Company
Barbecue, TX

Dear People:

In June of this year, I purchased a Smith Gas Grill Model 289 from your Web site. I am enclosing a copy of my receipt.

Right from the start, the grill did not work properly. Among the failures have been the connecting pipe from the gas tank to the burner, and the burner itself. The glass viewing window cracked, and most recently two of the wheels fell off.

Your terms of sale state that an unsatisfactory item should be taken to an authorized repair shop. I have done so three times. Each trip involved a roundtrip of thirty miles and loss of the use of the grill for about a week.

Although you have authorized a fourth visit to the repair facility, I think it is time to declare this grill a lemon.

I want the Smith Gas Grill Company to pick up this grill and replace it with a functioning model, or send me a check for the cost of the unit so that I can buy a new grill. I am willing to give Smith Gas Grill Company another chance, provided the replacement unit performs properly.

Please advise.

Sincerely,
John Diamond

Second letter about problems with product

Customer Service
Smith Gas Grill Company
Barbecue, TX

Dear People:

It has now been six weeks since I wrote to you about the problems I have been having with my Smith gas grill, but I have not received a response. I have attached a copy of my previous letter to you.

Please advise by return mail what you plan to do about my defective grill.

Thank you.

Sincerely,
John Diamond

Third letter about problems with product

Henry Heisler
Customer Service
Smith Gas Grill Company
Barbecue, TX

Dear Mr. Heisler:

I am in receipt of your letter of August 12, sent in response to my complaint about continuing problems with my Smith gas grill.

I find your offer of a $25 credit toward the purchase of a new grill to be inadequate and nonresponsive to a serious problem of product quality. The grill I purchased six months ago has never functioned properly and has been taken into the repair shop three times already.

As I indicated in my previous letters, copies of which are attached, I expect Smith to replace this defective unit or send me a full refund for the purchase of the grill.

I have already contacted the Smalltown Better Business Bureau and obtained information about my legal rights as a consumer. If I do not receive a satisfactory response within two weeks of the date of this letter, I plan to proceed with a Lemon Law case.

I look forward to hearing from you immediately.

Sincerely,
John Diamond

Acceptance of product settlement

Henry Heisler
Customer Service
Smith Gas Grill Company
Barbecue, TX

Dear Mr. Heisler:

Thank you for your prompt reply to my most recent letter about the problems we have had with our Smith gas grill.

Per your instructions, we delivered the faulty unit to the service center, where they will pack it up for return to your factory. And we have used the credit memo from Smith Gas Grill Company to purchase a new—and tested—grill from a local retailer here in Smalltown. Thus far, the grill seems to be performing properly.

Sincerely,
John Diamond

Returning item to catalog seller under satisfaction guarantee

Customer Service
The Cutting Edge
East Weston, SC

Dear People:

A year ago this past March, I ordered the enclosed jacket from your catalog. I removed the jacket from the box it was delivered in and hung it in my closet. I never wore it.

Recently, I came across the jacket. Either my taste has changed or I made a bad mistake when I placed the order. In either case, I do not want to keep the jacket.

In your catalog your guarantee states that an item can be returned at any time, for any reason. I do not have my original paperwork, but the tags are still attached to the jacket.

Please credit my account for the purchase price of the jacket.

Sincerely,
Morgan Diamond

Follow-up on return of item under satisfaction guarantee

Customer Service
The Cutting Edge
East Weston, SC

Dear People:

You have made a believer out of me.

I recently returned a jacket to you more than a year after I purchased it because I had decided that the original purchase was a mistake. Although your guarantee of satisfaction promises a return can be made at any time for any reason, I wasn't sure the promise was for real. Now I know that it is, because you credited my account for the full purchase price of the jacket.

The Cutting Edge has won me as a customer from now on.

Sincerely,
Morgan Diamond

Returning appliance under satisfaction guarantee

Customer Service
Sweep Well Vacuum Cleaning Company
Smalltown, OH

Dear Customer Service:

I am returning the Sweep Well Vacuum Cleaner I purchased recently. Under the terms of your guarantee, I am able to do so within three months of purchase for any reason.

I have no great dissatisfaction with the vacuum cleaner, but feel that it just doesn't perform well enough to justify its price. Please credit my charge card with the purchase price plus shipping.

Sincerely,
Laura Diamond

Canceling magazine subscription with prorated refund

Subscription Services
Modern Quilting Magazine
Big Town, NY

Dear People:

Please cancel my subscription immediately. Please send me a check for the issues still due, as promised under terms of your satisfaction guarantee.

I have attached a copy of the address label from the most recent issue.

Thank you.

Laura Diamond
Smalltown, OH

Asking for full refund for magazine

Subscription Services
Beekeeping Monthly
Flyover, MT

Dear People:

Please cancel my subscription to Beekeeping Monthly and send me a full refund under your "total satisfaction guarantee."

I have found that it is against the bylaws of my community to keep bees in the backyard, and therefore have no need for the publication.

Thank you.

Morgan Diamond
Smalltown, OH

16 Automotive Issues

Dear Reader:

For many of us, a car is the second most expensive property we purchase, after a home and the garage in which we park the vehicle.

Speaking for myself, I hate the process of shopping at car dealerships. I dislike the pressure tactics that some of them use, and I resent the gamesmanship that is built into negotiating for the best price. And so, I have resorted to written communications for the purchase of my last few cars.

In the following letters, you'll see an example of a bidding war I set up among several car dealers. I conducted the bidding by letter and fax, and only after I had accepted a bid did I have to visit the dealership to sign the papers.

You'll also find some of the written documentation that accompanies a complaint on the repair of a used car.

Best of luck.

Sincerely,
Corey Sandler

Soliciting bids for purchase of personal car

Steven Rehm, Sales Manager
Smalltown General Megamotors
Smalltown, OH

Dear Mr. Rehm:

I am ready to purchase a new car and would like to give your dealership the opportunity to submit a bid for my business. I would like to conduct this purchase by mail and fax; I do not need to come to the dealership until we have reached a firm agreement on price and specifications.

We are interested in the following vehicle, which we have seen for sale at several area dealerships:

2005 General Megamotors Puttputt All-Terrain, 2.6 V6 engine, AWD, LX Trim with Consumer Value Package.

We will accept any available color, but would prefer red or brown. We *do not* want any dealer add-ons such as pinstriping, undercoating, rustproofing, or paint sealant.

According to our research, this vehicle has a manufacturer's suggested list price of $28,895, and the dealer invoice cost is $24,007.

At this time we are interested in a cash price for the vehicle. We will consider other options including trade-in, financing, or leasing *after* we have accepted the best price.

I have sent this same letter to several other General Megamotor dealers in the area. I intend to buy a car from the dealership offering me the best price and service.

I look forward to hearing from you soon. We will consider all bids received no later than noon on Friday, July 7.

Sincerely,
Michael Diamond

Second round of bidding on purchase of new car

Steven Rehm, Sales Manager
Smalltown General Megamotors
Smalltown, OH

Dear Mr. Rehm:

Thank you for your bid, in the amount of $25,200, for the sale of a 2005 General Megamotors Puttputt All-Terrain with a 2.6 V6 engine, AWD, in LX Trim with the Consumer Value Package.

Your bid is about $750 higher than the best offer we have received.

We would be happy to give you our business because we have made previous purchases through your dealership. Therefore, we would be willing to accept one final bid from your company. We must receive your bid no later than noon on Monday, July 10.

Sincerely,
Michael Diamond

Response to bid for purchase of new car

Aaron Sanders, Sales Manager
Nearby General Megamotors Superstore
Nearby, OH

Dear Mr. Sanders:

Thank you for your bid, in the amount of $22,700, for the sale of a 2005 General Megamotors Puttputt All-Terrain with a 2.6 V6 engine, AWD.

I note, however, that your bid does not indicate that the vehicle includes LX Trim with the Consumer Value Package.

If in fact your bid is for exactly the vehicle we have specified, I would like to proceed with purchase at that price. You have my permission to call me for that purpose only.

On the other hand, if your bid is for a vehicle that does not meet our specifications, we will allow you one last opportunity to offer a vehicle that does. We will accept a written bid from your company no later than noon on Monday, July 10.

Sincerely,
Michael Diamond

Accepting bid for purchase of new car

Steven Rehm, Sales Manager
Smalltown General Megamotors
Smalltown, OH

Dear Mr. Rehm:

Thank you for your revised bid, in the amount of $24,250, for the sale of a 2005 General Megamotors Puttputt All-Terrain with a 2.6 V6 engine, AWD, in LX Trim with the Consumer Value Package.

We will be happy to buy the car at that price. Please draw up a sales agreement.

We have been offered financing through the Smalltown Credit Union at an annual percentage rate of 4.05 percent for forty-eight months. If your dealership can improve on that rate, we would be happy to finance the car through your dealership.

Please advise.

Sincerely,
Michael Diamond

Complaint to dealer about repair

General Manager
Ed Sell Newmobile
Smalltown, OH

Dear General Manager:

Two weeks ago, I brought in my 1999 Newmobile Scimitar for service because of serious hesitation problems when accelerating from a stop. I paid $320 for a tune-up and cleaning of the fuel injectors. I have attached a copy of the invoice.

The next day I experienced the very same problem, nearly causing a rear-end collision as I attempted to merge onto I-895.

I drove the car directly back to the shop and left it overnight for attention. I was told the injectors needed to be readjusted. At one point, your service adviser attempted to convince me that this was a normal condition for this model. I can't imagine any customer accepting such a dangerous and annoying "condition."

Although I had my misgivings about the work performed, I drove the vehicle for another week. Today the car hesitated and finally stalled on Main Street in Smalltown.

I have called to make an appointment for the day after tomorrow, June 6. I'm writing this letter to make you aware of this situation before I bring the vehicle in for further repair.

I have thus far paid $320 and lost many hours in taking the car to the shop repeatedly for the same problem. Although my family has purchased four cars from Ed Sell Newmobile in the past years, any future sales to me, my family, and my friends are going to be dependent upon a satisfactory solution of this problem.

I look forward to hearing from you.

Sincerely,
Joshua Diamond

Follow-up to district manager about repair problem

District Manager
Newmobile Auto Company
Nearby, OH

Dear District Manager:

I am writing to request your assistance in resolving an ongoing problem with one of your company's cars, a 1999 Newmobile Scimitar. The VIN is 3FALC15P7VR159289.

The vehicle was purchased new from Ed Sell Newmobile in Smalltown, OH. It performed well during its warranty period.

Within a few months after going out of warranty, the vehicle began exhibiting serious hesitation problems when accelerating from a stop. I have taken the vehicle to

Ed Sell Newmobile three times, and have paid for a complete tune-up and a cleaning of the fuel injectors.

As of this morning, the car is still stalling or hesitating quite severely when I accelerate rapidly from a standstill.

I have no confidence that the dealer is able to fix this persistent problem. I would like to know:

1. Is there a technical service bulletin related to this particular problem on a Newmobile Scimitar?
2. Have there been any recalls or unpublished extended warranties for this vehicle?
3. Can you arrange for a technical consultant to advise Ed Sell Newmobile on a strategy to repair this problem?

I look forward to hearing from you soon.

Sincerely,
Joshua Diamond

Objection to Better Business Bureau about repair issue

Consumer Advocate
Better Business Bureau
Smalltown, OH

Dear Advocate:

I am writing to register a complaint against Ed Sell Newmobile here in Smalltown. I have attempted to resolve a problem with the repair of my vehicle for three months now, and I do not feel that this business has any intention of repairing the vehicle to my satisfaction.

I have enclosed copies of several letters sent to Ed Sell Newmobile as well as those to the car manufacturer's district manager.

I would like other potential customers here in Smalltown to be aware of the inadequate service offered by this company.

Sincerely,
Joshua Diamond

17 School Policies

Dear Reader:

As a parent, you are a consumer of an essential product called "education" for your children. Unless you are very complacent—or very lucky—chances are you are going to need to get involved in managing your child's school career.

Nearly every teacher and school administrator we have ever met has been a dedicated professional. But not every one has been flexible enough to deal with every child on an individual basis. Some children have special needs; some families are organized in a different manner than others; and some children learn differently. Any of these may require adjustments in the classroom or curriculum.

In this chapter, we'll go through common letters regarding enrollment, absences from school, and some objections to and suggestions for change of school policies. The key here is to keep the communication on a professional and polite basis while you also exercise your right to be insistent as your child's best advocate.

Sincerely,
The Authors

Request information on preschool

Good Friends Preschool
Fairview, PA

Dear People:

We will be moving into the Fairview area shortly. Our daughter Hannah will turn 5 in June, and we want to enroll her in preschool in the fall.

Good Friends has been highly recommended to us. We would like to get information about the school and about enrollment for this September.

Please call me at (xxx) xxx-xxxx to discuss Good Friends, and to arrange a time for my daughter and me to visit.

Sincerely,
Karen Diamond

Nursery school health issue

Bitsy Collins, Headmistress
Wee Kids Nursery School
Fairview, PA

Dear Ms. Collins:

Hannah is very much enjoying her first weeks at nursery school. We are very pleased that she has become so comfortable with her new surroundings.

I hope you can help us with one small problem. Hannah is still somewhat shy about asking to use the bathroom. We would appreciate it if you or one of the other teachers would suggest to her that she take a break and use the facilities a few times each day.

We look forward to meeting you at Parents Day next week.

Sincerely,
Karen Diamond

Enrolling child in elementary school

Principal
Fairview Elementary School
Fairview, PA

Dear Principal:

We will be moving to Fairview this summer. I will need to enroll my son, Brian, into the third grade. I have requested that the Smalltown Elementary School, Smalltown, Ohio, send my son's records directly to you.

Brian's birth date is June 6, 20xx. If there is anything else you need, please call me at (xxx) xxx-xxxx. I would also be interested in bringing him over sometime this summer to acquaint him with the school and possibly meet some of the teachers. Please advise if this is possible.

Sincerely,
Karen Diamond

To school notifying of emergency contact for child

Fran Murphy, Ph.D.
Principal
Fairview Elementary School
Fairview, PA

Dear Dr. Murphy:

Please list Pam Nicklaus as the emergency contact for our son, Brian. Pam can be reached at (xxx) xxx-xxxx.

If I am not available, she has our permission to pick up Brian and take him to her home in case of illness.

Sincerely,
Karen Diamond

Notifying school of parents' differing names

Lydia Gordon, Director
Tiny Tots Preschool
Smalltown, OH

Dear Ms. Gordon:

My daughter, Ashley Morgan, has been accepted as a student in your school. My husband and I use different last names for professional reasons, so I want to be sure you know that Steven Morgan is her father and Donna Tyler is her mother.

Either one or both of us will be taking her to school and picking her up. As her legal parents, either one or both of us should be notified if any medical emergencies arise.

Sincerely,
Donna Tyler

Complaint about scheduling of teachers' days at school

Fran Murphy, Principal, Ph.D.
Fairview Elementary School
Fairview, PA

Dear Dr. Murphy:

My son, Brian, is a third-grade student at Fairview. In looking at the school calendar for the month of October, I notice that there are four days when the children will be released at noon, to allow for teachers' meetings on those days.

My experience with half days for school children has not been positive. I don't believe much happens academically, and it certainly creates havoc in the schedules of working parents.

Is there any reason not to schedule teachers' meetings for full days? I think it would make more sense to have an extended weekend with my children than to disrupt the schedule on two working days.

An alternative would be to arrange for special programs at school for the children during those afternoons, while teachers participate in training sessions. Perhaps some parents could volunteer to assist teachers' aides and administrative staff on those days.

Sincerely,
Karen Diamond

Excuse from school for medical appointment

Fran Murphy, Ph.D.
Principal
Fairview, PA

Dear Dr. Murphy:

Please excuse my son, Brian Diamond, from school on Tuesday, March 6, at 9:45 A.M. He has a dental appointment and will return to school as soon as possible when it is completed.

Sincerely,
Michael Diamond

Excuse from school for family needs

Jack Miller, Principal
Smalltown Elementary School
Smalltown, OH

Dear Mr. Miller:

My son, Brian, a student in Ms. Gordon's second-grade class, will be absent from school on Monday, Tuesday, and Wednesday, May 7 through 9.

We have a family situation that requires us to travel out of state. We will ask Ms. Gordon to assign him reading and homework to keep up with the class while he is away.

Brian will be back in school on Thursday, May 10.

Sincerely,
Karen Diamond

Medical excuse for absence

Jack Miller, Principal
Smalltown Elementary School
Smalltown, OH

Dear Mr. Miller:

Please excuse my son, Brian Diamond, for his absence from school from March 5 through 9. He had the chickenpox, and Dr. Tannenbaum advised bed rest.

Brian is now recovered, and Dr. Tannenbaum says he is no longer contagious and able to return to school.

Sincerely,
Michael Diamond

Medical excuse for absence with special needs

Patrick Norton, Principal, Ph.D.
Smalltown High School
Smalltown, OH

Dear Dr. Norton:

Please excuse my daughter, Heather Diamond, for her absence from school October 5. She sprained her ankle in an afterschool dance class.

Although she is able to return to school, our doctor has asked that she not participate in gym class for the next week. Would you please tell her physical education teacher about this?

Sincerely,
John Diamond

Excuse from school because of death in family

Patrick Norton, Principal, Ph.D.
Smalltown High School
Smalltown, OH

Dear Dr. Norton:

Please excuse Heather Diamond from school on September 28 and 29. We have had a death in the family and will be traveling out of town for the funeral.

Heather will check with her teachers and do all assignments and homework for the time she is away.

Sincerely,
Laura Diamond

Child will be absent for religious observance

Fran Murphy, Principal, Ph.D.
Fairview Elementary School
Fairview, PA

Dear Dr. Murphy:

This is to inform you that my son, Brian Diamond, will be out of school on October 12. We will be observing Yom Kippur.

Sincerely,
Michael Diamond

Permission for elementary school class trip

David Fisher
Fairview Elementary School
Fairview, PA

Dear Mr. Fisher:

I hereby give permission for my son, Brian Diamond, to attend the overnight field trip at the Natural History Museum on Monday, November 16. Our telephone numbers are listed below in case of an emergency.

It sounds like a great experience, and Brian is very excited.

Please call if anything further is needed.

Sincerely,
Karen Diamond

Objecting to fire drill schedule

Fran Murphy, Principal, Ph.D.
Fairview Elementary School
Fairview, PA

Dear Dr. Murphy:

My son, Brian, is a third-grade student at Fairview. I fully support the necessity for fire and safety drills; however, I must object to the lack of thought that went into the recent drill on Tuesday, November 16.

On that morning, the weathercasters warned parents throughout the area to bundle up their kids for a frigid and wet day. The drive to school was a messy and somewhat dangerous trip.

When I picked up my son that afternoon I was amazed to find that the school had gone ahead with a fire drill at 10 A.M., in the middle of the worst of the weather. Everyone at the school had been out in the bitter cold and sleet with no hat, coat, or gloves.

Did no one consider the possibility of postponing the drill until a later day? I'm sure the school has enough flexibility in its schedule to wait for a less threatening day.

Sincerely,
Karen Diamond

Suggesting a new high school course

Patrick Norton, Ph.D.
Principal
Smalltown High School
Smalltown, OH

Dear Dr. Norton:

I am writing to suggest that Smalltown High School add a course aimed at helping graduating seniors adjust to the specific demands of college life.

I am writing this letter from two perspectives—as the mother of a student at SHS, and as a college instructor. As you know, my daughter Heather is an incoming senior, and I teach political science at Smalltown Community College.

So much of Heather's junior year has been focused on preparation for the SATs, ACTs, and advanced placement exams, as well as the college application process. But we do not feel that much attention has been paid to college life itself, which is very different from high school.

I have seen many very bright and enthusiastic college freshmen overwhelmed with the academic and social challenges of their first year at college. Most are on their own for the first time and are not well prepared to handle that responsibility. And the biggest academic challenge is learning how to manage their time properly.

I strongly recommend that SHS develop a course for seniors aimed at giving them practical information about that first year at college.

I have many ideas that I would be happy to share with you and the school board. I strongly believe that this type of course would help students prepare for their critical first year of college.

Sincerely,
Laura Diamond

Asking about safeguards on Internet at school

Patrick Norton, Ph.D.
Principal
Smalltown High School
Smalltown, OH

Dear Dr. Norton:

My daughter Heather is a senior at Smalltown High School. We are very pleased that the school has upgraded all of its facilities to bring Internet access to classrooms and the library.

However, as a parent I am very concerned about some of the material—and some of the users—that one finds on the Internet. Here at home we are able to monitor the sites Heather visits and to set firm rules about what sort of information she discloses to people she meets in chat rooms.

What sort of safeguards are in use at the high school? Is there any filtering software to prevent access to inappropriate Web sites? I know the Student Handbook instructs students to notify a teacher if they mistakenly access such information, but I think this is unrealistic and comes too late.

Sincerely,
Laura Diamond

Follow-up on safeguards on Internet at school

Patrick Norton, Ph.D.
Principal
Smalltown High School
Smalltown, OH

Dear Dr. Norton:

Thank you for your response about Internet usage at school.

You can count on my support at the next meeting of the school board when you present your plan for filtering and monitoring all Internet usage at the school.

Sincerely,
Laura Diamond

Complaining about a school policy

Patrick Norton, Ph.D.
Principal
Smalltown High School
Smalltown, OH

Dear Dr. Norton:

I am writing to voice my displeasure with a dangerous and disruptive policy at Smalltown High School: the mad noontime dash of seniors driving to pick up lunch.

I don't see the value in allowing seventy teenagers to get in their cars in the middle of the day, dash to a fast-food restaurant, and hurry back to school. For those who don't leave, the drivers take orders and collect money, spending a considerable amount of class time just planning for lunch.

The lunchtime break lasts only forty minutes. These young people are not experienced enough to handle all the traffic and weather situations they may encounter and still be back in time for their first class of the afternoon.

I believe this practice began as a reward for good grades and special achievements. It has escalated to being considered an upperclassman's right.

This was a bad idea in the first place and has only gotten worse. Students should be concentrating on class work, not on racing to McDonald's.

I would be happy to meet with you and the school board to discuss this matter.

Sincerely,
Laura Diamond

To school board about vacation policy

Smalltown Board of Education
Smalltown, OH

Dear Members of the School Board:

I understand that for the coming year, the school board is considering a major change to two of the three vacation periods that are part of the school calendar.

In past years there was a week off from just before Christmas through New Year's Day. A second week off was scheduled for winter break in late February, and a third week for spring break was given in April.

The new proposal would do away with the winter break entirely and instead give at least two weeks off around the Christmas to New Year's Day period.

I think this would be a huge mistake. If the purpose of a break is to give families time to spend together, a week from Christmas to New Year's is a sufficient time to see family and friends. As far as traveling on a vacation is concerned, this is the least efficient and most expensive time to travel.

I think this proposal should be given a lot more thought. I would be willing to serve on a committee to investigate options to see if there is, indeed, a better use of precious time off.

Sincerely,
Laura Diamond

Complaint about school lunch

Fran Murphy, Ph.D.
Principal
Fairview Elementary School
Fairview, PA

Dear Dr. Murphy:

Brian is settling in well as a third-grade student at Fairview.

I do have a concern, though, about the food offered in the school cafeteria. The choices do not seem to have any relation to recognized medical studies about such things as excessive fat, sugar, and useless junk food.

A recent menu included fried fish with fried potato nuggets, a hot dog with potato chips, and fried chicken with French fries. The most healthful piece of food seemed to be a small piece of green pepper floating on a sea of cheese on a pizza.

I don't feed my child this sort of junk at home, and I don't think it's appropriate for school.

I would very much like to talk to the school dietitian about the offerings at school.

Sincerely,
Karen Diamond

Complaint about class schedule

Patrick Norton, Ph.D.
Principal
Smalltown High School
Smalltown, OH

Dear Dr. Norton:

We just received Heather's senior year class schedule and find that it does not include two very important courses that she selected in preparation for college. I am writing to ask that her schedule be reworked to include both Advanced Placement Calculus and Advanced French.

As you know, Heather is a dedicated and accomplished student, and we are very proud of the fact that she does not intend to take the lazy way out in her senior year. She intends to major in math in college, and the calculus course is essential. And the colleges to which she is applying all require three years of a foreign language.

We look forward to hearing from you before the start of the school year about these changes.

Sincerely,
Laura Diamond

Objection to disciplinary action

Patrick Norton, Ph.D.
Principal
Smalltown High School
Smalltown, OH

Dear Dr. Norton:

I am writing to object to an inappropriate disciplinary action by a substitute teacher in Mr. Harrison's British Studies class.

The substitute, Helen Wagner, took charge of the third-period class last week. I believe she has been assigned to the class for the remainder of the term while Mr. Harrison attends to personal business.

My daughter Heather tells me that from the moment the class began, Ms. Wagner did not seem to have control, and some of the students became very unruly.

In no way do I condone unruly behavior in the classroom. But I do think Ms. Wagner overreacted when she gave the entire class a week's detention plus a reduction in every student's final grade by five points.

This is a combination of collective punishment of every student for the behavior of a few, and an inappropriate academic sanction. It is important to separate behavioral penalties from the objective assignment of academic grades.

This is an Advanced Placement course, very important to the college-bound students in the class.

I hope you will discuss this incident further with Ms. Wagner and come to a less drastic conclusion. I would be happy to come to school for a meeting about this matter. I know that a number of other parents of children in the class would also want to attend.

I look forward to hearing from you soon.

Sincerely,
Laura Diamond

Supporting teacher in dispute

Patrick Norton, Ph.D.
Principal
Smalltown High School
Smalltown, OH

Dear Dr. Norton:

I understand from my daughter Heather that the school and the school board have become involved in a controversy over the teaching methods and curriculum in the advanced placement twelfth-grade English class taught by Robert Barlow.

I am aware of the reading list for that class, and although I do not endorse all of the choices and the ideas expressed by all of the authors, I applaud Mr. Barlow for challenging our students to think about things that are not part of their ordinary lives.

As our children near graduation from high school, one of the most important lessons we can teach them is that they will not always be comfortable with everything and everyone they come in contact with. Mr. Barlow has always treated his class as young adults and been very intellectually demanding of them.

He is a very valuable teacher, and to disrupt his course or to lose him would not only cause great harm but send the wrong message to a group of young adults who are less than a year away from being on their own in college.

Sincerely,
Laura Diamond

Objecting to discipline of teacher by school board

B.J. Bush, Chairman
Smalltown School Board
Smalltown, OH

Dear Mr. Bush:

I am writing to register my strong support of Bob Barlow, twelfth-grade English teacher at Smalltown High School. Mr. Barlow is a teacher of the highest caliber, and we should be honored that he is a member of the faculty here.

In the six months that my daughter Heather has been in his class, her appreciation and knowledge of literature has increased tremendously. She has not always enjoyed every selection Mr. Barlow required her to read, but she has always understood its place and significance.

Mr. Barlow taught her to think for herself, which is a lesson she must master if she is to be successful in life.

I plan to be at the next meeting of the school board, along with a group of other parents, to support Mr. Barlow and object to any disciplinary action against him by the board.

Sincerely,
Laura Diamond

Accepting advisory board appointment

Patrick Norton, Ph.D.
Principal
Smalltown High School
Smalltown, OH

Dear Dr. Norton:

I am pleased that the matter concerning English teacher Bob Barlow has been satisfactorily resolved.

As an educator myself, I am always very quick to get involved in school issues, especially when they involve freedom of expression. I am pleased to accept your request to become involved in a parents advisory council.

Sincerely,
Laura Diamond

Starting a memorial scholarship fund

Dear members of Smalltown Senior Center:

It has been almost one year since Kent Davenport passed away. As all of you know, Kent was the guiding hand behind the creation of this center.

Through sheer determination and hard work, Kent and those who gathered around him brought the center to life. We owe a lot to Kent; he was smart, kind, and on a personal note, my oldest and best friend. Many of us miss him every day.

Kent was largely self-educated. After World War II he had to go to work to support his brother's widow and young nephew, and he built a successful cartage company here in Smalltown.

All through the years, he was an avid reader and was always encouraging young people to stay in school, and those of our generation to go back to school and learn as much as possible.

We have decided to set up a scholarship at Smalltown High School in his name. We anticipate this to be a yearly gift to a deserving senior. We are sure this is something Kent would be proud of, and is a fitting reminder of his appreciation of learning.

We have allocated $2,000 from the community service fund of the center, and a group of us have contributed several thousand dollars more as the initial endowment for the scholarship fund. We would be happy to accept additional donations. Please make checks payable to the Kent Davenport Scholarship Fund and send them along to me at the senior center.

Incidentally, the lawyer who has volunteered his time to help us with the technicalities is Ben Davenport, Kent's nephew.

In Kent's memory, I am,

Sincerely yours,
Harold Diamond, President
Smalltown Senior Center

Announcing a memorial scholarship fund

B.J. Bush, Chairman
Smalltown School Board
Smalltown, OH

Dear Mr. Bush:

I am proud to announce that the Smalltown Senior Center and individuals in our community have established the Kent Davenport Memorial Scholarship Fund.

Kent was the guiding hand behind the creation of the senior center. Through sheer determination and hard work, Kent and those who gathered around him brought the center to life.

Beginning this May, we plan to offer an annual scholarship to the graduating senior who demonstrates the best dedication to community service here in Smalltown.

I look forward to working with the school board to set up the procedure to award the scholarship.

Sincerely yours,
Harold Diamond, President
Smalltown Senior Center

Complaint about location of school bus stop

Fran Murphy, Ph.D.
Principal
Fairview Elementary School
Fairview, PA

Dear Dr. Murphy:

My son, Brian, is a third-grade student at Fairview Elementary School. The closest bus stop for him would be the corner of Hill Street and Fourth Avenue, in front of 16 Hill Street.

I'm writing to ask that you consider moving that pickup spot to a safer location.

Hill and Fourth is a major intersection in Fairview and also on a truck route to the electrical plant. At 7:30 A.M. there is a tremendous amount of rush hour traffic.

All of the kids have been warned to be careful while waiting for the bus, but I don't think we can guarantee that one of them won't stray into the road.

Can I suggest the stop be moved around the corner onto Fourth Street, near the Keefe Playground? There is more room there, less traffic, and a play area to occupy the kids.

Sincerely,
Karen Diamond

18 Classroom Issues

Dear Reader:

Most teachers we know welcome the participation of parents and guardians in the education of their children. Let them know of your concerns, and be persistent in getting them resolved, whether it means requesting a meeting or setting up a program or activity that your student can pursue.

Your message to the teachers is this: We care, and we want to be involved.

Sincerely,
The Authors

Requesting a meeting with child's grade school teacher

Ms. Emily Gordon
Smalltown Elementary School
Smalltown, OH

Dear Ms. Gordon:

I would like to meet with you soon so that we can work together to resolve a problem Brian is having this year.

As you know, he is a conscientious student. But he seems to be overwhelmed by the workload, and specifically the amount of time he spends on homework.

He comes home from school and sometimes spends as much as two hours a night on homework, and then he worries whether he should do more. I believe he brings on much of this pressure himself, but I need your help in getting him to understand that he is doing well and does not have to be so hard on himself.

I'm sure we agree that we don't want to discourage a good student who has a great deal of potential, but we also want to allow a young child to enjoy school and his life outside of school.

Please call me at (xxx) xxx-xxxx as soon as convenient so that we may set a time to get together.

Sincerely,
Karen Diamond

To teacher about child's academic difficulty

Ms. Emily Gordon
Smalltown Elementary School
Smalltown, OH

Dear Ms. Gordon:

Our son, Brian, is enjoying his school year thus far, and has had many good things to say about you and his classmates.

However, as I am sure you know, he does seem to be struggling with math. I would appreciate your thoughts on how we can help him get a better grasp on the concepts of math before he falls too far behind the rest of the class.

I would appreciate a call.

Sincerely,
Karen Diamond

Follow-up on child's academic difficulty

Ms. Emily Gordon
Smalltown Elementary School
Smalltown, OH

Dear Ms. Gordon:

Thanks for your note about Brian's schoolwork. It is good to hear about his strengths in reading comprehension and writing.

I appreciate your suggestion about hiring a tutor for extra lessons after school. I will contact your classroom aide, Shannon Graham, and see what we can set up.

Sincerely,
Karen Diamond

Hiring a tutor for child's academic difficulty

Ms. Shannon Graham
Smalltown Elementary School
Smalltown, OH

Dear Ms. Graham:

Thank you for agreeing to tutor Brian in math. Ms. Gordon has many good things to say about you. The fact that you work directly with her in the classroom should help Brian a great deal.

Ms. Gordon has offered to help you plan a specialized enrichment course for Brian.

We look forward to seeing you at our house on Saturday, October 12, at 10 A.M.

Sincerely,
Karen Diamond

Requesting extra class work for absent child

Ms. Emily Gordon
Smalltown Elementary School
Smalltown, OH

Dear Ms. Gordon:

Brian will be absent from school on Monday, Tuesday, and Wednesday, May 7 through 9, as we attend to some important family matters out of state. We have already informed the principal.

Could you please assign him reading and homework to keep up with the class while he is away? Feel free to call me if you'd like to discuss the assignments.

Brian will be back in school on Thursday, May 10.

Thanks again for your help. We are very happy with Brian's academic progress this year.

Sincerely,
Karen Diamond

Requesting help for classroom problem

Deborah Smith
Fairview Elementary School
Fairview, PA

Dear Ms. Smith:

My son, Brian, is a student in your fourth-grade class. We have been looking forward to meeting you during parent-teacher conferences next month.

However, I would like to set up an appointment with you for the coming week to discuss a matter that is causing us a great deal of concern.

When we moved to Fairview over the summer, Brian left behind a number of good friends and was quite apprehensive about starting in a new school. We spent a considerable amount of time assuring him that when he started school he would find new friends and fun things to do.

However, from the first day of school we found that Brian was having a problem with several children in the class who have chosen to tease him constantly. Brian comes home quite upset every day and does not want to go back.

I am sure you would not tolerate such behavior if you were aware of it. We hope you will intervene now. We would like to meet with you to discuss the best way to deal with this problem.

Knowing my son as I do, I am sure that given a chance, he will fit in and do well.

Sincerely,
Karen Diamond

Requesting child be assigned to another class

Fran Murphy, Ph.D.
Principal
Fairview Elementary School
Fairview, PA

Dear Dr. Murphy:

I am writing to request that my son, Brian, be transferred to a different third-grade class and that we meet to discuss conditions in his classroom.

Brian has been the subject of nearly constant teasing from some of the other students in Ms. Smith's classroom, and it is making him miserable and unable to learn.

The problem began right at the start of the school year. I have been in contact with Ms. Smith by letter and met with her two weeks ago, but the problem has not been resolved.

It is now a month into the school year and Brian is still the target of the other children. I am asking that Brian be placed in another classroom immediately so that he does not fall farther behind in his schoolwork.

We specifically chose to move to Fairview because of the excellent reputation of the school district. I am disappointed that an elementary school teacher could not settle a problem as basic as one child being cruel to another.

I look forward to hearing from you very soon to schedule a meeting and to discuss Brian's new classroom assignment.

Sincerely,
Karen Diamond

Thanks to principal for help in resolving problem

Fran Murphy, Ph.D.
Principal
Fairview Elementary School
Fairview, PA

Dear Dr. Murphy:

I just wanted to thank you for your help in resolving the problem our son, Brian, was having in his third-grade classroom. I am happy to report that he is doing very well with his new teacher, Mr. Fisher, and is returning to the happy, well-adjusted little boy we knew him to be.

Sincerely,
Karen Diamond

19 Pre-College and Job Preparation

Dear Reader:

By the time your child reaches high school—and especially in their senior year—the focus shifts to life beyond secondary school to college and career. In this chapter, we'll look at some of the necessary pre-college details. In the next chapter, we'll look at the college application process itself.

Of course, not every child goes to college; some go into the trades, or the military. With these paths come a whole other set of details.

Wishing you great success in your child's college or job search, we are,

Sincerely yours,
The Authors

Request for transcript for college

Mary Mustby, Guidance Counselor
Smalltown High School
Smalltown, OH

Dear Mrs. Mustby:

I have applied for admission to Smalltown University. Thanks for your assistance in helping me prepare for college.

Would you please send an official transcript of my grades to the Admissions Department of Smalltown University? The transcript must include grades for the first quarter of my senior year. The information should be sent to the following address:

Director of Admissions
Smalltown University
Smalltown, OH

Thank you.

Sincerely,
Heather Diamond

Request for letter of recommendation for college

Robert North
Smalltown High School
Smalltown, OH

Dear Mr. North:

Believe it or not, I'm off to college in the fall. And I wanted you to be one of the first to know that I have decided to major in mathematics in preparation for a career in teaching.

Math has always been my favorite subject in high school, and your eleventh-grade trigonometry course was one of the most challenging (and enjoyable) classes I took. You motivated us to work especially hard . . . until trig became so very easy!

I have applied to Smalltown University. I would be honored if you would write a letter of recommendation on my behalf. The deadline for my application materials is January 1.

Thanks again.

Sincerely,
Heather Diamond

Thanks for letter of recommendation for college

Robert North
Smalltown High School
Smalltown, OH

Dear Mr. North:

Thank you so much for your wonderful letter of recommendation to Smalltown University! I think it was exactly what I needed, because in today's mail I received my acceptance letter and an academic scholarship from the SU Math Foundation.

I promise to name my first original math theorem in your honor!

Sincerely,
Heather Diamond

Registering for college open house

Office of Admissions
Smalltown University
Smalltown, OH

Dear Admissions Office:

My daughter, Amy, is very interested in attending Smalltown University next fall. We would like to attend the scheduled open house on Saturday, October 18.

Please send a list of accommodations in the area.

Sincerely,
Walter Rogers

Thanks for job reference

Mary Mustby, Guidance Counselor
Smalltown High School
Smalltown, OH

Dear Mrs. Mustby:

Thank you for being a reference for me when I applied for a summer job at the Smalltown Historical Foundation. I was just offered the job and plan to start as soon as school is over.

Sincerely,
Heather Diamond

Thanks for academic award

Lt. Robert Zimmerman
Police Benevolent Society
Smalltown Police Department
Smalltown, OH

Dear Lt. Zimmerman:

Thank you for your generous scholarship. I will be attending Smalltown University in the fall, and this money will go a long way toward helping with my expenses. I assure you I will do my best to live up to your expectations.

Sincerely,
Heather Diamond

About high school job fair

Dear Smalltown business leaders:

The annual Smalltown High School job fair will be held on Friday, June 2, from 10 A.M. to noon in the school gymnasium.

Those of you who have been involved in the past know that this is a great opportunity for businesses in need of summer help to meet our very impressive group of students.

Please notify Ms. Ranny in my office that you will be joining us this year, and tell her what your space requirements will be. We will provide folding tables and chairs, and will try to accommodate any other special requests.

We hope to see you at the fair.

Sincerely,
Patrick Norton, Principal
Smalltown High School

Request for audiovisual equipment at school fair

Patrick Norton, Ph.D.
Principal
Smalltown High School
Smalltown, OH

Dear Dr. Norton:

We are pleased to once again participate in the job fair. Please reserve a large booth for us.

If possible, we would like to be able to use a videotape player and large television screen to play some promotional videos from some of the musical instrument companies we deal with. We have found these tapes to be very attractive to high school students. We'll also need access to an electrical line, of course.

For your information, we expect to have three summer jobs available, beginning immediately after the end of the high school term.

Sincerely,
John Diamond
Diamond Music Hall

Inquiry about company scholarship

Human Resources Department
Stop and Save Supermarket
Smalltown, OH

Dear People:

I am a high school student and have worked part-time at Stop and Save Supermarket in Smalltown, Ohio, for the past two years. I understand that there is an employee college scholarship program for which I might be eligible.

Please send me information and applications for any scholarship opportunities.

Sincerely,
Heather Diamond

Asking union about scholarship possibilities

Member Benefits Manager
International Supermarket Employees Union
Bigtown, NY

Dear People:

I am a part-time employee at Stop and Save Supermarket in Smalltown, Ohio. I have been a union member for the past two years. My union membership number is: xxxx-xx-xxx.

I will be graduating from high school in June and going on to college in September. My union steward informs me that there are a number of college scholarships for which I may be eligible.

Please send me information and applications for available scholarships.

Sincerely,
Heather Diamond

To guidance counselor about child not going to college

Mary Mustby, Guidance Counselor
Smalltown High School
Smalltown, OH

Dear Mrs. Mustby:

My son Dennis is a senior at Smalltown High School. He is smart and a good student with a lot of potential, but at this point he does not plan to attend college after high school. He plans to seek an apprenticeship in the plumbing or electrical trades.

Although the school does a good job of advising students who expect to attend college, it does not appear that there is a lot of help for students who will be going directly to work or a trade apprenticeship. Dennis is by no means the only senior in this year's graduation class with such plans.

I think Dennis has what it takes to succeed as a tradesman, and we would appreciate some guidance in getting him on the right track.

Sincerely,
Brenda Trainer

Follow-up to guidance counselor about child not going to college

Mary Mustby, Guidance Counselor
Smalltown High School
Smalltown, OH

Dear Mrs. Mustby:

Thank you for your letter in response to my request for assistance for our son Dennis, who plans to seek a trade instead of going on to college directly from high school. We appreciate your kind words about Dennis.

The information you provided about counseling for apprenticeship programs is very valuable, and we would like to take you up on your offer to schedule a meeting to discuss the various options. Please coordinate with Dennis to pick a time that works for his class schedule.

Sincerely,
Brenda Trainer

Request for military recruiter

Mary Mustby, Guidance Counselor
Smalltown High School
Smalltown, OH

Dear Mrs. Mustby:

I am considering a career in the U.S. Coast Guard or U.S. Navy. Please let me know about any upcoming visits by recruiters, scholarships, and ROTC.

Please also add my name to the list of students who have indicated they are considering a military career. You have my permission to notify recruiters of my interest.

Sincerely,
Martha Waters

Request for information about recruitment college programs

U.S. Coast Guard Recruiting Station
Old Canal Street
Smalltown, OH

Dear Recruiter:

I recently read about a scholarship program called the College Student Precommissioning Initiative (CSPI) that pays for a college education and provides entrance into the U.S. Coast Guard as a commissioned officer upon graduation.

I am a senior at Smalltown High School, with a 3.2 GPA. I have always been interested in the Coast Guard, especially in the area of marine sciences and pollution control.

Please send me information about the CSPI program and any other scholarship and ROTC opportunities that might be appropriate.

Sincerely,
Martha Waters
Smalltown, OH

Request for information about union apprenticeship

Apprenticeship Coordinator
Ohio Building Trades Council
Columbus, OH

Dear Apprenticeship Coordinator:

I am a graduating senior at Smalltown High School, and I am interested in pursuing a career as a plumber or pipefitter.

Can you please provide me with information about available apprenticeships and training programs in these fields? I am available to relocate for training and work.

Sincerely,
Mason Grommet
Smalltown, OH

Among parents planning rock concert trip

To: Kathleen Vega, Linda Wilson, Chris Davenport, Lisa Khan
Smalltown, OH

Dear Parents

I'm writing you all with an update on plans by Heather and some of her friends to go to Cincinnati to see a rock concert by something called Twisted Peanut next month.

Not only do I not have a clue about Twisted Peanut, but Heather has never gone by herself or with a group of friends to a rock concert. I am hoping you have some more information, or that between us we can fill in the gaps about what is going on.

Heather says they are staying at Lindsey Kelso's grandmother's house, and that a friend of Lindsey's will be giving them a ride to the all-day show. The friend also supposedly will pick them up and take them back to the grandmother's house to spend the night. They plan on traveling by bus back to Smalltown the next morning.

I have been unable to reach Lindsey's parents to confirm these arrangements. Have you been able to obtain more details?

If Heather goes on this trip, we will make sure she carries her cell phone. We contacted the concert promoters, and they assured us that there will be adequate security provided inside and outside the arena.

Please let me know your thoughts and plans.

Sincerely,
Laura Diamond

To parents of students on school trip

Dear parents:

Well, we've given them permission to go, raised the money for their tickets and rooms, and if you're like me, helped pack the bag. The last thing for us to do is see the members of the French Club off on their grand trip, wish them well, and wonder why we're not going along.

The entire group (parents, students, and chaperones) will meet outside the main entrance to the Smalltown Airport on Saturday, May 15, at noon.

Some of us are doing silly things like making banners and signs; we'll do whatever it takes to embarrass our kids and help them remember there's no place like home.

We hope to see you at the airport.

Sincerely,
Laura Diamond

To host family for school trip

Danielle Dubois-Jovan
Ecole St-Germaine
Albertville
France

Dear Danielle:

Thank you for your very kind letter. I am looking forward to meeting you and your family when I visit Albertville with the Smalltown French Club in May.

Please allow me to tell you a bit about myself. I am seventeen years old, and in my last year in high school. I plan to go to college in September at Smalltown University to study math and become a teacher.

I have an older brother who is married and has two children, and another brother in college about to enter law school. My sister is going to be married next year.

I know a little about Albertville because of a book I read about ski resorts. How close are you to the mountains? Is there still any snow in May?

I can't wait for your next letter. I hope you can understand my French.

Sincerely,
Heather Diamond

To host family for school trip in French

Cher Danielle:

Merci de votre lettre très aimable. J'attends avec intérêt de rencontrer vous et votre famille quand je visite Albertville avec le club français de Smalltown en mai.

Svp permettez-moi de vous dire un peu au sujet de moi. J'ai 17 ans, et au cours de mon année dernière dans le lycée. Je projette aller à l'université en septembre à l'université de Smalltown pour étudier des maths et pour devenir un professeur.

J'ai un frère plus âgé qui est marié avec deux enfants, et un frère différent dans l'université environ pour entrer à l'école de droit. Ma soeur va être mariée l'année prochaine.

Je sais au sujet d'Albertville en raison d'un livre que j'ai connaissance des stations de sports d'hiver. Êtes-vous combien étroitement aux montagnes? Y a-t-il toujours de la neige en mai?

Je ne peux pas attendre votre prochaine lettre. J'espère que vous pouvez comprendre mon français.

Sincèrement,
Heather Diamond

Offer of donation of software to school

Patrick Norton, Ph.D.
Principal
Smalltown High School
Smalltown, OH

Dear Dr. Norton:

As you know, my daughter Heather graduated from Smalltown High School this June—the last of the Diamond children in the school system.

While doing some empty-nest housecleaning, I came across a great deal of educational computer software that my children have used through the years. There are many programs including basic letter and number drills, a history and science series, and a box full of SAT preparation courses.

All of the software will work on current PCs, and the boxes include all disks and instruction manuals.

I would be happy to donate them to the school system. Please let me know if you can use them.

Sincerely,
Laura Diamond

20 Collegiate Matters

Dear Reader:

For many young students, the first day of college is the first day of life as an adult. You've got a roommate and a dining plan and books to buy and a class schedule to meet.

But let's back up a few steps: First you have to get in. In the first part of this chapter we'll look at letters to request a college catalog and application, inquire about a scholarship, and schedule a college admission interview.

Later, we'll look at letters that deal with some specific issues related to studies in college, internships, and college semesters abroad.

Best of luck,
The Authors

Requesting catalog and college application

Admissions Office
Smalltown University
Smalltown, OH

Dear Admissions Office:

I am a high school senior at Smalltown High School and I am considering attending Smalltown University next fall.

Please send a college catalog and application kit. Please also add me to your mailing list so that I will know about open houses or events that I might want to attend.

Please send the information to:

Heather Diamond
81 Meadow Street
Smalltown, OH 45601

E-mail: heather@sol.com

Sincerely yours,
Heather Diamond

Request for private college scholarship application

Academic Scholarship Committee
Smalltown Chamber of Commerce
Smalltown, OH

Dear Committee Members:

I am a senior at Smalltown High School and will graduate this June. I plan to continue my education at Smalltown University.

Please send me information about the academic scholarships given annually by the Chamber, and please also send application forms.

I appreciate the opportunity to be considered for this award and thank the Chamber for its support of local students.

Sincerely,
Heather Diamond

Cover letter for scholarship application

Academic Scholarship Committee
Smalltown Chamber of Commerce
Smalltown, OH

Dear Committee Members:

Enclosed please find my completed application form and essay for the Smalltown Chamber of Commerce Academic Scholarship.

Smalltown has been a great place to grow up and go to school, and I hope to make a contribution to the community in future years. Thank you for considering my application and for your support of advanced education for local students.

Sincerely,
Heather Diamond

Thanks for scholarship

Academic Scholarship Committee
Smalltown Chamber of Commerce
Smalltown, OH

Dear Committee Members:

I am thrilled to accept your offer of an academic scholarship for the upcoming year.

I want to take this opportunity to thank the Smalltown Chamber of Commerce for its support of my college dream, and for its assistance to other students at Smalltown High School. I hope all of us can contribute to the community after we complete our education.

Sincerely,
Heather Diamond

Request for college scholarship information

Office of Admissions
Smalltown University
Smalltown, OH

Dear People:

I am a graduating senior at Smalltown High School, interested in attending Smalltown University in the fall, majoring in mathematics. Could you please send me information about scholarships available to incoming students?

Thank you.

Sincerely,
Heather Diamond

Cover letter with scholarship application

Office of Admissions
Smalltown University
Smalltown, OH

Dear Scholarship Committee:

Enclosed please find my application for a scholarship to Smalltown University.

It has been my goal to attend SU for as long as I can remember. My brother Joshua Diamond and sister Morgan Diamond have already graduated from Smalltown.

I believe that my high school record shows me to be a dedicated and accomplished student. I've been deeply involved in community service, and I hope to continue volunteer work while I am a college student.

I have enclosed the requested financial information. As the third in my family to head off to college, I find that our resources are pretty thin. I do hope the committee can assist me in fulfilling my dreams at Smalltown University.

Sincerely,
Heather Diamond

Cover letter with application for admission

Director of Admissions
Smalltown School of Law
Smalltown, OH

Dear Director:

Enclosed please find my application for admission as a first-year law student for the fall 2005 class of Smalltown School of Law.

I am a graduate of Smalltown University and I very much want to continue my education with studies at the law school.

Looking forward to a favorable review of my application, I am,

Sincerely yours,
Joshua Diamond

Request for college admission interview

Director of Admissions
Smalltown University
Smalltown, OH

Dear Director:

I have recently applied for admission to the freshman class of 2005.

I am writing to request an interview to supplement my application. Smalltown University is my first choice for college, and I am confident that with a personal meeting I can communicate this and answer any questions the applications committee may have regarding my application.

I would appreciate a call to set an appointment. I can be reached at (xxx) xxx-xxxx.

Thank you.

Sincerely,
Heather Diamond

Request for clarification of course description

Dr. Albert Tustein, Chairman
Department of Mathematics
College of Liberal Arts
Smalltown University
Smalltown, OH

Dear Dr. Tustein:

I am entering Smalltown University as a freshman math major this fall. I plan to use part of my summer to get a jump-start in preparing for the courses I will be taking.

I would appreciate it if you would please clarify the descriptions of the three available freshman calculus courses: Pre-calculus, Introductory Calculus, and Basic Calculus.

I have taken two semesters of high school calculus (receiving a B+ and A-).

Which college course would be most appropriate for me?

I look forward to meeting you when I arrive on campus this fall.

Sincerely,
Heather Diamond

Inquiry about college housing

Office of Student Life
Smalltown University
Smalltown, OH

Dear People:

My daughter Heather has been accepted into this year's freshman class at Smalltown University. We are all very excited for her.

Heather applied for a room in Sonya Hall, the smoke-free dorm. We have just received her room assignment and find she has been placed in Daniel Common instead.

My daughter is presently taking prescription medication for allergies and is particularly sensitive to cigarette smoke. We can provide a doctor's note if necessary.

Please advise us as soon as possible about a change in her dorm assignment to Sonya Hall or another smoke-free environment.

Sincerely,
Laura Diamond

Follow-up on student housing request

Ariane Hitchcock, Office of Student Life
Smalltown University
Smalltown, OH

Dear Ms. Hitchcock:

Thank you for resolving the problem with my daughter's housing assignment so quickly. It is very important for her to live in a smoke-free environment.

Sincerely,
Laura Diamond

Inquiry about off-campus college housing

Office of Student Life
Smalltown University School of Law
Smalltown, OH

Dear People:

I plan to attend Smalltown University as a graduate student in the School of Law this fall but have decided against living in campus housing.

Can you provide a list of private residences or apartments that are near the university?

Sincerely,
Joshua Diamond

Inquiry about sports scholarship

Simon Dit, Admissions Counselor
Smalltown University
Smalltown, OH

Dear Mr. Dit:

Thank you for meeting with me last week during your visit to Smalltown High School. Your input on Smalltown University, and college in general, was very valuable.

I have been on the Smalltown High School varsity lacrosse team for the past two years and hope to continue playing at the college level. I have followed the Smalltown University's women's team over the years and am very impressed with their accomplishments.

Does the university offer any athletic scholarships? How would I go about applying for such an award?

Sincerely,
Heather Diamond

Request for recommendation for sports scholarship

Pam Edwards, Women's Lacrosse Coach
Smalltown High School
Smalltown, OH

Dear Pam:

As you know, I have applied for admission to Smalltown University this September and would like to continue playing lacrosse on the university's team.

I have been in contact with the admissions office about sports scholarships and I intend to apply for one. A letter of recommendation from my coach is required as part of the application package.

Would you please write a letter of recommendation? The school would like to know about my experience and skills on the team. According to the application, the coach especially values leadership qualities and dedication to both academic and athletic pursuits.

I hope you'll tell the college coach about my position as team co-captain for the past two years. I've also enclosed a copy of my academic transcript, which shows my current GPA of 3.2.

Thank you for all the help and guidance you have given me over the last few years. You've really made me appreciate the sport.

Sincerely,
Heather Diamond

Thanks for letter of recommendation

Pam Edwards, Women's Lacrosse Coach
Smalltown High School
Smalltown, OH

Dear Pam:

Thank you for writing the letter of recommendation for a sports scholarship at Smalltown University. I hope I can live up to all of the wonderful things you had to say about my potential.

I will keep you posted on my application, and I will always treasure your coaching and friendship over the years.

Sincerely,
Heather Diamond

Inquiry about computer requirements on campus

Office of Computer Services
Smalltown University
Smalltown, OH

Dear People:

I will be attending Smalltown University this fall, and will reside in Sonya Hall.

What kind of computer hardware do I need to connect to the school's network and the Internet?

Please also provide me with the name of a contact from your computer center to answer any further questions I might have.

Sincerely,
Heather Diamond

Follow-up about computer requirements on campus

Office of Computer Services
Smalltown University
Smalltown, OH

Dear People:

Thank you for the information about hardware requirements to hook up my computer to the university's network.

In the materials you provided I noticed mention of a 25 percent discount on the purchase of a new system from Spaceway Computers. Would you please provide me with the necessary special offer number to obtain the discount?

Sincerely,
Heather Diamond

Preordering college textbooks

Campus Bookstore
Smalltown University
Smalltown, OH

In re:
Student ID xxxxxxxx
VISA credit card xxxx-xxxx-xxxx-xxxx (Expires xx/xx)

Dear People:

I will be entering Smalltown University this September as a math major. I understand that I can preorder my college textbooks to avoid the long lines on the first day of school.

Enclosed is a copy of my class schedule, including course numbers, class sections, and the names of professors. Please set aside the appropriate books for me. Used books are preferred if available.

Please charge them to my credit card. The number is listed above.

I would appreciate a confirmation of my order by mail or e-mail, addressed as listed on this letterhead.

Sincerely,
Heather Diamond

Seeking vegetarian meals

Dining Services
Smalltown University
Smalltown, OH

Dear People:

I will be attending Smalltown University this fall. I have reviewed your meal plan options with my parents so we can decide which arrangement is best for me. I see many mentions of pizza, deli sandwiches, rotisserie meats, and even Asian stir fries.

What I don't see is mention of vegetarian meals, which is a requirement for me. Do you offer a nutritionally sound vegetarian option for students at every meal?

I would appreciate it if someone would contact me before school starts. I don't want my parents paying for a meal plan I can't or will not use.

Sincerely,
Heather Diamond

To prospective new college roommate

Amy Rogers
Big Mountain, ME

Dear Amy:

I've just learned from the Director of Housing at Smalltown University that we have been assigned to be roommates. I wanted to introduce myself before September, and also find out if there is anything we can do before school starts to make our room the best place on campus.

I've lived near Smalltown U all my life. I know you're probably wondering why I would choose to go to college here. The truth is that it's just a good school.

My older brothers and sister both went to SU and had great experiences. I grew up rooting for the football team and going to all the concerts, and it just seemed a good fit for me to be here. I will be glad to be your experienced guide and show you all the important spots, like the mall and the best vegetarian places in town. (I'm a vegetarian, by the way).

I am a math major (a semi-nerd), plan on playing lacrosse, and will join at least the Drama Club. Before I commit to anything else, I want to see how heavy my course load is. I like MTV, garage bands, any movie with Adam Sandler in it and BASEBALL. I am secretly a Red Sox fan. Maybe you are too, since you are from New England.

I went skiing with my family at Sunday River once. It was really cold but we had a great time and Maine was beautiful. I'd like to learn to get off the bunny slope someday.

I like going to clubs but don't drink or do drugs. I know that neither of us smokes, since we are in the smoke-free dorm.

I'd love to hear from you before school starts. Let me know if there are any questions I can answer about Smalltown.

Your roommate,
Heather Diamond

Response to introductory letter from roommate

Heather Diamond
Smalltown, OH

Dear Heather:

Thanks for breaking the ice. I was sooo nervous about meeting you. I've lived in Maine for the past six years. We moved around a lot before that because of my father's job (he's an engineer), including one year in London (way cool).

I am a journalism major, so the newspaper and the university magazine will be my first choices for extracurriculars. I think it's great that you want to go to college so close to home. You'll get to see your family as often as you want but still have your own life.

I know I will miss my family. Besides my mother and father I have one younger (somewhat annoying) sister. I will still miss her, though.

I love going to clubs, don't smoke, drink, or do drugs either, and don't want to be with people who do. We differ somewhat in music and movie crushes, but what the heck. And, I LOVE the Red Sox. GO Pedro! In fact my second choice for college was BU so I would be near Fenway Park. I don't have a boyfriend but certainly like to look.

And, Heather, I also am a vegetarian. Let's keep in touch and when we meet in September we will be like old friends.

Amy

Inquiry about internship for law school

Pickwick and Chuzzlewit
Attorneys at Law
Smalltown, OH

Gentlemen:

I am a first-year student at Smalltown University School of Law and I am looking for a summer internship. My academic advisor, Prof. Jerry Dunn, recommended your firm.

I have maintained a 3.5 GPA through my college career. I am particularly interested in corporate law, which fits in well with my undergraduate degree in finance.

I am available for an interview at your convenience.

Sincerely,
Joshua Diamond

Inquiry about dorm move-in

Office of Student Life
Smalltown University
Smalltown, OH

Dear People:

I am an incoming freshman at Smalltown University. Since I live out of state, I would like to arrange to ship some of my belongings by freight ahead of the move-in date of August 30.

I will be living in room 12-C of Sonya Hall.

I plan to use United Parcel Service to send boxes.

Could you please tell me your policy on shipping to the dorms? Where should the packages be sent? Where will the boxes be stored until my arrival?

Thank you.

Sincerely,
Amy Rogers

Acceptance of invitation to sorority pledge breakfast

Cary Meback, Pledge Coordinator
Alpha Alpha Alpha Sorority
Smalltown University
Smalltown, OH

Dear Cary:

I am pleased to accept your invitation to the Alpha Alpha Alpha Pledge Breakfast on Sunday, September 14.

Since coming to Smalltown University I have investigated the many different sororities on campus and have been particularly impressed with Tri-Alpha. I am looking forward to meeting the members and viewing the sorority house.

Sincerely,
Amy Rogers

Acceptance of membership in sorority

Cary Meback, Pledge Coordinator
Alpha Alpha Alpha Sorority
Smalltown University
Smalltown, OH

Dear Cary:

I am thrilled to accept your offer of membership in Alpha Alpha Alpha. I am sure that when my college career is over, one of the highlights will be that I was a sister at Tri-Alpha.

Sincerely,
Amy Rogers

Declining sorority meeting

Cary Meback, Pledge Coordinator
Alpha Alpha Alpha Sorority
Smalltown University
Smalltown, OH

Dear Cary:

Thank you for your invitation to attend the freshman breakfast at the Alpha Alpha Alpha sorority house on Sunday, September 14.

With my participation on the field hockey and lacrosse teams and my heavy workload of academics, I don't feel I have the time to devote to pledging a sorority this term. I will certainly consider Alpha Alpha Alpha in the future.

Sincerely,
Heather Diamond

Inquiry about Parents Weekend at college

Office of Student Life
Smalltown University
Smalltown, OH

Dear People:

Our daughter Amy is a freshman at Smalltown University. We are excited about joining her for the upcoming Parents Weekend.

Is there any arrangement made for sleeping accommodations for parents either at the school or at hotels or motels in the area? As we are coming from Maine, we want to make sure we have everything arranged in advance.

Sincerely,
Helen Rogers

Inviting parents of daughter's roommate to dinner

John and Laura Diamond
Smalltown, OH

Dear Mr. and Mrs. Diamond:

Your daughter Heather and my daughter Amy are roommates at Smalltown University. Although we have never met, I feel that I know Heather very well. She and Amy seem to be hitting it off nicely, and we are very happy about that.

My husband, Walter, and I will be attending the Parents Weekend and we would very much like to meet you and perhaps go out for dinner. If the girls would like to join us that would be fine as well.

Sincerely,
Helen Rogers

Accepting invitation to dinner at Parents Weekend

Helen Rogers
Big Mountain, ME

Dear Helen:

Thank you for your kind note.

We would be very happy to meet you and join you for dinner during Parents Weekend. Since we live here, I hope you'll allow us the liberty of selecting an appropriate restaurant.

I'll ask Heather and Amy to coordinate on date and time. John and I look forward to seeing you then.

Sincerely,
Laura Diamond

Requesting meeting with college professor

Professor Susan Jones
Smalltown University
Smalltown, OH

Dear Professor Jones:

I would like to request an appointment to meet with you soon. I am concerned about my midterm grade this semester in Criminal Justice 101 and I would like to find out how I might improve it.

This course is very important to me, and I am willing to do whatever I can to bring it up to the level of the rest of my marks.

I am available any day after 3 P.M., and on Mondays and Wednesdays from 9 A.M. to 11 A.M. My campus phone is (xxx) xxx-xxxx and my e-mail address is *jdiamond @smalltown.com*.

Sincerely,
Joshua Diamond

Thank you for meeting with professor

Professor Susan Jones
Smalltown University
Smalltown, OH

Dear Professor Jones:

Thank you for meeting with me last Thursday. You helped clarify some of the concepts of the course, and I appreciate your pointers on ways to raise my grade.

I do intend to write the extra term paper you suggested. I will submit the outline for the paper to you by November 14 as you requested.

Sincerely,
Joshua Diamond

Asking for more work-study hours

George Slacker, Work-Study Administrator
Smalltown University School of Law
Smalltown, OH

Dear Mr. Slacker:

As part of my financial incentive package at Smalltown University School of Law I have been granted a part-time position of twelve hours per week at the library desk. In the first term, I chose to work for only eight hours per week.

I now find that my schedule is more flexible than I anticipated, and I am available to work four more hours per week.

I appreciate the opportunity to work to help pay for my law school education.

Sincerely,
Joshua Diamond

Letter from student asking to observe police at work

Chief Selwyn Norton
Smalltown Police Department
Smalltown, OH

Dear Chief Norton:

I am a first-year student at the School of Law at Smalltown University. I am writing a term paper about community policing, and would very much appreciate it if I could spend a few days at the department and accompany an officer on routine patrol.

My professor, Ted Grundy, tells me that students have been able to make similar arrangements in previous years.

I am available from 3 P.M. to midnight any day. I look forward to hearing from you.

Sincerely,
Joshua Diamond

Follow-up on request to observe police at work

Chief Selwyn Norton
Smalltown Police Department
Smalltown, OH

Dear Chief Norton:

Thank you for your offer to shadow one of your patrol officers for an afternoon and evening. I appreciate the opportunity.

I will be available on Wednesday, November 23, and will be in your office at 3 P.M.

Sincerely,
Joshua Diamond

Informing professor about visit to police at work

Professor Ted Grundy
School of Law
Smalltown University
Smalltown, OH

Dear Professor Grundy:

Thanks for your suggestion that I contact Chief Norton at the Smalltown Police Department to arrange to shadow a patrolman. He agreed, and I will be there on November 23 for the afternoon and evening.

Chief Norton asked me to sign a release of liability, and to have you do the same on behalf of the School of Law. I have enclosed the form and a stamped, addressed envelope.

Sincerely,
Joshua Diamond

Inquiry about semester abroad

Department of International Studies
Smalltown University
Smalltown, OH

Dear People:

I am in my first year of study at Smalltown University as a math major with an interest in architecture. I am considering the Semester Abroad program for my sophomore or junior year. Please send me information.

Sincerely,
Heather Diamond

To academic adviser about semester abroad

Professor Jane Gordon
College of Liberal Arts
Smalltown University
Smalltown, OH

Dear Professor Gordon:

Thanks for your assistance in helping me plan my first year at SU. I'm very much enjoying my classes and university life.

I am considering applying for the Semester Abroad program in Rome for my sophomore or junior year. I would appreciate your thoughts on the best way to plan my academic schedule so that courses offered in Rome are credited toward my requirements for graduation.

Sincerely,
Heather Diamond

21 Medical Care

Dear Reader:

Your doctor and hospital may be the best in the world, but when it comes to quality of care there is no better advocate than you or your immediate family.

Gather your personal information, understand your conditions and medications, and be prepared to clearly and directly state your needs and wants.

The first letter in this chapter is one of our favorites. How many times have you gone to see a doctor with several concerns, and then forgotten to ask about them all? Try writing a letter ahead of your visit, or prepare a note to bring with you to the appointment.

Another critical area of communication involves medical insurance and billing. A cooperative insurance agent, health provider, or consumer advocate in your community may be able to assist you in crafting a precise and direct letter in pursuit of proper coverage and services.

Wishing you good health, we are,

Sincerely yours,
The Authors

To doctor in advance of appointment

Dr. Timothy Todd
Smalltown Medical Center
Smalltown, OH

Dear Dr. Todd:

In preparation for my appointment on Friday I am sending a list of all the questions and concerns I would like to discuss with you.

I sometimes find that when I go in for my visit we either don't have time to discuss everything or I forget to bring something up. I would appreciate it if you could review this letter before my appointment.

Sincerely,
Harold Diamond

Thanking doctor for review of concerns

Dr. Timothy Todd
Smalltown Medical Center
Smalltown, OH

Dear Dr. Todd:

Thank you for the extra effort when we met for my exam yesterday. I was concerned you would be taken aback by my letter of questions; instead you responded with a checklist of answers and suggestions.

I am already at work on all of your suggestions. Thanks again.

Sincerely,
Harold Diamond

Inquiring about medical facilities aboard ship

Customer Service
GoldenSeas Cruiseline
Fort Lauderdale, FL

Dear Customer Service:

My wife and I are interested in booking your three-month Around-the-World Cruise.

Approximately four months ago I suffered a minor heart attack. I am on medication and am now in good health. However, before we commit to such a lengthy stay on the ship, I would like to know more about the medical facilities aboard.

I know there will be a doctor available, but is the ship equipped with an EKG machine? Is the ship's hospital capable of conducting periodic exams and transmitting the results to my doctor at home? Can my doctor communicate with the ship's doctor to adjust medication if needed?

What procedures are used if someone is in need of more extensive medical help than is available in the ship's hospital?

Please advise.

Sincerely,
Langley Clinton

Inquiry about prescriptions while traveling

Customer Service
Most States Insurance Company
Big Town, NY

Concerning: Policy xxxx-xxxx

Dear People:

I am presently taking a medication prescribed by my doctor for my heart condition. Under the terms of my health insurance policy, I am able to fill this prescription one month at a time.

This coming January, my wife and I plan to be out of the country for three months on a cruise ship. How do I handle getting refills? Please advise.

Sincerely,
Langley Clinton

To doctor about medical care during cruise

Dr. Timothy Todd
Smalltown Medical Center
Smalltown, OH

Dear Dr. Todd:

As we discussed last week, I am planning to take a three-month around-the-world cruise in January. You said you felt that I was in good condition to take the cruise, but expressed concern about your plans to monitor my EKG during that period and make adjustments to my medication.

I have exchanged letters with the medical services staff of GoldenSeas Cruise Line. They told me that all of their ships include state-of-the-art EKG machines, and the ship's doctor is able to interpret the results. They also are able to transmit the EKG file via e-mail to you for review.

Assuming this is acceptable, please provide me with a letter outlining any special instructions for the ship's doctor as well as your e-mail address for transmission of the report.

I also will need a four-month supply of my heart medication. Would you please send me a written copy of my prescription so that I can arrange to have the order filled in advance directly through my medical insurance company?

Thank you.

Sincerely,
Langley Clinton

Permission for school nurse to dispense over-the-counter medication

Cathy Merrill, RN
Nurse's Office
Smalltown High School
Smalltown, OH

Dear Ms. Merrill:

By this letter, I grant permission for the nurse's office at Smalltown High School to dispense the following over-the-counter medications as necessary for my child, Heather Diamond:

- Tylenol or acetaminophen for headaches and pain;
- Benadryl or similar for colds and allergies, and
- Pepto-Bismol or similar for stomach upset.

We have checked each of these medications with her physician, Dr. Timothy Todd, and he has given his approval.

Sincerely,
Laura Diamond

Permission for school nurse to dispense prescription medication

Cathy Merrill, RN
Nurse's Office
Smalltown High School
Smalltown, OH

Dear Ms. Merrill:

Our daughter Heather has been prescribed fexofenadine HCl (Allegra) to treat her allergies. Accompanying this letter is a container with thirty pills.

Heather takes one pill in the morning before school and can take a second after 1 P.M. if needed.

Per Smalltown High School policy, please hold her medication in the nurse's office. She will come to your office if she needs to take a second pill after lunch.

Thanks for your help.

Sincerely,
Laura Diamond

Changing dentists

Robert Owens, D.D.S.
Smalltown Dental Clinic
Smalltown, OH

Re: John Diamond, Laura Diamond, Morgan Diamond, Joshua Diamond, Heather Diamond

Dear Dr. Owens:

Please transfer all of my family's dental records to Dr. Perkins:

Josephine Perkins, D.D.S.
Smalltown Office Park
100 Main St.
Smalltown, OH 45601

Thank you for your services over the years.

Sincerely,
Laura Diamond

Notifying pastor of hospitalization

The Reverend Peter Hall
Smalltown Congregational Church
Smalltown, OH

Dear Mr. Hall:

I just wanted to let you know that I will be missing services for the next couple of weeks. I am scheduled to have some minor surgery on my back.

I don't think you will have any trouble getting someone else to take up the collections at the noon service on Sunday. I expect to make a full recovery and be back in about one month.

Regards,
Harold Diamond

Notifying insurance agent of upcoming surgery

Patricia Paulson
Small Help Insurance
Smalltown, OH

Dear Pat:

I will be undergoing back surgery on November 25 at Smalltown General Hospital.

I would appreciate any help you can give to guide me through what I anticipate to be a flood of insurance paperwork in coming weeks. Our policy is with Most States Insurance, No. xxx-xxx-xxxx.

Sincerely,
Harold Diamond

Seeking physical therapist to coordinate charges with insurance schedule

Helga Knutson, Physical Therapist
Smalltown Medical Associates
Smalltown, OH

Dear Ms. Knutson:

I have just received a notice from my insurance company that your charges for physical therapy exceed their definition of customary fees in this area, and that there will be an outstanding bill of $350 for your services.

While I am deeply appreciative of your good work in helping me recover from my back surgery, I must ask that you coordinate all charges with Most States Insurance. Patricia Paulson at Small Help Insurance can assist in putting you in touch with the proper department; her phone number is (xxx) xxx-xxxx.

Sincerely,
Harold Diamond

Thanks to physical therapist for insurance coordination

Helga Knutson, Physical Therapist
Smalltown Medical Associates
Smalltown, OH

Dear Ms. Knutson:

Thank you for working with Pat Paulson at Small Help Insurance to restate your charges to coordinate with the customary fees paid by my insurance company.

I realize that dealing with insurance companies is just as frustrating for health-care professionals as it is for consumers. As senior citizens, though, we already pay an outrageous portion of our fixed income on health care.

Thanks for your consideration and your assistance in helping me recover from my back surgery.

Sincerely,
Harold Diamond

Asking insurance agent to check on benefits

Patricia Paulson
Small Help Insurance
Smalltown, OH

In re: Emma Miller
Most States Insurance Company
Policy xxxx-xxxx-xxxx

Dear Pat:

My mother, Emma Miller, was hospitalized last week and treated for a heart condition. She will be released shortly and we want to have a nurse in to see her two times a week.

Would you please consult her Most States Insurance policy and advise us about available in-home benefits?

Sincerely,
Laura Diamond

Complaint about drugstore not filling prescription generically

Pharmacy Supervisor
Ellison's Drug Store
Smalltown, OH

Dear People:

I recently had a prescription for Ultramaxitor filled at the Smalltown branch of your drugstore.

We have used this drug regularly over the past year and the order has always been filled with the generic equivalent drug, disodium hyperglycophosphate. Dr. Todd here in Smalltown always writes his prescriptions to allow fulfillment with the generic equivalent.

In this case, though, the pharmacist on duty dispensed fifty Ultramaxitor pills. My husband, who was picking up my prescription, did not realize that the bill for $45 was unusual.

My insurance coverage, through Most States Insurance, has a copayment of $10 for generic drugs and a sliding scale for brand names of as much as $45. We did not want to pay $35 extra to receive pretty purple pills and support an obnoxious television advertising campaign.

If your pharmacy was out of the generic drug we should have been notified so that we could have waited until a new shipment arrived, or we could have taken our prescription across the street to MegaDrugs to be filled there.

I will appreciate a refund of the extra charge for the brand-name drug.

Sincerely,
Monica Diamond

22 Elderly and Special Care

Dear Reader:

There are many special programs and benefits available to senior citizens, but often you've got to ask for them and sometimes pursue them.

Contact your state and local Office for the Aging for information about available programs, and obtain addresses and contact names for the letters you'll write. In your letters, try to be as specific as possible in any references to federal, state, and local programs.

And sometimes you merely need some special consideration—asking for a parking space or a special meal. Put your request in writing to make sure your communication is clear and direct.

Sincerely,
The Authors

Requesting handicapped parking permit information

Smalltown Police Department
City Hall
Smalltown, OH

Dear People:

Please send the necessary forms for a permanent handicapped parking permit to my father at the address listed on this letter.

My mother has significant arthritis and uses a walker. As I understand it, the permit would be for her and could go with whatever car she occupies as a passenger.

Sincerely,
Laura Diamond

Asking for Meals on Wheels

Meals on Wheels Coordinator
Mega County Office for the Aging
Smalltown, OH

Dear Coordinator:

I am requesting that someone from the Office for the Aging get in touch with my parents to arrange enrollment in the Meals on Wheels program.

My father, Ronald Miller, and my mother, Emma Miller, are eighty-six and eighty-four, respectively. They are not as mobile as they used to be, and this service would be excellent for them.

Please call them at (xxx) xxx-xxxx to arrange an appointment.

Sincerely,
Laura Diamond

Thanks to Meals on Wheels

Meals on Wheels Coordinator
Mega County Office for the Aging
Smalltown, OH

Dear Coordinator:

My husband and I have been receiving Meals on Wheels for the past two months and I wanted to take a moment to put down my fork and write you a letter of thanks.

The food is excellent, and we also appreciate the contact with the cheerful volunteers who deliver our meals.

I was at first reluctant to use the program. I have been making dinner for my family for more than sixty years, a habit that's hard to break. But it has become more and more difficult for us to shop and cook, and we have realized what a wonderful service you provide.

Please pass along our thanks to everyone involved.

Sincerely,
Emma Miller

Requesting information about availability of services

Services Coordinator
Mega County Office for the Aging
Smalltown, OH

Dear Services Coordinator:

I am a retired seventy-five-year-old resident of Mega County. I will be undergoing back surgery in November and expect to be limited in my mobility for several months.

I would appreciate it if you would advise me of any services I could receive from your agency and others that assist the elderly.

Sincerely,
Harold Diamond

Thanks for information from agency

Emmet Jordan, Services Coordinator
Mega County Office for the Aging
Smalltown, OH

Dear Mr. Jordan:

Thank you for your prompt response to my letter inquiring about available services after my back surgery.

The offer of van service to and from my physical therapy after the operation is exactly what I was hoping to find. It will certainly relieve my wife of some of the stress this operation will cause.

Please send me any forms I need in order to sign up for the transportation service.

Sincerely,
Harold Diamond

Asking about special diets for Meals on Wheels

Meals on Wheels Coordinator
Mega County Office for the Aging
Smalltown, OH

Dear Coordinator:

I am very happy with the quality of the Meals on Wheels service.

I do, though, have a question: Is it possible to request low-sodium food? The other day the dinner consisted of a jumbo hot dog, and today the meal was chili with potato chips. Although the food was very tasty, it violates my doctor's instructions to avoid sodium.

Sincerely,
Monica Diamond

Requesting large-print library books

Lorraine Shayes, Librarian
Smalltown Public Library
Smalltown, OH

Dear Ms. Shayes:

My wife and I have been card-carrying members of the Smalltown Public Library for more than fifty years and have participated in half a dozen fundraising campaigns for the library.

We are now both in our mid-eighties, and our eyes aren't as good as they once were. I was surprised to find that the Smalltown Public Library does not subscribe to any of the magazines or newspapers now available in large print and that the number of large-print books on the shelves is very small.

It would not take a large expenditure of money to build an adequate selection for those who still want to enjoy the services of the library but are presently unable to do so. We would both be happy to assist in making selections and recommendations to cover a wide range of tastes.

Sincerely,
Ron Miller

Arranging for rental of wheelchair

Smalltown Medical Supplies
Smalltown, OH

Dear People:

My mother is currently a patient at Smalltown General Hospital, where she is being treated for a heart condition.

She will need to use a wheelchair for a period of time when she is released from the hospital next week. I was referred to your store to arrange this. We would like a lightweight chair that can be easily folded for storage in a car.

My mother has private insurance in addition to Medicare.

Please give me a call to discuss our options.

Sincerely,
Laura Diamond

Arranging home aide for convalescent

Home Services Coordinator
Mega County Office for the Aging
Smalltown, OH

Dear Coordinator:

My mother, Emma Miller, is presently a patient at Smalltown General Hospital. She is recovering from a heart condition, and will be released shortly.

Her primary caregiver is my father. Both are in their eighties.

For a period of time while she is convalescing, my father will need some in-home care to relieve him for periods of time while he runs errands and does the shopping.

I understand that the Office for the Aging administers a program that sends home aides to the elderly for exactly this sort of situation. We would like to arrange for an aide to be with my mother two or three times a week for a period of two hours at a time.

Please contact my father, Ron Miller, directly at the number listed to arrange dates and times.

Sincerely,
Laura Diamond

Confirming physical therapy appointment

Physical Therapy Department
Smalltown General Hospital
Smalltown, OH

Dear People:

I am writing to confirm that my wife, Emma Miller, will begin a period of physical therapy at 3 P.M. on Tuesday, October 16.

My instructions were to bring her to the reception room at the hospital.

I would appreciate a call to confirm our appointment.

Sincerely,
Ron Miller

Requesting assistance for handicapped at theater

Ron Donald, General Manager
Smalltown Playhouse
Smalltown, OH

Dear Mr. Donald:

My wife and I will be coming to see the December 6 production of A Christmas Carol at 8 P.M.

My wife has recently begun using a wheelchair, and we would appreciate whatever assistance can be provided to deliver her to the theater and take her to her aisle seat with as little difficulty as possible.

Could you please give me a call to discuss the best way for us to accomplish this?

Thank you.

Sincerely,
Ron Miller

Explaining handicapped accessibility

Morgan Diamond
Smalltown, OH

Dear Ms. Diamond:

We are very happy that you are considering celebrating an occasion as important as your wedding here at Leonard's.

Handicapped access is readily available throughout our facility, from the front door to the reception hall and even out onto the grand balcony, where the bride can toss her bouquet to the bridesmaids.

All of the public rooms of the museum have wheelchair ramps and handicapped restrooms, and we will make certain that you have as many reserved parking spaces out front as you need.

Sincerely,
Sharon Leonard

Asking for wheelchair on bus

Customer Service
Seymour Tour Company
Nearby, OH

Dear People:

My wife and I are interested in taking your day trip to visit the International Cornhusker Museum, followed by lunch at the Mountainside Restaurant.

My wife uses a wheelchair. Is the bus equipped to hold a wheelchair? Also, would the museum and restaurant be able to accommodate her?

Please let me know about this trip and any others that may be appropriate for us.

Sincerely,
Ron Miller

Asking that magazine subscription be changed to large print

Customer Service
Readers Monthly Magazine
Bigtown, NY

Dear People:

I presently have more than a year to go on my subscription to Readers Monthly. I would like to begin receiving my magazine in the large-print edition. If there is any difference in price, please let me know.

I have attached the mailing label from my current subscription.

Sincerely,
Ron Miller

Requesting doctor sign form for handicapped parking permit

Dr. Timothy Todd
Smalltown Medical Center
Smalltown, OH

Dear Dr. Todd:

I would appreciate your assistance in obtaining a handicapped parking permit to assist Emma.

I am enclosing the required application from the Smalltown Police Department. I have filled in all information required of me and signed the form. I would appreciate it if you would sign as our physician to confirm our need for the permit.

I have also enclosed an addressed, stamped envelope for the form, which is to be filed with the police department.

Sincerely,
Ron Miller

Seeking special menu

Chow Main
345 Main Street
Smalltown, OH

Dear People:

On February 23 we will be attending an engagement party at your restaurant for my granddaughter Morgan Diamond and her fiancé.

My wife is on a special low-cholesterol, nonfat, low-sodium diet. Can you accommodate her with something interesting so she does not feel singled out on this special evening?

A steamed vegetable or rice and vegetable plate would be fine. Feel free to call to discuss menu items.

Sincerely,
Ron Miller

23 Health Clubs

Dear Reader:

Health clubs are good for your health . . . and sometimes a source of stress. There are contracts and membership rules and fees and charges to deal with, and sometimes to contest.

Most clubs offer discounts to members who sign up for multiyear commitments, especially those who pay in advance. As attractive as that may be, it may be a better idea to join as a month-to-month member or agree to a shorter term.

Be sure you understand the details of a membership contract, and ask for written notice of any amendments to that agreement.

Sincerely,
The Authors

Request for information about health club

Stay Fit Health Club
Smalltown, OH

Dear People:

I am considering joining a health club. Please send me full details about your facilities.

I have one question in particular: During the course of the next year, I expect to be traveling away from Smalltown for a period of three months; do you have a policy that allows suspension of membership when I am away for an extended period?

Sincerely,
Roger Hamilton

Inquiry about coordination of health club with physical therapist

Chuck Satlas, Manager
Worldwide Health Club
Smalltown, OH

Dear Mr. Satlas:

I would like to arrange a conference, by telephone, to include me, a representative of your personal training staff and my physical therapist at Smalltown General Hospital. I recently suffered a pinched nerve in my shoulder, and my therapist offered to assist me in choosing exercises that will promote healing and not aggravate the condition.

I look forward to hearing from you soon.

Sincerely,
Joshua Diamond

Complaint about health club membership

Stay Fit Health Club
Smalltown, OH

Dear People:

In May of last year I paid for a one-year membership at your club. At the time I joined I was given permission to suspend my membership for three months, from October to December, while I did a great deal of traveling for my job. I was told by the former manager, Steve Jones, that my membership would be extended by three months.

On June 1 I was informed that the new owners will not honor that agreement. I am asking you to reconsider and extend my membership through September of this year.

I work nearby, and many of my friends and coworkers are considering joining your club. I hope that I can recommend they do so. I'd rather not have to spread the word about an uncooperative attitude at the club.

Sincerely,
Roger Hamilton

Cancellation of health club membership

CERTIFIED MAIL

Chuck Satlas, Manager
Worldwide Health Club
Smalltown, OH

Dear Mr. Satlas:

I joined the Worldwide Health Club seven weeks ago, mostly on the basis of your television and print ads. I also was told when I joined that there would be aerobics, Tae Bo, and other classes I could attend in addition to using all of the exercise equipment and pool.

I have yet to find any aerobics or Tae Bo classes, and the equipment I want to use is either continually busy or out of service. And the pool was unexpectedly closed for five days last week for some sort of maintenance.

The bottom line is that I have gotten nothing out of my membership for the past seven weeks.

As advertised, and as included in the contract, I am hereby taking advantage of your "money-back guarantee," which allows me to cancel my membership within the first sixty days and receive a full refund.

Please send a check in the amount of $500, the first year's membership dues, to me at the address on this letter.

Thank you.

Joshua Diamond

Canceling membership at health club for medical reasons

C. Satlas, Manager
Worldwide Health Club
Smalltown, OH

Dear Mr. Satlas:

In January of this year I signed a contract for a one-year membership at your club. In August, I was involved in an automobile accident. I sustained neck injuries and am seeing a physical therapist.

Per doctor's orders I am not to use exercise facilities for at least the next twelve months.

Under the terms of my agreement with the club, I am due a refund of the unused portion of the membership if I have a doctor's letter advising against use of the facilities.

I am enclosing a letter to that effect from my physician.

Please mail the balance of my membership to me at the above address.

Thank you,
Joshua Diamond

24 Senior Associations

Dear Reader:

Seniors represent an important component of our society, culturally, politically, and economically.

In this chapter, you'll find some examples of letters from a senior association. We also include some related letters in the chapter about clubs, organizations, and religious institutions.

Sincerely,
The Authors

Welcoming new tenants to association

Dear Emma and Ron:

It's my pleasure to welcome you to the Lakeview Apartments community. I would be delighted to introduce you to all of our members and to the many activities and services we have available to us at Lakeview.

I am enclosing our weekly newsletter, which gives you an idea of what's going on. Our Thursday evening social is especially popular, and I would recommend you take that opportunity to get to know us. I would be happy to accompany you and make the introductions.

Please call me at your convenience.

Sincerely,
Pete Carter, President
Seniors Association

Response to association letter of welcome

Pete Carter, President
Seniors Association
Lakeview Apartments
Smalltown, OH

Dear Pete:

Thank you for taking us under your wing. We thoroughly enjoyed Thursday evening. It was quite a big step for us to sell our home and move to a retirement community, and we were very anxious about it.

We will take a bit of time to settle in and then start taking advantage of all that is going on at Lakeview. We are very excited about the possibilities.

Sincerely,
Emma and Ron Miller

Announcement of new column in senior community newsletter

Dear Members:

I'm the new guy in town. My lovely wife, Emma, and I recently moved to Lakeview Apartments after we sold our home.

I have been asked by the editors of this esteemed publication to fill this space each week with a column. Perhaps it's because I spent more than forty years as editor of the Smalltown Banner, but more likely it's because everyone who's met me here has quickly discovered that I can be counted on to have an opinion on something, anything, and everything.

We have met many of the residents of Lakeview, but there are quite a few of you who have managed to avoid us thus far. If you happen to see two unfamiliar faces wandering the grounds, it's probably us; please introduce yourself.

I will be counting on all of you to give me some ideas for columns.

Please contact me at the phone number listed on the masthead. If we are away, you can leave a message. Or, if your grandchildren have shown you how to use a computer, please send me an e-mail message.

Sincerely,
Ron Miller

Asking computer store to give demonstration

Spaceway Computer Systems
Smalltown, OH

Dear People:

I am writing to you as a representative of a large group of senior citizens living in the Lakeview Senior Apartment Complex. As a group you will find us to be very interested in current technology and much younger than our accumulated years might suggest.

We have earmarked some funds in our budget to buy several computers to be installed in our center for Internet and e-mail.

I would like to know if someone from your store would be available to come to the senior center to give us a presentation about current computer technologies. I can't promise you a sale, but I expect that the budget committee will want to deal with a local company willing to help us set up and maintain the system.

Sincerely,
Ron Miller

Follow-up on computer demonstration

Norman Frates
Spaceway Computer Systems
Smalltown, OH

Dear Mr. Frates:

Thanks so much for your visit last week to demonstrate computers to members of the senior center. The talk around here since then has been almost exclusively bits and bytes, which is a lot more interesting than aches and pains.

Our budget committee authorized me to ask Spaceway for a formal bid for the following equipment and services:

- Three (3) personal computers. Pentium 4 at 1.5 GHz with 256 MB of memory. The computers must include graphics, audio, and Ethernet cards, plus keyboard and mouse.
- Three (3) 22-inch flat-screen monitors.
- One (1) combination hub, firewall, and gateway.
- Installation of the machines, plus a three-year service and maintenance agreement.

In addition, we expect the successful bidder to arrange for installation of a broadband cable link to the recreation room and high-speed Internet service.

We are asking for receipt of a bid no later than 9 A.M. on March 15.

Please feel free to call me to discuss the specifications.

Sincerely,
Ron Miller

Accepting bid for computer installation

Norman Frates
Spaceway Computer Systems
Smalltown, OH

Dear Mr. Frates:

On behalf of the budget committee of the Smalltown Senior Center, I am pleased to accept your bid, in the amount of $4,250, for installation and maintenance of three computers.

We have decided to go with your Option C, which substitutes a lower-cost Celeron processor for the Pentium 4, and also includes three trackballs, which you have convinced us are easier to use than mice.

I have attached a copy of your bid with the full description of Option C.

Please contact me at your earliest convenience to discuss a timetable for preparation of the recreation room and installation of the computers.

Sincerely,
Ron Miller

Soliciting bids for hairdresser to visit senior complex

Cathy Gillette
Cathy's Cutting Corner
Smalltown, OH

Dear Ms. Gillette:

I am writing on behalf of a group of several dozen women living at the Lakeview Senior Apartment Complex. We all like our hair to look good, but some of us find it difficult to get out to a beauty shop.

We are seeking bids from several area salons to have a hairdresser visit the complex once a week, and on an appointment basis, perform the same services that would be done in the shop. We have arranged to make available the crafts room at the complex, which includes several sinks and adequate electrical power and lighting.

If you are interested, please respond with a proposal that includes rates for common services.

Sincerely,
Emma Miller, Chair
Hairdressing Committee

Accepting bid for hairdresser to visit senior complex

Cathy Gillette
Cathy's Cutting Corner
Smalltown, OH

Dear Ms. Gillette:

We are pleased to accept your proposal to provide hairdressing services at the Lakeview Senior Apartment Complex. The crafts room will be available every Thursday from 9 A.M. to 5 P.M.

Per your request, the receptionist at the complex will maintain a sign-up list for appointments between visits. You will be responsible for setup and cleanup.

By a resolution of the Hairdressing Committee, this arrangement will be continued on a month-by-month basis. Any changes in hours or prices must be approved by the committee at least one month in advance. Our members understand that payments may be made in cash, check, or approved credit card.

We look forward to your first visit on Thursday, June 4.

Sincerely,
Emma Miller, Chair
Hairdressing Committee

25 Pets

Dear Reader:

For many of us, pets are part of the family. They give at least as much as they take.

But with this joy comes responsibility; pet owners must speak for their dogs, cats, birds, and other animal co-residents, and ensure that they receive the best possible care.

In this section, we present some common notes to pet-care providers.

Sincerely,
The Authors

Thanks to veterinarian for assistance

Monica Lewis, D.V.M.
Smalltown Veterinary Institute
Smalltown, OH

Dear Dr. Lewis:

Thank you again for all you did for Manny—and for us—when he was in your care recently. It was quite a shock when we came home and saw his eye bleeding.

You calmed us all down and handled the situation expertly. He is recovering nicely. I guess being a good vet means you treat the owner as well as the patient. Thanks again.

Sincerely,
Laura Diamond

Thanks to veterinary staff

Monica Lewis, D.V.M.
Smalltown Veterinary Institute
Smalltown, OH

Dear Dr. Lewis:

Would you please pass along our family's thanks for your staff's considerate care of our cat Frisky last week?

It is so sad when a much-loved member of the family reaches the end of the line. He was well cared for at the institute, and we greatly appreciate the way we were treated.

Our daughter Heather will treasure the sympathy card from the staff.

Sincerely,
Laura Diamond

Request to animal shelter for kitten

Smalltown Animal Shelter
Smalltown, OH

Dear People:

I am hoping to adopt a kitten sometime in the near future. Would you please keep me in mind and let me know if the shelter receives any cats with Russian Blue or Persian bloodlines?

Thank you.

Sincerely,
Laura Diamond

Seeking information about pet-care insurance

Customer Service
Best Friends Pet Care
Dogtown, IL

Dear People:

I saw your ad for pet health insurance in a magazine.

We have two pets, a dog and a cat, and the idea of pet-care insurance sounds very interesting. Please send me full information and enrollment forms.

Sincerely,
Laura Diamond

Inquiry to veterinarian about pet-care insurance

Monica Lewis, D.V.M.
Smalltown Veterinary Institute
Smalltown, OH

Dear Dr. Lewis:

I am considering purchasing pet-care insurance to help us with the care of our dog and cat.

The company is Best Friends Pet Care, located in Illinois. From the little I read in the ad it sounded interesting, and I have contacted them to send me brochures and forms.

Can you tell me if the Smalltown Veterinary Institute has had any experience with this insurance company? Are there other companies offering better coverage?

I'd appreciate your comments.

Sincerely,
Monica Diamond

Thanking veterinarian for information about pet-care insurance

Monica Lewis, D.V.M.
Smalltown Veterinary Institute
Smalltown, OH

Dear Dr. Lewis:

Thanks for your thoughts about pet-care insurance. It sounds as though the policies are pretty good when it comes to expensive, catastrophic problems like cancer, but of less value for more common problems like broken bones and minor diseases.

I will take your suggestion and call Sarah Hitchcock to find out her experiences with the policy she holds.

Sincerely,
Laura Diamond

To acquaintance about experience with pet-care insurance

Sarah Hitchcock
Smalltown, OH

Dear Sarah:

I understand that you are the unofficial pet expert in Smalltown. Dr. Lewis at the Smalltown Veterinary Institute suggested I contact you with my question.

I am considering purchasing pet-care insurance to cover my dog and cat. The best coverage I have found is from Best Friends Pet Care in Illinois. Do you know anything about this company, or have suggestions about other carriers?

Sincerely,
Laura Diamond

26 Complaints

Dear Reader:

I've got a complaint, and I want you to do something about it.

Not you personally, actually. But I do want to let the animal control officer know about my neighbor's unruly and unleashed dog, tell the headquarters of my preferred supermarket about a local decline in quality, and let my once-favorite restaurant know why I haven't been in lately.

A complaint should be politely stated, and unless you are merely venting your unhappiness, the letter should include a clearly stated request for action. Remember to use the active voice: I want you to fix the mess you made; I expect a refund or a rebate, or I want you to make a change in your policy.

It is pretty easy for a business to dismiss an unclear complaint and an irrational demand. It is much harder to ignore a clearly presented description of a problem and a reasonable request to make it right.

Best of luck.

Sincerely,
Corey Sandler

Dear Reader:

Many years ago I worked as an editor for a major New York magazine publisher. There I was introduced to one of the company's most valuable employees: the in-house copywriter. You know his work quite well.

This is the guy whose most famous writing includes such bestselling short novellas as: "Congratulations! You may have won a million dollars!" and "Hurry! Time is running out on this exclusive free offer."

And he also was responsible for dark and sinister works, like "This is the third time we have written to you about the outstanding balance for your magazine subscription. If we don't hear from you soon we will have no choice but to turn this matter over to a collection agency."

One of the first things I learned from the copywriter was what I call the Ladder of Complaint.

The first letter he wrote would be sweet and levelheaded, laying out the facts, and making a reasonable request. The second letter would be polite but insistent. The third letter, still polite and insistent, would add a consequence.

Before we go on to some examples, let's review the basics of letters of complaint about products we covered in Chapter 1:

1. Organize all of your supporting documents, including receipts, warranties, and advertising fliers and materials.
2. Find the right department (or person, if possible) to address.
3. Lay out your complaint in plain language: The product does not work. The product

does not work as advertised. The quality of the product was less than I expected. I was charged too much.

4. Decide what you want the recipient of the letter to do: Send a replacement. Make a refund. Make a repair.

Best of luck,
Corey Sandler

Complaint about receiving unordered subscriptions

Customer Service
Morgan Publishing
Bigtown, NY

Dear People:

I recently started receiving four of your company's magazines: Travel Digest, Children and Parents, Pets Monthly, and Golf Travel.

I did not order any of these magazines, and I will not pay the invoice.

I have attached the mailing labels from each of the four magazines.

I am assuming this was a prank by someone unknown. If you continue to send me invoices I intend to notify the state attorney general's consumer fraud division and the Better Business Bureau.

Thank you.

Ron Miller

Error in wedding invitation

Edward Strunk, Manager
Quality Printing Services
Nearby, OH

Dear Mr. Strunk:

I just received the invitations for my daughter Morgan's wedding in May. I was horrified to find that throughout the invitation her name is printed as Marian. We went over all the details when my daughter and I were in your office to personally place this order. If you check your copies, you will find that she is indeed listed as Morgan.

Please rush the corrected invitations to me as soon as possible. I am not even mentioning this mistake to my daughter. She does not need any more prewedding stress.

Sincerely,
Laura Diamond

Returning shoes dyed to match dress

Manager
Regal Shoes
Smalltown, OH

Dear Manager:

I am returning a pair of shoes I purchased two weeks ago. They were to be dyed to match the dress I will wear at my daughter's May wedding. I provided a swatch of the material at the time I purchased the shoes and was assured that they would indeed match the dress.

I am again providing a swatch of the dress. As you will see, the shoes do not even come close to matching the dress.

Please correct this mistake and let me know when I can pick up the shoes. They must be ready no later than May 1.

Sincerely,
Laura Diamond

Complaint about incompetent bridal consultant

Customer Service
Miller's Department Store
Smalltown, OH

Dear People:

My daughter Morgan is engaged to be married in May, and we are in the process of planning for her wedding.

We called your store recently and made an appointment with your bridal consultant, Samantha Jones. Morgan wanted to establish a bridal register for gifts. My daughter was not asking for anything out of the ordinary—just some help with silver patterns, china, and crystal, as well as basic pots and pans.

Not only was Ms. Jones unprofessional in keeping us waiting almost an hour because she forgot about our appointment, but she knew nothing about any of the items that interested us.

Our time was wasted and the experience was most unpleasant. We will take our business and the wedding register elsewhere.

Sincerely,
Laura Diamond

Complaint to neighbor about children ruining flowers

Jane and Bruce Silver
Smalltown, OH

Dear Mr. and Mrs. Silver:

My husband, Harold, and I live two doors up the road, at 18 Meadow Street. We haven't had the chance to meet you yet, but we look forward to the opportunity.

I hope by now you and your family are settling into life in Smalltown. I think you will find it a very welcoming and supportive community.

There is one issue, though, that I hope we can resolve. I have spoken to your children a number of times in the past two weeks about not picking the flowers along the edge of the sidewalk that passes in front of our house. On a few occasions the plants have been pulled out by the roots.

Would you please speak to them about this? I have four grandchildren of my own and am aware that some things are hard for little ones to resist, but my husband takes great pride in his garden and is most particular about it. If you or your children admire the flowers, we would be most happy to give you a bouquet. Just ask one of us.

It is important to us to be good neighbors. I look forward to hearing from you soon.

Sincerely,
Monica Diamond

Response about children ruining flowers

Monica Diamond
Smalltown, OH

Dear Mrs. Diamond:

Please accept my apologies for the damage done to your flowers by our children. I have spoken to them about this, and they have promised to respect your garden.

The kids are so thrilled to be in a new home and neighborhood, visiting new neighbors, and playing with new cats and dogs. They kept bringing me lovely bouquets of flowers; now I know where they came from.

I hope to come by to meet you soon. In the meantime, would you please accept these pictures of your garden, created by my children? The words, in case you can't read them, say "Sorry."

Sincerely,
Jane Silver

Complaint to catering company

Bonnie Bodacious
Bonnie's Catering
Smalltown, OH

Dear Ms. Bodacious:

On January 23 we engaged your company to cater the refreshments for an open house at the Smalltown Senior Center. Our requirements were simple, and since we met with you on two occasions in advance of the event, we thought they were crystal clear.

We requested platters of finger sandwiches and two dips with accompanying vegetables. The dips and vegetables were very good. But we requested that the finger sandwiches be shrimp and avocado, and chicken and watercress—a pair of dishes specifically requested by our entertainment committee.

Instead, the fillings turned out to be several varieties of unidentified mystery meat. Not only was the food less than inspired, it was not what we ordered.

I will be very happy to discuss this incident with you. The Senior Center is withholding payment until after we meet.

Please call me at the above telephone number, or leave a message at the Senior Center.

Sincerely,
Monica Diamond

Complaint about discount not given

Manager
Philips Variety Store
Smalltown, OH

Dear Manager:

I am a regular shopper at Philips Variety Store.

On February 7 I purchased a number of items at Philips. Attached is a copy of my sales receipt in the amount of $99.80. Because Wednesday is Senior Citizens Day, I requested my 10 percent discount. The cashier asked for and scanned my senior card.

It was not until I got home and studied my receipt that I realized I did not receive the discount, which would have come to $9.98. Since I went to the trouble of shopping on Wednesday and using my card, I want to be reimbursed for that amount.

Please advise.

Sincerely,
Monica Diamond

Second letter about discount not given

Manager
Philips Variety Store
Smalltown, OH

Dear Manager:

Five weeks ago I wrote to you complaining about the fact that I did not receive my senior citizen discount on a recent visit, despite the fact that I asked for the discount and the cashier scanned my senior card. I have attached a copy of my original letter.

I have not received a response from you in that time.

I am involved in a number of committees at the Smalltown Senior Center, including our Pennypinchers Club. I would be disappointed to remove Philips Variety Store from our list of recommended retail outlets, but I will do so if I do not hear from you soon.

Sincerely,
Monica Diamond

Follow-up on discount not given

Charles Crippendorf, Manager
Philips Variety Store
Smalltown, OH

Dear Mr. Crippendorf:

Thank you for your response to my letter about the error that resulted in my not receiving the senior discount at Philips. I trust all of your personnel now know to check the date on their cash registers each morning when they start work.

I will pass along the word to members of the Smalltown Senior Center that you will extend a double discount of 20 percent to seniors on every Wednesday in June as a special salute to our members.

Sincerely,
Monica Diamond

Complaint about quality of flowers received as a gift

Manager
Beautiful Blooms Flower Shop
Smalltown, OH

Dear Manager:

On May 10, I received a dozen long-stemmed red roses from Beautiful Blooms. They were a Mother's Day gift from my grandson, who lives out of town.

I am sure the flowers I received were not the ones my grandson thought he was paying for. The roses arrived wilted and limp. Even when I put them in water they could not be revived enough to last longer than three days.

My grandson is a college student and his funds are extremely limited. I cannot stand by and let him pay for shoddy merchandise.

I will appreciate a call at the above number. I trust that your store stands behind its products.

Sincerely,
Monica Diamond

Complaint about deteriorating service at supermarket

Manager
Super Shop Supermarket
Smalltown, OH

Dear Manager:

I am a lifelong resident of Smalltown, and I've been a patron of your supermarket ever since it opened some twenty years ago.

For nearly all of that time, Super Shop has been my favorite place to shop here in Smalltown. Until now, I have been quite satisfied with the quality and service.

Regretfully, I find it necessary to bring to your attention the deterioration of both the quality and service. For the past six months, grocery shopping at your store has become a chore rather than something to which I look forward.

The parking lot is regularly littered with abandoned carts. The shelves are increasingly sloppy, and the store seems to be operating with more closed checkout aisles than open ones.

Last week, I had to bring to the attention of an uninterested stock person the fact that there was milk on the shelves that was outdated by several days. I also have found open packages of meat in the cooler.

I hope that I will not need to take my business out of town to the Mega Market on the state highway, but I will do so if conditions do not improve soon.

I look forward to hearing from you soon.

Sincerely,
Monica Diamond

Second complaint about deteriorating service at supermarket

Regional Manager
Super Shop Supermarket
Corporate Headquarters
Bigtown, NY

Dear Manager:

I am writing to advise you about deteriorating conditions at your supermarket in Smalltown, Ohio.

Attached is a letter I sent to the local manager three weeks ago. As of this date, I have not received a response from the manager.

Sincerely,
Monica Diamond

Response to letter from executive about deteriorating service at supermarket

Daniel Keese, Vice President of Public Affairs
Super Shop Supermarket
Corporate Headquarters
Bigtown, NY

Dear Mr. Keese:

Thank you for your quick response to my letter about conditions at the Smalltown Super Shop Supermarket. I do understand how difficult it is to hire staff, but the people in your store represent your company in everything they do.

I will be happy to meet with you the next time you are in town to share my concerns and ideas about bringing the store back to what it used to be.

Please call me to arrange a time when we can meet.

Sincerely,
Monica Diamond

Complaint about rental car

Customer Service
Speedy Car Rental
Corporate Headquarters
Heartland, KS

Dear People:

On September 6 of this year, I rented a car from your company for pickup at the airport in Sacramento, California. My morning flight from the East Coast got me to California at approximately noon local time, after a six-hour flight.

I then had to wait in line at your agency for more than an hour because there was a huge line of very unhappy people in front of me, and only two clerks handling all the paperwork. Halfway through the experience, one of the clerks left the counter for exactly half an hour. It seemed obvious to many of us in line that she had ducked out for a lunch break.

After finally getting my rental car and exiting the lot to the freeway, I noticed that the gas tank was nearly empty. I had to leave the highway to fill the tank.

At the end of the day, I called the Speedy toll-free number to report the problem with the gas tank. I was told that my credit card billing would be adjusted.

My bill has arrived, and no adjustment was made. I am enclosing my receipt for the gas.

I make many business trips, and in recent years I have used Speedy Car Rental many times. This past trip makes me seriously consider taking my business elsewhere.

Sincerely,
John Diamond

Complaint about neighbor's noise

Mr. and Mrs. Herbert Saul
Smalltown, OH

Dear Mr. and Mrs. Saul:

Please let me take this opportunity to introduce myself and to welcome you to the neighborhood. My wife, Monica, and I live at #18, just up the road from your new home.

We have lived on Meadow Street for the past twenty years. Most likely because I'm older than everyone else around here, I am often addressed as the unofficial "mayor" of the neighborhood.

Speaking for all of us, I wish you and your family many happy years here. We all pitch in to help each other any time we can, and do what we can to keep our community a safe and peaceful place to raise our families.

I have been asked by several of our neighbors to communicate their wishes about a problem that has arisen since you moved in. We all love music, and most of us have had, or will have, teenagers. We would, though, appreciate it if you would ask your teens to turn down the volume.

We all look forward to meeting and greeting you properly after you have the chance to settle in.

Sincerely,
Harold Diamond

Second letter complaining of noise

Mr. and Mrs. Herbert Saul
Smalltown, OH

Dear Mr. and Mrs. Saul:

I recently communicated a request by some of your neighbors to ask your teens to tone down their music. Two of your adjacent neighbors have small children, and even those four houses down have trouble sleeping at night because of the noise.

As in a family, we in this neighborhood try to resolve all issues amongst ourselves whenever possible. Please ask your children to respect the fact that we don't all want to listen to their music, especially at all hours of the night.

Sincerely,
Harold Diamond

Third letter complaining of noise

Mr. and Mrs. Herbert Saul
Smalltown, OH

Dear Mr. and Mrs. Saul:

It has been more than a month since I communicated the problems your neighbors have been having with the continuous noise emanating from your house. I understand that a number of your closest neighbors have personally appealed to you to do something about it.

I must bring to your attention the fact that we do have a noise ordinance in Smalltown that is enforced by the police department on the basis of complaints received from the neighborhood. We hope you will allow us to resolve this without the intervention of the legal system.

Sincerely,
Harold Diamond

Requesting road repair from highway department

Department of Highways
Smalltown, OH

Dear People:

I am writing to bring to your attention a dangerous situation at the very busy intersection of Broad Street and Third Avenue. A pothole there has been growing almost daily, and now is nearly four feet wide and deep enough to bottom out the suspension of passing cars.

To avoid this hole, motorists have to veer out into oncoming traffic. Pedestrians cannot cross at the crosswalk but must take their chances between parked cars.

This is a serious accident waiting to happen.

Please advise when we can expect a road crew to fix the hole.

Sincerely,
John Diamond

Complaint about unleashed dogs

Animal Control Officer
Smalltown Town Hall
Smalltown, OH

Dear Officer:

I am writing to report two aggressive dogs in our neighborhood that are regularly left to roam without leashes.

Approximately one month ago I was out for my evening walk near 26 Pleasant Street when two large black mixed-breed dogs came bounding out of the yard. When I yelled for help, a young man came out of the house and took them inside without saying anything to me.

Similar incidents have happened several times in the past few weeks, including one confrontation between these two dogs and a child who was walking a puppy on the street.

I know that we have a leash law in Smalltown, and these dogs and their owner are in regular violation of it. I would appreciate it if you would follow up on this to make sure these animals are not a danger to anyone.

Please give me a call to update me on the situation.

Sincerely,
Harold Diamond

Complaint about lack of handicapped parking spaces

Manager
Stop and Save Supermarket
Smalltown, OH

Dear Manager:

I am a long-time, frequent customer of Stop and Save. I am also a senior citizen who has recently undergone back surgery. Until I personally experienced the need for a handicapped parking space, I had no idea how few there are and how rudely some drivers misuse the ones that are there.

By my estimate, the Stop and Save parking lot in Smalltown has space for more than 300 cars. Why is it that there are only four spaces designated for the handicapped? Please increase that number.

Please also assign one of the kids who collects shopping carts in the parking lot to checking for handicapped parking permits on the cars in those spaces. A phone call to the police department is all it will take for them to come by and issue tickets to the owners of the illegally parked cars.

Sincerely,
Harold Diamond

Follow-up on response to lack of handicapped parking spaces

Jim Jepperson, Manager
Stop and Save Supermarket
Smalltown, OH

Dear Mr. Jepperson:

I wrote to you a while ago about the lack of handicapped parking spots in your store's lot, and I'm very appreciative of the fact that five additional spaces were since designated for handicapped use only.

But on my trip to the market today I was very disappointed to see that four of those new spaces were given over to a display of gardening supplies and plants for the upcoming spring season.

Please find another place for this material, and free up these much-needed spots for those who need some extra help to get to the store.

Sincerely,
Harold Diamond

Complaint about garbage collection

Public Works Department
Smalltown, OH

Dear Commissioner:

For many years, I have been pleased with the service we have received from the public sanitation staff here in Smalltown. In the past two months, however, the service has deteriorated markedly.

The crew that is now collecting the trash in this neighborhood seems extremely careless in their work. Every Tuesday the road is littered with trash that misses the trucks, and many of the trash cans are in the street or tossed in haphazard fashion onto the lawns of the houses.

Some of the neighbors have spoken to the crew, but nothing has changed.

As taxpayers we deserve better treatment. I will appreciate your attention to this matter.

Sincerely,
John Diamond
cc: Mayor Meyer Minor

Complaint about snow removal

Department of Public Works
Fairview, PA

Re: 17 Southbury Road

Dear People:

This is our first winter in Fairview. So far your department's work in removing the snow from the main streets and highways has been very efficient.

But for whatever reason, the snowplow drivers seem to have decided to deposit much of the snow from up the street in the small cutout that leads to our driveway. Both times we had to dig through a wall of snow left by the plows.

This morning, I was unable to get out of my driveway in time to get the children to school, and had to prevail on a neighbor for help.

I want to set up a meeting with a supervisor at your department to discuss the situation and find a better solution for snow removal in this neighborhood. Please call me at the number listed on this letter.

Sincerely,
Karen Diamond

Complaint about restaurant

Ernie Caruso, Owner
Caruso's Italian Restaurant
Smalltown, OH

Dear Mr. Caruso:

We have been regular customers at Caruso's Restaurant for the past several years. Regrettably, after our most recent visit, we are uncertain if we want to return.

Last week my husband and I met with a group of three other couples to celebrate the eightieth birthday of one of our group. Instead of our usual enjoyable dinner, we ran into trouble at every step.

We made a reservation for a table for eight several days in advance, and told the maitre d' that it was for a special occasion. When we arrived for the dinner, we were made to wait about thirty minutes and finally shown to a very crowded round table designed for six people.

The table was in the middle of the dining room, surrounded by three noisy groups around us. We were unable to hear each other talk, and apparently the waiter could not hear us very well, either. Our order was hopelessly mixed up, with four of the eight orders in error. Two of the men asked for their steak rare and had to send it back once because it was overcooked and a second time because the potatoes and vegetables were cold.

Overall, we were very disappointed with our night out. I'm writing in hopes that this will help you return to your previous level of excellence.

Sincerely,
Monica Diamond

Thanking restaurant for response

Ernie Caruso, Owner
Caruso's Italian Restaurant
Smalltown, OH

Dear Mr. Caruso:

Thank you very much for your prompt response to my letter of June xx. We were truly disappointed with our last dining experience at Caruso's, perhaps especially so because we have been quite happy every other time we have dined there.

I appreciate your suggestion that we try to choose a weekday rather than a weekend, and that we reserve a table for early in the evening instead of prime time at 8 P.M. And we especially appreciate your request that we give you a second chance.

We will be pleased to take you up on your offer of a free dinner for our group. We will call the maitre d' soon to make a reservation for a return visit.

Thank you again. I appreciate dealing with people who know the value of a satisfied customer.

Sincerely,
Monica Diamond

Complaint about emergency room service

Administrator
Smalltown General Hospital
Smalltown, OH

Dear People:

On July 16, 20xx, I took my seven-year-old son, Brian, to the emergency room of Smalltown General Hospital for treatment of a bee sting. This was the first time he had been stung, and his arm swelled so severely that we were concerned he might be allergic.

Although there were no other patients in the waiting room, and there seemed to be many nurses and doctors in the area, it was more than an hour before we were shown to an examining room. If the hospital had been very busy this might have been understandable, but there was no evidence of this.

My family has lived in Smalltown for many years, and we all have been involved in the many fundraising campaigns for the hospital, including the recent expansion of the emergency room facilities. A lot of money was spent to improve the facilities; isn't there also some way to improve the service?

Sincerely,
Karen Diamond

Follow-up on complaint about emergency room service

Harold Dennis, Administrator
Smalltown General Hospital
Smalltown, OH

Dear Mr. Dennis:

Thank you for your reply to my letter about our unhappy experience in the Smalltown General Hospital emergency room last month.

I hope your plan to stagger work schedules for nurses and doctors will eliminate the problem of a gap in noncritical care at the start and end of each shift.

Sincerely,
Karen Diamond

Expressing concern about safety on college campus

Campus Security Department
Smalltown University
Smalltown, OH

Dear Security Office:

Last week we took our daughter Heather, an incoming freshman, to her dorm at Sonya Hall. We are very familiar with Smalltown University, because Heather is the third of our children to attend the school. That's why I was quite concerned by what I perceived as a decrease in security around campus.

The first thing we noticed was that the entrance to the dorm was not locked. In previous years, all students had to use a key to enter. A locked front door seems to me to be a vital first step in making the young people who live in the dorm feel secure.

We also were unhappy to see that many of the outside lights on the grounds of the campus were not lit. We are not at all comfortable knowing that our daughter will be walking around a dimly lit campus at night.

We have to face the fact that our children are growing up in a less secure world than the one we enjoyed. I hope that Smalltown University will improve the safety environment before there are problems on campus.

Sincerely,
Laura Diamond

Thanks for response to safety concerns

Captain Harold Remy
Campus Security Department
Smalltown University
Smalltown, OH

Dear Captain Remy:

Thank you for your quick response to my letter about the security issues at Smalltown University.

My daughter and I are quite relieved to hear that new locks will be installed at the entrance to all dorms. Heather tells me that Sonya Hall was one of the first to receive the new hardware.

I am somewhat less reassured about the outdoor lighting. As we walked the campus that night we noticed many lights that were not functioning, and my daughter reports that this continues to be the case.

The increase of safety patrols at night and the call boxes throughout the campus are very good additions. I also think your idea of getting the students involved in an advisory committee is very helpful. We will encourage our daughter to join.

Thank you,
Laura Diamond
cc: Fred Sanchez, Chancellor, Smalltown University

Requesting reimbursement for missing parts

Customer Service
Home Supply Corporation
Smalltown, OH

Dear People:

I recently purchased a bathroom vanity from your store. I am enclosing a copy of the receipt and the parts listing from inside the box.

After struggling to bring this large carton home and removing the old vanity, we discovered that several pieces of critical hardware were missing: a locking ring for the plumbing connection, caulk, and a screw to hold the hot-water knob in place.

Returning the vanity at that time was not an option, so I purchased what was needed at a local hardware store, and we completed the job. The total expense was $12.83.

I want Home Supply Corporation to reimburse me for the cost of purchasing the missing hardware. The alternative is for me to return a slightly used vanity to your store.

I am enclosing the bill for the hardware. You can send a check to me or, since I paid initially by credit card, you can credit my account for that amount.

Sincerely,
Harold Diamond

Second letter requesting reimbursement for missing parts

Customer Service
Home Supply Corporation
Smalltown, OH

Dear People:

I recently sent a letter regarding some parts that were missing for a vanity I purchased at your store. I am enclosing a copy of my letter.

To date I have heard nothing from you. I purchase a good deal of merchandise from the Home Supply Company, and this vanity represents a considerable amount of my fixed income.

It was not possible to return the vanity to the store, and the amount I had to pay out-of-pocket was only a small amount of the purchase price.

I believe it is only fair that I be reimbursed. I want to continue to do business with Home Supply Company, and hope to hear from you soon.

Sincerely,
Harold Diamond

Response regarding reimbursement for missing parts

Charles Maitland, Manager
Home Supply Corporation
Smalltown, OH

Dear Mr. Maitland:

Thank you for the reimbursement for the cost of purchasing missing hardware for a bathroom vanity I purchased at your store. I will use the credit check the next time I shop at Home Supply Corporation.

I appreciate your response.

Sincerely,
Harold Diamond

Returning item of clothing

Customer Service Department
J. Briggs Clothing
Oldtown, ME

Dear Customer Service:

Enclosed is a blouse I purchased from your Web site last month.

I wore it twice, and then washed it. I followed the instructions on the tag precisely. It was washed separately, in cold water, and line dried.

The blouse shrank several sizes, and the lining of the collar disintegrated.

I have attached a copy of the invoice and shipping documents.

Under terms of your ninety-day satisfaction guarantee, please issue a credit for the full price of the blouse.

Sincerely,
Morgan Diamond

Objecting to partial credit for return

Customer Service Department
J. Briggs Clothing
Oldtown, ME

Dear Customer Service:

Earlier this month I returned a blouse that shrank when I washed it. I asked that the full amount of the purchase price be credited to my account.

I have just received my credit card bill, and I see that I was not given full credit for the purchase price. I paid $45 for the blouse and received a credit of $36. Please credit the additional $9 to my account.

I have enclosed copies of my previous letter, invoice, and shipping documents.

Sincerely,
Morgan Diamond

27 Newspaper, Cable Television, Telephone, Utilities, and Mail

Dear Reader:

When it comes down to it, there are only a few services that actually touch you in your home. These include newspaper delivery, cable television and telephone providers, electric and water utilities, and mail delivery.

Now, tell us: Does your newspaper sometimes end up in a puddle (or not show up at all)? Does your cable television service perform perfectly at all times? Does your telephone bill always make sense?

If your world is anything like ours, you experience at least some problems with home delivery services and utilities. Just as for other complaints, your letters should be specific and direct, and any remedies you request should be reasonable and clearly stated.

Sincerely,
The Authors

Error on newspaper delivery bill

Smalltown Banner
Circulation Department
Smalltown, OH

Re: Morgan Diamond
23 Evergreen Street, Apt. 5B
Smalltown, OH

Dear Circulation Department:

I just received the bill for delivery of the daily and Sunday editions of the Smalltown Banner for the month of March.

I did not receive the Sunday edition of the Banner on March 2 and 9. I called the circulation number on both occasions and was told I would receive credit on my bill.

Please send an adjusted bill.

Sincerely,
Morgan Diamond

Response to newspaper circulation department

James Olsen, Circulation Manager
Smalltown Banner
Smalltown, OH

Dear Mr. Olsen:

I received your apology for the poor delivery service we experienced in recent weeks. Thank you for the note, and for the offer of a free month's delivery.

I accept the offer, and look forward to trouble-free delivery of the paper. If service is acceptable, I will continue beyond the free month.

Sincerely,
Morgan Diamond

Complaint about newspaper delivery during hold

Smalltown Banner
Circulation Department
Smalltown, OH

Dear Circulation Department:

I called the newspaper circulation department on May 1 to arrange to have my delivery suspended while I was on vacation from May 4 through 11.

When I got home I found eight newspapers piled on my doorstep. I expect my account to be credited for the week I was away. But more important, I am annoyed that anyone who passed by my apartment door knew I was gone.

Please advise.

Joshua Diamond

Canceling newspaper subscription

Smalltown Banner
Circulation Department
Smalltown, OH

Re: Morgan Diamond
23 Evergreen Street, Apt. 5B
Smalltown, OH

Dear Circulation Department:

Please cancel my subscription to the Smalltown Banner, effective immediately.

For the fourth time in the past two weeks, my newspaper has not been delivered. I am tired of calling the circulation department. Because nothing has been done to rectify the situation, I have decided to do without the newspaper.

Sincerely,
Morgan Diamond

Asking for blocking of pay-per-call phone numbers

Customer Service
Ma Bell Telephone Company
Smalltown, OH

Concerning: (xxx) xxx-xxxx

Dear Customer Service:

Please block all calls to talk lines, adult entertainment and information, and other pay-per-call phone numbers as follows:

550 Group conversation lines
554 Adult information services
920 General business applications and information services
940 Adult programs (prerecorded)
976 General information services (prerecorded)

I understand there is no charge for blocking access to these numbers from my residential phone.

Sincerely,
Laura Diamond

Request for analysis of local calling plan

Customer Service
Ma Bell Telephone Company
Smalltown, OH

Concerning: (xxx) xxx-xxxx

Dear People:

Enclosed please find a copy of the last three bills I received for local and regional telephone service.

I would appreciate an analysis to find out if there is a billing plan that would better match our usage patterns. I am available to discuss changes on Wednesdays and Fridays from 3 to 5 P.M. by telephone. I also would be happy to receive a letter outlining available options.

Sincerely,
Morgan Diamond

Requesting list of available calling plans and services

Customer Service
Ma Bell Telephone Company
Smalltown, OH

Concerning: (xxx) xxx-xxxx

Dear Customer Service:

Please send me a copy of the full listing for all available residential calling plans and services.

I have attached a recent copy of our phone bill for your analysis.

Sincerely,
Morgan Diamond

Request for analysis of cellular usage

Customer Service
Over the Rainbow Wireless Telephone Company
Truro, MA

Concerning: (xxx) xxx-xxxx

Dear People:

In the past five months we have exceeded our base allotment of minutes on our digital telephone service, costing us an average of about $20 extra with each bill.

Please analyze the attached bills and advise us of another rate plan that is better suited to our regular usage.

I note that Horizon Digital is offering a plan in our local calling area with 600 minutes of calling during the week plus unlimited weekend usage for $40 per month, which seems to be a much better deal than our present plan with your company. Do you have a similar—or better—plan?

I would like to stay with Over the Rainbow if we can receive the best available service plan.

Sincerely,
Laura Diamond

Requesting out-of-town telephone books

Customer Service
Ma Bell Telephone Company
Smalltown, OH

Concerning: (xxx) xxx-xxxx

Dear People:

I would like to have current copies of phone books for these towns:

Fairview, PA
Nearby, OH
Bigtown, NY

Please send me a listing of the prices for the books and shipping, or call me to discuss the order.

Sincerely,
Karen Diamond

Requesting cable television rates

Customer Service Department
Megamonopoly BroadCable Corporation
Smalltown, OH

Dear People:

I will be moving into a new apartment near Smalltown University in the fall and want to have cable television installed.

I have been unable to find a complete listing of installation charges and available cable television, broadband Internet, and other services. Please send me the information so that I can review it and make my decision.

Sincerely,
Joshua Diamond

Requesting clarification on pay-per-view policies

Customer Service Department
Megamonopoly BroadCable Corporation
Smalltown, OH

Concerning: customer number xxxx-xxxx

Dear People:

I recently had cable installed in my apartment. So far, I have been unable to get my questions answered on your pay-per-view option. The information provided onscreen does not give me prices, and your customer service representatives have given me three different prices for movies.

Please provide me with a current price list for pay-per-view movies.

Sincerely,
Joshua Diamond

Requesting credit for cable outage

Customer Service Department
Megamonopoly BroadCable Corporation
Smalltown, OH

Concerning: xxxx-xxxxx

Dear People:

My cable television service was out on January 6, 7, and 8. After repairs were made, I was told I would receive credit for the time when the service was not available.

I have just received my bill and do not see a credit for these days. Please review and see that my next bill reflects this credit.

Sincerely,
Morgan Diamond

Requesting additional cable channel

Customer Service Department
Duopoly Cable Company
Fairview, PA

Dear People:

We have just moved to Fairview and are new customers of Duopoly Cable Company. At our previous address in Smalltown, our basic cable included the 24-hour Fly Fishing Channel, which was our favorite station.

Here in Fairview, we are unable to find that among our basic channels. Please explain how we can add FFC to our lineup here.

Sincerely,
Karen Diamond

Requesting refund for cable box

Customer Service Department
Megamonopoly BroadCable Corporation
Smalltown, OH

Concerning: customer number xxxx-xxxx
26B Woodlake Apartments, Smalltown, OH

Dear People:

On July 27 I canceled service to the above address and returned my cable box. Enclosed is a photocopy of the receipt I was given at your local office.

It has now been one month and I have not received the return of my $65 deposit. Please send a check to my present address, which is listed below, as soon as possible.

Sincerely,
Morgan Diamond

Complaining of poor signal

Customer Service Department
Megamonopoly BroadCable Corporation
Smalltown, OH

Dear People:

In August I moved to my present address and had cable installed. For approximately one week after installation my reception was satisfactory, but since that time it has steadily declined. The signal is very weak and some channels do not come through at all.

Because I go to school and work I am not home during the day, and find it difficult to call when I can speak to a real human being. I have left a string of phone messages for your department, but have not heard from any of your representatives.

I can be reached at xxx-xxxx daily from 4 to 5 P.M. to set up an appointment for a service call.

I also expect my next bill to reflect a credit for my first month's charges.

Sincerely,
Joshua Diamond

Inadequate scrambling of adult channel

Customer Service Department
Duopoly Cable Company
Fairview, PA

Concerning: account number xxxx xxxx

Dear People:

I am writing to object to the inadequate "scrambling" of adult channels on our cable television service.

My family, which includes two young children, subscribes to the basic cable package. My husband and I strictly monitor the kinds of shows our children watch, but we can't be with them 100 percent of the time.

We were horrified to see our kids scan past Channel 50, an "adult" channel that is just a few clicks above the children's section. On Channel 50, the sound is not blocked at all and the picture moves in and out of the scramble at times.

Please let us know how we can remove that channel and ones like it from our cable service.

Sincerely,
Karen Diamond

Complaint about awkward remote

Customer Service Department
Megamonopoly BroadCable Corporation
Smalltown, OH

Concerning: customer number xxxx-xxxx

Dear People:

I will admit to not being a techno wiz, but I'm also not totally inept. However, the remote control you supplied for use with your cable box is just about the most unmanageable piece of hardware I have ever tried to use.

The design is awkward and the various buttons are so close together that you can never press just one.

I also find it extremely annoying that when I'm scrolling through the channels I can't remove the references to the ones that I don't subscribe to. I think that with the amount we are being charged for cable, the whole experience should be easier.

Please advise about alternatives to the clumsy hardware you have provided.

Sincerely,
Joshua Diamond

Requesting review of bill and senior discount

Customer Service Department
Megamonopoly BroadCable Corporation
Smalltown, OH

Dear People:

I have just received my first bill for our new cable service at Lakeview Apartments, and I do not understand all of the charges. A copy is attached.

First of all, there is a $14.95 charge for pay-for-view of a boxing match; we did not order that match and did not watch it. Second, we are being billed $20.95 for the Playboy Channel; again, we did not request this channel and do not intend to pay for it.

Finally, we are supposed to be receiving a senior discount on basic cable, and I do not see that reflected on the bill.

Please review these matters and send me a corrected statement.

Sincerely,
Ron Miller

Requesting electric power account

New Accounts
Smalltown Power Company
Smalltown, OH

Dear People:

I will be moving to the Shorewood Apartment Complex, Apt. 32B, on August 20, 20xx. According to management, each of the apartments in that complex is individually metered.

I need to have the electrical service established in my name as of that date.

Please let me know what you need to do this. I can be reached during ordinary business hours at (xxx) xxx-xxxx.

Sincerely,
Joshua Diamond

Vacation mail hold

Postmaster
Smalltown, OH

Dear Postmaster:

Please hold all mail addressed to:

Karen, Michael, Brian, or Hannah Diamond
123 Main Street
Smalltown, OH 45678

Start hold: Saturday, February 16
Resume delivery: Wednesday, March 6.

Sincerely,
Karen Diamond

Resume mail held for vacation

Postmaster
Smalltown, OH

Dear Postmaster:

We have returned early from our vacation.
Please resume delivery for all mail addressed to:

Karen, Michael, Brian, or Hannah Diamond
123 Main Street
Smalltown, OH 45678

Thank you,

Karen Diamond

Change of address

Postmaster
Smalltown, OH

Dear Postmaster:

Effective July 15, 20xx, please forward all mail addressed to Karen, Michael, Brian, or Hannah Diamond as follows:

FROM:
Diamond
123 Main Street
Smalltown, OH 45678

TO:
Diamond
789 New Avenue
Fairview, PA 23456

This is a permanent change. Thank you.

Karen Diamond

Complaint about damage to mailbox

Postmaster
Smalltown, OH

Dear Postmaster:

Our mailbox was damaged by a Postal Service truck making a delivery on March 5.

I happened to be looking out the window when the truck drove up to my mailbox and struck the supporting pole. I expected that the carrier would come to the door to tell me about the accident, but he drove on.

The pole was cracked and needs to be replaced, and the box is dented. I estimate the cost of repairs to be about $100.

Please let me know how to file a claim.

Sincerely,
Harold Diamond

Asking for removal from direct mail list

Mail Preference Service
Direct Marketing Association
P.O. Box 282
Carmel, NY 10512

Dear People:

Please add my name to the Mail Preference Service of the Direct Marketing Association and notify direct marketers that I do not want to receive unsolicited mail.

I understand that I must send a separate request for each name to be added to the list.

My name and address is as follows:

John Diamond
1234 State Street
Smalltown, OH 45601

My telephone number, to be used only for purposes of verification of my request, is (xxx) xxx-xxxx.

Sincerely,
John Diamond

28 Service Calls

Dear Reader:

My grandmother, who lived nearly 100 years, was born in a world in which the only appliance in the home was a wooden box that held a dripping block of ice to keep a bit of milk cool.

She lived to see modern homes with electric refrigerators, automatic heating, air conditioning, radio, television, VCRs, and personal computers. And she learned that—unlike an icebox—all of these extraordinary conveniences are subject to breakdowns and service calls.

Every time we add another device to our home we also start the clock toward the day when it will need to be maintained, repaired, or replaced. In this section, we look at some typical service-call letters.

Sincerely,
Corey Sandler

Repair call for dishwasher

Ed's Appliance Store
Smalltown, OH

Dear Ed:

Please call to arrange service on our Coldpoint Magic Dishwasher, purchased from your store ten months ago and still under warranty.

The unit seems to go through all of its cycles, but does not clean very well, especially for dishes and glasses on the upper shelves. Please call to arrange a repair visit. We are available most days from 3 to 5 P.M.

Sincerely,
Laura Diamond

Complaint about warranty expiration

Customer Service
Coldpoint Appliances
Northwest, IA

Concerning: Coldpoint Magic Dishwasher
Serial #xxxxxxxx

Dear Customer Service:

We purchased the above-noted dishwasher about fourteen months ago from Ed's Appliance Store in Smalltown, Ohio. The unit has been repaired twice since it was purchased, including a service call three months ago to repair a clogged filter.

The dishwasher is again showing problems—the pump makes a grinding noise when it first engages, and the upper cleaning arm appears to be clogged with debris.

Ed's Appliance Store informs us that the unit is now out of warranty, because more than twelve months have passed since it was purchased.

This is not acceptable to us. The unit has not performed properly since it was first installed, and in any case the repairs made to it just three months ago were not sufficient to bring it to a like-new condition.

We expect Coldpoint to stand behind its products and assist us here.

Sincerely,
Laura Diamond

Follow-up about warranty expiration

Martha Murray, Customer Service Supervisor
Coldpoint Appliances
Northwest, IA

Concerning: Coldpoint Magic Dishwasher
Serial #xxxxxxxx

Dear Ms. Murray:

Thank you for your offer to replace our Coldpoint dishwasher. You restored our faith in your company.

We have one request, though. We would like the new unit to be installed and maintained by Harbor Appliances in Nearby, Ohio. We do not feel that we received good service from Ed's Appliance Store and do not intend to do further business with them.

Sincerely,
Laura Diamond

Requesting estimate on major appliance repair

Inland Plumbing Services
Nearby, OH

Dear People:

I would like to receive an estimate on the cost of repair of our Beecheroil furnace before the onset of the winter season. The furnace is more than twenty years old and is exhibiting quite a few problems including vibration and excess soot. Most important, the ignition system sometimes does not function properly.

Please let us know the price for a complete overhaul of the system, and also for installation of a new high-efficiency system.

Sincerely,
Harold Diamond

Requesting information on service contract

Inland Plumbing Services
Nearby, OH

Dear People:

Please send a quote for the purchase of an annual service contract to maintain our Boldt oil furnace. The furnace has recently been fully overhauled by your company.

Please provide full details on services covered by the contract, along with any charges for parts or labor beyond the cost of the contract.

Sincerely,
Harold Diamond

Specifying problem with computer

Customer Service
Doorway Computer Company
Sioux Falls, SD

Concerning: RMA #xxxxxxx

Dear Service Department:

Enclosed please find my Doorway Bolo 2500 portable computer, returned for service under the extended warranty I purchased with the unit two years ago. Your RMA (Return

Merchandise Authorization) number, given to me by your service adviser, is listed above and on the package that contains the computer.

The screen on the computer is displaying blotches of color in the middle of text. The problem arose last week in the middle of work on a project. I had not installed any new software or made any changes to the operating system before I noticed the problem.

Under terms of the warranty, I expect that the computer will be repaired or replaced within ten days. Please advise me if there are any problems with service.

Sincerely,
Joshua Diamond

Dissatisfaction with repair of computer

Customer Service
Doorway Computer Company
Sioux Falls, SD

Concerning: RMA #xxxxxxxx

Dear Service Department:

Today I received my Doorway Bolo 2500 portable computer, which I had returned for service under the extended warranty.

I was disappointed to find that the problem has not been fully repaired. If you go to a word-processing screen, you will notice large blotches of color that move across the screen from right to left. They seem to become more prominent after the computer has been in use for a while, perhaps as the electronics become warmer.

I do need this computer to be repaired or replaced quickly. Please contact me upon receipt to advise status.

Sincerely,
Joshua Diamond

29 Names and Lists

Dear Reader:

In our modern lives we weave a complex web of addresses, subscriptions, and lists. And the entire network is subject to upset each time we move.

With each change we need to inform friends and business services of our mailing address, telephone number, cell phone number, e-mail address . . . have we left something out from your personal database?

To this section we also add the process of joining waiting lists for services and products: requesting dental appointments, asking for the next available post office box, and other details of modern life.

These letters are simple and to the point. They demand only precision.

Sincerely,
The Authors

Notifying friends of address and phone change

Dear friends:

The good news is that the moving van has left; the bad news is that I'm still surrounded by unopened boxes.

I have moved to a new address, and I have a new phone number:

1212 Delano Court
Smalltown, OH 45601
(xxx) xxx-xxxx

Please drop me a line, give me a call, or send me an e-mail at the address you already have.

Sincerely,
Josh

Notifying friends of change in phone number

Dear friends:

I just wanted to let you know I've gone high tech. I got tired of having my phone number change every time I moved, so I'm now using my cell phone only.

From now on I can be reached anywhere, any time . . . unless I run out of batteries. The phone number is a local call for you, no matter where I have strayed.

My new phone number is (xxx) xxx-xxxx.

Josh

From newly married woman to associates

Dr. Mark Albert
Smalltown Medical Associates
Smalltown, OH

Dear Dr. Albert:

I'm still here at the Smalltown General Hospital lab, but you'll find my name filed under a new letter of the alphabet in the directory.

I was married on May 20 (to Roger Hamilton, head of the physical therapy department) and I will now be known as Morgan Hamilton.

Sincerely,
Morgan Diamond Hamilton
cc: Tory Wolff, office manager
Renatta Beckett, nurse practitioner

To clubs about name change

Smalltown Professional Women's Association
Smalltown, OH

Dear members:

Since my marriage on May 20, I have decided to take my husband's last name. I will now be known as Morgan Diamond Hamilton.

I'm looking forward to many more years of membership in the club, but you'll have to learn to look for my name under a different letter of the alphabet in the club directory.

Sincerely,
Morgan Diamond Hamilton

To magazine about name change

Circulation Department
Fit and Healthy Magazine
Bigtown, NY

Dear People:

Please adjust your records to reflect a change of name. I will now be known as Morgan Diamond Hamilton.

I have attached a copy of the current subscription label.

Sincerely,
Morgan Diamond Hamilton

Notifying friends about keeping maiden name

Sharon and Ron Gilbert
New York, NY

Dear Sharon and Ron:

We wanted to tell you that Jack and I were married on October 16 in a small civil ceremony.

For professional reasons, I will keep my maiden name.

Sincerely,
Susan Eliot

Requesting notification of last-minute travel deals

Emily Redeker
Stay Away Travel Agency
Nearby, OH

Dear Ms. Baedeker:

My husband and I have used your agency on several occasions and were always satisfied with the service and advice. We are interested in taking a cruise sometime in the next year and would like to be notified about any last-minute special deals, cancellations, or spectacular sales.

Now that we are in our retirement, we are very flexible on travel dates, itineraries, and cruise lines. Our main interest lies in finding the best value.

We're not necessarily looking for the cheapest possible cruise; it would especially please us to travel on a super-luxury cruise at a steep discount. Please feel free to call us any time you spot something you think would interest us.

Sincerely,
Monica Diamond

Requesting notification of available dental appointment

Dr. William Dukenfield
Smalltown, OH

Dear Dr. Dukenfield:

On my last visit two weeks ago, you told me I needed to have extensive dental work including two crowns. The earliest available appointment was in four months.

Please put me on your waiting list if any cancellations occur before then. My schedule is relatively flexible.

Sincerely,
John Diamond

Request to schedule dental appointment during school break

Dr. William Dukenfield
Smalltown, OH

Dear Dr. Dukenfield:

My daughter Heather will be attending college this fall. I know from past experience with my son that you keep a few appointments open for students during college winter break which will be January 2 to the 14th.

I'd appreciate it if you could put her on your list for a cleaning and dental checkup during that time.

Sincerely,
Laura Diamond

Requesting safety deposit box at bank

Henry F. Potter, Manager
Smalltown Savings Bank
Smalltown, OH

Dear Mr. Potter:

Please put my name on your waiting list for a small safety deposit box and notify us when it is available. My wife and I have had various accounts at this branch for many years.

Sincerely,
Ron Miller

Requesting a post office box

Postmaster
Smalltown, OH

Dear Postmaster:

Please notify me when the next available small post office box becomes available. We currently receive mail at our home, but would prefer the security of a postal box.

Sincerely,
Morgan Diamond Hamilton

Requesting placement on waiting list for apartment in adult community

Lori Gross, Manager
Lakeview Senior Apartment Complex
Smalltown, OH

Dear Lori:

Thank you for showing us around the Lakeview complex last week. We were very impressed with everything we saw. So much so, that we have decided Lakeview is the place for us.

The unit that would accommodate us best is the one we saw with two bedrooms, equipped for wheelchair access. We would love a view of the lake but would accept a unit on the back side of the complex if that is all that is available.

Please put us on your waiting list. We hope to hear from you soon with encouraging news.

Sincerely,
Ron Miller

30 Banking and Credit Cards

Dear Reader:

Money makes the world go around, although sometimes it may seem that it places us on a treadmill: We have to keep track of savings accounts, checking accounts, mortgages, credit cards, debit cards, and the various credit reports that bring them all together.

Many of the interactions you have with banks and financial institutions must be in writing. This is for your protection and the institution's; you don't want someone else transferring funds or changing the name on your records.

You also should establish a filing system to keep copies of all written communication regarding your finances.

Letters concerning accounts should include essential details such as account numbers, the name that appears on the account, and clear and direct instructions. Letters should not include passwords and blank checks.

Sincerely,
The Authors

Request information on banking services

Henry F. Potter, Manager
Smalltown Savings Bank
Smalltown, OH

Dear Mr. Potter:

I am an incoming freshman at Smalltown University. Please send me information and a list of fees and charges on the various checking account options you have available, including the SU debit card offered to students.

Sincerely,
Heather Diamond

Asking for student line of credit

Henry F. Potter, Manager
Smalltown Savings Bank
Smalltown, OH

Dear Mr. Potter:

Thank you for the information about the various types of checking accounts available at your bank. I have applied for the SU debit card, linked to a checking account.

Is it possible to add a line of credit to the checking account so that I have a cushion in case I overdraw my available funds? My parents, John and Laura Diamond, are customers of the bank and are willing to cosign the application for the line of credit.

Sincerely,
Heather Diamond

Asking for payment of CD on maturity

Customer Service
Smalltown Savings Bank
Smalltown, OH

Concerning: CD #xxx-xxx-xxxx

Dear Customer Service:

Please send me a check for the proceeds of the certificate of deposit listed above when it matures on July 6, 20xx. Thank you.

Joshua Diamond

Asking for rollover of CD on maturity

Customer Service
Smalltown Savings Bank
Smalltown, OH

Concerning: CD #xxx-xxx-xxxx

Dear Customer Service:

The certificate of deposit listed above will mature on July 6, 20xx. I would like the proceeds to be rolled over into a short-term six-month CD.

Please mail confirmation of the rollover.

Thank you.

Joshua Diamond

Asking for information on savings bank life insurance

Life Insurance Department
Smalltown Savings Bank
Smalltown, OH

Dear People:

Please send me information and application forms for savings bank life insurance for myself (age fifty-six) and my wife (age fifty-two).

We are interested in comparing your rates to those for a ten-year level term policy from a commercial insurance company.

Sincerely,
John Diamond

Closing account

Henry F. Potter, Manager
Smalltown Savings Bank
Smalltown, OH

Dear Mr. Potter:

Please close our checking account (xxxx-xxx-xxxx) and savings account (xxxx-xxx-xxxx). We have brought the balances of both accounts to zero.

We are moving out of state and have established a new set of accounts. Thank you for your assistance over the years.

Sincerely,
Michael and Karen Diamond

Requesting copy of appraisal for mortgage

Ditechnic Mortgage Company
Bigtown, NY

Concerning mortgage PA-xxxx-xxxx-xx
Michael and Karen Diamond

Dear People:

We have recently received a mortgage through Ditechnic for our home in Fairview, Pennsylvania. At the closing we received a letter indicating that we could request a copy of the appraisal commissioned by the lender as part of the loan application process.

Please send a copy of the appraisal to us at the address on this letter.

Thank you.

Sincerely,
Michael and Karen Diamond

Contesting bank charge

Henry F. Potter, Manager
Smalltown Savings Bank
Smalltown, OH

Concerning account xxx-xxx-xxxx

Dear Mr. Potter:

I have just received my monthly statement for my checking account and debit card, and I see that I was charged $20 for a one-day overdraft that amounted to $5.25. Immediately after I was notified of the overdraft, I applied for and received a line of credit to protect against such a situation.

At the time I applied for the line of credit I was assured that any charges for the overdraft would be reimbursed. Please credit my account for the $20 fee for the overdraft.

Thank you for your assistance.

Yours truly,
Heather Diamond

Changing name on account

Henry F. Potter, Manager
Smalltown Savings Bank
Smalltown, OH

Concerning accounts xxx-xxx-xxxx and xxx-xxx-xxx1

Dear Mr. Potter:

I will be getting married next month, and will need to change the name on my checking and savings accounts to my married name, which will be Morgan Diamond Hamilton.

Please send whatever forms are necessary to update your records and order new checks.

Sincerely,
Morgan Diamond

Setting up custodial account

Henry F. Potter, Manager
Smalltown Savings Bank
Smalltown, OH

Dear Mr. Potter:

Our accountant has suggested that we make gifts to our great-grandchildren as part of their savings for college.

Please send whatever forms are appropriate for the establishment of two certificates of deposit, one each for Hannah Diamond and Brian Diamond. Our grandson Michael Diamond will be the trustee both for Hannah and for Brian. We are told both accounts should be set up under the Uniform Gift to Minors Act.

Thank you.

Sincerely,
Harold and Monica Diamond

Requesting copy of statement

Henry F. Potter, Manager
Smalltown Savings Bank
Smalltown, OH

Concerning account xxx-xxx-xxxx

Dear Mr. Potter:

I am writing to request a duplicate copy of the August statement for my checking account. The original statement apparently was lost in the mail when I moved from my dorm room to my new apartment in Smalltown.

I understand from the bank regulations that there is a $10 charge for a duplicate copy of the statement. I hope that fee can be waived because I never received the original copy.

Thank you.

Sincerely,
Joshua Diamond

Requesting copy of credit report

Equifax
Atlanta, GA

Concerning: Morgan Diamond, 123 Main Street, Smalltown, OH xxxxx
Social security number: xxx-xx-xxxx

Dear People:

I am writing to request a copy of my credit report to check for inaccuracies and errors.

I was turned down in my request for a line of credit at the Smalltown Savings Bank two weeks ago. According to the letter I received, federal law allows me to receive a free copy of the information you have on file about me within sixty days of having been denied credit, employment, or insurance as a result of a credit report.

My address is listed above.

Sincerely,
Morgan Diamond

Asking for analysis of mortgage

Arthel Watson, Account Executive
Bitech Mortgage Company
Smalltown, OH

Dear Mr. Watson:

Per your offer, enclosed is a copy of our most recent mortgage statement from Bigtown Bank. To summarize, we currently are twelve years into a thirty-year fixed-rate mortgage at an annual percentage rate of 9 percent. The original mortgage was for $200,000, and the current outstanding balance is about $150,000.

We estimate the current worth of our home to be about $300,000.

I would like to see your analysis of our mortgage, with suggestions on a possible refinance of the loan. We would consider a straight refinancing of the outstanding balance as well as a money-out mortgage that would give us about $50,000 at closing.

Please advise.

Sincerely,
John Diamond

Asking for comparison of mortgage refinance options

Arthel Watson, Account Executive
Bitech Mortgage Company
Smalltown, OH

Dear Mr. Watson:

Thank you for your recent analysis of our existing mortgage, in which you recommended a refinancing of the loan to a new fixed-rate thirty-year loan at a lower annual percentage rate. As I understand it, today's very low interest rates make adjustable-rate loans less attractive.

However, I would appreciate it if you would also provide us with costs and benefits of a fifteen-year fixed-rate mortgage to replace our existing loan.

Sincerely,
John Diamond

Granting authority to accountant to disclose information

Robert Kleinman, Certified Public Accountant
Snowdonia, OH

Dear Bob:

I have asked a mortgage broker to look into refinancing the loan on our home. I have told him he can consult with you about any appropriate details of our financial status, and with this letter I grant you permission to disclose information for this purpose only.

We are dealing with Arthel Watson of Bitech Mortgage Company here in Smalltown.

Sincerely,
John Diamond

Change of address for credit card

Customer Service
Universal Credit Card Company
Bigtown, NY

Re: Account xxx-xxx-xxxx

Dear People:

Please change your records for the above credit card account to reflect my new address:

Morgan Diamond
123 New Address
New Place, PA

Thank you.

Sincerely,
Morgan Diamond

Change of name for credit card

Customer Service
Universal Credit Card Company
Bigtown, NY

Re: Account xxx-xxx-xxxx

Dear People:

I will be getting married next month and would like to change the name on my credit card to my married name, which will be Morgan Diamond Hamilton.

Please update your records and send me a new card. I have enclosed a copy of our marriage license; please advise if you need any further documentation.

Thank you.

Sincerely,
Morgan Diamond

Cancel credit card

Customer Service
Universal Credit Card Company
Bigtown, NY

Re: Account xxx-xxx-xxxx

Dear People:

I have not used the credit card listed above in the last two years. Please cancel this card, as I no longer intend to use it.

Thank you.

Sincerely,
Morgan Diamond

Contesting a credit card service charge

Customer Service
Universal Credit Card Company
Bigtown, NY

Re: Account xxx-xxx-xxxx

Dear People:

When paying my last credit card bill I intended to pay the minimum amount due, which was $109.89. However, when I made out the check I misread the amount due, and paid $109.69, a mistake of only twenty cents.

The current bill includes a service charge of $10 for paying less than the minimum due.

This was obviously a mistake on my part, and I would like you to remove this $10 charge. I intend to pay off the entire outstanding balance next month.

Thank you.

Sincerely,
Morgan Diamond

Contesting a credit card purchase

Customer Service
Universal Credit Card Company
Bigtown, NY

Re: Account xxx-xxx-xxxx

Dear People:

I am writing to contest a charge for $250 paid to Mario's Prints in Rural, Ohio, and posted to my current credit card bill.

In October I purchased a signed lithograph from Mario's Prints. I am enclosing a copy of the sales receipt and credit card invoice.

I arranged to have the store ship the package to me at my home address. The item I purchased, as described on my invoice, was not the same as what was delivered to me.

I have attempted to resolve this with Mario's Prints, but they have refused to arrange to pick up the lithograph and issue a refund. I do not wish to keep the item I received, and I do not want to do further business with this company.

The credit card agreement and federal law state that I have the right not to pay the amount due on the property if I have made the purchase in my home state or, if not within my home state, within 100 miles of my current mailing address, and if the purchase price is more than $50.

Please remove the charge from my account and advise me what to do with the unacceptable product from Mario's Prints.

Thank you.

Sincerely,
Morgan Diamond

Submitting a claim under credit card purchase protection plan

Customer Service
Super Blue Card Company
Hometown, NJ

Re: Account xxx-x-xxxx

Dear People:

I am writing to submit a claim under the Purchase Protection Plan that is part of my credit card agreement.

My new camera, which I purchased with the card six weeks ago, was damaged when it fell from my hands to the pavement. I have attached a copy of the original purchase receipt for the camera and the credit card slip, both of which show the camera's price of $599.

Under terms of the plan, I understand you will pay for repair or replacement of any product purchased within the past ninety days.

Thank you for your assistance.

Sincerely,
Morgan Diamond

Requesting annual report of public company

Director of Investor Relations
Smalltown Amalgamated Industries, Inc.
Smalltown, OH

Dear Director:

I am considering buying stock in your company. Please send me a copy of your most recent annual report and 10-K filing.

Sincerely,
John Diamond

Requesting issuance of credit card to wife

American Excess Credit Card
Philadelphia, PA

Re: Account xxxx-xxxx-xxxx-xxxx

Dear Customer Service:

I will be married on May 20 of this year. Please issue a card for my wife in her name, Morgan Diamond Hamilton. Her social security number is xxx-xx-xxxx, and her date of birth is 05/31/1978.

Sincerely,
Roger Hamilton

Requesting issuance of credit card to child

Mastervisa Credit Card
Atlanta, GA

Re: Account xxxx-xxxx-xxxx-xxxx

Dear Customer Service:

Please issue an additional card under the above account for use by my daughter, Heather Diamond.

She will be an undergraduate at Smalltown University beginning in September. Her social security number is xxx-xx-xxxx, and her date of birth is 11/06/1985.

Sincerely,
John Diamond

31 Insurance Matters

Dear Reader:

Insurance is another part of modern life in which you need to get information in writing. Your policies and any decisions on claims will be communicated to you as official documents; any questions you pose or information you provide should be written as well.

If you have a good insurance agent, he or she should be able to assist you in crafting any formal letters to the insurance company. If you have any questions about your legal rights or if a lawsuit or other action is contemplated, you should consult an attorney before sending any letters of substance to an insurance company or adjuster.

The letters in this section deal with requests for information and straightforward challenges to decisions of the insurance company. Be sure to include your policy number and your name and address—as they appear on the policy—in your letters.

Yours truly,
The Authors

Transmittal of bills to insurance company

Patricia Paulson
Small Help Insurance
Smalltown, OH

Re: Homeowners Policy xxxx-xxx-xxx
28 New Street, Smalltown, OH

Dear Patricia:

We have completed the repairs to our house caused by the fall of the large oak tree in the front yard. As you know, the insurance adjuster visited the next day and authorized us to remove the tree and make repairs to the roof of the garage where limbs fell. He instructed us to send the bills to you for submission to the insurance company.

Enclosed please find copies of receipts for the tree surgeon and the carpenter. They total $1,750.

Please let me know if there is anything else I need to do to receive reimbursement for this loss.

Sincerely,
John Diamond

Changing status of health insurance

Most States Insurance Company
Bigtown, NY

Re: Policy No. xxxxxx-xxxxx

Dear People:

Please remove my daughter, Morgan Diamond, from the above-mentioned health insurance policy and adjust our monthly premium accordingly.

Morgan has taken a full-time job at a company that provides health insurance.

Sincerely,
John Diamond

Challenging ruling on health insurance

Patricia Paulson
Small Help Insurance
Smalltown, OH

Re: Most States Insurance
Policy xxxx-xxx-xxx

Dear Patricia:

Per our conversation earlier today, I am writing to document our appeal of a ruling by Most States Insurance regarding payment for physical therapy for our son, Joshua.

Joshua was involved in an automobile accident on April 25. He was taken to the emergency room and treated there for a sprained knee.

Dr. Martin Todd advised him to have physical therapy sessions on a weekly basis for a minimum of five weeks. At the end of the five weeks the therapist determined that he would have to come in for four additional sessions of therapy.

Joshua has now been released from therapy and the sessions are completed.

I received notification from Most States Insurance that the four additional therapy sessions would not be covered because they were not authorized at the time of the accident. Until the extent of the injury and the progress of my son's treatment were determined, there was no way of knowing just how many sessions he would need.

All the physical therapy is the result of the original accident and should be covered. According to the policy, insured clients are eligible to receive as many as twelve weeks of physical therapy for each covered incident.

Please assist us in having the insurance company re-evaluate its ruling and pay for the necessary physical therapy sessions.

Sincerely,
John Diamond

Inquiring about insurance coverage abroad

Patricia Paulson
Small Help Insurance
Smalltown, OH

Re: Most States Insurance
Re: Policy xxx-xxx-xxx

Dear Patricia:

My wife and I will be taking an extended cruise to Central America in April.

We want to find out what sort of medical coverage our present health insurance policy provides while we are aboard the cruise ship and on shore. We will be visiting Mexico, Honduras, Belize, and Panama. Does our policy cover visits to the ship's doctor? What if we need to visit an emergency room on shore?

We'd also like to find out about available travel insurance that would cover the cost of lost deposits if we were forced to cancel the cruise because of illness or family emergency. The cost of the cruise is $3,995.

Sincerely,
Harold Diamond

Inquiring about medical coverage abroad

Patricia Paulson
Small Help Insurance
Smalltown, OH

Re: Policy xxxxx

Dear Pat:

My daughter Heather will be going to France in May on a school-sponsored trip with the French Club. Please advise whether our medical policy will cover her while she is in Europe.

If it will not, I would like to purchase additional insurance for this one-time event. She will be leaving on May 15, so we need to have everything in place before then.

Sincerely,
John Diamond

Inquiring about travel insurance

On the Road Again Insurance
Hartford, CT

Dear People:

Please send me information about travel insurance. I am interested in a policy that includes medical coverage abroad, emergency transportation, and cancellation coverage in case a medical emergency forces us to cancel a trip before it begins.

The policy would be for my daughter Heather, age eighteen, for a high school class trip, departing May 15 and returning May 25.

Thank you.

Sincerely,
John Diamond

Asking for comparison of travel policies

Patricia Paulson
Small Help Insurance
Smalltown, OH

Dear Pat:

Thank you for researching our medical coverage to see if it would cover Heather on her upcoming European trip. It sounds as if the extremely limited coverage the policy offers while she is out of the country is not sufficient for our needs.

I have examined the travel policy you sent us, from TravelSafe Insurance. Would you please compare it with the enclosed proposal we received directly from On the Road Again Insurance?

Thanks for your help.

Sincerely,
John Diamond

Asking for review of all personal policies

Patricia Paulson
Small Help Insurance
Smalltown, OH

Dear Pat:

It has been several years since we last reviewed all of the coverage we have in our home, car, boat, and life insurance policies. Would you please go over all of the various policies we have in effect through your agency to determine whether any of them need to be updated, upgraded, or are no longer needed? In addition, of course, we would like to find out whether any lower-cost options are available.

Please give me a call when you have completed the review to schedule an appointment to go over all of our policies.

Sincerely,
John Diamond

Asking for review of all personal policies from new agency

Michael Harkit
Friendly Insurance
Nearby, OH

Dear Mr. Harkit:

I am considering moving our various insurance policies to a new agency, and your company has been recommended to me.

Enclosed are copies of our current home, car, boat, and life insurance policies. I would appreciate it if you would go over all of them and consider whether any need to be updated, upgraded, or are no longer needed. In addition, of course, we would like to find out whether any lower-cost options are available.

Please give me a call when you have completed the review to schedule an appointment to meet with you and receive a proposal for new policies.

Sincerely,
John Diamond

Asking advice about teenage drivers

Patricia Paulson
Small Help Insurance
Smalltown, OH

Dear Pat:

Our daughter Heather is about to begin driver's education classes at Smalltown High School.

I would appreciate your advice on the best way to properly cover Heather and the entire family after she receives her driver's license.

I have a few specific questions:

1. Should we purchase an umbrella policy to increase the liability coverage for the family?
2. If Heather buys her own car, would it be best to register it in her name, or mine? Which would result in a higher insurance rate? Which exposes the family to greater liability?
3. One of our cars is leased. Will Heather be allowed to drive that vehicle?

Thanks for your help.

Sincerely,
John Diamond

Asking insurance agent's advice about new car purchase

Patricia Paulson
Small Help Insurance
Smalltown, OH

Dear Pat:

We are shopping for a new car to replace our elderly Ford. I read in a personal finance book that different makes and models of cars can have significantly different collision and comprehensive insurance costs. The author recommended checking with your insurance agent before buying a new car. Would you please give me an estimate on insurance costs for the following vehicles?

20xx Mercury Melange SUV, 3.0 V8 engine, 4WD.

20xx General Megamotors Puttputt All-Terrain, 2.6 V6 engine, AWD.

20xx Mercedes Bombastisch, 2.8 V8 engine, 4WD, sunroof, 36-CD player.

Let's assume that we will want coverage identical to what we have now. I'd appreciate your advice as soon as possible, because we plan to buy the car within the next two weeks.

Sincerely,
John Diamond

Name change for marriage

Charles Preston
Preston Insurance Company
Smalltown, OH

Re: Automobile policy xxxx-xxxx
Most States Insurance

Dear Mr. Preston:

Please update my automobile insurance policy to reflect the fact that I am now married and have taken my husband's name.

Please also add my husband, Roger Hamilton, as an occasional driver of my car. I have attached a photocopy of his driver's license.

Sincerely,
Morgan Diamond Hamilton

32 Retirement and Estate Planning

Dear Reader:

Every one of us hopes to live long and well, to be able to enjoy a comfortable old age, and to be able to take care of our loved ones when we pass.

We're not going to tell you how to plan your finances. But we can offer one piece of very important advice: Get it in writing.

Do not rely on any verbal promises of services or performance. Insist upon written descriptions of the work that will be performed by an attorney or accountant. And for clarity, pose your own questions and issue your own instructions in writing.

Cordially,
The Authors

Asking employer for pension update

Karen Krow, Director
Office of Personnel Management
Smalltown Community College
Smalltown, OH

Dear Karen:

I am writing to request an update on my pension portfolio. While I do not plan to retire any time soon, I would like to do some long-range planning.

Please provide a statement of my contributions, the college's matching payments, and current investments.

Sincerely,
Laura Diamond

Seeking retirement advice

John B. Tipton
Smalltown Trust Company
Smalltown, OH

Dear Mr. Tipton:

I am considering hiring a financial adviser to help me prepare for retirement. You have been recommended to me by a colleague as someone who can deal with the complexities of retirement planning for a self-employed businessperson.

I currently am fifty-six years old. I have owned my own business, a retail music store, for the past thirty-five years.

Please contact me to discuss your services and arrange for a consultation.

Sincerely,
John Diamond

Requesting financial planning assistance

J.C. Nickel
Copperplate Financial Advisors
Nearby, OH

Dear Mr. Nickel:

My wife and I would like to make an appointment to discuss our finances. We are both in our early thirties. We want to set up a college fund for our two young children and prepare for our eventual retirement.

I have a statement of net worth and copies of all of our investments available to share with you. Please give me a call to set up an appointment.

Sincerely,
Michael Diamond

Inquiring about estate planning

Howard Black
Black & White, Inc.
Smalltown, OH

Dear Mr. Black:

You were recommended to us as someone who specializes in estate planning.

My wife and I are both in our eighties. We have recently sold our house and moved to a retirement community in Smalltown. We are both in good health for our age, but my wife is confined to a wheelchair.

At this point in our lives, I would like to see that the money we have is being handled properly. I have grandchildren I would like to give gifts to, but I am unsure of how to do it with the best possible tax advantage. I also want to see that my wife is provided for should something happen to me.

And there is one additional gift of money my wife and I would like to make. Our son Donald passed away almost thirty years ago when he was a student at Smalltown High School. I would like to endow a college scholarship in his name.

I look forward to hearing from you soon. We would appreciate it if you could meet with us at our apartment.

Sincerely,
Ron Miller

Hiring an estate planner

Howard Black
Black & White, Inc.
Smalltown, OH

Dear Howard:

Thank you for meeting with us at our apartment. We liked your ideas and want to engage you to help us plan our estate matters.

Please call me to discuss the next step.

Sincerely,
Ron Miller

Giving instructions to an estate planner

Howard Black
Black & White, Inc.
Smalltown, OH

Dear Howard:

In response to your questions, Emma and I have decided as follows:

1. You will structure our estate so that we can take advantage of the maximum tax-free gift provisions for our grandchildren;
2. Our finances will be structured so that it is minimally impacted by estate taxes, and

3. We will be able to make a substantial gift to endow a college scholarship at Smalltown High School in the name of our late son, Donald.

I look forward to hearing from you once you are under way on establishing our plan.

Sincerely,
Ron Miller

Question to accountant

Robert Gross
Gross Income Tax Accounting Services
Smalltown, OH

Dear Bob:

I have engaged Howard Black for estate planning. He may be contacting you for some details about our holdings; this letter will serve as permission for you to disclose appropriate information to him.

On the tax front: Are fees paid to an estate planner tax-deductible? Are there any other steps I should take for tax purposes?

Sincerely,
Ron Miller

33 Charitable Contributions

Dear Reader:

It is a most worthy goal to be wealthy enough to be able to help those less fortunate. It is also worthy to make sure that your contributions—large or small—are put to proper use.

In this chapter, we include letters written to check on the activities of charities, to accompany a gift, and to respond to an appeal.

We appreciate your efforts.

Sincerely,
The Authors

Checking on charitable organization

Charitable Trust Bureau
Office of the Attorney General
State Capitol
Street Address, State, ZIP Code

Dear People:

I am considering making a contribution to a group called Citizens for a Better Smalltown, a registered charity in this state.

Please send me a copy of the most recent report filed with the state, along with your guidelines to help me interpret the filing.

Sincerely,
John Diamond

Requesting annual report of charitable organization

Citizens for a Better Smalltown
Smalltown, OH

Dear Executive Officer:

I received a copy of a solicitation for a contribution to your charitable organization.

Please send me a copy of your most recent annual report and federal form IRS 990 or IRS 990PF along with information about the percentage of funds raised that are paid to professional fundraisers.

Sincerely,
John Diamond

Change in sponsorship level

Aimee Poulet
Friends of the Piping Plovers
Smalltown, OH

Dear Aimee:

For the past five years my husband and I have been active supporters of your organization. We deeply believe that piping plovers need to be protected from uncaring ATV drivers. Throughout that time, we have been able to give at the highest level of sponsorship.

We now find that we must reduce somewhat the amount we are able to contribute. We remain committed to the goals of the FPP.

Please accept our donation, and keep up the good work.

Sincerely,
Monica Diamond

Seeking sponsorship status

Aimee Poulet
Friends of the Piping Plovers
Smalltown, OH

Dear Aimee:

We are pleased to once again support the good work of the Friends of the Piping Plovers. We deeply believe that piping plovers need to be protected from uncaring ATV drivers.

We would like to increase our contribution from the Fledgling to the Mother Hen level. As I understand it, this level of gift includes front-row seats at the upcoming concert by Jackson and the Shelties at the Smalltown Bandstand.

Keep up the good work.

Sincerely,
Laura Diamond

Thanks for contribution made in name

Dear Monica and Harold:

I just received notification from the Arthritis Foundation of the contribution you made in my name. I couldn't have asked for a better birthday gift.

I have been fighting this condition since I was a young girl, which I will admit was many, many years ago.

I support the good work of the Arthritis Foundation. Your gift—with my name on it—will help them find treatments and cures for all of us who suffer from the condition.

Sincerely,
Betty

Thanks to company for matching contribution

John Klein, President
Klein Graphics Company
Fairview, PA

Dear Mr. Klein:

I am a new employee at Klein Graphics, and very happy with the company and my supervisors and coworkers. I want to express my thanks for the company's policy of matching contributions to a number of community organizations.

I have just become a member of the local Public Radio station WFVW-FM, and am very pleased to find that Klein Graphics will match my contribution.

Sincerely,
Karen Diamond

Asking charity to pick up items

Habitat for Smalltown
Smalltown, OH

Dear People:

My wife and I will be moving from our house at the above address to a much smaller apartment in May. We have a number of items including furniture, clothing, and household items we would be glad to donate to Habitat for Smalltown for fundraising.

I'd appreciate a call to arrange pickup of the items.

Sincerely,
Ron Miller

Confirming pickup of items

Ray Carter
Habitat for Smalltown
Smalltown, OH

Dear Mr. Carter:

Thank you for your letter about the items we are donating to Habitat for Smalltown.

Of the dates and times you proposed, April 16 at 2 P.M. works best for us. Would you please call to confirm that time?

We are happy to make this contribution to a worthy cause.

Sincerely,
Ron Miller

Declining to make alumni contribution

Patsy MacGovern, '01
Smalltown University Alumni Association
Smalltown University
Smalltown, OH

Dear Patsy:

Thank you for putting me on the Smalltown University Alumni list. I appreciate receiving the magazine and newsletter.

Unfortunately, I am unable to send a contribution at this time. I just graduated in June, and have enrolled at Smalltown University School of Law.

At some time in the future, though, I hope to be able to give back to the university.

Sincerely,
Joshua Diamond

Declining to make alumni contribution, alternate version

Patsy MacGovern, '01
Smalltown University Alumni Association
Smalltown University
Smalltown, OH

Dear Patsy:

Thank you for putting me on the Smalltown University Alumni list. I appreciate receiving the magazine and newsletter.

Until I pay off my college loans, though, I don't expect to be able to make a contribution to the university. I hope to do so at some time in the future.

Sincerely,
Joshua Diamond

Clothing collection for flood victims

Dear members of the congregation:

As you all know from seeing the pictures on television and in the newspaper, Central America has been devastated by a series of hurricanes. Tens of thousands of people are homeless and without food, adequate clothing, and even the barest necessities for survival.

I feel that we are being called upon to do something to help.

We are designating Saturday, September 19, as "Help from Smalltown" day. We will be happy to accept canned goods, warm clothes and blankets, and cash of any denomination. Please bring all donations to the church grounds between 10 A.M. and 4 P.M.

Thank you for helping your fellow human beings in their time of desperate need.

Sincerely,
Rev. Peter Hall
Smalltown Congregational Church
Smalltown, OH

Asking for volunteers for Thanksgiving soup kitchen

Dear members of the congregation:

As we give thanks this coming Thursday, many of our parishioners will be giving of their time at the annual Smalltown Soup Kitchen Thanksgiving Day Dinner.

Marcy and I will be there, and we would love to see as many of the members of our congregation as possible. Anyone who has participated in the past will tell you it has been one of the most rewarding experiences of their life. Some even bring the entire family, making the soup kitchen a part of their own day of thanksgiving.

We need cooks, sous-chefs, servers, and cleanup staff. Please contact me and I will set you up with the appropriate people.

Thank you.

Sincerely,
Rev. Peter Hall
Smalltown Congregational Church
Smalltown, OH

Establishing memorial scholarship

Patrick Norton, Ph.D., Principal
Smalltown High School
Smalltown, OH

Dear Dr. Norton:

My wife, Emma, and I have been residents of Smalltown for most of our lives. Our three children attended Smalltown High School, and two of them graduated with honors. Our son, Donald, died of juvenile leukemia when he was a junior more than thirty years ago.

Donald was a very special person. He never gave in to his illness. When he passed away the whole town grieved with us. We were especially touched by the dedication of a plaque outside the gymnasium, where he was all too briefly a star on the basketball court.

We have decided we would like to establish a memorial college scholarship in his name. In this way, we hope to extend the memory of Donald and help a new generation of Smalltown kids spread their wings.

Please let me know when I may come in to discuss this with you.

Sincerely,
Ron Miller

Follow-up on memorial scholarship

Patrick Norton, Ph.D., Principal
Smalltown High School
Smalltown, OH

Dear Dr. Norton:

Thank you for meeting with me on Thursday to discuss the Donald Miller Memorial Scholarship.

We expect to be able to establish a perpetual fund that will generate at least $2,000 per year to benefit a student who best typifies Donald's determination to overcome life's challenges. In the scholarship's initial years, my wife and I will serve on a committee with a representative appointed by the school district to choose the winner.

I have asked Howard Black, our estate planner, to get in touch with you and the school district's financial officer to work out the details.

Sincerely,
Ron Miller

Authorization to financial adviser to meet with school

Howard Black
Black & White, Inc.
Smalltown, OH

Dear Howard:

We have worked out the basic structure for the Donald Miller Memorial Scholarship with Smalltown High School.

Would you please call the principal, Dr. Patrick Norton, to arrange a meeting to work out the details of the creation of the trust fund for the scholarship and to set up the award committee?

Thank you.

Sincerely,
Ron Miller

Announcing matching contribution for radio station

Dear employees:

As all of you know, Diamond Music Hall has been a sponsor of radio station WSMA for many years. In fact, it is the official background music heard throughout the store.

We have decided to increase our level of support during the station's annual pledge drive by matching any contribution by an employee of Diamond Music Hall up to $500.

We hope you appreciate the quality of music and information that WSMA provides as much as we do, and that you will join with us in helping the station reach its goal during its fundraising campaign.

Sincerely,
John Diamond

Asking if contribution to charity can be matched

John Diamond, President
Diamond Music Hall
Smalltown, OH

Dear Mr. Diamond:

I have been a full-time employee in the shipping department of Diamond Music Hall for the past six years. I very much enjoy the opportunity to work here and hope to explore other opportunities within the company in the future.

I read your recent memo in which you announced that the company would match any contribution to WSMA radio. I, too, am a fan of that station and appreciate the company's willingness to encourage employees to contribute to a worthy cause.

My choice for a personal charity, though, happens to be the Smalltown Boys & Girls Club. This organization did a lot for me when I was growing up, and I am sure that many of the kids of Smalltown would tell you the same.

Would Diamond Music Hall be willing to make the same very generous offer to match gifts to the Smalltown Boys & Girls Club?

Sincerely,
Roberta Corkin

Response to employee request to match contribution

Roberta Corkin
Smalltown, OH

Dear Roberta:

Thank you for your letter. We are very appreciative of your service with the company.

I agree with everything you say in your letter. We are truly fortunate in Smalltown to have such a fine facility as the Boys & Girls Club. I am very familiar with it as my son, now in law school, played baseball and soccer there.

You may not know that Diamond Music Hall already gives a substantial cash contribution to the club each year, and we also support its annual fall clambake by buying a block of tickets, which we offer to our employees.

Our policy here is to spread out our contributions to as many worthy charitable institutions as we can. Since we already make a donation to the Boys & Girls Club, a matching program would take away from some other community institution.

We're going to keep to our budget for this year, but I would welcome your participation on our charitable contributions committee in the fall. That group advises the board of directors on donations for the coming year. If you'd like to be on the committee, please let me know.

Sincerely,
John Diamond

Appointment to charitable contributions committee

Roberta Corkin
Smalltown, OH

Dear Roberta:

I am pleased to appoint you to the charitable contributions committee of Diamond Music Hall. We are dedicated to supporting our community institutions in every way we can. In the current fiscal year, our company plans to donate $50,000 to area charitable organizations.

As a member of the committee, you will advise me and the board of directors on the best way to make a positive impact in Smalltown.

The first meeting of the committee is scheduled for just after Labor Day. You'll receive a schedule and agenda a few weeks before the session.

Thank you so much for your participation.

Sincerely,
John Diamond

34 Real Estate Matters

Dear Reader:

For most of us, buying a home is the biggest single purchase of our life, and selling it is one of the most significant events. Although you can buy or sell a home on your own, it often makes sense to hire a professional real estate agent to assist you.

In this section, we'll cover some common real estate matters regarding agents, attorneys, moving companies, and the new owners.

Sincerely,
The Authors

Asking for real estate appraisal

Smalltown Real Estate Company
Smalltown, OH

Dear People:

After forty years here in Smalltown, we are considering selling our home and moving into a condominium or retirement community.

We would like to meet with you to hear your suggestions about the best way to market our home.

Please contact us to make an appointment to view the house and give us an appraisal.

Sincerely,
Ron and Emma Miller

Engaging a real estate agent

Jane Gordon
Smalltown Real Estate
Smalltown, OH

Dear Jane:

Thanks for coming over on Tuesday. We enjoyed meeting you and feel confident you will represent us well in the sale of our house.

This is a major step for us. We have been very happy here for forty years. We hope the next owners love it as much as we have.

Sincerely,
Ron Miller

Seeking bid for moving

Armstrong Moving
Smalltown, OH

Dear People:

We will be moving from our house at 18 Meadow Street, Smalltown, to the Lakeview Apartments in May. Would you please contact us about an estimate of the cost of moving our furniture to the new address?

Thank you.

Sincerely,
Ron Miller

To new owners of house

Dear Lisa and Tom:

Now that the papers have been signed and the moving trucks have come and gone, Ron and I wanted to drop you a note wishing you well as the new owners of 18 Meadow Street.

We hope that you will be as happy as we were during the forty years we lived there. We built the house soon after we were married, and we saw our children grow from infants to college students to young adults with lives of their own.

We are now moving on to a simpler way of life but leave feeling confident that our home will be cared for by a family who will cherish it as we did.

Sincerely,
Emma Miller

Assistance for job-related move

Julie Stanton
Human Resources Department
Moneysworth Investment Group
Fairview, PA

Dear Ms. Stanton:

I have just accepted a position as a financial consultant with Moneysworth Investment Group. I begin work on July 15.

Roger Harrison instructed me to contact you for assistance in moving my family from Smalltown, Ohio, to the Fairview area.

We will need a moving van to clear our possessions from our apartment and place them into storage while we look for a home in Fairview.

My wife and I have two children, ages 4 and 6. We would appreciate any assistance your office can provide, including references to real estate agents, recommendations on schools, and any other advice about life in Fairview.

My wife, Karen, will be managing our move. Please call her at home at (xxx) xxx-xxxx.

Thank you for your assistance.

Sincerely,
Michael Diamond

Requesting assistance from relocation agency

Paula Quinn
Quality Home Real Estate
Fairview, PA

Dear Ms. Quinn:

I have accepted a position with Moneysworth Investment Group, beginning July 15. Julie Stanton in the human resources department there recommended that I contact you to begin the process of looking for a home in the Fairview area.

I am married with two children, ages 4 and 6. My son will be entering second grade, and has attended a public school in Smalltown, Ohio. Our daughter will be starting preschool.

My wife has previously been employed part-time as a business consultant. She will explore job opportunities in and around the Fairview area.

We would like to concentrate our search on a house with at least four bedrooms in a suburban location. We prefer a two-story home with a porch or deck for the children. This will be our first home, so we expect to be looking at entry-level prices.

I would prefer a commute to Moneysworth of no more than one hour each way.

My wife, Karen, is managing our move. Please call her at (xxx) xxx-xxxx to arrange a time when we can go house hunting.

Sincerely,
Michael Diamond

Follow-up letter to agent about house hunting

Paula Quinn
Quality Home Real Estate
Fairview, PA

Dear Paula:

Thank you for your time last Saturday. It certainly was a whirlwind tour, but it did give us a good overall view of the area.

We agree with your assessment that we will get more for our money if we concentrate on an area outside of Fairview. We were impressed with Southville. It would mean a commute of about fifty-five minutes for my husband, which is about as far as he is willing to go.

Southville also appears to have a good public school system and some high-tech companies where I might explore job opportunities.

For round two, then, let's concentrate on Southville in the price range we discussed.

Sincerely,
Karen Diamond

Confirming moving arrangements

John Boxer, Relocation Specialist
Moveit Moving & Storage
Smalltown, OH

Dear Mr. Boxer:

This will confirm arrangements for the move of our possessions from our apartment in Smalltown, Ohio, to our new home in Southville, Pennsylvania.

All arrangements have been made through the office of Julie Stanton of the human resources department at Moneysworth Investment Group, which will be paying all expenses associated with the move.

We understand that the moving van will be at our apartment at 16 Pine Street, Apartment 2B, in Smalltown, Ohio, between 7 and 8 A.M. on July 28. Your crew will box up our possessions and load the truck that day.

The van will deliver the contents to 84 Willow Street, Southville, Pennsylvania, between 7 and 8 A.M. on July 29.

Please let us know if there are any changes to the schedule.

Sincerely,
Karen Diamond
cc: Julie Stanton, Human Resources Department
Moneysworth Investment Group

Claim for damages during move

John Boxer, Relocation Specialist
Moveit Moving & Storage
Smalltown, OH

Dear Mr. Boxer:

On July 28 your company moved our possessions from Smalltown, Ohio, to Southville, Pennsylvania.

For the most part, the move was successful. However, a few items were damaged, including a framed mirror that was cracked. I have enclosed a list of the damaged or broken objects and their estimated value.

All of the items on the list were packed by your employees, and none were marked on the inventory sheet as being damaged prior to the move.

Please advise us of your claim procedure.

Sincerely,
Karen Diamond
cc: Julie Stanton, Human Resources DepartmentL
Moneysworth Investment Group

Compliment to real estate agent

Paula Quinn
Quality Home Real Estate
Fairview, PA

Dear Paula:

We have moved into our new home in Southville, and eventually we expect to get back to our new version of normal. It's been quite hectic, but we love the new house and neighborhood.

I wanted to thank you again for all your help. It may sound trite, but we couldn't have done it without you. I will certainly pass on my positive feedback to the people at Moneysworth Investment Group.

Sincerely,
Karen Diamond

Hiring attorney for sale of house by owner

Arthur Kirk, Esq.
Smalltown, OH

Dear Mr. Kirk:

We have received an acceptable offer for the purchase of our house in Smalltown. The deal was arranged without the involvement of a real estate agent.

We would like to hire an attorney to handle the closing of the real estate transfer. Please contact us to arrange a time when we may meet.

Sincerely,
Sylvia and Donald Kay

35 Apartments

Dear Reader:

A lease is a legally binding contract, and regardless of whether your relations with the landlord are friendly or combative, informal or formal, you should conduct much of your business in writing. Before you repaint your bathroom in Day-Glo green, you should ask for permission in writing; when it comes time to give notice about ending the lease, you should do so in a formal letter to protect yourself.

In this section, we'll include some common communications to landlords as well as letters of inquiry in search of an apartment.

Sincerely,
The Authors

Asking for repairs in apartment

Jack Whalen, Manager
Evergreen Apartments
Smalltown, OH

Re: Apartment 16A

Dear Jack:

I have noticed a spreading water stain on the ceiling of my living room. I suspect there is a leak in the roof.

I'd suggest you have maintenance check the attic above my apartment and the ceiling as soon as possible to avoid serious damage. At the very least, I'm going to need a touchup of the paint on the ceiling.

Thank you.

Sincerely,
Morgan Diamond

Second letter asking for repairs in apartment

Jack Whalen, Manager
Evergreen Apartments
Smalltown, OH

Re: Apartment 16A

Dear Jack:

As you know, it has been raining for much of the past two weeks, and the apparent leak in the roof above my apartment seems to be getting worse. I am concerned that a section of the ceiling may fall.

I have heard nothing from you since I notified you of the problem ten days ago. I do need to have the problem tended to soon.

Sincerely,
Morgan Diamond

Serious problem in apartment

Jack Whalen, Manager
Evergreen Apartments
Smalltown, OH

Re: Apartment 16A

Dear Jack:

I must have the leak in the ceiling of my apartment tended to immediately. It has spread across an entire corner of the living room and extended into the kitchen, and I fear that a section of the plasterboard may fall at any time.

I have brought this to your attention twice in the past three weeks, and nothing has been done to make repairs.

I have consulted with the City Housing Department, and they said they will send an inspector to the apartment next week. They told me that they may withdraw the certificate of habitability for the entire apartment building if they find serious structural or health defects.

Please call me immediately to advise when repairs will be undertaken.

Sincerely,
Morgan Diamond

Requesting apartment painting and cleaning

Manager
A Different Place Apartments
Smalltown, OH

Re: Apartment 10A

Dear Manager:

In September of this year I will be getting married, and my wife will be moving into my apartment.

I have occupied my apartment for four years. Under terms of the rental agreement, I am entitled to a paint job and carpet cleaning once every three years.

I would like to have this work done before our wedding in mid-May. Could you please advise when maintenance can spruce up my apartment?

Sincerely,
Roger Hamilton

Thanks for arranging painting and cleaning

Roger Williams, Manager
A Different Place Apartments
Smalltown, OH

Re: Apartment 10A

Dear Mr. Williams:

Thank you for your kind note about my upcoming marriage. I look forward to introducing you to my new wife.

Per your letter, you will be repainting the interior walls and ceiling of the apartment. The windows and screens will be cleaned from the outside, and the wall-to-wall carpeting is to be shampooed.

Please advise as to the timetable for such work to begin.

Sincerely,
Roger Hamilton

Asking for permission to make alteration to apartment

Roger Williams, Manager
A Different Place Apartments
Smalltown, OH

Re: Apartment 10A

Dear Mr. Williams:

I would like permission to add a deadbolt lock to the front door of my apartment.

I understand this is to be done at my own expense and I must provide the office with a key to this lock. Please advise whether you want me to engage a locksmith for this job or whether you would prefer to have the maintenance department install the lock.

Sincerely,
Roger Hamilton

Asking for permission to paint apartment

Manager
Shorewood Apartment Complex
Smalltown, OH

Dear Manager:

Thank you for your assistance in finding a one-bedroom unit for me. I now have enough space.

For some reason the previous tenant must have enjoyed a purple bedroom. I don't. I would like to repaint the room—at my own expense—in a more neutral color. Under the terms of my lease, I must get permission. Please advise.

Sincerely,
Joshua Diamond

Safety complaint at apartment

Roger Williams, Manager
A Different Place Apartments
Smalltown, OH

Dear Mr. Williams:

I am writing to make you aware of a serious fire threat caused by one of the tenants in the building.

The tenants directly above me in 11A have a small gas grill on their deck, which they use quite often. This is in violation of the terms of the rental agreement and of the Smalltown fire code.

I have brought this to my neighbors' attention on numerous occasions but they refuse to do anything about it.

I am very uncomfortable about a barbecue on a wooden deck in a wooden apartment building. I would appreciate your attention to this matter as soon as possible.

Sincerely,
Roger Hamilton

Complaint about occupancy of apartment

Manager
Shorewood Apartment Complex
Smalltown, OH

Dear Manager:

I have just moved into Apartment 32B, and am enjoying my stay here. However, I do have a concern about one of my neighbors.

When I signed my lease it was emphasized to me that there could be no more than two persons living full-time in a studio apartment. That is definitely not the case in the apartment directly above mine, 33B.

During the one month I have been here, there must have been at least six adults and three young children somehow squeezed into that studio apartment at any one time. The constant noise, the traffic into and out of the apartment, and the four cars they use is very annoying.

Please look into the matter and advise me of the resolution as soon as possible.

Sincerely,
Joshua Diamond

Requesting additional parking space

Roger Williams, Manager
A Different Place Apartments
Smalltown, OH

Re: Apartment 10A

Dear Mr. Williams:

As you know, my wife will be moving into my apartment with me after our marriage this May.

We will need a second parking space in front of our unit. Please advise.

Thank you.

Sincerely,
Roger Hamilton

Asking for notification if another apartment becomes available

Manager
Shorewood Apartment Complex
Smalltown, OH

Re: Apartment 32B

Dear Manager:

I recently moved into a studio apartment at Shorewood.

I now find that I need more space. Would you please advise me if a one-bedroom apartment becomes available?

I prefer a ground floor unit, but would consider an apartment on the second or third floor.

Sincerely,
Joshua Diamond

Asking for short-term renewal of lease

Jack Whalen, Manager
Evergreen Apartments
Smalltown, OH

Re: Apartment 16A

Dear Jack:

The lease on my apartment expires this June. As you know, I will be getting married about that time, and plan to move to a new apartment with my husband.

I would like to extend the lease on my present apartment by one month, until the end of July, while our new home is being painted.

Please advise if this is possible and what the rent would be for the extra month.

Sincerely,
Morgan Diamond

Accepting apartment

Lori Lei, Manager
Lakeview Apartments
Smalltown, OH

Dear Lori:

Thanks for your call. As you requested, I am writing to formally accept tenancy of the one-bedroom lake-view unit at Lakeview Apartments on May 1 of this year.

We will be in shortly to sign the lease and deliver our security deposit and first month's rent as required.

Thank you again.

Sincerely,
Ron Miller

Notice of intent to move

Jack Whalen, Manager
Evergreen Apartments
Smalltown, OH

Re: Apartment 16A

Dear Jack:

My lease expires on July 31, 20xx. I will vacate the apartment on or before that date and will not renew my lease.

Sincerely,
Morgan Diamond

Notice of intent to sublet

Jack Whalen, Manager
Evergreen Apartments
Smalltown, OH

Re: Apartment 23B

Dear Jack:

I am writing to notify you that I intend to sublease my apartment, as permitted under the lease agreement.

Beginning on February 1, 20xx, the apartment will be occupied by Manuel Martinez. I have attached the required sublease form provided by the management office.

I understand that as the original lessee, it is my responsibility to see that monthly payments are made through the end of my lease agreement on June 30. I have made Mr. Martinez aware of all of the regulations of the apartment complex.

Sincerely,
Morgan Diamond

Asking for return of apartment security deposit

Sanjit Patel, Manager
Woodbridge Apartments
Smalltown, OH

Dear Mr. Patel:

When I moved with my family into apartment 12B of Woodbridge Apartments on August 1, 1999, I signed the standard rental agreement and paid the required security deposit of $1,000.

We vacated the apartment and turned in the keys for the door, mailbox, and storage locker on July 30 of this year. The apartment was in perfect condition, exactly as it was when we moved in.

As of this date, I have yet to see the return of my security deposit.

According to the terms of the rental agreement, the deposit was to be placed in escrow in an interest-bearing account, and was to be returned within sixty days of vacating the apartment. That deadline passed two weeks ago.

Please send a check for the full amount of the security deposit plus accrued interest to my new address—listed above—as soon as possible.

Sincerely,
Michael Diamond

Second letter asking for return of security deposit

Sanjit Patel, Manager
Woodbridge Apartments
Smalltown, OH

Dear Mr. Patel:

It is now four months since my family moved from apartment 12B at Woodbridge Apartments, and I have not yet received the return of my security deposit plus interest.

Under terms of the rental agreement, this deposit was to have been returned within sixty days.

I expect to receive a check from you by December 15, or I will be forced to take legal action.

Sincerely,
Michael Diamond

Asking for payment of interest on security deposit

Sanjit Patel, Manager
Woodbridge Apartments
Smalltown, OH

Dear Mr. Patel:

Today we received a check in the amount of $1,000 representing the return of the security deposit for apartment 12B of Woodbridge Apartments.

Under terms of the rental agreement, the deposit was to be held in an interest-bearing escrow account and the interest was to be sent to us along with the deposit.

According to Smalltown Savings Bank, the standard interest rate on an escrow account is 3 percent. Based on that rate, we are owed $92.73 in compounded interest for the three years you held our deposit.

Please send a check for the accrued interest to my new address—listed above—as soon as possible.

Sincerely,
Michael Diamond

Inquiry about housing

Lakewood Chamber of Commerce
Lakewood, N.J.

Dear People:

I am considering attending Clifton Law School in the fall and would like to know about the availability of suitable rental housing. Would you please send me a list of apartments and rental agencies in the Lakewood area?

Thank you.

Sincerely,
Joshua Diamond

Inquiry to Better Business Bureau about apartment

Smalltown Better Business Bureau
Smalltown, OH

Dear People:

I will attend the Smalltown University School of Law in the fall. I expect to put a deposit on an apartment in the Shorewood Apartment Complex.

Are there any complaints on file about this business that I should be aware of before committing to rent this apartment?

Sincerely,
Joshua Diamond

Thanking friend for use of truck to move

Dear Nick:

Thanks for the use of your truck last Thursday. I was able to get all my stuff to the new apartment in one trip.

Call me when you have an evening free. I want to take you to dinner and have you see my new place.

Josh

Thanks for helping with move

Dear Ed:

Thanks for all the help on Thursday. I couldn't have moved without you.

I love my new apartment; it sure beats living in a dorm room.

I owe you a ball game and a beer . . . and a strong back when it is your turn to move.

Josh

36 Home Services

Dear Reader:

If you want to hire a neighborhood kid to mow your lawn—just once—you might consider it safe to make a verbal contract. But when it comes to more complex assignments like installing a fence, hiring a painter, or engaging a handyman, you should protect yourself by asking for a written agreement.

The elements of the contract should include the specifics of the work to be performed, the price, and the starting or ending date, or both. The agreement should also specify how and when payments will be made.

If you experience any problems with the work performed, you should document your objections in writing to protect yourself should the dispute result in a legal proceeding.

Best of luck,
The Authors

Seeking bid for fencing

Ralph Barb
Enclose Fencing Company
Fairview, PA

Dear Mr. Barb:

We have just moved to a new home in Fairview and would like a quote on the construction of a stockade fence in the backyard.

Please call me at (xxx) xxx-xxxx to arrange a time to view the property and to discuss available fence designs.

Sincerely,
Michael Diamond

Seeking bid for painting

Smith Painting Company
Fairview, PA

Dear People:

We have just purchased a home in Fairview. We have seen your advertising and would like a quote on repainting the interior of the house.

Please call at (xxx) xxx-xxxx to arrange a time to view the property.

Sincerely,
Michael Diamond

Asking for free offer with painting bid

Ed Smith
Smith Painting Company
Fairview, PA

Dear Mr. Smith:

Thank you for your visit the other day and the estimate for repainting our new home.

I noticed in today's newspaper that your company is running an ad offering a free cleaning of rain gutters with any paint job. We would like to include that service in the work to be done on our home.

Please advise that this can be included in your bid.

Sincerely,
Michael Diamond

Accepting bid for house painting

Ed Smith
Smith Painting Company
Fairview, PA

Dear Mr. Smith:

I am writing to accept your bid for the painting of our house at 234 Home Street, Fairview.

The rooms to be painted are the living room, dining room, family room, kitchen, master bedroom, and two smaller bedrooms. The paint is to be provided by you, and colors have been agreed on. I have attached a copy of the specifications and your bid for our business.

Work is to start the last week of August (approximately August 27) and will be completed on or about the second week in September, but not later than September 30. It is very important that this schedule be kept. We have various commitments that require the painting to be finished by the end of September.

Per our phone conversation, your crew will also clean the rain gutters of the house at no additional charge.

A deposit of $500 is enclosed with this letter. One-half of the remainder is to be paid on September 16, providing that the work is on schedule, and the remainder will be paid upon satisfactory completion of the job.

Sincerely,
Michael Diamond

Problem with timely completion of house painting

Ed Smith
Smith Painting Company
Fairview, PA

Dear Mr. Smith:

As you know, your company is in the process of painting the interior of our house at 234 Home Street in Fairview.

I am very concerned that the job will not be completed before the contracted deadline of September 30.

The job was to have begun during the last week of August. Your crew did not start until September 5. It is now September 15, and as of this morning, only the kitchen has been painted.

We are due to make a second payment, in the amount of $x,xxx, on September 16. I intend to withhold that payment until at least half of the job has been completed, as stated in the contract.

I am trusting that your company will value its agreement—and its reputation in the community—and will complete the job to our satisfaction by September 30.

Thank you.

Sincerely,
Michael Diamond

Praising contractor

Ralph Barb
Enclose Fencing Company
Fairview, PA

Dear Mr. Barb:

Enclosed is the balance due under our contract.

The fence looks wonderful. Beyond that, I wanted to pass along our appreciation of the professional and conscientious work performed by your crew.

Please feel free to use us as a reference. We would be happy to share our experience with others.

Sincerely,
Michael Diamond

Inquiry to handyman about repairs

A Man Around the House
Smalltown, OH

Dear People:

I saw your ad in the Smalltown Banner offering your services for small household jobs and repairs. My wife and I are putting our house on the market and would like to have a number of minor repairs made.

The house has been well maintained over the years but needs some sprucing up before we show it to prospective buyers. Please call at the number above to arrange an appointment.

Sincerely,
Ron Miller

Hiring handyman

Ed Harrington
A Man Around the House
Smalltown, OH

Dear Ed:

Thank you for meeting with us on Thursday. We would like to engage your services to do the following:

- Clean rain gutters.
- Repair broken soffit near porch.
- Replace handrail to basement.
- Replace broken step in basement stairs.
- Apply asphalt sealer to driveway.
- Make three trips to town dump to dispose of contents of basement and storage shed.

Based on my notes of our conversation, the total cost for labor for these jobs will be $800. We will pay for any lumber and materials on a cost-plus-15-percent basis.

Please call as soon as possible to set up a schedule for the work.

Sincerely,
Ron Miller

37 Caring for Children

Dear Reader:

Sooner or later, you've got to trust someone else to watch over your precious children: a baby sitter, a preschool, a teacher, or a family member.

For a brief night on the town, a note to the baby sitter should go over the ground rules for the kids (and the sitter) and provide information about where you will be for the evening, in case of emergency. For a lengthier trip, we recommend you write an operating manual for your kids with full details about schedules, behavior, medical matters and permissions, and your itinerary and contact numbers.

Best regards,
The Authors

Note to baby sitter

Dear Debbie:

Here is our schedule for the evening, and all important telephone numbers:

We are going with Jane and Phil Stevens for dinner at Antonio's Restaurant and from there will be seeing a show at the Repertory Theater. We should be home before midnight.

Both kids have already had dinner but could have some small snack before bed (a piece of fruit, yogurt, or graham crackers and milk).

They can watch TV or a videotape (they will show you our collection). Bedtime is 9 P.M., and that is not negotiable.

Hannah should go right to sleep, but Brian will want you to read him a chapter from his book (The Scarecrow of Oz). Then it's lights out, good night, see you in the morning.

Feel free to help yourself to anything in the refrigerator.

Please keep the telephone free in case we call.

We will have our cell phone, but we may have to turn it off inside the theater. Here are some phone numbers:

Cell phone (xxx) xxx-xxxx
Antonio's Restaurant (xxx) xxx-xxxx
Repertory Theater (xxx) xxx-xxxx

Thanks for your help.

Karen Diamond

Thanks to grandparents for child care

Dear Mom and Dad:

Thank you so much for "volunteering" to stay with Brian and Hannah while I accompany Michael on a business trip. I have to pinch myself to make sure I am not dreaming: two weeks in Paris and London!

Michael keeps reminding me he will be there on business. But I'm studying Econoguides for museums, restaurants, and nightlife. I am sure we will reach some kind of balance.

I'll send you a note soon with some of the details of care and feeding.

Love,
Karen

To grandparents about children's schedule

Dear Mom and Dad:

Here's the operating manual for Brian and Hannah. I've tried not to overwhelm you with too many details; obviously, you're quite experienced as parents!

I've divided the schedule into weekdays and weekends.

WEEKDAYS

Brian

Brian's school day is from 7:50 A.M. to 2:30 P.M. He sets his own alarm clock to get up at 6:30 A.M. (You can check that the alarm is on when he goes to bed.)

I lay out his clothes on his dresser each night. He usually picks out a favorite shirt on his own. He has cereal for breakfast.

We drive him to school, leaving at 7:30 A.M. sharp.

We pick him up Monday, Wednesday, and Friday at 2:30 P.M.

Tuesday: He has soccer practice right after school. He needs to be picked up at 4 P.M. at the field.

Thursday: After school he has an Art Appreciation class at the museum. I have arranged for Ann McGarrity to take him to the museum with her son Garrick, and to drop him off at home about 5 P.M.

Hannah

Hannah goes to preschool at the Community Church on Main Street five days a week from 8 A.M. to 12:30 P.M.

Sarah Schmidt, who lives across the road, will pick up Hannah at 7:45 A.M. every day and take her to preschool with her daughter Marianne.

Please pick up Hannah and Marianne at the church every day at 12:30 P.M. and drop off Marianne at her house.

Hannah gets up at the same time as her brother but needs more help in getting ready. We lay out her clothes the night before. She will not eat cereal; most mornings she eats a jelly sandwich for breakfast. Sometimes she'll accept French toast—you'll find some in the freezer.

WEEKENDS

Brian

On the weekends he can go to a friend's house (any of the ones we have listed on the telephone list) or, with your consent, he can invite someone over for a few hours. Do yourself a favor and limit the time—don't leave it open-ended.

If he has anyone over, tell them they have to have their own ride home. Don't be a chauffeur.

We have told him there are to be NO sleepovers while we are away, either at our house or at a friend's house.

MEDICAL

I have notified Dr. Todd that we will be away and you will be in charge. If you have any questions, there is a nurse on duty who can help.

I have attached a photocopy of our health insurance card. It is also on file with Dr. Todd, and at Smalltown General Hospital.

Both kids can take child-strength acetaminophen (not aspirin) for headaches and slight fevers.

They each take one multivitamin per day, which I have left in the locked cabinet with the medicines.

MEALS

Please give Brian $2.50 per day to buy lunch at school. I have left a jar with cash above the refrigerator.

Hannah takes a small peanut butter and jelly sandwich to school for snack time. They provide milk there.

Whatever you fix at dinner time is fine. They like chicken dishes of almost any description. For treats, pizza or takeout Chinese is a great reward for good behavior. (I hope you see some.)

BEDTIME

Lights out at 9 P.M. during the week and 9:30 on weekends. I read them a chapter from their current book before they go to bed.

BEHAVIOR

Try not to let them fight with each other. We have warned them under penalty of grounding until their eighteenth birthday to not give you a hard time.

The best nonviolent punishment is loss of television privileges. The more specific, the better: “Stop fighting now, or there’s no Nickelodeon tonight.”

KEEPING IN TOUCH

We have attached our schedule, including the flight numbers and times, and the phone numbers at our hotels in Paris and London.

We will be six hours ahead of you in Europe. We’ll try to call you every day around 5 P.M., which will be 11 P.M. our time.

I know that Michael has shown you how to turn on the computer and read the e-mail. If you run into trouble, Brian can help. (Really!) We will be sending e-mails from Internet cafés every day, and you can reply to them.

On a separate sheet I have listed all the names and phone numbers for the children’s friends. I’ve also listed the phone numbers for all of the neighbors; they’ve all been alerted to be available to help you in any way they can.

Finally, I’ve attached a legal letter giving you authorization to approve medical treatment for the children in case of emergency.

We can’t begin to tell you how much we appreciate your pitching in with the kids. We really need a break—and so will you when we return.

Love,
Karen and Michael

To preschool about grandparents in charge

Mary Millinocket, Director
Time Out Preschool
Fairview Community Church
Fairview, PA

Dear Mary:

Michael and I will be out of the country for two weeks, October 12 through 26.

My husband’s parents, Laura and John Diamond, will be taking care of Hannah and are authorized to act on our behalf in all matters regarding her care.

Sincerely,
Karen Diamond

To teacher regarding absence of parents

Karen Stacy
Fairview Elementary School
Fairview, PA

Dear Ms. Stacy:

My husband and I will be out of the country for two weeks, from October 12 through 26.

Brian's grandparents, John and Laura Diamond, will be staying in our home. Please feel free to contact them with any concerns in our absence.

Sincerely,
Karen Diamond

To school advising that baby sitter will pick up child

Mary Millinocket, Director
Time Out Preschool
Fairview Community Church
Fairview, PA

Dear Mary:

This letter will serve as notice that my daughter, Hannah, will be picked up by her baby sitter on Monday, Tuesday, and Thursday each week until further notice. The baby sitter's name is Carol O'Brien. I will introduce you to her before she begins picking up Hannah.

Sincerely,
Karen Diamond

Reschedule doctor appointment while parents are away

Laura Nevens, M.D.
Fairview, PA

Dear Dr. Nevens:

My son, Brian, has an appointment on October 14 for a routine visit.

My husband and I will be out of the country at that time and his grandparents will care for Brian. Please contact me to reschedule his appointment for any time after October 27.

Sincerely,
Karen Diamond

38 Very Personal Letters

Dear Reader:

We don't always follow this good advice ourselves, but here it is: Don't make loans to friends or family. Or at the very least, don't lend more than you can easily afford to forget about.

If you've not followed the advice, though, here are some letters about this matter and others that are very personal: asking for repayment of a loan, offering advice, and pushing a young adult toward a better path in college.

A personal letter should be no less direct than a business letter, although the tone should be warmer and less formal.

Warm regards,
The Authors

Asking for repayment of personal loan to friend

Dear Fred:

I'm writing to ask that you fulfill your promise and repay the money I loaned to you last year.

You asked for the money as a friend, and I gave it to you in that spirit. Now the fact that it has not been repaid hangs like a dark cloud over our friendship.

I'd appreciate it if you would send me the money by return mail.

Sincerely,
Josh

To relative about unpaid loan and lifestyle

Dear Al:

It really troubles me to be writing to you again on the same subject. When you came to me last year asking for a loan to help you get by while you looked for work, I thought that this time you were sincere in trying to settle down.

But six months later, I see no evidence that you have made good use of the help your family has offered. You still have not found a steady job. And you have done absolutely nothing to even attempt to repay the loan.

Your sister, Laura, constantly worries about you. And your mother and father, at this stage of life, should not be subjected to such constant stress.

Your family loves and cares for you, Al, but you are ultimately responsible for yourself. We will continue to offer as much emotional support as we can give, but we cannot continue to enable you to live an irresponsible lifestyle.

We are all here for you, but first you have to help yourself.

Love,
John

Reply to letter about family loan

Dear John:

I hope you will believe me when I say that I appreciated your letter. It was tough, but I know you're right. I hate being a burden and worry to those who care about me.

I really am trying to get back on track. I have contacted a career planner and he is helping me get my resume to the appropriate people. In the meantime, I've taken a part-time sports reporting job at the Smalltown Banner. It won't pay much, but it will be a paycheck.

I have always intended to pay you back, but I can't promise to be able to pay much in the short term.

Thanks for caring. One of the best things I have going for me is the support of a great family.

Sincerely,
Al

Thanks for reply to letter about family loan

Dear Al:

Thanks for the update. I like what you're saying.

Believe me, Al, it was never about the money. You have so much potential and so much going for you that it was hard for us to see you drifting.

Please keep us posted on your progress.

Sincerely,
John

From parent to child about problems in college

Dear Amy:

Your father and I are very pleased that you like Smalltown University so much. We think it is a very good fit for you.

We are also glad that you have made so many friends already. Heather sounds delightful and we look forward to meeting her. You also talk a lot about spending time with Kevin. I hope we can meet him when we come for Parents Weekend.

On a more serious note, Amy, we have received a notice from the college that you are in danger of not passing two very important subjects. You have always been a very good student, and we find it hard to understand how someone who was on the honor roll throughout high school could have such difficulty.

Before you left for college we discussed with you what was expected of you academically. You need to maintain a B average in order to keep the academic scholarship you received. We all agreed this was not unrealistic.

Your father and I worry that you may be devoting too much time to social activities and not enough to academics.

This is a very serious point in your college career. You are close to failing.

We know you are capable of doing much better. We're here for you for any support we can offer, but ultimately you have to be responsible for yourself.

Love,
Mom and Dad

Response to parents about college grades

Dear Mom and Dad:

Thanks for the letter. I'm sorry you were upset and surprised by the notice.

First of all, I'm pretty sure I've gotten my grades back on track. I pulled my grade in journalism up to a B- and I just got an A- on an economics test. I've spoken to both of my professors and they gave me extra work that will help me get back up to and above the B average.

You were more or less right about social activities interfering with academics. This is the first time I've been completely on my own, and it is very easy to get distracted.

My adviser has been helping me learn how to budget my time, and I've got a pretty good handle on it now.

I can't wait to see both of you at Parents Weekend. You will love Heather. She is so sweet. I invited her to come skiing with us on Winter Break. You will not be seeing Kevin, though. We don't see each other anymore; he was too immature. I have decided that a steady boyfriend and college just don't mix right now.

Love,
Amy

39 Contests

Dear Reader:

Congratulations! Your name is among those that will be on the final list that will include the winner of the Publisher's Bleating House Sweepstakes.

A careful reader, of course, will note that you have won exactly nothing, at least at this stage of the game. But then again, someone is going to win, and you can't win if you don't enter.

In this section, you'll find letters submitting an entry (with and without a purchase) and a request for the results of a contest.

Best of luck,
The Authors

Submitting recipe for contest

Great Thanksgivings Contest
Great Housekeeping Magazine
Bigtown, NY

Dear Editor:

Enclosed please find my family recipe for Oh-So-Garlicky Potatoes, submitted for consideration in the "Great Thanksgivings" contest.

My grandmother was famous in our family for these high-powered potatoes. We all grew up looking forward to Thanksgiving dinner, when she would wheel out a tub full of spuds. Sometimes we almost forgot to carve the turkey.

Today, I am seventy-two years old and the family comes to my place for Thanksgiving . . . and garlic potatoes.

I'm happy to share the recipe with your readers.

Sincerely,
Monica Diamond

Asking for results of contest

Design Your Dream Wedding Contest
Modern Weddings Magazine
Bigtown, NY

Dear Editor:

Several months ago I entered your "Design Your Dream Wedding" contest. According to the entry form, the winners were due to be selected by this date. Please send me a list of the winning entrants.

Sincerely,
Morgan Diamond

Submitting contest entry without purchase

Christmas with the Family at Sea Contest
Second Best Foods
Carmel, CA

Dear People:

Enclosed please find a 3" x 5" index card with my name and address as an entry to your "Christmas with the Family at Sea" contest. The rules state that no purchase is necessary, and I have complied with all other requirements.

Sincerely,
Harold Diamond

40 Employment Letters

Dear Reader:

When you apply for a job, you are selling your experience and background. Think about your marketable skills and your personal enthusiasm and attitude, and try to communicate—in a short and direct letter—what makes you best suited for an available position.

In most business settings, the job application process begins with a preliminary interview at the human resources or personnel department and then proceeds to department heads and supervisors. One way to help your application stand out above the others is to follow each step with a thank-you or a confirmation. Let the company know that you are interested in the job, that you know how to communicate clearly, and that you observe common courtesy and professional behavior.

When you are offered a job, you should follow up with professional written communication. If the offer was verbal, you should reiterate the essential points—salary, job title, major benefits, and starting date—in your letter of acceptance. If you were given an employment contract or a letter of offer, make reference to it in your acceptance and include a copy with your correspondence.

If you decline a job offer, do so politely and professionally. You may want to apply to that company again some day.

And when it comes time to resign your present job—to take another or for other reasons—do so in a polite and professional manner. You may want to use your former employer as a reference some day, or even go back to work for that company. Burn no bridges, no matter how tempting it may be to tell your boss what you really think.

Best of luck,
The Authors

Cover letter with resume for nonspecific job opening

Personnel Department
American Credit Company
Bigtown, NY

Dear People:

Enclosed please find my resume, submitted in application for an appropriate opening at American Credit Company.

I will graduate this June from Smalltown University in Ohio with a Bachelor of Science degree in business management. As you will see from my resume, I have had extensive training in finance, business administration, and business law. In my junior year I served an internship at the Ohio Credit Bureau.

I am willing to relocate to Bigtown or to any of your offices around the country. I will be available for an interview at your convenience.

American Credit Company is at the top of my list of places to work. I would be honored to have the opportunity to interview.

Sincerely,
Joshua Diamond

Cover letter with resume for advertised job opening

Human Resources Department
Moneysworth Investment Group
16 Computer Plaza
Fairview, PA

Dear People:

Enclosed please find my resume, submitted for consideration for the position of financial consultant that was advertised in the Smalltown Banner on May 23.

I have been an account executive with Amalgamated Business Software in Smalltown,

Ohio, for the past four years. In this position I supervise relations between Amalgamated and our accounting firm and banking clients.

I am ready for new challenges and feel that my background and employment experience are perfect for the financial consultant position at Moneysworth Investment Group.

I am available to come for an interview at your convenience, and look forward to hearing from you soon.

Sincerely,
Michael Diamond

Cover letter with resume for blindly advertised job opening

Box 6SJ7
Help Wanted Ads
Smalltown Banner
Smalltown, OH

Dear Sir or Madam:

I am writing to apply for the position of personal secretary, as advertised in the Smalltown Banner.

I have more than thirty years of experience in major corporations and government agencies, and in my career I have written thousands of personal and business letters.

Attached is a copy of my resume. I would be happy to provide references from employers and members of the community.

The job, as described, sounds very much like what I am looking for. I know I would provide excellent service.

Looking forward to hearing from you soon, I am,

Sincerely yours,
Martha Waters
Smalltown, OH

Confirming interview appointment

Roger Harrison, Director of Human Resources
Moneysworth Investment Group
Fairview, PA

Dear Mr. Harrison:

Thank you for your telephone call this morning. I am very excited about the possibilities of working for Moneysworth Investment Group. The job we discussed seems very appropriate for my experience and interests.

I look forward to meeting with you on Monday, June 19, at 10 A.M.

I have attached the list of references that you requested. As we discussed, I would prefer you not contact my present employer before we meet.

Sincerely,
Michael Diamond

Thank you for job interview

Roger Harrison, Director of Human Resources
Moneysworth Investment Group
Fairview, PA

Dear Mr. Harrison:

Thank you for meeting with me on Monday to discuss the financial consultant position at Moneysworth Investment Group. I hope the level of my interest in the job came through in the interview; I am very excited about the possibility of working for Moneysworth.

I have informed my current employer that I plan to move from Smalltown to pursue other job opportunities, and you can now contact my supervisor and the head of personnel at Amalgamated Business Software for references. Both expressed their wishes that I would stay, but understand my interest in working for a much larger company.

I look forward to hearing from you soon.

Sincerely,
Michael Diamond

Accepting job with employment contract

Roger Harrison, Director of Human Resources
Moneysworth Investment Group
Fairview, PA

Dear Mr. Harrison:

I am very pleased to accept your offer of the financial consultant position at Moneysworth Investment Group. I am enclosing the signed contract. I look forward to beginning work on Monday, July 15.

I accept the terms of your relocation package and will contact Julie Stanton in the human resources department to begin the process of moving my family to Pennsylvania.

I am very excited about being a part of the Moneysworth team, and eager to begin.

Thank you again.

Sincerely,
Michael Diamond

Accepting job and reiterating details of offer

Harold Scheib
Scheib Family Trust
Smalltown, OH

Dear Mr. Scheib:

I am pleased to accept your offer of employment as your personal secretary.

I very much enjoyed meeting you and learning about your needs for secretarial help at the Scheib Family Trust. I look forward to being of assistance.

As we discussed, the salary is $50,000 per year, paid weekly. The ordinary work week will be Tuesday through Saturday, from 9 A.M. to 5 P.M. I understand that days and office hours may vary from week to week based on your travel schedule, and that I will be paid time-and-a-half overtime for any week in which my services are required for more than forty hours.

As we discussed, I am covered under my husband's medical insurance policy and will not require coverage from Scheib Family Trust. I am happy to accept your offer of a leased company car in lieu of medical insurance.

After six months, I will be entitled to one week of paid vacation, with a second week offered at the end of one year of service. Salary and benefits will be reviewed on the one-year anniversary of employment.

I look forward to the start of work on Monday, September 16, 20xx.

Sincerely yours,
Martha Waters
Smalltown, OH

Declining a job offer

Alfred Oldman, Director of Personnel
Amerex Credit Corporation
Parklot, WV

Dear Mr. Oldman:

Thank you for your letter of June 25, 20xx, in which you offered me the position of senior auditor at Amerex.

I was very impressed with Amerex when I met with you two weeks ago, and I very much appreciate the offer. However, I have accepted a position with another company and will begin work there in mid-July.

Sincerely,
Michael Diamond

Resignation from job

Howard L. Canard, Director of Personnel
Amalgamated Business Software
Smalltown, OH

Dear Howard:

With this letter, I am resigning my position as account executive for Amalgamated Business Software, effective May 24, 20xx. Pursuant to my employment contract, I am giving two weeks' notice.

I have valued my association with Amalgamated Business Software for the past four years and appreciate the opportunities given me. However, at this time I must take advantage of what I believe is an important step forward in my career.

Would you please provide me with whatever forms are necessary to transfer my retirement and profit-sharing funds to new accounts? I have asked my accountant, Robert Klein, to contact you directly on my behalf if there are any questions about procedures.

Thank you.

Sincerely,
Michael Diamond

Notifying supervisor of resignation

Martin Vineyard, Director of Sales
Amalgamated Business Software
Smalltown, OH

Dear Martin:

As you know, I have resigned my position as account executive for Amalgamated Business Software, effective May 24, 20xx.

I just wanted to thank you for the opportunities you have given me over the years. I learned a great deal working for you, and I value your mentorship and friendship.

I hope we can remain in touch.

Sincerely,
Michael Diamond

Accepting letter of resignation

Chris Reagan
Smalltown, OH

Dear Chris:

It is with regret that we accept your resignation. Your tenure at Diamond Music Hall has been most satisfactory, and you will be missed.

We all wish you the best of luck in whatever paths you pursue. Feel free to use my name as a reference.

Sincerely,
John Diamond

Acknowledging receipt of resume

Laura Hudson
Smalltown, OH

Dear Ms. Hudson:

Thank you for sending a copy of your resume in application for a job at Diamond Music Hall. We appreciate your kind words and desire to work here.

Unfortunately, at this time we have no openings that would fit your qualifications. We will keep your resume on file and will be happy to consider you should anything become available.

Sincerely,
John Diamond

Invitation to applicant for an interview

Laura Hudson
Smalltown, OH

Dear Ms. Hudson:

Last spring you sent us your resume for a position in the advertising department. At that time we had no jobs available that would meet your qualifications.

We have just received word that one of our advertising representatives is leaving. If you are still interested, we would like to set up an interview.

Please call our Advertising Manager, June West, to schedule an appointment.

Sincerely,
John Diamond

Congratulating new employee

Laura Hudson
Smalltown, OH

Dear Laura:

Congratulations! June West tells me you will be joining our company as an advertising representative on August 14.

On behalf of the entire company, I want to welcome you and extend our wishes that your tenure here will be most enjoyable and satisfying. Please know that my door is always open, should there be anything I can do to help you succeed in your job.

Sincerely,
John Diamond

Confirming appointment for interview

Marsha Taylor, Advertising Director
Klein Graphics Company
Fairview, PA

Dear Ms. Taylor:

Thank you for your call today inviting me to come in for a job interview. I am very much interested in working at Klein Graphics Company.

I will be at your office at 9 A.M. on Monday, August 29. If there is anything else you need from me, please let me know.

Sincerely,
Karen Diamond

Declining job as presented

Marsha Taylor, Advertising Director
Klein Graphics Company
Fairview, PA

Dear Ms. Taylor:

I received your letter today offering me a job in the graphics department at Klein Graphics. While the job as outlined in your letter sounds challenging and professionally rewarding, I cannot accept it at this time.

When I was interviewed, I thought I made it clear that with my obligations at home, including two small children, I am available only for a part-time position of no more than twenty hours per week, or one that I could do in some measure from my home.

My husband and I have made the commitment that while our children are small, it is best that one of us be readily available to them.

Thank you again for the offer. It is very tough to decline.

If your requirements in the graphics department ever include part-time work or flexible hours, please let me know. I would still love to be a part of your team.

Sincerely,
Karen Diamond

Accepting job as amended

Marsha Taylor, Advertising Director
Klein Graphics Company
Fairview, PA

Dear Ms. Taylor:

I am happy to accept the position in the graphics department outlined in your letter. I very much appreciate your flexibility in helping me take care of my family obligations.

The mix of two days at the office and two days working from home works very well for me. I promise you that I will be an excellent employee.

I will be available to start on Monday, September 10. Please let me know if I should come in sooner to fill out any paperwork, or for meetings.

Thank you again.

Sincerely,
Karen Diamond

41 Introductions and References

Dear Reader:

A personal contact or reference can open the door to a new job or career, and if you know someone well and can offer honest praise, you can do that person a tremendous favor by helping in his or her quest for employment.

However, don't cheapen the value of your good name by offering references about someone you do not know well, or positive words about someone not worthy of your recommendation.

Many companies, fearful of lawsuits, do not offer references about former workers other than confirmation of job title and dates of employment. Our policy has been to give a good reference when it is warranted, and to decline to comment about workers we could not recommend. Most people making hiring decisions are smart enough to read between the lines.

In any case, tread carefully here. Remember that when you write a letter of recommendation you are attaching your own reputation to someone else's resume, personal history, and even their future performance. Be especially cautious if you are recommending someone to one of your own clients, friends, or business associates.

Our advice is to only make recommendations when you know someone very well, and, even then, only if you are fully comfortable with all of the details of the situation: where they are currently employed, where they are looking to work, and the nature of your own business. (Do you want to have to explain to one of your own clients why you helped a valuable employee jump ship to one of their competitors?)

And you should never offer false or misleading information in your recommendation. At the very least you risk damage to your reputation; at worst, you're opening yourself to legal action from a company that makes a hiring decision based on your words.

If the person asking you for a reference requests you to falsify information, he or she certainly is not worthy of your recommendation.

And think twice or thrice or more before you respond to a request for a reference for someone for whom you have nothing good to say. You could be opening yourself to a lawsuit for libel or other allegations of damages.

To put it another way: If you're willing to offer a reference but can't find anything nice to say, say nothing at all.

Sincerely,
The Authors

Asking for job contacts

Laura Diamond
Smalltown, OH

Dear Laura:

I just realized that it must be at least five years since we last spoke. I hope you and the family are well. I miss our times together, and I even miss those awful faculty meetings at Smalltown Community College. Not a lot, just a little.

How are things at SCC? Your children must be on their own now. Is Heather in college yet?

I am still here in Florida at Citrus Community College, but I'm looking to move on at the end of this school year. I'd like to be nearer to my family, and I also find that I really miss the change of seasons.

I have heard that Mystic Junior College in Rhode Island is going to enlarge its Political Science department, and that perhaps there are some possibilities for me. I remember you taught there briefly. Was it right after college? Do you still have contacts there? I was hoping you could steer me in the right direction.

My best to John.

Sincerely,
Kay Smith

Suggestions on job contacts

Kay Smith
Soggy Bottom, FL

Dear Kay:

How good to hear from you. Just a few weeks ago John and I were wondering how the person who always was complaining about the slightly warm summers in Boston could possibly tolerate summer in Florida.

As far as Mystic Community College is concerned, here's what I know: The place is expanding like crazy, serving as a feeder school to the big universities in Providence. Most of the people I worked with have moved on, but when I checked the directory I found that Billy Legrande is still there—you may not have known him, but he was one of the best teachers at the school and is a good egg. He is now the vice provost for academic affairs.

I called Billy this morning. After he gave up trying to recruit me to go back there to teach, I told him you were looking to move back north. He said he would be thrilled to hear from you. I'd suggest you get a letter and curriculum vitae in the mail to him immediately.

Keep me posted.

Best regards,
Laura Diamond

Unable to offer introduction

Kay Smith
Soggy Bottom, FL

Dear Kay:

How good to hear from you. Just a few weeks ago John and I were wondering how the person who always was complaining about the slightly warm summers in Boston could possibly tolerate summer in Florida.

As far as Mystic Community College is concerned, I'm afraid my contacts are way out of date. I made a few phone calls and checked the college directory, but couldn't find anyone I knew from my time there.

I have heard good things about MCC, and I know it has grown considerably in the past few years.

While I can't give you any contacts, count me as a reference if you need it. Maybe a recommendation from a former professor would carry some weight.

And I'll let you know if I hear of any other PoliSci departments in need of a spirited rabble-rouser like you.

Good luck, and keep me posted.

Sincerely,
Laura Diamond

Request for reference

Robert Simmons
Guidance Counselor
Smalltown High School
Smalltown, OH

Dear Mr. Simmons:

I am applying for a summer job at the Smalltown Historical Foundation. I would like to use your name as a reference.

Please let me know if that is okay with you, and let me know which telephone number you would like me to list on the reference form.

Thank you.

Sincerely,
Heather Diamond

Declining to be a reference

Dear Jim:

It was good to hear from you recently. It certainly has been a long time since we last talked. I wish you well in your job search.

At this time, however, I don't feel that I should be listed as a reference for you.

Sincerely,
John Diamond

Declining to be a reference for reason

Dear Jim:

I have received your letter asking me to serve as a reference for you in your job search.

Based on the unhappy end to your employment here, I don't think any reference I might offer would help you find another job. I would suggest you ask someone else to be a reference.

Good luck.

Sincerely,
John Diamond

Enthusiastic reference

PDQ Jones, President
Sing Song Musical Sales
Albany, New York

Dear Mr. Jones:

I am writing to commend to your attention a most extraordinary young man. Scott Carter has worked as senior salesman for Diamond Music Hall for the past five years.

During that time he has consistently exceeded all sales quotas while at the same time scoring the highest with our customers.

Scott has extensive knowledge of the music business and first-rate skills in dealing with people. I have found him completely reliable and enthusiastic in performing whatever he is asked to do.

I will personally be very sorry when Scott moves on, but am confident that wherever he goes he will be a great addition. I enthusiastically recommend him.

Sincerely,
John Diamond
Owner

Noncommittal reference

Leonard Stein
Record's End Musical Sales
Troy, New York

Dear Mr. Stein:

I have been asked by your company to provide some details about the employment of Janet Smith. Ms. Smith worked here until approximately one year ago. While I am not personally familiar with her work while at Diamond's, a check of company records indicates she was a clerical assistant in the order-processing division for two years.

Sincerely,
John Diamond

Employer requesting reference

Marion Russell, Advertising Director
The Grand Piano Music Company
Hightone, MN

Dear Ms. Russell:

Sandra Miller has applied to our company, Diamond Music Hall, for a position in the advertising department. She would be assistant advertising manager reporting to the director of the department, managing an annual budget of about $300,000 for print and radio buys.

Ms. Miller gave us your name to contact as a reference. I understand she has worked for the Grand Piano Music Company for a number of years in a similar position.

We would appreciate whatever guidance you can give us about her employment history and record.

Thank you.

Sincerely,
John Diamond

Submit resume with referral

Marsha Taylor, Advertising Director
Klein Graphics Company
Fairview, PA

Dear Ms. Taylor:

I am a graphic artist with more than eight years of professional experience in agencies in the Ohio area, working on print advertisements, Web sites, and catalogs.

I have just moved to the Fairview area, and I am looking for a job that will allow me to put my skills to good use.

Nancy Harrison, one of your current employees, suggested I contact you about current openings. Nancy and I worked together on several ad campaigns in Ohio, and she has offered to be a reference for me in my job search.

I am enclosing my resume and will be available for an interview at your convenience.

Sincerely,
Karen Diamond

Advising use of name as referral

Nancy Harrison
Klein Graphics Company
Fairview, PA

Dear Nancy:

Thank you again for your suggestion that I consider applying for a job at Klein Graphics. I have sent a resume and letter to Marsha Taylor, and hope to hear from her soon.

As you suggested, I said in the letter that you would serve as one of my references. I really appreciate your assistance. I hope we can work together again.

Sincerely,
Karen Diamond

Thanks for referral

Nancy Harrison
Klein Graphics Company
Fairview, PA

Dear Nancy:

Greetings from the newest employee of Klein Graphics. I got the job!

I interviewed last week with Marsha Taylor and was just offered a position tailor-made for my very busy life.

Marsha was very accommodating. I will work two days from the office and two days from home.

Your reference made the difference. Marsha told me they were looking for a full-time employee, but based on my background and your recommendation, they rewrote the job description.

Thanks again, Nancy. It will be great working together again.

Sincerely,
Karen

Asking for letter of reference for volunteer work

Randolph Webster, Director
Smalltown Literacy Center
Smalltown, OH

Dear Randy:

I've only been gone a week, and already I miss the opportunity to volunteer at the literacy center. I hope to return soon.

In the meantime, I am putting together my application for graduate school. Would you be willing to serve as a community reference for me?

I have enclosed the form from Smalltown University, and a self-addressed, stamped envelope for its return. If you would like to add a letter with more details about my work (I would really appreciate it if you would), you can attach it to the form.

Thanks again.

Sincerely,
Morgan Diamond

Thanks for letter of reference for volunteer work

Randolph Webster, Director
Smalltown Literacy Center
Smalltown, OH

Dear Randy:

I've just been accepted to graduate school, with a merit scholarship. The admissions department made special note of my involvement with the literacy center and your effusive letter of praise about the quality of my work. Thank you so much!

I expect to have a handle on my school schedule in a few weeks and will contact you then to find out if you'd like me to work for a few hours each week during the term.

Sincerely,
Morgan Diamond

42 Legal Letters

Dear Reader:

Contrary to what you might think about our modern society, it is not necessary to have a lawyer approve every last jot and tittle we write. With a bit of common sense any of us can learn to avoid slander, threats, and other illegalities.

And it is also not essential that you hire a lawyer to help you draft simple contracts and agreements. In this section you'll find a set of basic letters to accompany the sale of an item, make an agreement with a repair person, authorize another to take care of your child in your absence, give someone the power of attorney to act on your behalf in a financial transaction, and authorize other arrangements.

That said, let us emphasize a few very important points:

1. We are not lawyers, and we are not offering legal advice in this book.
2. The letters in this section should only be used when there is absolutely no question about the ownership of an item, the guardianship of a minor, or the right of an individual to enter into a legally binding agreement.

3. These letters should *not* be used if the item that is the subject of the agreement is very valuable, or if the nature of the agreement is more complex than can be properly described in one of the letters.
4. The letters should *not* be used for the transfer of real estate or for issues of guardianship of a minor.
5. You should not use one of these sample letters if you think it is likely that the other party is not going to comply with its terms. If you expect to end up in a legal dispute, you should involve an attorney in the transaction from the very start.

If you do use one of the letters in this section, be very specific when you describe a person, place, or thing. If you are selling a television set, include the details of the manufacturer, model number, and serial number. If you are giving someone power of attorney to act on your behalf, describe precisely the rights you are granting.

Sincerely,
The Authors

General bill of sale, payment in full, immediate pickup

Date of sale:____________________

This letter constitutes the entire agreement between the Seller ____________________ and the Buyer ____________________

for the sale of the following Goods: ____________________ The full purchase price for the Goods is $ ____________________. The Buyer has paid the Seller the full purchase price in one payment.

The Buyer shall take immediate possession of Goods.

The Seller warrants that he or she is the legal owner of the Goods and that the Goods are free of all liens and encumbrances.

The Seller believes the Goods to be in good condition except for the following known defects: ____________________.

The Seller disclaims any implied warranty of condition, merchantability, or fitness for a particular purpose. The Goods are sold as is and the Seller makes no express warranties.

Seller's name: ______________________________
Seller's address: ______________________________
Buyer's name: ______________________________
Buyer's address: ______________________________

Signed by the Buyer: ______________________________
Date:______________________________

Signed by the Seller: ______________________________
Date:______________________________

General bill of sale, payment in full, scheduled pickup

Date of sale:__________________

This letter constitutes the entire agreement between the Seller __________________ and the Buyer ________________ for the sale of the following Goods: ________________

The full purchase price for the Goods is $__________________ .

The Buyer has paid the Seller the full purchase price in one payment.

The Buyer shall pick up the goods from the following location __________________ on or before the following date: __________________.

The Seller warrants that he or she is the legal owner of the Goods and that the Goods are free of all liens and encumbrances.

The Seller believes the Goods to be in good condition except for the following known defects: __________________.

The Seller disclaims any implied warranty of condition, merchantability, or fitness for a particular purpose. The Goods are sold as is and the Seller makes no express warranties.

Seller's name: ____
Seller's address: ____

Buyer's name: ____
Buyer's address: ____

Signed by the Buyer: ____
Date:____

Signed by the Seller: ____
Date:____

General bill of sale, payment in installments, immediate pickup

Date of sale:__________________

This letter constitutes the entire agreement between the Seller __________________ and the Buyer ________________ the sale of the following Goods: ________________.

The full purchase price for the Goods is $ __________________ .

The Buyer has paid the Seller $__________________ as a down payment. The balance of purchase price, $__________________ , is due by __________________ [date].

The Buyer agrees to make installment payments of not less than $________________ per month, due on the __________________ day of each month, until the purchase price is paid in full.

The Buyer shall take immediate possession of Goods.

The Seller warrants that he or she is the legal owner of the Goods and that the Goods are free of all liens and encumbrances.

The Seller believes the Goods to be in good condition except for the following known defects: ___________________.

The Seller disclaims any implied warranty of condition, merchantability, or fitness for a particular purpose. The Goods are sold as is and the Seller makes no express warranties.

Seller's name: ____

Seller's address: ____

Buyer's name: ____

Buyer's address: ____

Signed by the Buyer: _____________________________________

Date: ____

Signed by the Seller: _____________________________________

Date: ____

General bill of sale, payment in installments, scheduled pickup

Date of sale: ___________________

This letter constitutes the entire agreement between the Seller ___________________ and the Buyer _______________ for the sale of the following Goods: _______________.

The full purchase price for the Goods is $___________________.

The Buyer has paid the Seller $___________________ as a down payment. The balance of purchase price is due by ___________________ [date].

The Buyer agrees to make installment payments of not less than $_______________ per month, due on the ___________________ day of each month, until the purchase price is paid in full.

The Buyer shall pick up the goods from the following location ___________________ on or before the following date: ___________________.

The Seller warrants that he or she is the legal owner of the Goods and that the Goods are free of all liens and encumbrances.

The Seller believes the Goods to be in good condition except for the following known defects: ___________________.

The Seller disclaims any implied warranty of condition, merchantability, or fitness for a particular purpose. The Goods are sold as is and the Seller makes no express warranties.

Seller's name: ____

Seller's address: ____

Buyer's name: ____

Buyer's address: ____

Signed by the Buyer: _____________________________________

Date: ____

Signed by the Seller: _____________________________________

Date: ____

Agreement for home maintenance

Contractor ____

Address ____

Address ____

The following represents the full agreement between ________________ [Homeowner] and ________________ [Contractor] for the performance of maintenance work on the property located at ________________.

Contractor agrees to perform the following work: _____________________ ____.

Homeowner agrees to pay to the Contractor the total of $________________ for the work, as follows: one-half at the beginning of specified work and one-half upon satisfactory completion of the job. Payment will be made by check.

Contractor agrees to obtain any necessary permits or permissions to perform the work. Contractor will carry workers' compensation and liability insurance. Homeowner will be relieved of liability to the full extent of the law.

Contractor's state or local license or registration for repair and construction work is of the following description and number: ________________

The work to be performed under this agreement shall begin on or before ________________ [date] and shall be completed on or before ________________ [date]. Time is of the essence.

In addition, Homeowner and Contractor also agree that: ____________________.

Homeowner's signature: ___________________________________

Print name: ____

Date: ____

Address: ____

Address: ____

Contractor's signature: ___________________________________

Print name: ____

Date: ____

Limited power of attorney

I, ____________________ [full legal name], residing at ____________________ [full permanent address], hereby appoint ____________________ [full legal name] of ____________________, ____________________, ____________________ as my Attorney-in-Fact to act in my place for the purposes of: ____.

This limited power of attorney takes effect on the following date: ________________, and shall continue until ____________________, or before then if terminated in writing.

I hereby grant my Attorney-in-Fact full authority to manage and conduct the foregoing powers, and I ratify all lawful acts that my Attorney-in-Fact performs in exercising those powers.

Any third party who receives a copy of this document may act under it, for the limited purposes listed. I agree to indemnify a third party for any claims that arise against the third party because of reliance on this power of attorney.

If this power of attorney is revoked, such revocation is not effective upon a third party until the third party has received notification of the revocation.

Signed:
This ____________________ day of ____________________, 20xx.
State of: ____________________ County of: ____________________
Signature of principal: ____________________
Print name: ____________________
Social Security Number: ____________________

Signature of Attorney-in-Fact: ____________________
Name of Attorney-in-Fact: ____________________

Witnesses: ____________________
Notary Public: ____________________

For a broader power of attorney, be sure to consult a lawyer for advice. In most states, a notary public must witness the signatures of both parties; in some states, you will also need one or two third-party witnesses to the signing of the agreement. A notary public, a bank officer, or a real estate broker should be able to tell you whether witnesses are required in your state.

As this book went to press, the following states required witnesses for any power of attorney: Arizona, Arkansas, Connecticut, Florida, Georgia, Illinois, Ohio, Oklahoma, Pennsylvania, South Carolina, and Wisconsin. Additionally, the following states require witnesses if the power of attorney is to be officially recorded with a government agency: Michigan and Vermont, plus the District of Columbia. Check with your home state because laws can change.

Revocation of power of attorney

I, __________________ [full legal name], residing at __________________ [full permanent address], hereby revoke the power of attorney dates __________________ [date] appointing __________________ [full legal name] of __________________, __________________, __________________ as my Attorney-in-Fact.

I revoke and withdraw all power and authority granted under that power of attorney.

Signed:

This __________________ day of __________________, 20xx.

State of: __________________ County of: __________________

Signature of principal: __________________

Print name: __________________

Social Security Number: __________________

Notary Public: __________________

Authorization to drive your car

I am the registered owner of the following vehicle: __________________ [make, model and year of vehicle], license plate number __________________, registered in __________________, [state]. The vehicle is insured by ________________ [insurance company] under policy number __________________.

I hereby give my authorization and consent for the borrower identified on this letter to use this vehicle as follows:

From __________________ [date] to __________________ [date].

Under the following restrictions: __________________.

Vehicle Owner

Name: ____

Address: ____

Address: ____

Daytime phone: ____

Authorized Borrower

Name: ____

Address: ____

Address: ____

Daytime phone: ____

Owner's signature: ____

Print name: ______________________ Date: ______________________

Temporary authorization for care of minor

To Whom It May Concern:

Regarding:
Child's name: ______________________________
Address: ______________________________
Address: ______________________________
Date of birth: ______________________________

I affirm that the above-named minor child is my child and that I have legal custody.

I hereby give full authorization and consent for my child to live with the temporary guardian named here:
Guardian name: ______________________________
Address: ______________________________
Address: ______________________________

I give the temporary guardian permission:

a. ______________________________a.
To authorize medical and dental care as recommended by a qualified doctor, dentist, or other medical practitioner.

b. ______________________________b.
To act in all matters relating to educational and recreational activities.

c. ______________________________c.
To pay such living expenses, medical, and dental expenses as are necessary and to sign on my behalf any insurance forms necessary for services provided.

This temporary authorization shall be in effect from ________________ , 20xx, to ________________ , 20xx.

Parent's signature: ______________________________
Print name: ______________________________
Date:______________________________

Authorization for minor to travel abroad with non–family member

Under penalty of perjury under the laws of the state of ________________ I affirm that the following is true and correct.

Regarding ________________, [Child's name]

a citizen of the United States, born on ______________ [date] in______________ [city, state], who carries United States passport number ________________, I hereby affirm that I have legal custody of the child and that there are no active or pending child custody or divorce rulings or proceedings that involve the child.

I hereby give full authorization and consent for my child to travel outside of the United States with ________________ [name of adult], who carries United States passport number ________________. The purpose of travel is ________________.

The trip will commence on ________________ [date] and include the following destinations: ________________.

__________ [name of adult] is authorized to modify the travel plans as necessary.

Parent's signature: ______________________________

Date: ______________________________

Print name: ______________________________

Address: ______________________________

Address: ______________________________

[Notary Seal]

Request for copy of your birth certificate

Town Clerk/Department of Vital Statistics/Department of Health

Address ______________________________

Address ______________________________

Dear Registrar:

Please send me a certified copy of my birth certificate. As required, I have enclosed a check in the amount of $________________ and a stamped, self-addressed envelope.

Name on birth certificate: ______________________________

Father's name: ______________________________

Mother's maiden name: ______________________________

Date of birth: ______________________________

Sex: ______________________________

Hospital or other place of birth: ______________________________

Location: ______________________________

Thank you.

Signature: ______________________________

Print name: ______________________________

Address: ______________________________

____

Request for copy of someone else's birth certificate

Town Clerk/Department of Vital Statistics/Department of Health
Address ______________________________
Address ______________________________

Dear Registrar:

Please send me a certified copy of the following birth certificate. As required, I have enclosed a check in the amount of $__________ and a stamped, self-addressed envelope.

Name on birth certificate: ______________________________
Father's name: ______________________________
Mother's maiden name: ______________________________
Date of birth: ______________________________
Sex: ______________________________
Hospital or other place of birth: ______________________________
Location: ______________________________
Thank you.

Signature: ______________________________
Print name: ______________________________
Address: ______________________________
____

My relationship to person named on birth certificate: __________

Loan repayable in lump sum, without interest

The following letter includes the full details of a promissory note agreement between __________ [Borrower] and __________ [Lender].

The Borrower promises to pay to the Lender the amount of $__________ on or before __________ [due date].

If the Lender must undertake legal action to collect the amount due and is successful, the Borrower agrees to pay reasonable attorney and court fees incurred by the Lender.

Signed at: __________ [location: city, town, or county]

Borrower's signature: ______________________________
Print name: ______________________________
Date of signature: ______________________________

Lender's signature: ______________________________
Date of signature: ______________________________

Borrower's name: ______________________________
Print name: ______________________________
Borrower's address: ______________________________
Borrower's address______________________________

Lender's name: ______________________________
Print name: ______________________________
Lender's address: ______________________________
Lender's address ______________________________

Loan repayable in lump sum, with interest

The following letter includes the full details of a promissory note agreement between ____________ [Borrower] and ____________ [Lender].

The Borrower promises to pay to the Lender the principal of the loan in the amount of $____________ on or before ____________ [due date].

In addition, the Borrower will pay simple interest which shall be charged on the amount of principal specified above, at the rate of ____________ percent per year from the date this agreement is signed until the amount is paid in full.

If the Lender must undertake legal action to collect the amount due and is successful, the Borrower agrees to pay reasonable attorney and court fees incurred by the Lender.

Signed at: ____________ [location: city, town, or county]

Borrower's signature: ______________________________
Date of signature: ______________________________

Lender's signature: ______________________________
Date of signature: ______________________________

Borrower's name: ______________________________
Borrower's address: ______________________________
Borrower's address ______________________________

Lender's name: ______________________________
Lender's address: ______________________________
Lender's address ______________________________

Loan repayable in installments, with interest

The following letter includes the full details of a promissory note agreement between __________________ [Borrower] and __________________ [Lender].

The Borrower promises to pay to the Lender the amount of $ __________________ on or before __________________ [due date] at the interest rate of __________________ percent per year from this date until the amount borrowed is paid in full.

The Borrower agrees to make installment payments, which include principal and interest, of not less than $________________ per month, due on the ________________ day of each month, until the outstanding principal and interest are paid in full.

If any installment payment due under this note is not received by the Lender within __________________ days of the specified monthly due date, the Lender may demand immediate repayment of the entire unpaid principal.

If the Lender must undertake legal action to collect the amount due and is successful, the Borrower agrees to pay reasonable attorney and court fees incurred by the Lender.

Signed at: __________________ [location: city, town, or county]

Borrower's signature: ______________________________________
Date of signature: ______________________________________

Lender's signature: ______________________________________
Date of signature: ______________________________________

Borrower's name: ______________________________________
Print name: ______________________________________
Borrower's address: ______________________________________
Borrower's address ______________________________________

Lender's name: ______________________________________
Print name: ______________________________________
Lender's address: ______________________________________
Lender's address ______________________________________

Demand to make good on bad check

Regarding:
Check# ______________________
Bank ______________________
Dated ______________________
Amount $ ______________________

Dear Mr. Jones:

Your check was returned to our bank and refused payment because of insufficient funds in the account to cover the amount of the check.

Please let us know at once how you intend to make good on the amount you owe. If there is a problem with paying the amount due, please contact us to discuss possible options.

If we do not hear from you within ten days from the date of this letter, we will be forced to begin legal proceedings for collection of the amount due plus any legal expenses incurred.

Sincerely,
John Diamond
President
Diamond Music Hall

Notice of intent to move out of rented apartment or home

Landlord or Manager
Address: ______________________
Address ______________________
Regarding rental unit: ______________________
Unit number: ______________________
Address: ______________________
Address ______________________

Dear Manager:

This is to notify you that we intend to vacate the above indicated rental unit on [date] ______________.

As required under the rental agreement, we hereby are giving at least ______ days' advanced written notice.

Tenant 1 signature ______________ Print name______________
Tenant 2 signature ______________ Print name______________
Date:______________ Date: ______________

43 Letters to Government Officials and Religious Leaders

Dear Reader:

When we write to a friend, we typically use their first name in an informal salutation. If the letter is addressed to someone we don't know personally, or with whom we have a formal relationship, we use their title plus first name and surname: Mr., Mrs., Ms., Miss, or Dr.

But some personages bear more lofty titles, and require more complex forms of address. The president of the United States, for example, is referred to by his or her job; Dear Mr. President or Dear Madam President. A member of congress can be addressed as Representative Keefe or Senator Beecher. Various religious officials have other salutations that differ by position and sect.

In the section that follows, we have brought together some examples of proper forms of address for government officials and religious leaders. In most forms of address you'll find an alternate form or a female version *in italics*. For these formal letters, you should add your address at the top of the letter, as described in Chapter 1.

Best regards,
The Authors

Formal or business letter to the president of the United States

The President
The White House
Washington, D.C. 20500

Dear Mr. President:
Dear Madam President:

I am writing to tell you of my appreciation for your support of a global campaign to end hunger. I am following closely the progress of Senate Bill 18, which I hope will pass both houses and make its way to your desk for signature soon.

Sincerely,
Laura Diamond

Social letter to the president of the United States

The President and Mrs. Surname
The President and Mr. Surname
The White House
Washington, D.C. 20500

Dear President and Mrs. Surname:
Dear *President and Mr. Surname:*

I want to compliment you on your recent joint appearance at the fundraiser for Global Hunger Campaign. I am a volunteer at my local food bank, and it made me very proud to be thanked by the president and first lady for my small efforts.

Sincerely,
Laura Diamond

Formal or business letter to the vice president of the United States

The Vice President
The White House
Washington, D.C. 20500

Dear Mr. Vice President:
Dear Madam Vice President:

On behalf of the United Garden Clubs of Ohio, I want to thank you for your efforts on behalf of the National Arboretum of Washington. This is a most important campaign, and we appreciate your support.

Sincerely,
Laura Diamond
Smalltown, OH

Social letter to the vice president of the United States

The Vice President and Mrs. Surname
The Vice President and Mr. Surname
The White House
Washington, D.C. 20500

Dear Vice President and Mrs. Surname:
Dear Vice President and Mr. Surname:

Thank you so much for the signed photograph of the both of you at the ribbon-cutting ceremony of the National Arboretum. The picture will take a place of honor at our club headquarters.

Sincerely,
Laura Diamond
Smalltown, OH

U.S. senator

The Honorable Firstname Surname
United States Senate
Washington, D.C. 20510

Dear Senator Surname:
Dear Mr. Senator:
Dear Madame Senator:

On behalf of the United Garden Clubs of Ohio, an organization of 72 clubs with 6,500 members across your home state, I am writing to ask your support for the Unified Pesticide Control Bill, due for a vote in coming weeks.

Our members, along with hundreds of thousands of other gardeners across the nation, feel that this bill is essential to ban the production and use of certain dangerous pesticides that kill friendly bugs and birds that are essential for a healthy and balanced environment. We look forward to hearing from you.

Sincerely,
Laura Diamond
Smalltown, OH

U.S. representative

The Honorable Firstname Surname
United States House of Representatives
Washington, D.C. 20515

Dear Mr. Surname:
Dear Ms. Surname:
Dear Congressman Surname:
Dear Congresswoman Surname:

On behalf of the Smalltown Garden Club, I am writing to ask you to reconsider your opposition to the Unified Pesticide Control Bill, due for a vote in coming weeks.

Our members, along with hundreds of thousands of other gardeners across the nation, feel that this bill is essential to ban the production and use of certain dangerous pesticides that kill friendly bugs and birds that are essential for a healthy and balanced environment.

We here in Smalltown intend to monitor closely your position on this essential bill. Your vote will be a critical element of our decision-making at election time.

Sincerely,
Laura Diamond
Smalltown, OH

Attorney general of the United States

The Honorable Firstname Surname
Attorney General
Department of Justice
Constitution Avenue and 10th Street NW
Washington, D.C. 20530

Dear Mr. Attorney General:
Dear Ms. Attorney General:

I am writing to protest the recent actions of the Department of Justice regarding lack of enforcement of the Alien Species Act.

This important law was intended to prevent the unintended importation of plant and animal species that could do damage to domestic agriculture and gardens.

In a recent speech you referred to the proponents of this law as "fruits and nuts." I would first of all remind you that as the chief law enforcement officer of the United States you are bound to enforce the laws whether you agree with them or not. And I would also remind you that gardeners vote, too; we will remember your actions when it comes time to make a decision in the upcoming congressional elections and two years from now when we elect a new president.

Sincerely,
Laura Diamond, President
Smalltown Garden Club
Smalltown, OH

State governor

The Honorable Firstname Surname
Governor of State
Statehouse, State Capital

Dear Governor Surname:

On behalf of the United Garden Clubs of Ohio, I would like to invite you to speak at our plenary session, scheduled for May 2, 20xx at the Smalltown Convention Center.

We expect more than 500 gardeners from across the state to attend.

We would be honored if you would speak to our members at the opening session, scheduled for 9 A.M., or at the grand award ceremony, which begins at 7 P.M.

I look forward to hearing from you.

Sincerely,
Laura Diamond, President
Smalltown Garden Club

Mayor

The Honorable Firstname Surname
Mayor of City
City Hall
City, State

Dear Mayor Surname:

We are thrilled that Governor Hart has accepted our invitation to be the keynote speaker at the upcoming convention of the United Garden Clubs of Ohio, which will be held here in Smalltown on May 2 at the Smalltown Convention Center.

We would be honored if you would join the governor at the head table during the plenary session at 9 A.M. and make short welcoming remarks to the attendees. The governor will be introduced by our state president, Marcy Vine, from Ashtabula.

I look forward to hearing from you.

Sincerely,
Laura Diamond, President
Smalltown Garden Club

Priest (Roman Catholic or Episcopal)

The Reverend Firstname Surname
The Reverend Dr. Firstname Surname
Our Lady of Faith Church
Smalltown, OH

Dear Father Surname:

We would be honored if you would give the opening invocation at the grand plenary session of the United Garden Clubs of Ohio on May 2 at 9 A.M. at the Smalltown Convention Center.

We expect about 500 avid gardeners from around the state, and Governor Hart is scheduled to give the keynote speech.

We look forward to hearing from you.

Sincerely,
Laura Diamond
Smalltown Garden Club
Smalltown, OH

Rabbi

Rabbi Firstname Surname
Rabbi Firstname Surname, D.D. (with a doctorate)
Smalltown Jewish Center
Smalltown, OH

Dear Rabbi Surname:
Dear Dr. Surname:

We would be honored if you would give the closing prayer at the awards ceremony of the United Garden Clubs of Ohio on May 2 at 7 P.M. at the Smalltown Convention Center.

We expect about 500 avid gardeners from around the state.

We look forward to hearing from you.

Sincerely,
Laura Diamond
Smalltown Garden Club
Smalltown, OH

Formal or business letter to member of president's cabinet

The Honorable Firstname Surname
Secretary of Agriculture
Washington, D.C.

Dear Mr. Secretary:
Dear Madam Secretary:

I wish to express my appreciation for the Agriculture Department's continuing efforts to improve the guidelines for the labeling of ingredients in our food. We have a right to know what we are eating, and we depend on your efforts to ensure that this happens.

Sincerely,
Monica Diamond

Formal letter to chief justice of supreme court

The Chief Justice of the United States
The Supreme Court of the United States
Washington, D.C. 20543

Dear Mr. Chief Justice:
Dear Madam Chief Justice:

I am writing to tell you how much I enjoyed your recent letter to the editor of The New York Times, "Patriotism Knows No Party."

In stressful periods such as these, we need reassurance that love of country and patriotism are still important and relevant.

Sincerely,
Harold Diamond

Formal letter to associate justice of supreme court

Mr. Justice Firstname Surname
Madam Justice Firstname Surname
The Supreme Court of the United States
Washington, D.C. 20543

Dear Mr. Justice:
Dear Madam Justice:

I wanted to tell you how much my husband and I enjoyed your talk at the Smalltown Public Library. We, along with everyone fortunate enough to attend, were thrilled to hear of the inner workings of our highest court.

Sincerely,
Monica Diamond

Formal letter to speaker of the House of Representatives

The Honorable Speaker of the House of Representatives
The Honorable Firstname Surname
Speaker of the House of Representatives
United States House of Representatives
Washington, D.C. 20515

Dear Mr. Speaker:
Dear Madam Speaker:

I am writing to you on behalf of the Smalltown Senior Center, a group of very active and vocal senior citizens in Smalltown, Ohio. We would very much appreciate your support of H.R. 3, which will be coming up for a House vote shortly. This bill would be an important first step in helping the elderly get relief from the sometimes intolerable and prohibitive cost of prescription medications.

Sincerely,
Harold Diamond, President
Smalltown Senior Center

Formal letter to United Nations ambassador

The Honorable Firstname Surname
U.S. Ambassador to the United Nations
United Nations Plaza
New York, NY 10017

Dear Mr. Ambassador:
Dear Madam Ambassador:

I am writing in support of the United Nations's continuing efforts to supply food and much-needed medicine to the victims of famine and other environmental catastrophes worldwide. We need to have a conscience, and for that we need the United Nations.

Sincerely,
Ronald Miller

Formal letter to foreign ambassador

His Excellency Firstname Surname
Her Excellency Firstname Surname
The Ambassador of Canada
Washington, D.C.

Excellency:
Dear Mr. Ambassador:
Dear Madam Ambassador:

We were greatly impressed with your recent speech here in Smalltown about some of the lesser-known attractions of Canada, including the restoration of Pier 21 in Halifax, Nova Scotia. My father's family arrived in Canada from Poland through Pier 21, and we were fascinated to hear about its history. We are already making plans to visit Halifax this coming summer. Thank you again for your visit.

Sincerely,
Ronald Miller

Formal letter to American ambassador abroad

The Honorable Firstname Surname
The Honorable Firstname Surname
Ambassador of the United States
American Embassy
Reykjavík, Iceland

Sir:
Madam:
Dear Mr. Ambassador:
Dear *Madam Ambassador:*

While visiting Iceland recently we were fortunate to hear your remarks at the Reykjavík library. We were the only Americans in attendance and must say we were happy to share in the favorable impressions of the audience. You made us proud.

Sincerely,
Ronald and Emma Miller

Formal letter to state legislator

The Honorable Firstname Surname
The Honorable Firstname Surname
House of Representatives
State Capitol
Address, State

Dear Mr. Surname:
Dear Ms. Surname:

The residents of the Smalltown Senior Center wish to voice our unqualified support of the proposed legislation to reduce the school tax for senior citizens. We recognize the importance of education for our young people, but the existing school tax rates impose an unfair burden on those living on a fixed income.

We appreciate your efforts in this area.

Sincerely,
Harold Diamond, President
Smalltown Senior Center

Formal letter to judge

The Honorable Firstname Surname
The Honorable Firstname Surname
Justice, Appellate Division
Supreme Court of the State of Ohio
Address
Columbus, OH

Dear Judge Surname:

The Smalltown Senior Center in Smalltown, Ohio, will hold its annual "Get Out the Vote" dinner on Saturday, October 13, at 7 P.M. in the new dining room at our center.

We know how important Smalltown is to you, and we would be honored if you could join us that evening and give us the benefit of remarks after dinner. This dinner is one of our most important events of the year.

Please let me know if the date and time is acceptable to your schedule. We look forward to your appearance.

Sincerely,
Harold Diamond, President
Smalltown Senior Center

Formal letter to the pope

His Holiness, The Pope
His Holiness Pope Name
Vatican City
Rome, Italy

Your Holiness:
Most Holy Father:

We were most fortunate to be at Castel Gandolfo recently and were among the privileged to be in the audience you addressed from your balcony.

We carried home with us your blessing and the Holy Spirit.

Sincerely,
Ronald and Emma Miller

Formal letter to cardinal

His Eminence Firstname Cardinal Surname
Archbishop of Columbus
Columbus, OH

Your Eminence:
Dear Cardinal Surname:

Thank you for your appearance at the Interfaith Breakfast last Wednesday at the Smalltown Synagogue. The support we received from so many eminent representatives of different faiths made this year's event an outstanding success.

Sincerely,
John Diamond, Chairman

Formal letter to bishop (Roman Catholic)

The Most Reverend Firstname Surname
Bishop of (Diocese)
Address
Columbus, OH

Most Reverend Sir:
Your Excellency:
Dear Bishop Surname:

Thank you for your help and that of your staff during our recent clothing drive to help victims of the hurricane in Central America. With so much red tape and bureaucracy to overcome, it was invaluable to have the expertise of those skilled in handling such operations.

Thank you,
Harold Diamond, Chairman
Smalltown Senior Center

Formal letter to bishop (Episcopal)

The Right Reverend Firstname Surname
Bishop of (Diocese)
Address

Right Reverend Sir:
Dear Bishop Surname:

Thank you for the very inspirational letter you wrote recently to the Smalltown Banner. Your remembrances of aiding the hurricane victims in Central America was motivating indeed.

Sincerely,
Harold Diamond

Formal letter to bishop (Protestant excluding Episcopal)

The Reverend Firstname Surname
Bishop Firstname Surname
Address
Columbus, OH

Reverend Sir:
Dear Bishop Surname:

On behalf of the Smalltown Genealogical Society I would like to thank you for your gift of a bound set of Smalltown Banner newspapers from the nineteenth century. We will put them to great use in our studies.

Sincerely,
Monica Diamond, Chairperson

Formal letter to monsignor

The Reverend Monsignor Firstname Surname
Address
Columbus, OH

Reverend Monsignor Surname:
Dear Monsignor Surname:

Thank you for giving the invocation at the annual Smalltown Chamber of Commerce Dinner. Your remarks were very inspiring, and we appreciate your participation.

Sincerely,
John Diamond, President
Smalltown Chamber of Commerce

Formal letter to Protestant clergy

The Reverend Firstname Surname
The Reverend Dr. Firstname Surname (with a doctorate)
Churchname
Address
Columbus, OH

Dear Mr. Surname:
Dear Mrs. Surname:
Dear Ms. Surname:
Dear Dr. Surname:

Thank you for addressing our group at the Lakeview Senior Apartment Complex. We found your remarks funny, inspiring, and thought provoking—a wondrous combination.

Please be our guest again whenever your time permits.

Sincerely,
Ron Miller, Spring Reception Committee

Formal letter to religious brother

Brother Firstname, [Name of Order]
Brother Firstname
Monastery of Saint Jackson
Address
Nearby, OH

Dear Brother Firstname:

Thank you for your help with our local efforts on behalf of the victims of the hurricane in Central America. Your guidance was just what we needed to make this endeavor a success.

Sincerely,
Ron Miller

Formal letter to religious sister or nun

Sister Name, [Name of Order]
Sister Name
St. Mary's School
Address
Waterford, OH

Dear Sister Name:

I wanted to tell you how much I appreciated your remarks at Lisa Decker's memorial service. We all loved Lisa, and you captured her essence so very well.

Thank you.

Sincerely,
Laura Diamond

Formal letter to college president

President Firstname Surname
Smalltown Community College
Smalltown, OH

Dear President Surname:

Congratulations on your appointment as president of Smalltown Community College. As one who has lived in Smalltown for the past twenty years and worked at the college for the past ten, I know that you have chosen a fine place to live and work.

I look forward to working with you in the future and doing what I can to make your administration a great success.

Sincerely,
Laura Diamond, Chairperson
Political Science Department

Formal letter to college dean

Dean Laura Diamond
Smalltown Community College
Smalltown, OH

Dear Dean Diamond:

Thank you for your letter of support. I am excited about being associated with such a fine school as Smalltown Community College, and my family looks forward to being part of the community.

I look forward to meeting you soon.

Sincerely,
James Jillson, President
Smalltown Community College

Formal letter to professor

Professor Hal Wood
Smalltown University
Smalltown, OH

Dear Professor Wood:

I am a student in your Wednesday morning Introduction to Statistics class. Before we are too far into the term, I would appreciate the opportunity to meet with you to discuss my progress in the class.

I am available at your convenience.

Sincerely,
Heather Diamond

44 Government Affairs

Dear Reader:

I'm a taxpayer and a voter and you work for me. That's the unstated bottom line any time you communicate with a government official. You don't have to be so blunt, and you should avoid making threats, but you should nevertheless be direct and to the point.

You can politely remind an elected official of a promise, or an administrator of a policy. One very effective tactic is to send a copy of a letter to an administrator to his or her elected supervisor. For example, if you write to the parks commissioner, send a copy to the mayor.

Wishing you the best of luck, we are,

Sincerely yours,
The Authors

Requesting handicapped parking permit

Community Relations
Smalltown Police Department
Smalltown, OH

Dear People:

I will be undergoing back surgery in a few days, and I expect to be on crutches for several months afterwards.

I am writing to apply for a handicapped parking permit valid for the next three months, through September 15. As requested in my telephone conversation with Lt. Jock Gibson, I have attached a copy of a note from Dr. Timothy Todd attesting to my medical condition.

Please advise me when the parking permit is available.

Sincerely,
Harold Diamond

Complaint about lack of handicapped parking spaces

Lt. Jock Gibson, Community Relations
Smalltown Police Department
Smalltown, OH

Dear Lt. Gibson:

I underwent disk surgery in June. At that time I applied for and received a handicapped parking sticker from the city with your assistance.

The problem now is that there are very few parking spaces designated for use by the handicapped within the city. I have found a handful of spaces behind City Hall and at the Memorial Library, but we have had little success parking at shops, the doctor's office, and the theater.

Is there anything that can be done to add more spaces around town?

Until I found myself on crutches, I had no idea how difficult it was to get around town with a handicap. I hope to be back on my own feet soon, but I'd like to make it easier for those who are permanently disabled.

Sincerely,
Harold Diamond
cc: Mayor Meyer Minor

Complaint about illegal parking in handicapped spaces

Lt. Jock Gibson, Community Relations
Smalltown Police Department
Smalltown, OH

Dear Lt. Gibson:

Once again, I am writing about problems with handicapped parking spaces in Smalltown. In the last few weeks I have been unable to park downtown because all of the spaces have been taken. We have discovered that many of the cars do not have the required handicapped parking permit displayed.

I can only conclude that our parking enforcement squad is not paying attention to the cars using the handicapped spaces, including the four directly in back of the police station. What can be done to help the handicapped make use of downtown?

Sincerely,
Harold Diamond
cc: Mayor Meyer Minor

Advising mayor of problem with parking

The Honorable Meyer Minor
Mayor of Smalltown
Smalltown Town Hall
Smalltown, OH

Dear Mayor Minor:

I am enclosing a copy of a letter sent to Lt. Jock Gibson of the Smalltown Police Department about the lack of law enforcement regarding use of handicapped parking spaces in downtown.

I will appreciate your attention to this matter.

Sincerely,
Harold Diamond

Request for information about absentee ballot

Commissioner, Board of Elections
City of Smalltown
Smalltown, OH

Dear Commissioner:

We will be out of town on the upcoming primary election day. Please advise as to how we may obtain absentee ballots.

Sincerely,
Laura and John Diamond

Requesting absentee ballots

Commissioner, Board of Elections
City of Smalltown
Smalltown, OH

Dear Commissioner:

Per your instructions, I am requesting that absentee ballots for the September 5 special election be sent to John Diamond and Laura Diamond. I understand that we will need to have our signatures on the ballots witnessed by a third party and that the ballots must be postmarked before September 5.

Sincerely,
Laura Diamond
John Diamond

Requesting information on registering to vote

Commissioner, Board of Elections
City of Smalltown
Smalltown, OH

Dear Commissioner:

On August 19 of this year I will turn eighteen. Please send me information and whatever forms are necessary for me to register to vote.

Sincerely,
Heather Diamond

Complaint about skateboarders in downtown

The Honorable Meyer Minor
Mayor of Smalltown
Smalltown Town Hall
Smalltown, OH

Dear Mayor Minor:

I recently had some business to conduct at town hall. As I attempted to ascend the concrete steps at the front of the building, I was almost knocked down by half a dozen young skateboarders who were using the steps and the steel rails of the plaza as launching ramps.

I can't believe these kids were allowed to engage in this type of dangerous behavior on public property. This situation is an accident—and a lawsuit—waiting to happen.

What happened to the plans to open a skate park at one of the town's recreation facilities?

Sincerely,
Harold Diamond

Response to mayor's reply about skateboarders

The Honorable Meyer Minor
Mayor of Smalltown
Smalltown Town Hall
Smalltown, OH

Dear Mayor Minor:

Thank you for your prompt reply to my letter about skateboarders using the steps of town hall.

I understand the dilemma faced by the government—if the parks department built a skate park it would be considered an endorsement of the activity and acceptance of liability for problems there. And it is also true that our police have better things to do than to stand guard over a set of steps.

I like your idea of installing a new set of trash receptacles, strategically placed to block use of the steps for skateboarding. It will be interesting to see where the skateboarders move next, though.

Sincerely,
Harold Diamond

Complaint about placement of a stop sign

Mega County Highway Department
Smalltown, OH

Dear People:

I would like to add my voice in opposition to the new stop sign on South Road at the intersection with Meadow Lane.

Although the idea of slowing drivers along that stretch of highway is a good one, the stop sign is more of a hazard than is a straightaway. I have seen four or five instances of drivers overlooking the sign and speeding through the intersection or being surprised when the car in front of them slowed down and stopped at the intersection.

I think a better idea would be a flashing caution light, a lowered speed limit on the entire stretch of road, or even a series of well-marked speed bumps.

I would be happy to get involved with a traffic advisory committee.

Sincerely,
John Diamond

Requesting passport renewal

Fairview Town Clerk
Fairview Town Hall
Fairview, PA

Dear Town Clerk:

My husband, Michael, and I are planning a trip to France in April.

We both need to renew our passports. Please send the appropriate papers.

Sincerely,
Karen Diamond

Seeking permission to use park for holiday gathering

Commissioner of Parks
Smalltown Parks Department
Smalltown, OH

Dear Commissioner:

I am writing on behalf of a group of residents in the Overbrook neighborhood. We would like permission to have a July 4 family celebration in Freer Park from 1 P.M. until the conclusion of the fireworks display at 10 P.M.

We plan to set up tables for food and use the park's barbecue pits for cooking. We will conduct games and activities for children nearby.

According to the mayor's office, we need to apply for a permit for the use of a portion of the park for our group. Please send us any needed forms and instructions.

Sincerely,
Harold Diamond

Requesting information about summer programs

Parks and Recreation Department
Fairview, PA

Dear People:

We will be moving to Fairview in a few weeks.

Please send me information about the various programs offered by the parks and recreation department for Granger Park and other facilities.

I am interested in hours, events, activities for children, and fees.

Sincerely,
Karen Diamond

Thanks for use of park

Commissioner of Parks
Smalltown Parks Department
Smalltown, OH

Dear Commissioner:

On behalf of the Overbrook neighborhood, I wanted to thank the department for the use of Freer Park facilities for our neighborhood Fourth of July party. Your staff was very helpful in preparing the Meadows picnic area and assisting us in safely managing the barbecue pits.

We had a real old-fashioned celebration and everyone who attended said it was one of their best neighborhood parties ever.

Sincerely,
Harold Diamond
cc: Mayor Meyer Minor, Smalltown City Hall

Suggestion for parks program

Fred White, Community Relations Department
Parks and Recreation Department
Fairview, PA

Dear Mr. White:

Thank you for sending me the information about Granger Park. I was impressed with the beautiful facilities including the pool, but did not find any information about swimming lessons for children. Are there any swimming programs available through parks and recreation or from private instructors?

Sincerely,
Karen Diamond

Praising city employee

Fred White, Community Relations Department
Parks and Recreation Department
Fairview, PA

Dear Mr. White:

We recently moved to Fairview and are enjoying Granger Park very much. I recently had a special reason to appreciate our new home, and would like to give credit to a very impressive employee.

I was at the pool recently with my two young children. While I was involved in a "time-out" with my six-year-old son, my daughter took the opportunity to wander off. We are new to the area, and she immediately became lost.

A parks and recreation employee, Laura Norton, noticed that my daughter was in distress and handled the situation perfectly. Hannah was back with us before we had time to become very worried. This young woman was courteous and thoughtful, and we appreciate everything she did.

Thank you,
Karen Diamond
cc: Laura Norton

Asking for skate park

Smalltown Parks Department
Smalltown, OH

Dear People:

I enjoy living in Smalltown while I attend law school at the university. I have been acquainting myself with town facilities but have not as yet found a place where I can work out on my inline skates. Does Smalltown have a designated skate park?

Every college town I have visited has this type of facility, and I can vouch for their popularity. If there is not such a park in town, are there any plans to build one? I would be happy to become involved in any design committee for that purpose.

Sincerely,
Joshua Diamond

Complaint about lack of enforcement of dog regulations

Smalltown Parks Department
Smalltown, OH

Dear People:

I would like to bring to your attention a situation at Freer Park that is jeopardizing the enjoyment of that lovely facility for many of us.

In Smalltown we have a law stipulating that dogs must be on leashes in all public areas and that the owners must clean up after them. It is impossible to take a walk in the park without dodging a running group of barking, unleashed dogs, or their leavings.

What can be done to see that dog owners take responsibility for keeping the park in a condition we can all enjoy?

Sincerely,
Harold Diamond
cc: Mayor Meyer Minor

Complaint about walking path in park

Commissioner of Parks
Smalltown Parks Department
Smalltown, OH

Dear Commissioner:

My wife and I have lived in Smalltown for more than sixty years and have enjoyed Freer Park for all that time. When we were young and didn't have the money to go anywhere else we would walk there almost every day. Our children grew up going to family picnics and Fourth of July fireworks there.

Now we are seniors, and my wife must use a wheelchair for any extended walk. We find that the beautiful walking paths through the park are all but impassable to her. The paths are cracked and littered with rocks and debris that make it impossible to roll her chair from place to place.

More so than any other public facility, outdoor parks should be completely accessible to the handicapped.

We hope you will devote resources to restoring the walking paths in Freer Park for all visitors.

Sincerely,
Ron Miller
cc: Mayor Meyer Minor

Response to mayor's letter about walking path in park

The Honorable Meyer Minor
Mayor of Smalltown
Smalltown Town Hall
Smalltown, OH

Dear Mayor Minor:

Thank you for your kind note in response to my letter to the commissioner of parks. Emma and I completely agree with you about the need to make all public facilities accessible to the handicapped.

I would be honored to accept a position on the Mayor's Task Force on Handicapped Access. At my first meeting, I will ask the commissioner to present a plan to restore the walking paths to their original condition.

Sincerely,
Ron Miller

Asking excuse from jury duty because of travel

Jury Commission
Justice Center
Smalltown, OH

Dear Commission:

I have received a summons for jury duty beginning October 5, 20xx. A copy is attached.

Unfortunately, I will be out of the country from September 30 through October 15. Please reschedule my jury duty for another time. My preferred date would be early December.

Sincerely,
John Diamond

Asking excuse from jury duty for medical reason

Jury Commission
Justice Center
Smalltown, OH

Dear Commission:

I have been summoned to jury duty on October 8. A copy of the summons is attached.

Enclosed is a letter from my physician, Dr. Timothy Todd, regarding a medical condition that makes it impossible for me to serve on a jury in October. As indicated, I do not expect to be available for the next six months.

Please remove my name from the October list of jurors.

Sincerely,
Harold Diamond

Asking excuse from jury duty because of move out of state

Jury Commission
Justice Center
Smalltown, OH

Dear Commission:

I have received the attached summons for jury duty.

I have moved from Mega County and now make my permanent residence in Fairview, Pennsylvania.

Please remove my name from the juror list.

Sincerely,
Michael Diamond

Asking excuse from jury duty for out-of-state student

Commissioner of Jurors
Warren, ME

Dear Commissioner:

My daughter, Amy Rogers, has received a summons for jury duty. A copy is attached.

Because she is a full-time college student at Smalltown University in Smalltown, Ohio, she will not be able to meet this obligation.

At this time, I am not aware of her plans for the summer, and do not know whether she will be back in Maine. Please postpone or cancel her jury summons, and advise us of any future obligation.

Sincerely,
Walter Rogers

Advising of availability for commission appointment

The Honorable Meyer Minor
Mayor of Smalltown
Smalltown City Hall
Smalltown, OH

Dear Mayor Minor:

I see in the public service announcements section of the Smalltown Banner that there is an open position on the Airport Commission.

I have always been interested in aviation and was a private pilot in my younger days. I would be honored to be considered for a position on the airport board.

Sincerely,
Harold Diamond

Resigning from advisory board due to illness

Harry Dalton, President
Smalltown Cable Television Advisory Board
Smalltown, OH

Dear Harry:

With regret, I must tender my resignation as a member of the Smalltown Cable Television Advisory Board because of illness.

It has been my pleasure to serve for the past three years as a member of this important community commission. I will continue to follow the progress of the board and its important issues.

Sincerely,
Ron Miller

45 Political Matters

Dear Reader:

Politicians need you: They want your money and your vote. In theory, you will be repaid with representation at city hall, the statehouse, or in Washington.

In this section you'll find some letters of response to fundraising letters, and letters related to the establishment and conduct of a local political campaign.

Remember that you will weaken your message if it is unclear, indirect, or abusive. Put yourself in the recipient's position. Are you more likely to respond to a polite and reasonable letter or to a rude rant?

Sincerely,
The Authors

Asking to be removed from political mailing list

Mary Smith
Candidate for State Senator
Smalltown, OH

Dear Ms. Smith:

I received your literature in the mail, along with your request for a contribution. Your values and point of view do not coincide with mine.

Please remove my name from your mailing list and do not contact me again.

Sincerely,
Morgan Diamond

Sending political donation

Jane Jones
Candidate for State Senator
Smalltown, OH

Dear Ms. Jones:

Thank you for the literature regarding your candidacy for the state senate. You can count on me as a most enthusiastic supporter.

I have watched your career in politics over the past several years. Though I don't agree with you on everything, I think you will be a valuable advocate for the people of our district.

Please accept my donation and best wishes for success.

Sincerely,
Morgan Diamond

Requesting information on seeking office

Board of Elections
Smalltown Town Hall
Smalltown, OH

Dear People:

I am a registered voter, residing in Smalltown. I am considering running for a seat on the Town Council.

Please send me all of the forms and petitions I would need to file should I decide to run for office this fall.

Please send information to my attention at the address above.

Thank you,
John Diamond

Request for political introduction

John Diamond
Smalltown, OH

Dear John:

For years I've sat back and let others do all the heavy lifting. I've voted in all the elections, sent my contributions, and even stuffed a few envelopes from time to time.

But now I find myself wanting to do more. As you may know, Bob Stevens is going to retire this fall as town treasurer, and I'm giving serious consideration to running for that position.

With my background as an accountant I think I could do a heck of a job. I also have some good ideas that I would like to run past an astute politician like you.

And, of course, I will want the backing of Citizens for a Better Smalltown. I am hoping you will be able to arrange some introductions and advise me on campaign tactics.

I have believed in you and your positions for years, John. Any help you can give me will be most valuable.

Sincerely,
David Paul

Agreeing to provide political introduction

David Paul
Smalltown, OH

Dear Dave:

Yes, yes, a thousand times yes! You will make a fine candidate for town treasurer, and I think your chances of being elected are very good. I'll be happy to do what I can to make it happen.

Although I can't speak on behalf of Citizens for a Better Smalltown before the board formally endorses a candidate, I can tell you that I would be glad to sponsor you. And as the chairman, I do have a bit of influence in the association.

I know from our previous informal discussions that you agree with our platform of fiscal responsibility and open government. I've enclosed with this letter our most recent party statement.

We have been searching for someone with your expertise and integrity to run for office. Call me next week, and we'll get together for lunch.

Sincerely,
John Diamond

Seeking political advice from friends

Dear Gloria and Jim:

Can an old friend tap into the wisdom of two valued and trusted confidants?

As you know, over the past several years I have been involved in grassroots politics here in Smalltown. I am now considering whether to take the next step—a run for Town Council.

I hope you'll join me and Laura, as well as some other close and trusted friends and acquaintances, to brainstorm this possibility.

We will get together on Monday, June 6, at 8 P.M. at my house.

Sincerely,
John Diamond

Asking someone to join election committee

Fred Blaine
Smalltown, OH

Dear Fred:

Thank you for being part of the group of trusted friends and associates who met at my house on Monday to give me guidance as I contemplate a run for Town Council.

It probably will come as no surprise to anyone who attended the gathering that I have decided to toss my hat in the ring. I plan to make a formal announcement next week.

Out of all the fine minds giving me some direction, I was particularly impressed with your focus and vision regarding not only what I can contribute as town councilman, but also to the community as a whole. I think we are very much on the same page when it comes to what is best for Smalltown.

I have a request to make of you. I would be honored if you would be my campaign manager. I think the two of us as a team would be very hard to beat.

I ask this knowing it would require a large commitment of your time and energy. As we discussed last week, if something is important it is worth the sacrifice required to make it happen.

Sincerely,
John Diamond

Seeking newspaper coverage for announcement of candidacy

Jerry White, Editor
Smalltown Banner
Smalltown, OH

Dear Mr. White:

On Tuesday, July 15, at noon, I will be making a formal announcement regarding my candidacy in the upcoming election for Smalltown Town Council.

I will hold a rally on the steps of Town Hall and will take questions from reporters afterwards to explain my platform.

I would appreciate coverage by the Banner.

Sincerely,
John Diamond

Invitation to announcement of candidacy

Dear friend:

I am so appreciative of the support of many friends and acquaintances as I have considered a possible run for Town Council this fall.

This is probably not much of a secret to you by now, but here goes: I plan to throw my hat in the ring next week. I hope I can count on all of you to help me win, and more important, to help me accomplish the changes in town government that we all agree we need.

I will make a formal announcement of my candidacy at noon on Tuesday, July 15, on the steps of Town Hall. We've invited the press to cover the event.

If you can, I hope you'll spend your lunch hour at the rally, and then begin to spread the word about the campaign.

Sincerely,
John Diamond

Invitation to cocktail party for supporters

Dear Barbara and Tom:

I hope you will join Laura and me on Tuesday, July 15, at 8 P.M. at our house for cocktails. This will be the first real event of my campaign for Town Council.

Earlier that day, at noon on the steps of Town Hall, I will reveal the worst-kept secret in town with a formal declaration of candidacy. (You're invited to that event, too, of course.)

I know that you are two of our town's most concerned and committed citizens. I am eager to share with you my plans and ideas for the future growth of Smalltown.

Please join us on Thursday.

Sincerely,
John Diamond

Campaign letter

Dear Citizen of Smalltown:

Please allow me to take a minute of your time to introduce myself. My name is John Diamond, and I am running for Smalltown Town Council.

I first came to Smalltown more than thirty years ago to attend Smalltown University. There I met my lovely wife, Laura, and the two of us never left.

After college I started my own business, Diamond Music Hall, which I am proud to say has been a fixture of downtown Smalltown for more than fifteen years. Laura is a professor of political science at Smalltown Community College.

Laura and I raised our family here: our son Michael, who is married to Karen and has two small children; our daughter Morgan, who is married to Roger Hamilton and works at Smalltown General Hospital; our son Joshua, who will graduate this year from Smalltown University; and our daughter Heather, who will be a freshman at Smalltown University in the fall.

I am committed to the growth and vitality of Smalltown. At the heart of my platform is a belief that we must all work to strengthen the economic underpinnings of downtown Smalltown.

Every business that pays taxes and employs workers and attracts shoppers to Smalltown helps support our schools, police force, fire department, parks and recreation department, and other essential services of our community. Anything we do that weakens downtown—including support of unincorporated subdivisions and shopping malls that draw buyers but do not contribute to the support of our town—hurts us all now, and will continue to hurt us in the future.

I am enclosing a pamphlet that lays out more of my ideas.

I hope you will honor me with your vote in November.

Sincerely,
John Diamond

Get-out-the-vote letter

Dear Voter:

On Tuesday, November 6, the voters of Smalltown once again will enjoy the privilege of casting a vote to determine the course of our government.

I would be honored to receive your vote for my candidacy for a seat on Town Council.

One thing we can all agree on is that it is a gift to be a resident of such a wonderful place as Smalltown. But we have to work hard to keep it that way and to make growth acceptable to all residents.

If you need any assistance in getting to the polls, or in casting an absentee ballot, please contact my campaign committee at (xxx) xxx-xxxx.

Sincerely,
John Diamond

Thanks for endorsement

Editorial Board
Smalltown Banner
Smalltown, OH

Dear Editorial Board:

Thank you for your endorsement of my candidacy for Town Council.

I hope your readers, and all voters in Smalltown, will honor me with their votes on election day.

Sincerely,
John Diamond

Accepting newspaper endorsement with reservations

Editorial Board
The Times of Smalltown
Smalltown, OH

Dear Editorial Board:

Thank you for your endorsement of my candidacy for Town Council.

Although our ideological visions are almost always directly opposite, I accept your endorsement of my background and commitment to meaningful change in Smalltown.

I hope your readers, and all voters in Smalltown, will honor me with their votes on election day.

Sincerely,
John Diamond

Victory letter in newspaper

The Editor
Smalltown Banner
Smalltown, OH

To the Editor:

I want to thank the voters of Smalltown who honored me with election to the Town Council.

In the course of my campaign, I heard your thoughts on what your government is doing right and what you think we can do to be better. Beginning today, I will work to put into effect the programs that were the basis of my campaign.

Smalltown was built with the hard work of all who have lived here. Its future begins today.

Sincerely,
John Diamond

Letter to newspaper regarding unsuccessful campaign

The Editor
Smalltown Banner
Smalltown, OH

To the Editor:

I want to thank the voters of Smalltown for their support. Unfortunately, I did not receive enough votes to win a seat on Town Council, but I was honored to have the opportunity to run for office.

I am most grateful for the support and commitment of all my fine, dedicated workers. Your enthusiasm and tireless effort makes the political process work.

Although I will not be taking a seat on the council in January, I promise to remain involved in local government. Let us now support our elected officials with constructive efforts for change.

Sincerely,
Mark McDonald

Thanks to newspaper for coverage

Jerry White, Editor
Smalltown Banner
Smalltown, OH

Dear Mr. White:

As I prepare to take office on the Smalltown Town Council, I want to express my thanks to the newspaper for the coverage of my campaign. Although I didn't agree with everything written about me and my campaign, I never questioned your dedication to honest journalism and to Smalltown.

I expect that we will also have our agreements and disagreements over the coming two years of my term on the council. I promise I will always respect the independence of the journalist, and trust that in return, the Banner will respect my dedication to constructive change in Smalltown.

Sincerely,
John Diamond

To victorious opponent

John Diamond
Smalltown, OH

Dear John:

Although the election did not turn out the way I had hoped, please allow me to offer my congratulations to you on your victory.

I am proud of the way we both handled our run for office.

I'm not going away—you can expect to see me at Town Council meetings and other public events, pushing for the constructive change I asked for in my campaign. I hope I can find many opportunities to work with you on common goals.

Sincerely,
Mark McDonald

Expression of support for friend running for office

Dear Mary:

State Senator Mary Williams? That sounds just right to me.

Congratulations on throwing your hat in the ring. You have been the voice of reason and fiscal responsibility in this community for years. I am so glad you are taking the next step.

You have my full support. Please let me know what I can do to help you win election this fall.

Sincerely,
Laura Diamond

Supporting former opponent's position

John Diamond
Smalltown, OH

Dear Councilman:

I wanted to express my support of your stand opposing the proposed stop sign at State and Elm.

A stop sign at that intersection would just create more confusion and not alleviate any of the traffic problems we hope to solve.

A bandage on a broken arm is not the solution.

Sincerely,
Mark McDonald

Requesting advertising rates for political campaign

Robert Lynn, Advertising Director
Smalltown Banner
Smalltown, OH

Dear Mr. Lynn:

I am a candidate for town treasurer here in Smalltown.

I would like to receive a media kit and other information about paid advertising space in the Banner.

Thank you.

Sincerely,
David Paul

Asking for bulk political advertising contract

Robert Lynn, Advertising Director
Smalltown Banner
Smalltown, OH

Dear Mr. Lynn:

Thank you for the information on rates for political advertising in the Banner.

As I understand it, you offer a discount on total column inches for ads that exceed various specified levels. Your materials make it very clear that political ads must be paid in advance, which seems harsh, but this must be based on your experience with other candidates.

Please give me a call to schedule a meeting with me and my campaign manager, Fred Blaine.

Sincerely,
David Paul

Seeking assistance from advertising agency for political ads

Alex Stein
Stein Advertising Agency
Smalltown, OH

Dear Mr. Stein:

I am the campaign manager for David Paul, who is running for Smalltown town treasurer in the election this fall.

I would like to meet with you soon to discuss hiring your agency to develop some print, television, and radio ads for the campaign. I am available anytime the week of August 19.

Looking forward to hearing from you, I am,

Sincerely yours,
Fred Blaine, Campaign Manager
David Paul for Town Treasurer
Smalltown, OH

46 Clubs, Organizations, and Religious Institutions

Dear Reader:

Humans are social creatures—some more so than others—and many of us build our lives around clubs, organizations, and religious institutions in our community.

In this section we include letters about joining groups, resigning from them, running for office, and launching and managing activities. The tone of this type of letter is generally friendly and collegial; make sure that any requests or instructions are clearly and directly stated.

Best regards,
The Authors

Requesting information about club

Smalltown Extreme Ski Club
Smalltown, OH

Dear People:

I saw your flier in the supermarket. I am a pretty good skier and dream of becoming a better one—something that is not all that easy here in Ohio.

Please send me information about the club, membership requirements, and dues.

I will be attending the Law School at Smalltown University. Do you have any active members from the school?

Sincerely,
Joshua Diamond

Requesting membership information

Membership Committee
Classics for Young People
Southtown, PA

Dear Membership Committee:

I love classic books and am the mother of two small children, so I was delighted to learn of your organization. It is great to see our young children read, and it is wonderful to see them reading something worthwhile.

Please send me information about joining and getting involved in promoting good literature for youngsters.

Sincerely,
Karen Diamond

Accepting membership

Membership Committee
Classics for Young People
Southtown, PA

Dear Membership Committee:

I am happy to accept your offer of membership in Classics for Young People.

Because I'm a lover of classic books and the mother of two small children, I completely agree with your group's goals. I look forward to getting involved in activities in the community in support of reading.

Sincerely,
Karen Diamond

Soliciting membership in club

Dear Parent:

As the mother of a child at Smalltown Elementary School I know how thrilling it is to watch a youngster learn to read. Mine started with cereal boxes and stop signs.

Unfortunately, some of our schools and libraries seem to have decided that cereal box literature is good enough. Many of the books our children are being asked to read are all sugar, with no protein. The theory seems to be that getting a child to read anything at all is a success.

We think otherwise. Classics for Young People endeavors to get our children back to reading the great books: Charles Dickens, Jack London, Herman Melville, Jane Austen, and other great writers.

We need your help in getting our schools and libraries to again emphasize that quality and fine writing do matter. I am enclosing some literature about our organization and hope you will join me in becoming a member and volunteer.

Sincerely,
Karen Diamond

Declining membership offer

Membership Committee
Protect Our Outdoor Pets
Smalltown, OH

Dear Membership Committee:

Thank you for the information about your organization. I support your philosophy of safeguarding the rights of those who cannot speak for themselves.

However, at this time I am unable to commit time and money to another community organization, and must respectfully decline your invitation to be a member.

Sincerely,
Monica Diamond

Declining membership offer because of disagreement

Membership Committee
Protect Our Outdoor Pets
Smalltown, OH

Dear Membership Committee:

Thank you for the information about your organization. While I support your philosophy of safeguarding the rights of those who cannot speak for themselves, I completely disagree with your campaign to repeal Smalltown's pooper-scooper law. I feel that all residents need to be responsible for the acts of their pets.

I must respectfully decline your invitation to be a member.

Sincerely,
Monica Diamond

Resignation as officer

Smalltown Parent and Teachers Association
Smalltown, OH

Dear Board Members:

It is with regret that I must resign my position as president of the Smalltown Parent and Teachers Association. My husband has accepted a job in Pennsylvania and we will be moving in two months.

I am proud to have been involved with SPTA for all of these years, and feel that we have made a difference in the education of our children. We have a great group of parents and teachers, and I am sure SPTA will continue to thrive.

Sincerely,
Karen Diamond

Resigning club membership

Dear President:

I regret to inform you that I have decided to resign as a member of Citizens for a Better Smalltown.

As you know, I have been a vocal opponent of the direction in which the organization is going. I no longer feel that my membership makes a meaningful difference.

I know we all want the best for Smalltown, but our differences over the means of change make it impossible for us to work together.

Sincerely,
John Diamond

Rejoining organization

Membership Committee
Smalltown Historic Foundation
Smalltown, OH

Dear Membership Committee:

Please accept my application for membership in the Smalltown Historic Foundation.

I was an active member from 1980 to 1995 and was happy to contribute to this worthwhile organization. For a variety of personal reasons I dropped out of the group for the past few years.

I am free to rejoin, and look forward to becoming involved.

Sincerely,
Monica Diamond

Announcing dues increase

Dear Members of the Smalltown Garden Club:

At our annual meeting last Thursday the board of directors reluctantly came to the conclusion that we must increase dues in order to keep up with rising costs.

This will be the first increase we have asked for since 1999.

Our agenda for the coming year is an ambitious one, and we need the additional revenue to make it happen. Accordingly, we are setting the amount for an active membership at $110 per year, an increase of 10 percent over current rates.

We certainly hope this doesn't represent a hardship for any of our loyal members. If this should be the case, please let me know.

Sincerely,
Laura Diamond, President

Notification of change of meeting date

Dear Members of the Smalltown Garden Club:

Please be advised that the time and date of the next meeting have been changed because of a scheduling conflict with our speaker.

CANCELED: 7 P.M. Thursday, June 16, in the Media Room at the Smalltown Public Library.
NEW MEETING: 7 P.M. Tuesday, June 21, in the Community Room at the Smalltown Public Library.

We are looking forward to hearing from our guest speaker, Dr. William Parker, professor of botany at Smalltown Community College. He will tell us about "New Trends in Backyard Composting."

We look forward to seeing you all there.

Sincerely,
Laura Diamond

Notice of dress code for meeting

Dear Members of the Smalltown Garden Club:

I have received inquiries from several of you asking about the appropriate dress for our annual dinner meeting. The committee decided that this year's gathering would be a formal event. That means a gown or cocktail dress for the ladies and a tuxedo or dark business suit for the gentlemen.

Just to remind you, the event will be held at Sebastian's on the Lake on Saturday, June 9. We will meet for cocktails at 7 P.M., followed by dinner at 8 P.M.

It promises to be a delightful evening. Hope to see you there—dressed to the nines.

Sincerely,
Laura Diamond

Request for meeting room

Jack Miller, Principal
Smalltown Elementary School
Smalltown, OH

Dear Mr. Miller:

The Smalltown Garden Club hopes to hold its first meeting of this year on February 18. For the past several years Smalltown Elementary School has graciously allowed us to use a conference room for this purpose.

We would very much appreciate the same courtesy this year. If possible, we would like to use the conference room from 7 to 8:30 P.M. on February 18. We would expect a group of no more than fifty persons.

As in years past, we would be happy to contribute books about plants and gardens to the school library.

I look forward to hearing from you soon.

Sincerely,
Laura Diamond

Inviting members to meeting

Dear Member:

Though it's still the dead of winter, it's time to begin planning our spring gardens—and the spring fundraiser for the Smalltown Garden Club.

I am writing to invite you to attend our first meeting of the year. We will get together on Monday, February 18, at 7 P.M. in Conference Room B of the Smalltown Elementary School.

At this meeting we also will need to finalize our plans for planting daffodils at City Hall and select a speaker for our annual luncheon.

I have had the pleasure of speaking to many of you since the fall, and I know we have the seeds for many great ideas.

Sincerely,
Laura Diamond, Chairperson

Invitation to a speaker

Jonatha Smyth
Garden Columnist
Smalltown Banner

Dear Ms. Smyth:

The steering committee of the Smalltown Garden Club would be honored if you would accept our invitation to be the guest speaker at our spring fundraiser.

Your column on gardening in the Smalltown Banner is a must-read for our members. We would be thrilled to hear your thoughts on how the garden club can accomplish even more in the coming years.

The meeting will be held at Fitzgerald's Restaurant on Tuesday, March 18, beginning at 11 A.M. A delicious lunch will follow the business meeting about noon. We hope you will be available to speak for no longer than thirty minutes after the meal and to answer some of the questions I know our members are eager to ask.

Please let us know about any special requirements. Do you need a slide projector and screen? We also can provide a computer and projector for a PowerPoint show.

We would be happy to have someone pick you up at your office.

We hope you can find time in your busy schedule to meet with us. Having you as our speaker would be a special treat for our members.

Sincerely,
Laura Diamond, Chairperson

Acceptance of invitation as speaker

Laura Diamond, Chairperson
Smalltown Garden Club

Dear Ms. Diamond:

Thank you for your gracious invitation to be the guest speaker at the spring fundraiser of the Smalltown Garden Club. I am happy to accept the invitation.

I would like to speak about my particular interest, "Multilayer Compost Heaps." I will bring a tray of slides and would appreciate setup of a Kodak Carousel projector and screen.

You graciously offered to have someone pick me up for the meeting. I would appreciate that courtesy; I am hobbling around on a broken ankle. Please call me to set the time and discuss directions to my home.

Regarding lunch, I eat only organically raised vegetables and fruit. Can you arrange an appropriate meal for me?

Sincerely,
Jonatha Smyth

Acknowledgment of acceptance as speaker

Jonatha Smyth
Garden Columnist
Smalltown Banner

Dear Ms. Smyth:

We are so thrilled that you are able to accept our invitation to speak at our spring fundraiser.

Emily Carlson will call you soon to confirm arrangements to pick you up at your home on Tuesday, March 18, and bring you to the luncheon at Fitzgerald's Restaurant.

We will have a Kodak Carousel projector and screen set up for your use. We are already aware of your dedication to organically grown fruits and vegetables and have arranged a special meal for you.

Please let me know if there is anything else we can do for you.

We are very excited to have you address our group, and look forward to finally meeting one of our favorite writers.

Sincerely
Laura Diamond

Thanks to speaker

Jonatha Smyth
Garden Columnist
Smalltown Banner

Dear Ms. Smyth:

Thank you again for your stirring speech. Never again will we think of organic mulch—or lasagna—in the same way. The idea of layering organic material like an elaborate Italian pasta dish is a breathtaking concept.

Please know that you have a standing invitation to attend our meetings at any time. In the meantime, we will continue to read your column and follow your excellent advice.

Sincerely,
Laura Diamond

Follow-up to members after meeting

Dear Members:

Everyone I have spoken with is thrilled with the success of our spring fundraiser. Congratulations to everyone involved!

Our speaker, Jonatha Smyth, was marvelous. We hope she will come back to speak with us again someday.

Let's keep up the good work and come to the next meeting full of ideas for making this the best year ever. Details on our next get-together will be sent to you within the next two weeks.

Sincerely,
Laura Diamond, Chairperson

Declining invitation to speak at school

Mr. Gordon Fuller
Smalltown Elementary School

Dear Mr. Fuller:

Thank you for inviting me to address your seventh-grade history class. I commend you for your efforts to expose young minds to the excitement of history.

Unfortunately, I will be attending a conference in Boston at that time. Please give me a rain check. I would love to speak to your students.

Sincerely,
Laura Diamond

Invitation to open house

Dear Resident of Smalltown:

After ten long months of work, the beautiful new addition to the Smalltown Senior Center has been completed. This wonderful new space will serve as a library, conference room, and entertainment venue for our residents and the community.

We think this lovely space—with skylights and oversized windows—will also make a beautiful spot for functions such as weddings and parties.

We have had tremendous support from the community in raising funds for this project. To show our appreciation, we will have an open house on Sunday, January 23, from 1 to 4 P.M. We hope you'll join us for cake and punch.

Monica Diamond
Honorary Chairperson, Smalltown Senior Center

Declining invitation to speak at luncheon

Speakers Committee
Smalltown Professional Women's Association
Smalltown, OH

Dear Members of the Committee:

Thank you for your invitation to address the Smalltown Professional Women's Association at your luncheon on March 16. I appreciate the kind words.

Unfortunately, I have a prior commitment on that day.

Please do keep me in mind for a future meeting. I would love to address your group.

Sincerely,
Laura Diamond

Declining gift

Speakers Committee
Smalltown Professional Women's Association
Smalltown, OH

Dear Members of the Committee:

Thank you so much for the gift of a framed lithograph of downtown Smalltown as a token of appreciation for my recent speech to your group. I appreciate the thought and your generosity.

Unfortunately, Smalltown Community College policy prevents me from accepting such an expensive present from groups and individuals with which we have business and professional relationships.

Your thanks are payment enough.

Sincerely,
Laura Diamond

Refusing a position in organization

Search Committee
Smalltown Community Center
Smalltown, OH

Dear Members of the Search Committee:

Thank you for considering me for the position of president of the Smalltown Community Center. It is an honor to be deemed worthy of such an important post.

Unfortunately, I must ask that nothing further be done to advance this idea. With family commitments, health issues, and volunteer obligations, my wife and I have all we can handle at present.

Please be assured that this in no way diminishes our commitment to the community center. It remains a very important part of our life, and we will continue our involvement and support to the fullest extent we are able.

Sincerely,
Neil Steven

Asking to be considered for position in organization

Search Committee
Lakeview Apartments Senior Committee
Smalltown, OH

Dear Members of the Search Committee:

I would like to be considered for a position on the executive board of the Lakeview Apartments Senior Committee.

In the three months Emma and I have lived here, we have been very impressed with the wide range of interests and activities of the residents. I've seen the wish list posted on the community bulletin board—in fact, I've added a few ideas myself—and I'd like to help make more of them happen.

I would be honored to be nominated.

Sincerely,
Ron Miller

Accepting nomination and asking for votes

Dear Residents of Lakeview Apartments:

I am honored to be nominated for a position on the executive board of the Lakeview Apartments Senior Committee. My platform is simple: I plan to work as hard as I can to fulfill as many of the requests on the wish list as possible . . . and then some.

I hope you will vote for me at the community meeting on Tuesday, September 6.

Sincerely,
Ron Miller

Requesting better facilities at theater

General Manager
Smalltown Community Theatre
Smalltown, OH

Dear General Manager:

My husband and I are enthusiastic supporters of the Smalltown Community Theatre, and we look forward to every new production.

I do, though, have a complaint about the facilities: There is only one ladies' restroom in the entire theater, and this accommodates only six at a time. At intermission there is always a long line out the door and into the hallway, and sometimes theatergoers miss part of the second act.

I have noticed that on that same floor there is an additional restroom marked "Employees Only." Could that room be used at intermission time as an additional ladies' room?

Sincerely,
Monica Diamond

Request for information about consumer group

Member Services
National Automobile Association
Smalltown, OH

Dear People:

Please send me information about joining the association. I am interested in towing services, supplementary insurance, and trip planning books and maps.

I am interested also in home equity and mortgage refinancing services available through the association.

Do you offer membership discounts to senior citizens?

Sincerely,
Harold Diamond

Add family member to association membership

Member Services
American Automobile Association
Smalltown, OH

Re: Membership xxxx-xxxx

Dear Member Services:

Please add my daughter, Heather Diamond, to our AAA membership and send her a welcome kit and identification card.

Per association guidelines, I certify that my daughter is a family dependent, currently attending college full-time. Her date of birth is July 6, 1985.

Please send me a bill for the supplemental membership.

Sincerely,
John Diamond

Remove family member from association membership

Member Services
American Automobile Association
Smalltown, OH

Re: Membership xxxx-xxxx

Dear Member Services:

Please remove my son, Joshua Diamond, from our membership in the AAA, and refund to us the unused portion of his annual fee.

Joshua has graduated from college, and per association guidelines he is no longer eligible to be included in a family membership.

Sincerely,
John Diamond

Appreciation of sermon

The Reverend Peter Hall
Smalltown Congregational Church
Smalltown, OH

Dear Mr. Hall:

I always receive a great deal of comfort and inspiration from your sermons. But your message to the congregation last Sunday was truly motivational.

You challenged us all to get involved, using the perfect blend of soft-spoken gentleness and spirited urgings. You dared us to put aside our complacency.

Sometimes, Reverend, your flock needs to be prodded. Thank you for doing just that.

Sincerely,
Monica Diamond

Objecting to political sermon

The Reverend Peter Hall
Smalltown Congregational Church
Smalltown, OH

Dear Mr. Hall:

I have always been one of your foremost supporters, and expect to always be. You give the congregation the emotional support and strength we need from our religious leaders.

However, I believe your sermon last Sunday crossed the line dividing religion and politics. The pulpit is not the place to endorse a candidate.

I believe differently than you do about certain candidates, but I don't think we should use the church as the place to argue those beliefs. Please continue to be our spiritual leader, but leave politics out of the church.

Sincerely,
Harold Diamond

Notice of upcoming election

Dear Members:

The Smalltown Garden Club will hold its annual election of officers on Thursday, October 18.

We are now soliciting nominations for the positions of president, vice president, secretary, and special events coordinator. Nominees must be members in good standing and endorsed by at least five other members.

Enclosed with this notice is a nominating petition and instructions regarding the election process.

All nominations must be received by September 30 in order to be eligible for the election.

Sincerely,
Laura Diamond, President
Smalltown Garden Club

Reminder to submit nominating petitions

Dear Members:

This is to remind you that nominating petitions for club officers are due by September 30 in order for the candidate to be listed on the ballot.

The election will be held at our regular meeting on Thursday, October 18.

If you have any questions about the nomination process, please call me at (xxx) xxx-xxxx or contact Mary Haims, club secretary, at (xxx) xxx-xxxx.

Sincerely,
Laura Diamond, President
Smalltown Garden Club

Notice of club election

Dear Members:

The next meeting of the Smalltown Garden Club will be on Thursday, October 18, at 7 P.M. in the large conference room of the Smalltown Public Library.

At this meeting we will elect officers for the coming year. Attached with this notice is a list of nominees for the offices of president, vice president, secretary, and special events coordinator.

Please attend this very important meeting and make your vote count.

If you will be unable to come to the meeting, please contact club secretary Mary Haims at (xxx) xxx-xxxx to obtain an absentee ballot. You must request the ballot and return it in a sealed envelope to Mary on or before October 17.

Sincerely,
Laura Diamond, President
Smalltown Garden Club

Results of club election

Dear Members:

At the October 18 meeting of the Smalltown Garden Club the following people were elected as officers for the next year:

President: Louise Richards
Vice president: Angela Norman
Secretary: Geraldine Stern
Special events coordinator: Myrna Croft

The new officers will take their positions at the next meeting, scheduled for November 1 in the large conference room of Smalltown Public Library.

On a personal note, I want to express my gratitude for the opportunity to serve as club president for the past year. I enjoyed the challenge very much and hope to continue to assist the club and its officers in any way I can.

Sincerely,
Laura Diamond, Outgoing President
Smalltown Garden Club

Asking for reasons to reject new members

Dear Members:

The following individuals have applied for membership in the Neighborhood Improvement Association.

Barbara Thorn
Yvonne Mitchell
Beverly Matthews
Gail Bush

If any member has a reason why a proposed member should not be granted admission to the association, please respond to Membership Chairperson Colin Grant before March 2.

Sincerely,
Angela Norman, President
Neighborhood Improvement Association

47 Neighborhood Events

Dear Reader:

Every corner of America, from the smallest hamlet to downtown Manhattan, is made up of little communities. There are block associations, neighborhood watches, child-care cooperatives, and improvement societies almost everywhere.

Letters to groups like these are based on the recognition that the members are in this together. In general, community groups stay away from political campaigns and positions beyond their narrow scope; a block association may seek to put pressure on the department of public works or parks, for example, but stay out of the race for mayor.

Cheers,
The Authors

Organizing July 4 block party

Dear Neighbor:

Please join your friends and neighbors in an old-fashioned Fourth of July family celebration. We have permission from the city to use the Meadows at Freer Park from 1 to 10 P.M.

Our plans call for games and contests for kids of all ages. We will have tables with pies and salads and other great homemade food, and a few large grills where you can cook your own main course.

At 9 P.M., we'll move to the top of the hill to watch the fireworks from the town green.

We're still making plans, and we could use some more volunteers for the various committees. Please call me or one of the chairpersons on the enclosed list if you can help.

I'm looking forward to celebrating the Fourth in style with all of you.

Sincerely,
Monica Diamond

Seeking donations for block party

Dear Neighbors:

I'm writing with an update on plans for our old-fashioned Fourth of July family celebration. We have had tremendous response from the neighborhood; it really seems everyone is excited about our big party.

Our organizing committee has gotten some great ideas about different kinds of activities, and people are stepping up to run them.

One event that has a lot of appeal is a fundraising auction. We're going to use the proceeds to buy athletic equipment for the kids to use at Freer Park.

We need items to sell at the auction. Please check your basement, attic, and garage. Remember: one person's trash is another's treasure. Please call anyone on the enclosed list to make arrangements for someone to pick up your treasures.

Sincerely,
Monica Diamond

Organizing a babysitting cooperative

Cindy Martin
Fairview, PA

Dear Cindy:

I just saw a great story about a group of parents who have formed a babysitting cooperative in their town, and I think it would be a wonderful addition here in Fairview.

Here's the way it works: Several caregivers (mothers, fathers, single parents, grandparents) get together and pledge that they will be available to babysit for each other's children. An hour is credited to a member's account for every hour they act as babysitter for another member of the group. The members then can draw upon the hours banked in their accounts when they need babysitting for their own children.

As you know, finding a reliable babysitter around here is very difficult, and the good ones are in such demand that it is almost impossible to schedule them.

I know you're involved in the preschool and active in the parents organization at the elementary school. What do you think of setting up a cooperative?

Sincerely,
Karen Diamond

Response to organizing a babysitting cooperative

Karen Diamond
Fairview, PA

Dear Karen:

I think the idea of a babysitting cooperative sounds great. We've lived here all of our lives, and we have no better luck than you in finding a babysitter every time we need one.

I will start spreading the word, and will plan an organizational meeting.

Among the questions I have is about the inequity between caring for one twelve-year-old who stays in his room playing video games (like mine) or chasing after a set of fifteen-month-old triplets (like my neighbor's). Perhaps we'll need a variable point system.

I'll be in touch soon to discuss details.

Sincerely,
Cindy Martin

Follow-up on babysitting cooperative

Karen Diamond
Fairview, PA

Dear Karen:

Good news. The initial response has been great. I have already heard from ten families willing to give the babysitting cooperative a try.

I have set up an organizational meeting at Liza Miller's house (she's a single mom) on Sunday, August 8, at 2 P.M. She's got a big backyard, and we can bring our kids, which is a good thing since none of us can find a babysitter!

Best regards,
Cindy

Announcing picnic to kick off babysitting cooperative

Dear Members of the Fairview Babysitting Cooperative:

Thank you all for joining as charter members of the cooperative. We have accepted the applications of fifteen families to start, and once we have worked out the inevitable kinks, we expect to expand our membership.

The babysitting registry officially begins on October 1. But before then we have planned a family picnic for all charter members so that we can get to know each other.

Please come to our picnic at Thornden Park on Saturday, September 24, from noon until 4 P.M. The location will be as close to the playground as we can get, since we expect about twenty-four kids.

We will have a grill going; please bring something to cook for your family. Any contributions of salads and desserts will be appreciated.

Cindy Martin, Co-Chair
Fairview Babysitting Cooperative

48 Community Fundraisers

Dear Reader:

We don't know about you, but we hate to ask others for money. We also know, though, that money is the fuel for many community events and efforts.

The most difficult letter of all is a straightforward appeal for money. Make your case for the worthiness of your organization and its efforts and then directly ask the recipient for help: "We need your cash donation to continue our work." An indirect appeal, such as "we'd appreciate your support," may receive psychic kudos but no cash.

For many of us, it is easier to deal with benefits and fundraising events when some or all of the money goes to the sponsoring organization. "If you buy a ticket to this concert, you'll enjoy a great show and support a great local organization." Or, "Every purchase you make at our tag sale helps to raise funds for our group."

In the following section you'll find a series of organizational letters for events and fundraisers.

Best of luck,
The Authors

Soliciting funds for an organization

Dear Parent:

Classics for Young People is an organization that works hard to get our children to go beyond "junk food" books to appreciate the timeless classics of literature.

We encourage libraries and educators to promote the classics. We help the effort by donating books to schools and libraries across the region.

Unfortunately, it costs a great deal of money to back up our ideals with action. I'm writing to you to ask for your help.

We are asking for contributions in whatever amount you can afford so we can buy great literature for the great minds of the future: the children of Smalltown.

Please make checks payable to "Classics for Young People" and send them to the address on this letter.

Sincerely,
Karen Diamond

Fundraiser selling booths to artists and craftspeople

To Craftspeople and Artists of Smalltown:

The Smalltown Senior Center will host its annual Crafts Fair at the center on December 13 from 10 A.M. to 4 P.M.

We are proud to say that this very popular event is held in high regard by the community. Many people tell us they do all their Christmas shopping in one visit. All of the best artists and craftspeople of Smalltown and the surrounding area are represented each year.

As in years past, we will be providing booth space for rental. A five-foot table costs $50, and a U-shaped six-by-six-by-six booth costs $125.

To reserve your space, please call Helen Dwyer at (xxx) xxx-xxxx. We expect to sell out all available space soon, so don't be left out. All the proceeds for the rental of the booths go to support our activities at the center during the year.

We look forward to hearing from you soon.

Sincerely,
Emma Miller, Chairperson
Smalltown Senior Center Crafts Fair

Requesting booth at fundraiser

Helen Dwyer
Smalltown Senior Center
Smalltown, OH

Dear Helen:

Thank you for the information about available booths at the Crafts Fair on December 13 at the Senior Center. I make Nantucket Lightship baskets and presently supply some of the finer shops in Smalltown.

I welcome the opportunity to participate in this event and to meet some of the folks of Smalltown.

For my purposes a five-foot table will be sufficient. I am enclosing my check for $50. Please send me confirmation.

Sincerely,
Miranda Macy

Confirming booth rental

Miranda Macy
Smalltown, OH

Dear Miranda:

Thank you for your interest in our Crafts Fair. We have never had Nantucket Lightship baskets represented before, and we look forward to seeing your products. In fact, we've given you one of the most prominent tables.

The fair opens at 10 A.M. on December 13. Setup for sellers begins at 8:30 A.M. You have been assigned table #4. Look for the volunteers, dressed in purple T-shirts; they can help you unload your wares.

Sincerely
Helen Dwyer

Community radio pledge request

Dear Member:

It has been more than twelve months since you joined WSMA radio as a supporting member. I hope you take pride in your important role as a supporter for this valuable community resource, the home of Smalltown High School Goliaths football as well as the Classics for Young People Saturday night "readathons."

We hope that as a loyal friend of WSMA, you will once again show your support by making a pledge. We have many exciting plans for the coming year, but we need your help to make them happen.

Please take the time to fill out the enclosed pledge card and return it to us as soon as possible.

Thank you for your part in our success.

Sincerely,
Morgan Diamond
Development Director

Acknowledgment of pledge

Dear Member:

Thank you for responding so quickly to the WSMA pledge drive. We would much rather spend our time developing new and exciting programs than asking for money.

Enclosed is the pledge request card. Please decide how you want to make your payments, and return the card to us.

Sincerely,
Morgan Diamond
Development Director

Pledge follow-up

Dear Member:

Please forgive us for bothering you again, but it has been two months since you made a pledge to support WSMA, and we have not received your check.

As you know, we rely almost totally upon the contributions of our listeners to support the programming we have all come to enjoy and expect. May I ask you to please send your check as soon as possible?

Sincerely,
Morgan Diamond
Development Director

Seeking items for bake sale for fundraising

Dear Members of the French Club:

We will be having a bake sale at the Super Shop Supermarket on Saturday, May 4, from 9 A.M. to noon. The store has again agreed to let us set up our table at the entrance.

This is the last bake sale before we leave for our trip to France on May 15, so we want it to be our most successful. We will need volunteers in groups of two to work the table and, of course, we need great items to sell. We have had luck with all sorts of goods, but cookies and brownies seem to sell best. Please wrap them individually.

You may call me to sign up.

Sincerely,
Laura Diamond
Chairperson, French Club Trip Committee

Donating car to charity auction

White Elephant Auction
Smalltown Boys & Girls Club
Smalltown, OH

Dear Auction Committee:

We would be happy to donate our car to be sold at the annual White Elephant Auction to raise funds for the Smalltown Boys & Girls Club.

The vehicle is pretty special: a 1972 Ford Fairlane "woody" station wagon.

It's not quite in collectible condition, but still very usable. It would be a perfect restoration project. In recent years, we have used the Fairlane as a second car for occasional special outings but we no longer have need—or room—for it. I would estimate its value at about $10,000.

Please contact me soon to arrange transfer of the car to you for the fundraiser.

Sincerely,
Ron Miller

Giving car to school for repair shop

Thomas Click
Auto Maintenance Shop Department
Smalltown High School
Smalltown, OH

Dear Mr. Click:

If you're interested—and can send a tow truck—I would be happy to donate my old car to the auto maintenance class to be restored.

I have a 1985 Jeep that needs a bit of work in just about every area—new rings, new brakes, a major tuneup, and an assortment of dents and rust spots to be filled and painted. But the car runs, and when it is repaired I would expect it could be sold at a profit to buy more supplies for the class.

If you're interested, please contact me to make arrangements.

Sincerely,
Al Miller

Selling tables at fundraising dinner

Dear Community Leaders:

We would be honored by your presence at our annual fundraising dinner, scheduled for October 18 at Sebastian's on the Lake.

As you know, this is the principal fundraising event for the Smalltown Repertory Theater. The funds we raise at the dinner form the base of our budget for an entire year of great works at the Rep.

Our evening will start with cocktails at 7 P.M. At 8 P.M. we will move into the dining room. We have an exciting roster of speakers including our new president, Dr. Samuel Cooper, and a guest appearance by a mystery star from Broadway.

Tickets for the event are $150 per person. We encourage businesses and organizations in the Smalltown community to purchase one or more tables for eight, which sell for $1,000.

Chef Todd LaFleur promises to perform his usual magic and whip up an exceptional dinner. The wines will be personally selected by master sommelier Carl Watkins.

Please call us as soon as possible to reserve your tables.

Sincerely,
Agatha Green, Chairperson

Purchase of table at fundraiser

Agatha Green, Chairperson
Smalltown Repertory Theater
Smalltown, OH

Dear Ms. Green:

We are pleased to once again attend the annual fundraising dinner for the Smalltown Repertory Theater.

Please reserve two tables at the dinner. As we have in years past, we will be sending some of our most successful salespeople and their guests to the dinner. Laura and I will also attend.

Enclosed is a check in the amount of $2,000 for the tables.

Sincerely,
John Diamond, President
Diamond Music Hall

Follow-up on sale of tables at fundraising dinner

Dear Community Leaders:

Our annual fundraising dinner takes place in just two weeks, and we have only a few tables still available. Your company has contributed in the past, and we didn't want you to miss the opportunity to participate in this important community event.

As you know, this is the principal fundraising event for the Smalltown Repertory Theater. The funds we raise at the dinner form the base of our budget for an entire year of great works at the Rep.

Please contact me soon to reserve a table. Tickets for the event are $150 per person. We encourage businesses and organizations in the Smalltown community to purchase one or more tables for eight, which sell for $1,000.

Sincerely,
Agatha Green, Chairperson

Report on funds raised at dinner

Dear Community Leaders:

I am thrilled to report that—with your help—the Smalltown Repertory Theater raised more than $25,000 at the annual fundraising dinner on October 18.

Every table was sold, and we received an additional contribution from Sebastian's on the Lake, which hosted the event.

Thanks to all of the companies, organizations, and individuals who attended the dinner and supported the theater.

The curtain rises on our first production of the season on December 1. We look forward to seeing you there. Be sure to look for your name in the commemorative program that will be given to every playgoer.

Sincerely,
Agatha Green, Chairperson

Asking for contributions to high school booster club

Dear Business Leader:

Summer is almost over, and there's a hint of fall in the air. That means Smalltown High School football, soccer, and lacrosse time!

I hope you will join other fine businesses, families, and individuals in Smalltown in supporting our student athletes through the Booster Club. The funds we raise help pay for equipment, transportation to away games, and celebrations of our victories.

We welcome gifts of any size. Major contributors will be recognized by name in athletic programs in the following categories:

Champions: $1,000 and more
Superstars: $500 to $999
Sponsors: $250 to $499

Thank you for your support.

Sincerely,
Cliff Webber, President
Smalltown High School Booster Club
Smalltown, OH

Soliciting business ads for high school yearbook

Dear Smalltown Business Leaders:

Once again, we are preparing to publish the Smalltown High School yearbook.

This is an excellent opportunity for your company to show its support of the community by placing an advertisement to help underwrite the cost of the book. Students, parents, and community leaders will see your company's name many times, because few books are as closely studied and treasured as a high school yearbook.

A full-page commercial ad costs $250, a half page $130, and a quarter page $70.

The deadline for purchase of an ad and submission of all copy is February 15. Please contact me with any questions, and send checks and materials to my attention.

Sincerely,
Richard Levine
Yearbook Director
Smalltown High School
Smalltown, OH

Soliciting personal ads for high school yearbook

Dear Parents:

Here is your chance to show how proud you are of your graduating senior at Smalltown High School: an ad in the Smalltown Big Guys Yearbook.

Proclaim your pride! Declare your independence! Embarrass your kid!

For more than fifty years, parents have helped support the yearbook through the ads they purchase. We are happy to run your messages, baby photos, and poetry.

A full-page ad costs $150, a half-page $80, and quarter-page $45.

The deadline for purchase of an ad and submission of all copy is February 15. Please contact me with any questions, and send checks and materials to my attention.

Thank you.

Sincerely,
Richard Levine
Yearbook Director
Smalltown High School
Smalltown, OH

Seeking purchase of movie ticket books for fundraiser

Manager
Super Megaplex Cinema
Smalltown, OH

Dear Manager:

I am president of the Smalltown High School Booster Club. This organization consists of parents, family, and others who support Smalltown High School's athletes. We raise money to supplement what the school budget provides for equipment, uniforms, and transportation expenses.

We would like to consider selling your books of tickets as part of a fundraising drive.

Could you give us a price for the ticket books, including a discount to our organization?

We will be sure to give credit to the theater in any promotional material associated with this campaign.

Sincerely,
Joan Graham, President
Smalltown High School Booster Club

Announcing sale of movie tickets as fundraising effort

Dear Members of the Smalltown High School Booster Club:

The Super Megaplex Cinema has agreed to sell us books of movie tickets at a substantial discount as part of our fundraising effort.

Individual tickets to the theater sell for $9 each. A book of five tickets normally costs $40. The theater has agreed to sell ticket books to the booster club for $25 each.

We will sell the ticket books to the public at the list price of $40, earning a $15 profit on each.

We are hoping to sell at least 200 of the books, which makes this one of our major fundraising campaigns for the year.

We will have an organizational meeting on Wednesday, September 19, at 7 P.M. in the High School Auditorium. We look forward to seeing you there.

Sincerely,
Joan Graham, President
Smalltown High School Booster Club

Asking for bid to supply wines for fundraiser

Fern Carbo
Carbo's Wine Shoppe
470 Tipps Avenue
Smalltown, OH

Dear Ms. Carbo:

The Smalltown Business Association will host a fundraising wine-tasting party in November.

We are soliciting bids from area merchants for two cases of each of the following wines:

- Chateau Ste. Michelle 1999 Merlot
- Banfi 1998 Chianti Classico Riserva
- Dominus 1999 Estate
- Zenato 1998 Cabernet Sauvignon

Please advise us of your price by October 2. We will be happy to include mention of your company in the brochure advertising the event, and on a placard near the wines themselves.

Sincerely,
John Diamond, President
Smalltown Business Association

Announcing fundraising wine tasting

Dear Members:

It's time to break out your best enological adjectives for the annual SBA Wine Tasting Party.

We will gather in the oak-paneled conference room of the Smalltown Country Club on Friday, November 7, at 8 P.M. to try four unusual vintages chosen by our highly selective (and opinionated) wine committee. We will offer crackers, cheese, and other hors d'oeuvres.

Here are this year's special wines:

- Chateau Ste. Michelle 1999 Merlot
- Banfi 1998 Chianti Classico Riserva
- Dominus 1999 Estate
- Zenato 1998 Cabernet Sauvignon

This year the proceeds from the party will benefit the Smalltown Boys & Girls Club. Tickets are $50 per person, and are available through the SBA office. We will sell only 100 tickets, which in past years were all sold well in advance of the date of the party.

To purchase tickets, please call the office at (xxx) xxx-xxxx.

Sincerely,
John Diamond, President
Smalltown Business Association

Asking for items for fundraising tag sale

Dear Members of the Smalltown Senior Community Center:

We are planning a tag sale to raise money for the Kent Davenport Memorial Scholarship Fund on Saturday, September 21.

Think of this as an opportunity to clean out your closets and get rid of stuff you haven't made use of in years . . . and to give back to some of Smalltown's brightest hopes.

We will begin collecting items at the center starting September 16. We will donate everything that doesn't sell to the Salvation Army so that nothing you part with will come back to you.

Please see the attached sheet for various volunteer opportunities for the sale.

Sincerely,
Harold Diamond, President
Smalltown Senior Community Center

Asking for volunteers for tag sale

Jane Gold, Director
Community Services Organization
Smalltown University
Smalltown, OH

Dear Ms. Gold:

On Saturday, September 21, from 10 A.M. to 3 P.M. we will have a tag sale at the Smalltown Senior Community Center to raise money for a memorial fund established in honor of our founder, Kent Davenport.

The endowment will be used to grant college scholarships to students from Smalltown High School.

The seniors will be donating furniture, clothing, books, and other items for the tag sale. We could use some assistance in setting up the sale and loading vehicles for delivery.

We would very much appreciate any assistance from students at Smalltown University. Could you help us in recruiting some volunteers?

Sincerely,
Harold Diamond, President
Smalltown Senior Community Center

Report on results of fundraising sale

Dear Members of the Smalltown Senior Community Center:

I am happy to report that our tag sale for the Kent Davenport Memorial Scholarship Fund was a resounding success. We raised a total of $4,650.56. All of the money will be devoted to the endowment of the scholarship.

Thank you to all members who donated items for sale and who volunteered to work the tables.

Sincerely,
Harold Diamond, President
Smalltown Senior Community Center

Thanking volunteers at tag sale

Jane Gold, Director
Community Services Organization
Smalltown University
Smalltown, OH

Dear Ms. Gold:

Please extend our thanks to the delightful students who lent a hand and their strong backs to the Smalltown Senior Community Center fundraising tag sale for the Kent Davenport Memorial Scholarship Fund.

We raised nearly $5,000, all of which will be added to the endowment for the scholarship.

Sincerely,
Harold Diamond, President
Smalltown Senior Community Center

Advising apartment complex of Girl Scouts cookie sale

Dear Residents of Lakeview Senior Apartment Complex:

This is to let you know that Smalltown Girl Scouts Troop 41 has asked us for permission to allow their girls to sell cookies in the apartment building on Tuesday, February 16, from 3 to 5 P.M.

Instead of having the scouts go door to door, we have decided to allow them to set up a table in the lobby. If you decide to indulge in any of their delicious treats—and help them raise funds for their activities—they will be taking orders there.

Sincerely,
Ron Miller, President
Lakeview Senior Apartment Complex

Advising neighborhood of Girl Scouts cookie sale

Dear Neighbors:

We hope you will give a friendly welcome to the members of Smalltown Girl Scouts Troop 41, who will be going door-to-door selling cookies on Thursday, February 18, from 3 to 5 P.M. The profits from the sale of the cookies go to support the troop's activities.

The girls will be accompanied, at a discreet distance, by parents from the neighborhood.

We hope you will help support our neighborhood girls with a purchase.

Sincerely,
Hillie Brand

To office about Cub Scouts candy sale

Dear Staff:

As you may know, the Fairview Cub Scouts are holding a candy sale to earn funds to support their field trips. You can buy candy at local supermarkets and malls . . . and through the good services of my son, Brian, right from your desk (on your coffee break, of course).

Please let me know if you are interested.

Sincerely,
Michael Diamond

Suggesting fundraising for family suffering loss of house

The Reverend Peter Hall
Smalltown Congregational Church
Smalltown, OH

Dear Mr. Hall:

As you know, six members of our congregation, Rachael and Steve Phillips and their four children, suffered a devastating fire at their home last weekend.

We are so thankful they all survived without injury; however, their house and possessions are all gone.

I am confident that as a caring community we are giving them all the emotional support we can. But we need to give them a hand to get on their financial feet again as well.

I'd like to meet with you soon to discuss some ideas for a benefit or fundraiser for this wonderful family. I have some ideas, and many enthusiastic people willing to get to work.

Sincerely,
Laura Diamond

Planning fundraising house tour

Janice Reynolds
Smalltown, OH

Dear Janice:

As you know, the Phillips family suffered a devastating fire that destroyed their home and all their possessions. We all are thankful that no one was hurt.

Reverend Hall and the rest of us in the congregation have tried to support the family emotionally, but their material needs are tremendous.

We are in the process of deciding what type of fundraiser would be the most productive to help this young family get back on its feet. One idea that a lot of people support is a house tour of some of the beautiful old historic homes in Smalltown. Yours, of course, would be on the top of that list.

If we go ahead with this idea, may we add your home to those that would be visited? We were thinking of the Saturday after Thanksgiving as the date of the tour. Please call me or Reverend Hall to discuss. We all want to do what we can.

Sincerely,
Laura Diamond

Use of hall for Halloween fundraiser

Harry Johnson
VFW Post 675
Smalltown, OH

Dear Harry:

As you know, the Phillips family recently suffered a devastating fire that destroyed their home and all their possessions.

Right now, they are living at the Smalltown Motor Lodge in rooms generously donated by Jim and Lucy Grant, the owners. But you can imagine how difficult it is for a family of six to be confined to two small motel units.

A group of their friends and neighbors is trying to think of ways to get them back on their feet again. One suggestion we are considering is to conduct a Halloween Fun House on October 31. This event would be aimed at kids and have all the usual scary stuff, including a haunted house. There also will be games, prizes, and food.

Most people suggested that we hold the fundraiser at the V.F.W. hall.

Please call me to discuss whether this would be possible. We think it is our duty to help this wonderful family in their time of need.

Sincerely,
John Diamond

Granting permission to use home for house tour

Laura Diamond
Smalltown, OH

Dear Laura:

I am happy and honored to make my home available for the fundraising house tour. I was very affected by the Phillips family's loss and will be happy to do my small part in getting them back on their feet again.

Keep me up-to-date on details. The Saturday after Thanksgiving is fine.

Sincerely,
Janice Reynolds

Granting permission to use hall

John Diamond
Smalltown, OH

Dear John:

The VFW hall would make a great haunted house. Some of the young folks in town think of us old-timers as ghosts anyway.

We are pleased to pitch in to help a local family in need.

The place is yours. Let us know how we can help.

Sincerely,
Harry Johnson

49 Volunteerism

Dear Reader:

When you volunteer, you are making an irreplaceable gift of something unique: your time and skills. Any such gift is usually at least as valuable to the giver as to the receiver.

If you are offering your skills as a carpenter, make it clear that you're not volunteering to work the telephones at a fundraiser.

Thank you for your good efforts.

Sincerely,
The Authors

Seeking volunteers for fundraiser

Dear Members of the Parish:

As I write to you I am enjoying a perfect spring day. The sky is a wonderful cerulean blue, the early bulbs are starting to bloom, and I can feel a touch of warmth on my face. But I must take you away from this scene and get you to think of autumn and our annual Fall Festival.

If you have volunteered for this event in the past, you know that a tremendous amount of work goes into this much-anticipated fundraiser. If you have not already been involved, we hope that you will be this year.

We need people to chair several committees, ranging from tickets and entertainment to setup and cleanup. We need folks with a lot of enthusiasm to work the booths, and those with a culinary flair to help with the food.

The money raised each year goes to many worthy endeavors, both within our parish and throughout the community. In recent years we have provided new hymnbooks for the pews in our church, software for the computers in the local elementary school, and pots and pans for the soup kitchen.

Please call me to volunteer.

Sincerely,
Laura Diamond

Volunteering services to adult literacy program

Volunteer Services
Pennsylvania Adult Literacy Coalition
Fairview, PA

Dear People:

My husband and I have recently moved to Fairview. For a number of years I volunteered at the Adult Literacy Center in Smalltown, Ohio.

I would very much like to become involved in working with an adult reading program again. Please send me information about opportunities in the Fairview area.

Sincerely,
Karen Diamond

Offering to volunteer as high school aide

Patrick Norton, Principal, Ph.D.
Smalltown High
Smalltown, OH

Dear Dr. Norton:

I am a math major at Smalltown University and I am looking for some experience in teaching at the high school level. I understand that the school district welcomes volunteers as teacher's aides.

Will you please advise me about available opportunities for volunteers?

Sincerely,
Heather Diamond

Resigning from volunteer work

Randolph Webster, Director
Smalltown Adult Literacy Center
Smalltown, OH

Dear Randy:

I have greatly enjoyed my work as a literacy volunteer at the center for the past three years. I think I have received as much from the people I have worked with as I have given. It has been a gift to be able to make a difference in the lives of such wonderful people.

Unfortunately, though, I will have to suspend my involvement at least for the immediate future. I am getting married this spring, and with the arrangements for that, my full-time job at the hospital, and plans for graduate school, I am overwhelmed.

When my life returns to normal, I would love to come back. Thank you for giving me the chance to contribute.

Sincerely,
Morgan Diamond

Greetings to new volunteer

Monica Diamond
Smalltown, OH

Dear Mrs. Diamond:

Welcome to the family of volunteers at Smalltown General Hospital. Our fine hospital is vital to this community and it takes many, many dedicated persons to make it run as smoothly as it does.

I have asked Jim Wakefield, manager of the gift shop, to get in touch with you in the next few days to work out a schedule.

Thank you again for volunteering.

Sincerely,
Gretchen Reynolds, Volunteer Coordinator

Scheduling volunteer work

Monica Diamond
Smalltown, OH

Dear Mrs. Diamond:

I am very happy to hear that you will be available to volunteer some time here at the gift shop of Smalltown General Hospital. As you know, all of the profits from the store go to help pay for new equipment for the hospital. Over the past three years we have raised more than $250,000.

Gretchen Reynolds tells me you are available Monday, Wednesday, and Friday afternoons. I'd like to schedule you for those days from noon to 4 P.M.

Would you please give me a call to discuss your hours and duties?

And please pass along my regards to Harold; I know him through Rotary Club.

Sincerely,
Jim Wakefield, Manager
Smalltown General Hospital Gift Shop

50 Sports Leagues

Dear Reader:

Play ball! It's not such a big deal to play a game—or a season—of softball, soccer, touch football, or tennis. The challenge comes in organizing: signing up teams, finding a place to play, arranging for officials, and keeping track of it all.

Your letters about sports leagues don't need to convince someone to play—most of us have one or another sports dream or fantasy. The point of the letters is to *organize*. Be clear about meeting dates and purposes, and be direct in your requests of participants.

You can also use community newspapers, radio and television stations, and cable television announcement boards to gather players.

Good luck!

Sincerely,
The Authors

Organizing adult softball league

Dear Neighbor:

We may no longer be the boys (and girls) of summer, but many of us still daydream of swinging for the fences and executing a perfect double play.

A group of us have decided to get up from our easy chairs and back onto the field of dreams. We're in the beginning stages of planning Smalltown's first adult softball league.

We plan to invite sign-ups by men and women, ages twenty-five and older. Each team of twenty players must include at least seven women, and starting lineups must include at least three female players. We'll be approaching area businesses and organizations to ask them to sponsor teams and help defray the cost of uniforms and equipment.

We'll be announcing the date for sign-up for the teams in about a month, but before we reach that point we're going to need a lot of help on organizational issues. We need to obtain permits to use the diamonds in the Smalltown park system, set the schedule, seek sponsorships for teams, and arrange for umpires and equipment managers.

I am enclosing the names and telephone numbers of the members of the organizational committee. Please call one of us to get more information and sign up to help.

Sincerely,
John Diamond

Asking to use classroom for softball team planning

Ethel Rogers, Chief Librarian
Smalltown Public Library
Smalltown, OH

Dear Ms. Rogers:

I represent a group of men and women in Smalltown who are interested in starting a coed adult softball league for next summer. We have done our preparatory work and are ready to have our first meeting.

The large conference room on the second floor of the library would fit our needs perfectly. Would it be available for our use on Wednesday, January 18, from 7 to 9 P.M.?

We appreciate your assistance.

Sincerely,
John Diamond

Confirming meeting at library

Ethel Rogers, Chief Librarian
Smalltown Public Library
Smalltown, OH

Dear Ms. Rogers:

Thank you for the use of the conference room at the library on Wednesday, January 18, from 7 to 9 P.M. We anticipate having thirty to forty people in attendance and we hope for some newspaper coverage.

Sincerely,
John Diamond

To newspaper announcing organizational meeting of softball league

Sports Editor
Smalltown Banner
Smalltown, OH

Dear Editor:

We are excited to announce that we are organizing the first coed adult softball league in Smalltown. We expect to begin competition in the spring of this year.

On Wednesday, January 18, from 7 to 9 P.M., we will meet in the large conference room on the second floor of the Smalltown Public Library to make committee appointments for the new league.

We would appreciate an announcement of the meeting in the Banner's sports calendar section. We also would be happy to meet with a reporter to provide more information about this new league.

I can be reached at my home or work number. Both are listed on this letterhead.

Sincerely,
John Diamond

To community about softball organizational meeting

Dear Neighbor:

Here in the depths of winter, we're pretty far along in our dreams of spring . . . and softball.

The first official organizational meeting of the Smalltown Adult Softball League will be held Wednesday, January 18, from 7 to 9 P.M. in the large conference room of Smalltown Public Library.

We plan to invite sign-ups by men and women, ages twenty-five and older. Each team of twenty players must include at least seven women, and starting lineups must include at least three female players. We'll be approaching area businesses and organizations to ask them to sponsor teams and help defray the cost of uniforms and equipment.

I hope to see you there.

Sincerely,
John Diamond

Report on first meeting of new softball league

Dear Neighbor:

Thanks for signing up at the organizational meeting of the Smalltown Adult Softball League. We were thrilled to have more than fifty people in attendance.

We've elected officers, organized committees, and begun planning. Attached is a copy of the first draft of the minutes of the meeting, recorded by our elected secretary, Jeff Thomas.

Watch your mail for the first issue of our newsletter. This newsletter will keep you informed about what's going on, the date of the next meeting, and the needs identified by the various committees.

Please give me a call with any questions.

Sincerely,
John Diamond, President
Smalltown Adult Softball League

Requesting use of town park for league

Commissioner of Parks
Smalltown Parks Department
Smalltown, OH

Dear Commissioner:

I am writing on behalf of the new Smalltown Adult Softball League to request the use of the town softball diamonds for a series of scheduled games this summer. We expect to play a total of thirty games among six teams during a six-week season, from about June 15 through August 1, plus a three-game playoff and championship series about August 8.

We would also like to reserve the fields for workouts from June 1 through June 15.

We understand that the town requires that we post a certificate of liability insurance for the league. We are making arrangements through Patricia Paulson of Small Help Insurance in Smalltown for issuance of a policy, and it will be in place before the first organized workout.

Please give me a call with any questions.

Sincerely,
John Diamond, President
Smalltown Adult Softball League

To newspaper announcing softball tryouts

Ben Fraiser, Sports Editor
Smalltown Banner
Smalltown, OH

Dear Mr. Fraiser:

The Smalltown Adult Softball League will hold tryouts for the first six teams in our new league on Saturday, June 1, from 10 A.M. to 4 P.M. at Freer Park on the softball field adjacent to the bathhouse.

The league is open to men and women, ages twenty-five and older. Each team of twenty players must include at least seven women, and starting lineups must include at least three female players.

We are in the process of approaching area businesses and organizations to ask them to sponsor teams and help defray the cost of uniforms and equipment.

We would appreciate advance publicity of the tryouts in the Banner, and coverage of the league once it is under way.

Sincerely,
John Diamond, President
Smalltown Adult Softball League

Seeking sponsorship of softball league

Dear Business Leaders:

I hope you will join me in sponsoring one of the six teams in the new Smalltown Adult Softball League, which will debut this summer for a thirty-game season in Freer Park.

We are very excited about this new activity in town, aimed at men and women ages twenty-five and older. Each team of twenty players must include at least seven women, and starting lineups must include at least three female players.

We are seeking area businesses and organizations to sponsor teams in the league and otherwise contribute to the expenses of the season. Sponsors will have their names on the uniforms and in all of the coverage of the league in the newspaper and on our local radio and television stations. It's a very inexpensive way to generate goodwill for your company right here in Smalltown.

The cost of sponsorship for each team is $500, which pays for uniform shirts with your company name and also contributes to the cost of permits and other fees.

Please call me to arrange for sponsorship of a team.

Sincerely,
John Diamond
Diamond Music Hall
President, Smalltown Adult Softball League

To parents of soccer league players

Dear Parents:

Welcome to another season of youth soccer here in Fairview. We have more than 100 kids signed up for our eight teams.

On behalf of the parents booster club, I would like to invite you to attend a meeting to plan our activities to support the kids. In previous seasons we have organized car pools for players, snack and drink tables at games, and a gala picnic and awards ceremony at the end of the season.

I would love to see every mom and dad involved in this year's activities. Please contact me to sign up for one of our committees.

Sincerely,
Karen Diamond, Chairperson
Fairview Soccer League
Parents Booster Club

Organizing field trip for children's team

Dear Parents and Guardians:

Our fifth season of T-ball baseball is off to a great start. We're planning to celebrate our success with a field trip to Toledo to see a AAA baseball game between the Mudhens and the visiting Columbus Clippers on Saturday, June 5.

This is a great opportunity for our young players (and their families) to see professional baseball at not-quite-major-league prices. We plan to charter a bus that will leave from Fairview Elementary School early that day.

We have worked out a price of $32 per person, which includes transportation, a box lunch, and grandstand tickets to the game.

We want to have at least one adult for every four kids. If your child will attend the game without you, please sign the attached permission slip. Before the trip, we will be sure you know who will supervise your child.

Please make your check payable to the Fairview T-ball Trip and send it to me by May 15, along with the enclosed form to reserve your seats.

We hope to see you at the game.

Sincerely,
Michael Diamond, Coach
Fairview Boys & Girls Club T-ball Team

Details of field trip for children's team

Dear Parents and Guardians:

Our field trip to a Toledo Mudhens game has turned into a major community event, and we're thrilled with the participation. As of today, we have received seventy-five checks, which means we will fill up two buses.

Here are the details:

The buses will leave from the parking lot of Fairview Elementary School at 7:30 A.M. on Saturday, June 5.

The trip to Toledo will take about 4 hours, including a few stops along the way. We should arrive at the stadium in time to see batting practice. The game begins at 1 P.M.

The buses should return to Fairview about 8 P.M. We will be in contact by phone with the Boys & Girls Club during the day, and parents and guardians can call the front desk, (xxx) xxx-xxxx, for updated information about arrival time.

We suggest that children be given about $10 for snacks at the game and on the trip. Please make sure that each child also carries some identification with their name and address and home phone number.

We expect to make the trip rain or shine. Because we will be leaving so many hours before the game begins, we really can't predict the weather at game time. We will be in contact with the stadium by cell phone during the trip, and will make some sort of alternate arrangements in case of a rainout. Let's hope for clear skies.

Sincerely,
Michael Diamond, Coach
Fairview Boys & Girls Club T-ball Team

51 To the Editor

Dear Reader:

Trust us: Your community newspaper does not mind receiving a request for coverage of an event or an announcement of a new organization or campaign. Without news, a newspaper would be just ads—and the advertisements would soon go away without reader interest.

Read the newspaper and get a sense of the sort of letters it publishes, and check the local news section to gauge its style of coverage. Then match your letter or news release to the newspaper.

Check the masthead (the listing of editors that usually appears on the editorial page) for names of editors of the various sections, and consult the calendar page for deadlines. In general, weekly newspapers "close" their coverage two or three days before the date of publication. Special sections of daily newspapers may also require that much advance notice, although breaking news can make it into the local news section with just a day's notice.

Yours truly,
The Authors

Announcing memorial scholarship

Jerry White, Editor
Smalltown Banner
Smalltown, OH

Dear Mr. White:

My wife, Emma, and I have been residents of Smalltown for most of our lives. Our three children attended Smalltown High School, and two of them graduated with honors. And then there was our son, Donald, who died of juvenile leukemia when he was a junior, more than thirty years ago.

Donald was a very special person. He never gave in to his illness. When he passed away the whole town grieved with us. We were especially touched by the dedication of a plaque outside the gymnasium, where he was all too briefly a star on the basketball court.

We have decided to establish a memorial college scholarship in his name. In this way, we hope to extend the memory of Donald and help a new generation of Smalltown kids spread their wings.

The fund, which will be supported by a perpetual trust, will provide an annual scholarship of at least $2,000 per year to be awarded to a Smalltown High School senior who best typifies Donald's spirit and determination to overcome life's obstacles.

Sincerely,
Ron Miller

Asking permission to reprint article in newsletter

Jerry White, Editor
Smalltown Banner
Smalltown, OH

Dear Mr. White:

I am writing to ask permission to reprint an article from the February 6, 20xx, edition of the Smalltown Banner in the newsletter of the Smalltown Senior Citizens Center.

The article in the Living section entitled "No Rest for the Elderly," by Ellen Jones, discussed the thicket of red tape faced by the elderly when it comes to claims for medical insurance. Ms. Jones did an excellent job of guiding us through what at times seems like an insurmountable mountain of paperwork and frustration.

I want to make sure that the residents of our senior center read this piece.

Our publication is offered free of charge and we will, of course, credit the Smalltown Banner and Ms. Jones. Please advise.

Sincerely,
Harold Diamond

Complaint about editorial

Jerry White, Editor
Smalltown Banner
Smalltown, OH

To the Editor:

In your editorial of May 16, you correctly state that the problem of young people congregating and partying in our parks at night has gotten out of control. The police have established that underage drinking, illegal drug use, and crimes of a sexual nature have taken place.

However, your editorial takes issue not with the fact that these things are happening, but that the young people do not clean up after themselves.

The editorial page of the Smalltown Banner is an important influence in this community. What is going on in the park at night has the potential to become a community disaster. Don't trivialize either the situation or your voice.

Sincerely,
John Diamond

Supporting editorial position

The Editor
Smalltown Banner
Smalltown, OH

To the Editor:

Your editorial of July 28 was right on target. As much as I love Smalltown, I doubt it will ever be on very many visitors' lists of must-see vacation spots. However, the Chamber of Commerce is doing a good job of promoting Smalltown as a convenient stopover on the way from Columbus to Cincinnati.

By promoting our restaurants, shopping, fine dining, and small but impressive museums, the Chamber of Commerce has shown people that there is more than enough to make a stop worthwhile.

However, I don't think the next step is a tax break to those establishments that cater to tourists. We need to support all of our businesses equally, not one at the expense of another.

Sincerely,
John Diamond

Complaint about newspaper coverage of school board

The Editor
Smalltown Banner
Smalltown, OH

To the Editor:

I commend the Banner for its extensive coverage of school board meetings. It is important for all citizens to know how their schools are being run and where their tax dollars go.

However, at the most recent meeting one of your reporters created a problem where none had existed. One of the items on the agenda was an editorial in our school newspaper, The Truth. This editorial by our managing editor, Ben Rogers, made suggestions to balance the school budget without laying off teachers.

He wrote about saving money by trimming administrative salaries and eliminating perks enjoyed by some high-level employees. The editorial was not mean-spirited; it sought to encourage the debate and help find a solution to the deficit in this year's budget.

The school board, to its credit, discussed the editorial in an open debate.

However, the Banner reporter covering the meeting, Mary Shaw, seemed intent on creating conflict between the students and the school board. She seemed disappointed that she was unable to stir up trouble between the two sides. This was inappropriate and not helpful.

Sincerely,
Heather Diamond

Open letter about placement of a stop sign

Editor
Smalltown Banner
Smalltown, OH

To the Editor:

I hope readers of the Smalltown Banner will join me in opposing the new stop sign on South Road at the intersection with Meadow Lane.

Although slowing drivers along that stretch of highway is a good idea, the stop sign is more of a hazard than is a straightaway. I have seen drivers overlook the sign and speed through the intersection and have seen others forced to stop short when the car in front of them slows down and stops at the intersection.

I think a better idea would be a flashing caution light, a lowered speed limit on the entire stretch of road, or even a series of well-marked speed bumps.

Readers should send their comments to the Mega County Highway Department, Mega County Building, Smalltown, Ohio.

Sincerely,
John Diamond

Complaint about reporter

The Editor
Smalltown Banner
Smalltown, OH

To the Editor:

Our son was involved in a serious multiple-vehicle accident near the Crosstown Shopping Center last week. Fortunately, he sustained only relatively minor injuries. Others were not so lucky. One person died and several others were injured.

I realize this was a major news story and I fully appreciate the fact that a reporter had the right to be there and cover the incident.

However, your reporter at the scene, John Stevens, was extremely insensitive to those who were injured or trying to help. My husband and I arrived at the site just before our son was taken away in an ambulance. We had to push our way past your reporter to get to our son. Even as we tried to determine whether Joshua was all right, Mr. Stevens continued to ask questions and invade our privacy.

We asked him to leave us alone, but he persisted.

I teach political science at the college level and fully support First Amendment rights, but rudeness and obnoxious behavior should not be tolerated under any circumstances.

Perhaps Mr. Stevens was absent from class the day they were covering courtesy.

Sincerely,
Laura Diamond

Dedication of library collection

Editor
Smalltown Banner
Smalltown, OH

Dear Editor:

We hope the Smalltown Banner will send a reporter and photographer to cover a very special event at the Smalltown Public Library—one that celebrates the history of our town and one of its most celebrated journalists.

On April 5 at 10 A.M., we will dedicate the Ron Miller Collection at the library. Mr. Miller, the former editor of the Smalltown Banner, donated his collection of more than 1,000 books about Smalltown, our state, and the world.

Please call me with any questions about the collection and the ceremony.

Sincerely,
Ethel Rogers, Chief Librarian
Smalltown Public Library

Request for donations for senior class trip

Members of the Smalltown Chamber of Commerce
Smalltown, OH

Dear Members:

My name is Heather Diamond and I am president of the class of 20xx at Smalltown High School. On Saturday, April 14, we will have our annual Silent Auction at Smalltown High School to raise money for the senior class trip to Washington, D.C.

As you know, the trip to our nation's capital is a long-standing tradition here in Smalltown. We tour the Smithsonian Institution, see the government buildings, and meet with our congressional delegation.

In past years the Silent Auction has been very successful, not only in raising a very generous amount of money, but in rallying our community to support an important local event. We are very fortunate to be going to school and living in a place as special as Smalltown.

We are asking if you can make a donation to support us in our fundraising efforts. It can be a monetary contribution or an item we can auction. Typical auction items include dinner for two, admission to a movie or event, or a special service from your company. We are open to all suggestions.

All contributors are acknowledged at the auction and in publicity materials in the Smalltown Banner and on local radio station WSMA.

We would like to have all items in hand by April 1 so we can begin our advertising and publicity campaign before the event.

Please call me at (xxx) xxx-xxxx to discuss your involvement.

Thank you in advance for your important contribution.

Sincerely,
Heather Diamond
Senior Class President 20xx

Request for coverage of auction

Jerry White, Editor
Smalltown Banner
Smalltown, OH

Dear Mr. White:

I am writing to request advance coverage of the annual Silent Auction to benefit the Smalltown High School Senior Class Trip.

The auction will take place Saturday, April 14, at 5 P.M. in the auditorium of Smalltown High School. Items and services donated from local merchants will be on display in the lobby of the high school from 11 A.M. through the start of the auction at 5 P.M.

All funds raised from the auction will help pay for the class trip to Washington, D.C., in May. This will mark the eighteenth consecutive year that seniors have gone to our nation's capital. We will tour the Smithsonian Institution, government buildings, and meet with our local congressional delegation. Senator Hilary Nixon will join us for lunch on the final day.

The Smalltown community has been very supportive and generous in both the quality and amount of merchandise donated. Items up for auction include a private dinner party for eight at Chez Jimmy, seven days of chauffeured limousine service, and a ten-day Caribbean cruise.

We would very much appreciate your help to publicize this annual event. We hope that you will be able to print stories both before the auction on April 14 and afterward to present the fundraising results.

Please call me at (xxx) xxx-xxxx to discuss the event and allow me to answer any questions. Thank you.

Sincerely,
Heather Diamond, Senior Class President
Senior Class Trip to Washington

Thanks for fundraising success

Jerry White, Editor
Smalltown Banner
Smalltown, OH

Dear Mr. White:

On behalf of the Senior Class of Smalltown High School, I want to thank everyone involved in our Silent Auction on April 14. The event was a tremendous success; we raised more than $5,000 for the class trip to Washington in May.

Many of Smalltown's finest companies donated items and services, and many of our best citizens placed bids to help the senior class. A listing of the auction items and the successful bidders is posted on our Web site at www.shs-auction.com.

We are fortunate to live in a place like Smalltown, and hope to represent our home town well in Washington in a few weeks.

Sincerely,
Heather Diamond, Chairperson
Senior Class Trip to Washington

Requesting coverage of open house

Jerry White, Editor
Smalltown Banner
Smalltown, OH

Dear Mr. White:

On Sunday, January 23, we will have an open house in our new conference center, library, and entertainment venue at the Smalltown Senior Center.

The entire community was tremendously supportive of us as we raised funds for this important project, and we hope to open the space for community events whenever we can. The Smalltown Banner has been a good friend in keeping the community aware of our plans.

We would like to invite the Banner to visit the center before its formal opening, and to help us publicize the open house.

Please give me a call at the number on this letter to arrange for a visit and for full details of the open house.

Sincerely,
Monica Diamond, Chairperson Open House Committee
Smalltown Senior Center

Notice to newspaper about booster club fundraiser

Editor
Smalltown Banner
Smalltown, OH

Dear Mr. Editor:

The Smalltown Booster Club will begin its fundraising for the coming athletic season next week with the sale of ticket books to the Super Megaplex Cinema.

We want to thank the theater for its generous assistance to the club. Every purchase of a ticket book helps student-athletes at Smalltown High School . . . and also offers low-price admission to the theater.

Yours truly,
Joan Graham, President
Smalltown High School Booster Club

52 Radio and Television

Dear Reader:

Radio and television stations depend upon attracting and holding listeners in order to sell the ads that pay for the lighting, the radio station's library of sound effects, and the tremendous amount of hairspray that television newsreaders require.

Radio stations are generally relatively small operations, and the program director or news director may be very approachable. Most stations regularly give airtime to community organizations and are responsive to requests.

Television stations, though, are usually much larger operations and a bit more difficult to deal with. Watch the station, especially the local news, to find out what kind of stories it runs. Also look for community service programs, which often run early on Sundays or late at night during the week.

Sincerely,
The Authors

Dissatisfaction with new television anchorman

Fred Farnsworth, General Manager
WSMA-TV Channel 68
Smalltown, OH

Dear Mr. Farnsworth:

I have been a loyal viewer of WSMA Nightly News for many years. I generally appreciate your professional and sober reporting on local stories. Of all the local stations, your station has consistently been the most substantial.

This I why I am most puzzled with the station's choice of a new anchor, Jim Carter.

He seems to feel it is his job to either make us laugh or to trivialize every bit of information he presents.

I have begun to change the channel anytime Mr. Carter is on.

The news report is not the time for comedy or happy talk. I hope you will bring back the intelligent, straightforward reporting that made me a steady viewer over the years.

Sincerely,
John Diamond

Praising television coverage

General Manager
WBIG-TV
Smalltown, OH

Dear General Manager:

I am writing to commend WBIG-TV for their recent news series about the numerous traffic accidents near the Smalltown Mall.

My wife and family regularly drive through the intersection you highlighted, and we do so with great apprehension. The sight lines are terrible and the traffic signs are inadequate, especially when many drivers seem to ignore them.

I hope you will continue to bring this situation to the attention of the City Council in the hope they will install a traffic signal at the intersection.

Thank you.

Sincerely,
John Diamond

Requesting return of television program

Program Director
WSMA-TV
Smalltown, OH

Dear Program Director:

For the past several years on Labor Day weekend you have blessed us with a Fawlty Towers marathon. I am not an avid television watcher, but I can honestly say this is something I wait for from one year to the next.

The fact that I know each episode by heart does not detract from my enjoyment. (I will admit I hope each year that some long-forgotten episode will be discovered and aired.)

That is why when I saw the programming for this Labor Day I was heartbroken. There is no Fawlty Towers—none, not even one episode.

I guess it may be too late to change the schedule for Labor Day, but I hope you will consider satisfying some of your maniacal viewers. May I suggest a Thanksgiving marathon?

Sincerely,
Harold Diamond

Follow-up to response about programming request

Program Director
WSMA-TV
Smalltown, OH

Dear Program Director:

As Manuel would say, "Qué?" You honestly thought we had seen enough of Basil, Sybil, Polly, and Manuel?

I look forward to the midnight series of Fawlty Towers episodes you plan to begin in December. I promise to spread the word to every serious Fawltyphile in town.

Sincerely,
Harold Diamond

Objecting to new radio station format

Program Director
WSUR-FM
Smalltown, OH

Dear Program Director:

I have been a fan of WSUR-FM for decades, since I was a college student.

Your station has always been known for its devotion to folk music. On-air hosts had a reputation as extremely knowledgeable guides to past and current performers.

Lately, though, I have noticed a change in the selection of music. More and more airtime is being spent on contemporary and light rock instead of traditional folk.

If you have made a decision to alter your playlist to modern music, I'd like to know about it now so I can begin the search for a new station.

Please advise.

Sincerely,
John Diamond

Accepting membership on radio station advisory board

Wilson Guthrie, Program Director
WSUR-FM
Smalltown, OH

Dear Mr. Guthrie:

Thank you for your response to my letter inquiring about the playlist for my favorite radio station, WSUR-FM.

I am relieved to hear that the station does not plan to abandon its roots as one of the oldest and best folk music stations in the Midwest.

I would be honored to accept your offer to serve on the board of advisers of WSUR-FM. I look forward to receiving information about the next scheduled meeting.

Sincerely,
John Diamond

53 Library Matters

Dear Reader:

Though your local library is one of the community's treasures, it is often neglected. In this section you'll find some letters that deal with requests for assistance, suggestions for programs, and an offer of a donation of current books—something that is usually greatly appreciated by librarians.

Sincerely,
The Authors

Seeking assistance with research

Ethel Rogers, Chief Librarian
Smalltown Public Library
Smalltown, OH

Dear Ms. Rogers:

I have been asked by Mayor Meyer Minor to do some research for a commemorative booklet on the history of Smalltown. This booklet will be released in conjunction with the bicentennial celebration planned for next August.

I am a history buff, but I do find myself a little daunted by the responsibility of such an important undertaking. I know that the library has an extensive archive of old newspapers, documents, and personal writings that date back to the founding of the town by Uriah Small in 1804.

I hope that you will be able to steer me in the right direction and perhaps give me some guidance as I work my way through the project. I am available at your convenience to come in to discuss this with you.

Sincerely,
Harold Diamond

Returning long-overdue library book

Smalltown Public Library
Smalltown, OH

Dear People:

I graduated from Smalltown University in June of this year and plan to attend Law School in the fall. Because I will be moving into my first apartment in September I decided to finally weed out some of the stuff I've accumulated in my career as a high school and college student. To my horror, I discovered an overdue library book—very overdue, since it should have been returned March 13, 1996.

I have enclosed the book with this letter.

Since I hope to be an officer of the court someday, I want to make sure there are no skeletons lurking in my past. I am sure I owe something for the book and I apologize profusely for this oversight. I just hope I don't need to get an extra job to pay my library bill.

Please advise.

Sincerely,
Joshua Diamond

Thanks to library for amnesty

Ethel Rogers, Chief Librarian
Smalltown Public Library
Smalltown, OH

Dear Ms. Rogers:

Thank you so much for your kind letter.

I greatly appreciate the offer of unconditional amnesty on the fine for my seriously overdue book. That means a lot to a struggling college student.

As you suggested, I do plan to drop by the next time I am in Smalltown to make a contribution of old textbooks and other titles I collected (though not from the library!) while in college.

Sincerely,
Joshua Diamond

Complaint about misuse of library grounds

Ethel Rogers, Chief Librarian
Smalltown Public Library
Smalltown, OH

Dear Ms. Rogers:

My husband and I have lived in Smalltown for the past twenty-five years and have been members of the library for almost that long. I am very proud of our library and have volunteered for numerous fundraising activities.

I firmly believe that the library belongs to everyone, and certainly encourage young people to make the most of its valuable resources. However, I do want to object to an unpleasant recent problem: the misuse of the library grounds as a place for youngsters to hang out for much of the day and late into the night.

Patrons can no longer sit and read a book on one of the benches under the library's elm trees because these young people are either lying all over the benches or are so loud that no one else can concentrate. Because the youngsters smoke and use offensive language, they also have driven off the young parents who used to take their children to the library grounds to play.

May I suggest that the library ask the Smalltown Police Department's community relations officer to make suggestions about ways to return the grounds of the library to all visitors?

Sincerely,
Monica Diamond

Asking for more Internet access at library

Ethel Rogers, Chief Librarian
Smalltown Public Library
Smalltown, OH

Dear Ms. Rogers:

I am a senior citizen and a regular patron of the Smalltown Public Library.

I think we have a fine facility in Smalltown, but compared to other libraries in the area we are behind the times. Our library has only two computers connected to the Internet, and the last time I attempted to use the machines, there were six people ahead of me.

Are there any plans to get more computers? I would be happy to participate in a fundraising effort to add more machines and connections to the Internet.

Sincerely,
Harold Diamond

Suggesting special children's program

Eloise Kidd, Children's Librarian
Fairview Public Library
Fairview, PA

Dear Ms. Kidd:

I would like to take this opportunity to compliment you and the other staff at Smalltown Public Library on the wonderful job you have done with the Children's Room. Both my husband and I enjoy your facilities almost as much as our two children do.

We have taken advantage of many of your special programs and readings in the short time we have lived here, and I am especially impressed with the "Honor an Author on Their Birthday" series. I would like to nominate William Steig for that special treatment on his birthday, which is November 14.

Mr. Steig has written so many fine books for children that I just can't imagine a childhood without his literature as a part of it. I started reading these books to my daughter and found that I was enjoying them myself. Some of his most well-known titles include Shrek, Doctor DeSoto, Dominic, and my personal favorite, The Real Thief.

I would be happy to help you plan a special event in his honor.

Sincerely,
Karen Diamond

Offer of books to library

Ethel Rogers, Chief Librarian
Smalltown Public Library
Smalltown, OH

Dear Ms. Rogers:

My wife and I recently moved from our home to an apartment. We have had to downsize considerably, but are quite comfortable where we are now. The one room I miss most, though, is my personal office, which contained the books accumulated over half a century while I was a reporter and then editor of the Smalltown Banner.

Each wall had a bookshelf filled with books about Smalltown, Ohio, and the rest of the world.

I would like to make these books a gift to the library. If I can't have them with me, I'd like to at least be able to visit them from time to time. Please call me to discuss this if you are interested in taking them.

Sincerely,
Ron Miller

Follow-up on response to offer of books to library

Ethel Rogers, Chief Librarian
Smalltown Public Library
Smalltown, OH

Dear Ms. Rogers:

I am so pleased that the library will take my collection of books, and absolutely thrilled that you will be able to keep them together in a single room. I am struck speechless by your plan to give my stack of books a name: the Ron Miller Collection.

Sincerely,
Ron Miller

Asking for donation of books

Dear Members of the Smalltown Public Library:

Do you have a stack of current bestsellers alongside your easy chair?

Although we try to keep our collection up-to-date through purchases, I did want you to know that we welcome donations of current books and certain reference.

You can bring contributions to the main desk anytime during regular library hours. We will consider all titles, and those we cannot use will be donated to an appropriate charity.

I hope you will help us—and your neighbors—in this way.

Sincerely,
Ethel Rogers, Chief Librarian
Smalltown Public Library
Smalltown, OH

Thanks for donation of books

John Diamond
Smalltown, OH

Dear Mr. Diamond:

Thank you for your very generous donation of books to the permanent collection of the Smalltown Public Library. We appreciate your commitment to our community.

We will post a list of all donors on a special board by the checkout desk.

Sincerely,
Ethel Rogers, Chief Librarian
Smalltown Public Library
Smalltown, OH

54 Intraoffice Letters

Dear Reader:

For those of us of a certain age, the world of the office has undergone so much change during our professional lives as to make it almost unrecognizable. The rest of you have grown up in an era of word processors, e-mail, high security, family leave, equal opportunity, employment evaluations, and much more.

Don't get us wrong: These changes are all for the good. They're just . . . so very different.

In this section, we present a set of intraoffice letters and memos for the thoroughly modern workplace.

Sincerely,
Corey Sandler and Janice Keefe

Job vacancy

Dear Staffers:

We are pleased to announce the following job openings. We encourage any qualified employee to submit a letter of interest to the Human Resources Department on or before June 15 for any of these positions:

Executive secretary to the chairman
Front lobby receptionist
Payroll specialist

Full job descriptions are posted on the bulletin board outside the Human Resources Department along with the procedure for internal job transfers and promotions. Please review the details of the job, necessary qualifications, and other information before applying.

As always, we start our job search within the company. If one or more of these positions is not filled from within, we will advertise in the Fairview Banner beginning June 22.

Sincerely,
Tracey Branson
Human Resources Department

Announcing bonus for job referral

Dear Staffers:

Here at Klein Graphics we pride ourselves on the quality of our workforce, and we also know that our employees are the best recruiters we have for filling positions.

We hope you will help us find more excellent workers. We are pleased to announce that we have begun a "Bonus for New Hires" program. If you refer someone who is eventually hired as a full-time employee, you will receive a $250 bonus after that person has been on the job for six months.

I have attached a list of current job openings. We will distribute updates every two weeks.

Sincerely,
Tracey Branson
Human Resources Department

Welcoming new employee

Karen Diamond
Fairview, PA

Dear Karen:

Congratulations and welcome aboard! We're thrilled to have you join us. I'm sure you'll find Klein Graphics a challenging and supportive place to work.

I have enclosed a copy of the employee handbook, information about health and life insurance, and tax forms. Please stop by my office on or before your first day of work to file your paperwork.

I'm looking forward to seeing you again.

Sincerely,
Tracey Branson
Human Resources Department

Parking spaces

Dear Employees:

Just a friendly reminder from the company traffic cop: Please do not park your car in the "Visitors" spaces at the front of the office. These spaces are intended for use by our valued customers when they have business here at the office.

We have recently added new spaces at the rear of the building, and encourage you to use them. They are close to the loading dock entrance.

If you require a closer parking space for medical reasons or have any other concerns, please contact me to discuss alternatives.

Sincerely,
Leslie Fay
Security Manager

Changes in health insurance plan

Dear Employees:

Here at Klein Graphics we are proud of the package of benefits we offer, and we have every intention of continuing to take care of our valued employees and families as best we can.

As we are all aware, the skyrocketing cost of health insurance is a heavy burden on most companies. We have decided to make a change in the insurance program we offer employees to reduce costs; in doing so, we expect to maintain or improve the quality of care.

Effective September 1, we will no longer be using the Green Cross Insurance Company as our health insurance carrier. We will switch to a combination of self-insurance and a major medical policy from Coleman Assurance Corporation.

I have attached information about the new plans as well as information forms that must be filled out and submitted to Human Resources by August 15.

We will conduct a series of meetings with each department over the coming few weeks to explain the plan and answer any questions. Please feel free to contact me directly with any particular concerns you may have.

Sincerely,
Tracey Branson
Human Resources Department

Scheduling briefing on changes in benefits

Dear Employees:

Please join with other members of your department to attend a briefing on Tuesday, August 2, at 2 P.M. in the second-floor conference room to discuss upcoming changes in the health plan benefit. Perry Blank, our benefits manager, will conduct the thirty-minute session. A representative of Coleman Assurance Corporation, our new carrier, will also attend.

We encourage every employee to attend the meeting. If you cannot attend this meeting, please contact me for the schedule of sessions we are conducting with other departments.

Sincerely,
Tracey Branson
Human Resources Department

Request for unpaid leave

John Baker, Director
Marketing Department
Klein Graphics
Fairview, PA

Dear John:

My husband, Stan, was involved in a serious automobile accident this weekend while he was on a business trip in Seattle.

The good news is that he is doing well, but he will be hospitalized in Washington for a few weeks before he is stable enough to return to Pennsylvania.

I am requesting a three-week unpaid leave of absence to be with him while he recovers. I would be away from the office beginning Thursday, April 1, and would return on or about Monday, April 24.

As always, I am concerned that our department maintain its usual high level of efficiency and quality. I have already brought my colleagues up to speed on my important projects and will be available by phone in case of an emergency.

Thank you for your consideration.

Sincerely,
Esther Morgan

Granting unpaid leave

Esther Morgan
Klein Graphics Company
Fairview, PA

Dear Esther:

I am sorry to hear of Stan's accident and hospitalization. We certainly understand your need to be with him and can grant your request for unpaid leave.

To have such a terrible thing happen so far from home and family must certainly be stressful. Please let us know of anything else we can do to help you.

Thanks for your offer to keep in touch. I'd appreciate it if you would call in to the office daily to answer any questions.

Sincerely,
John Baker, Director
Marketing Department
cc: Tracey Branson, Human Resources Department

Request for vacation leave

Augustus Furze
Shipping Department
Klein Graphics Company
Fairview, PA

Dear Augie:

I would like to schedule my vacation for the period from June 30 through July 14.

According to my records, I have twelve accrued vacation days in my account; this request, which includes the July 4 holiday, would reduce that number to three days.

Thank you.

Sincerely,
Paul Webster

Denying request for vacation leave

Dear Paul:

I am afraid that we have to deny your request for vacation leave for the period from June 30 through July 14. As you know, we have a huge backlog of projects including banners and posters for the Fourth of July celebration, and we are unable to grant any leaves that would interfere with our ability to meet the commitments we have made to our customers.

We would be happy to grant vacation leave that begins on or after July 4.

Sincerely,
Augustus Furze
Shipping Department

Requesting summer vacation calendar

Dear Employees:

As we approach the busy summer season, I want to remind all staffers who plan to take vacations between May 1 and September 1 that all requests for that period must be submitted to the Human Resources Department no later than April 1.

We will carefully consider all requests, but keep in mind that if a particular department has a need for coverage that does not permit employee absence we will be unable to grant leaves.

Please refer to your employee handbook to find our policy on summer vacations. The company considers both individual workload and seniority level in filling requests.

Note also that any employee who schedules vacation time during the other eight months of the year receives a bonus of an additional day of personal leave.

Sincerely,
Tracey Branson
Human Resources Department

Salary increase

John Baker
Marketing Director
Klein Graphics Company
Fairview, PA

Dear John:

I am pleased to inform you that following your recent employee evaluation, the executive committee has authorized an increase in your salary.

Effective October 12, your new monthly gross salary will rise to $5,200. This reflects a 12 percent increase.

Please let me know if you have any questions, or if any changes need to be made on tax forms.

Congratulations.

Sincerely,
Tracey Branson
Human Resources Department

Scheduling employee evaluation

Eugene Bressee
Accounting Department
Klein Graphics Company
Fairview, PA

Dear Gene:

Your annual employee evaluation meeting has been scheduled for Tuesday, October 5, at 9 A.M., in the conference room of the Human Resources Department.

Please let us know immediately if you have a conflict.

In preparation for the session, please fill out the attached self-assessment form and return it to your supervisor, Harry Frazier, before October 1.

At the meeting Mr. Frazier will go over your self-assessment form and the employee evaluation he has prepared.

As you know, the purpose of the employee evaluation is to help you and the company assess your performance for promotion and salary purposes, and to point out any areas where improvement is needed.

Sincerely,
Tracey Branson
Human Resources Department

Recommending termination of probationary employee

Tracey Branson
Human Resources Manager
Klein Graphics Company
Fairview, PA

Dear Tracey:

I am recommending that we terminate the employment of Ruth Harris, a probationary employee, effective immediately. Ms. Harris was hired eight weeks ago as a shipping clerk. In that time she has repeatedly failed to meet minimum standards as laid out in the job description and she shows no likelihood of improvement.

I have met with Ms. Harris on six occasions to review her work performance; attached are the notes from those meetings.

Please let me know if there is anything else you need from me, and advise me of the date of termination and procedures to be followed.

Sincerely,
Augustus Furze
Shipping Department

Recommending termination of permanent employee

Tracey Branson
Human Resources Manager
Klein Graphics Company
Fairview, PA

Dear Tracey:

I am writing to recommend the termination of Scott Taylor, a senior account manager.

As you are aware, Mr. Taylor has received unacceptable ratings on three employee evaluation reports conducted in the past nine months. We continue to receive complaints from coworkers and clients about inappropriate language and behavior that reflects poorly on the company.

I have attached copies of the employee evaluations and notes from interviews with complaining staffers.

We have tried to work with Mr. Taylor on numerous occasions, but he has proven unwilling or unable to modify his behavior.

I suggest he be terminated effective at the end of business on Friday, which would cause the least disturbance in the office.

Please let me know your plans for Mr. Taylor.

Thank you.

John Baker, Director
Marketing Department

Request to attend seminar

Marsha Taylor, Advertising Director
Klein Graphics
Fairview, PA

Dear Marsha:

I am writing to request permission to attend a three-day seminar on "New Trends in Internet Marketing for Graphics Designers" in San Francisco, October 5 through 8.

Attached is a brochure describing the seminar. The cost of attending is $850 plus airfare, hotel, and meals.

I have spoken with Fred Black, who went to a training session sponsored by the same group last year, and he recommends the seminar highly.

Sincerely,
Karen Diamond

Accepting request for seminar

Karen Diamond
Klein Graphics Company
Fairview, PA

Dear Karen:

Your request to attend the Internet seminar in San Francisco in October has been approved. Attached is an authorization form for payment of the seminar fee; include it with the seminar registration form when you submit it to Human Resources.

Please contact Mary Maguire in Travel Services to make arrangements for your flight and hotel.

We look forward to hearing from you about the seminar.

Sincerely,
Marsha Taylor, Advertising Manager

No-smoking policy

Dear Employees:

As you know, Klein Graphics Company has a no-smoking policy throughout the building. There is a designated area in the back of the building near the loading dock where employees should go during scheduled breaks if they must smoke.

Please do not congregate outside the front entrance to the building or in other public areas other than the designated area.

Violations of this policy will be noted on employee evaluations.

Tracey Branson
Human Resources Department

Staggered work hours

Dear Employees:

The Ross County Commissioners have asked all major employers in the region to explore the possibility of staggering their work hours to reduce congestion on highways during the morning and evening rush hours.

Here at Klein Graphics Company we support this effort, and also endorse the idea of expanding the company's hours of operation for the convenience of our customers.

Therefore we encourage all employees to meet with their supervisors to consider adjusting daily starting times anywhere in the period from 8 A.M. to 10 A.M. daily, and to adjust ending times accordingly.

The final decision on work schedules will be made by the supervisors, who must assure that any changes do not affect our ability to meet deadlines.

Thank you.

Tracey Branson
Human Resources Department

Holiday office parties

Dear Employees:

As the end of the year approaches, we are aware that many departments plan to have small gatherings to share the holiday spirit.

We are happy to see our staff socializing in this way, but we do want to reinforce company policy on office parties:

1. All social events must be approved by the department head.
2. Parties must be scheduled for lunch break, or at the end of the day, so as not to interfere with work.
3. Alcohol is not permitted on company property.

Please also be considerate of your fellow employees in your plans.

Tracey Branson, Manager
Human Resources Department

Carpool registry

Dear Employees:

A number of employees have asked about the possibility of company sponsorship of carpools to and from work.

Our insurance policy prohibits us from direct involvement in such a program. However, we are happy to establish a bulletin board that will help interested employees find others with similar schedules and commuting routes.

The board will be posted in the company cafeteria.

Sincerely,
Tracey Branson, Manager
Human Resources Department

Request for exit interview

James Adams
Klein Graphics Company
Fairview, PA

Dear Mr. Adams:

Per your letter of resignation, your last day with the company will be Friday, July 20.

We appreciate your years of service here at Klein Graphics, and wish you well with your new employer.

Please visit the Human Resources Department on July 20 between 3 and 4 P.M. to sign insurance papers and to pick up your final paycheck. At that time, we would also appreciate it if you would allow an exit interview with one of our personnel specialists. We want to make sure we learn as much from our employees as we can, and we welcome suggestions on changes and improvements in our operations.

Sincerely,
Tracey Branson, Manager
Human Resources Department
Klein Graphics Company
Fairview, PA

Policy on inquiries from the media

Dear Employees:

I am writing to remind all staffers of company policy regarding inquiries from print, radio, and television reporters.

If you receive a call or written communication from a reporter, please politely inform them that they must direct all questions to our Public Relations Department. The phone number for that office is (xxx) xxx-xxxx.

This policy is in place to protect the company and all employees from difficulties that might arise from the release of misstatements or incorrect information. Violation of the policy is considered a serious infraction of the employee guidelines.

If you have any questions about this policy, please contact me.

Sincerely,
Lois Lang
Director of Public Relations

Notice of important visitor

Dear Employees:

On the morning of Tuesday, April 5, we expect a visit from Yoshii Watanabe, chairman of Ninteko Industries, one of our most important suppliers.

Mr. Watanabe will be touring the offices, and we know that all of our employees will demonstrate professionalism and courtesy in all contacts.

Sincerely,
David Klein

Announcement of family leave policy

Dear Employees:

As required by the Family and Medical Leave Act, we have expanded the provisions for personal leave included in the employee handbook here at Klein Graphics Company.

We are happy to assist any full-time staffer who requests unpaid leave for any of the following reasons:

Birth of a child to an employee or spouse.
Placement of a child with an employee for adoption or foster care.
Necessary care for a serious health condition for a spouse, son, daughter, or parent of an employee.
A serious health condition that makes the employee unable to perform his or her job.

Any employee granted family leave will receive full health benefits during the period away from work, and will be guaranteed a return to the job after the end of the leave.

If you have any questions, please feel free to contact me.

Sincerely,
Tracey Branson, Manager
Human Resources Department

Requesting family leave

Augustus Furze
Shipping Department
Klein Graphics Company
Fairview, PA

Dear Mr. Furze:

I am requesting a family leave to care for my son Christopher, who is hospitalized for treatment of a kidney disorder. I expect to be away from work for two to three weeks, and will be in touch with the department regularly.

Thank you for your consideration.

Sincerely,
Abigail van Stratton

Granting family leave

Abigail van Stratton
Klein Graphics Company
Fairview, PA

Dear Abigail:

Your request for family leave has been granted. Please contact Tracey Branson in Human Resources to fill out the necessary paperwork.

We hope your son recovers quickly. Please let us know if there is anything we can do to help you during this period.

Sincerely,
Augustus Furze
Shipping Department
cc: Tracey Branson

Policy regarding use of phones for personal calls

Dear Employees:

I am writing to remind you of company policy about the use of telephones for personal calls.

We realize that it is sometimes necessary for employees to contact family and businesses for personal needs during the course of the day. However, we ask that as many of these calls as possible be limited to your break periods, lunch hour, or before or after your working hours.

In addition, we ask that you use your own telephone credit cards for any long-distance calls.

Violation of this policy will be noted on employee evaluation forms.

Thank you.

Jay Georges
MIS and Telecommunications Director

Advisory about Internet usage

Dear Employees:

All staff are reminded that company policy prohibits the use of computers to access Web sites unrelated to the core mission. This includes personal shopping, music and entertainment pages, pornography, and chat pages.

Please be aware that the MIS department monitors all uses of the company's computers and will report infractions to your departmental supervisor.

If you have any questions, please contact me.

Thank you.

Jay Georges
MIS and Telecommunications Director

Telephone answering policy

Sonya Skoczylas
Receptionist
Klein Graphics Company

Dear Ms. Skoczylas:

We appreciate your exceptional efforts at the front desk; our customers regularly tell us they appreciate your warm and friendly manner.

Effective immediately, we would like you to answer the phone with a standard greeting:

"Thank you for calling Klein Graphics Company. This is Sonya speaking. How may I help you?"

Thank you.

Jay Georges
MIS and Telecommunications Director

Announcement of training session

Dear Staff:

On Wednesday, October 5, we will conduct training sessions on the use of our new computer network, which includes an improved e-mail system, a high-speed link to the Internet, and a corporate Intranet that will allow real-time access to all inventory, manufacturing, sales, and shipping reports.

The sessions will be conducted in the large conference room on the second floor at 10 A.M., 1 P.M., and 3 P.M.

All employees are expected to attend one of the training sessions. Please consult your supervisor to select the time that works best for your schedule, and notify us of your plans. We look forward to seeing you there.

If you will be unable to attend, please call me to schedule an alternate session at a later date.

Sincerely,
Jay Georges
MIS and Telecommunications Director

Expense report policy

Dear Staffers:

Effective immediately, we are making the following change in policy regarding the filing of expense reports.

1. Reports must be filed on or before the first business day of each month in order for payment to be made in that month. Reports received after the first business day will be held for the following month.
2. All expenses must be billed within sixty days of the date they were incurred, unless you receive a waiver of this rule from your department head for a specific project or expense.
3. All expenses must be accompanied by an itemized receipt. The only exception is gratuities, which shall be calculated according to the attached schedule.

Please review the section on allowable expenses that is included in the employee handbook.

If you have any questions, please give me a call.

Nora Hammermill
Expense Account Auditor

Change to employee ID system

Dear Employee:

Effective Monday, June 5, all employees will be required to wear an identification card at all times when on company property. The card, which will feature your picture, will also include a magnetic strip that will allow you to gain access to the building.

All employees will need to schedule an appointment to pose for a digital photograph. We will be available in the conference room on the third floor every day from 8 A.M. to 6 P.M. for the next two weeks. Please call Extension 5670 to schedule a five-minute appointment.

Along with your ID card you will receive a personal PIN code that you will need to enter into a card reader any time you enter the building other than during ordinary business hours.

If you have any questions, please contact me.

Simmie Harrison
Security Office

Announcement of Web teleconference

Dear Sales Staff:

Please plan to be at your desk on Wednesday, March 23, at 2 P.M. to take part in an important Web-based teleconference to introduce new products and services.

Before the start of the conference, please sign on to http://www.yourconferencecall.com/kleingraphics/products.

Please use your e-mail address as your ID, and enter the following as your password: kleinsales.

I will be available to answer any questions about the conference on the morning of March 23.

Jay Georges
MIS and Telecommunications Director

Announcing major new contract

Dear Employees:

I am pleased to announce that Klein Graphics has been awarded a major new contract to design and execute a national advertising campaign for Mrs. Roth's Pickles.

Congratulations to Erin Kelly and Chris Burtmen, who pitched our campaign.

And the next time you drop by my office, help yourself to a Mrs. Roth's pickle. We now get them wholesale.

Sincerely,
David Klein

55 Personal Notes to Employees

Dear Reader:

A lot of companies make the claim that they care for their employees as if they were family. Some even mean what they say.

In this section you'll find a series of letters that deal with congratulations, apologies, and expressions of sympathy to employees.

The goal in this sort of letter should be empathy and honesty. It's important that the writer express only honest emotions. A supervisor or executive of a company should not make claims of familiarity that don't ring true.

Most sincerely,
The Authors

To injured employee

Dear Ken:

Mary tells us that your recovery is going well and she will soon have to stop you from doing too much.

We miss you here, Ken, but don't want you to worry about work until you are back to 100 percent. Your job is secure, and we will do everything we can to help you get the most out of our employee benefits.

If there is anything we can do to make this time easier for you or your family, please let me know.

Sincerely,
John Diamond

To employee whose husband died in an accident

Dear Sandra:

All of us at Diamond Music Hall are saddened to hear of Paul's tragic death.

While our grief is small compared to yours, we feel the loss as well.

Please accept my condolences and those of the rest of the family here. Rest assured that we will help you take advantage of the benefits we offer to our employees. Please let me know if there is anything else we can do to help you.

Sincerely,
John Diamond

Business letter of holiday greetings

Dear Member of the DMH Family:

At this special time of the year, I'd like to express my personal thanks to everyone in our family of faithful employees. Your dedication, hard work, and creative spirit enable this company to grow and prosper.

Thank you for all you have done this past year, and for all you will contribute in the next.

Yours truly,
John Diamond

Congratulations to employee on birth of child

Michael Duggen
Smalltown, OH

Dear Mike:

You're a father! I just heard the wonderful news. I understand that Jerri and your son, Wilson, are doing just fine.

I wanted to make sure that you know about a tradition at Diamond Music Hall: When your child is old enough to start playing his first musical instrument, it's his free of charge.

Regards,
John Diamond

Congratulations to longest-serving employee

Conrad Quinn
Smalltown, OH

Dear Conrad:

Every year when the anniversary of your employment rolls around, it reminds me of those first months of business selling guitars from a booth at the county fair. We have come a long way together, and once again I congratulate you as the second-longest serving employee, just after me.

Thanks again, Conrad, for your service to Diamond Music Hall for sixteen years.

To show our appreciation, we would like you and your lovely wife, Lucy, to have dinner with our compliments at your choice of restaurants downtown. Just call Sylvia in Human Resources to work things out.

Sincerely,
John Diamond

Congratulations on employment anniversary

Helen Troy, Chief Buyer
Diamond Music Hall
Smalltown, OH

Dear Helen:

Ten years ago you started working as a clerk in our humble little music store in downtown Smalltown.

Diamond Music Hall has certainly grown in the past ten years, and it would not have been possible without the hard work and dedication of people like you.

Congratulations on your anniversary with us, Helen. We appreciate your service.

Sincerely,
John Diamond

Congratulations on birth of child to employee, letter accompanying gift

Abbie Short
Smalltown, OH

Dear Abbie:

On behalf of all of us at Diamond Music Hall, congratulations on the birth of your child.

We miss you here at the store and look forward to your return. In the meantime, get all the rest you can.

Please accept the enclosed gift. May I suggest you make it the first deposit in Sarah's college fund? Trust me, you'll be glad that you did.

Sincerely,
John Diamond

Congratulations to father of new child, letter accompanying monetary gift

Charles Martin
Smalltown, OH

Dear Chuck:

On behalf of all of us at Diamond Music Hall, congratulations on the birth of your son. Convey our congratulations to Susie; we look forward to seeing baby pictures. Please accept the enclosed gift. Man I suggest you make it the first deposit in William's college fund? Trust me, you'll be happy that you did.

Sincerely,
John Diamond

Congratulations to employee whose child received scholarship

Frank Nolan
Smalltown, OH

Dear Frank:

I just heard the great news about Tiffany's acceptance at the University of Ohio, with an academic scholarship.

Please pass along the congratulations from all of us here at Diamond Music Hall. I guess this leaves you and Susan with an empty nest; Laura and I face the same this fall.

Regards,
John Diamond

Thanking employee for referring new hire

Martha Bradley
Smalltown, OH

Dear Martha:

Congratulations! Adam Brock will be starting work at Diamond Music Hall in the accounting department. We think he will make an excellent employee.

Thank you for referring him to us. Under our company policy, you will receive a $50 bonus in your first paycheck after he has been with us for ninety days.

Sincerely,
Sylvia Carroll, Director of Human Resources

Congratulations to married employees on anniversary

Luke and Amelie Carter
Smalltown, OH

Dear Luke and Amy:

I just heard that two of our favorite staffers will be celebrating their twenty-fifth anniversary on Tuesday. Congratulations!

Amy, I hope you enjoy the flowers. After twenty-five years, Luke, you must understand that the lady always gets the attention.

Sincerely,
John Diamond

56 Employee Relations

Dear Reader:

Ancient mapmakers used to mark unknown territory with an all-purpose warning: there be dragons. We would consider doing the same when it comes to many employee relations communications.

If you are a business owner or a manager, be very careful to avoid unintended promises or insupportable claims. Don't make threats, either, unless they are clearly within the bounds of your company's published rules of conduct and employment.

As an employee, you should be similarly careful. Don't give out unnecessary personal information or make claims you can't support.

In other words, take great care in any communication that relates to employment. Stick to the facts, and err on the side of discretion and civility. As they used to warn us in grade school, this could end up on your permanent record.

Best regards,
The Authors

To acquaintance who lost job, offering interview for new position

Mary Byrnes
Nearby Music Sales
Nearby, OH

Dear Mary:

I was sorry to hear about the closing of Nearby Music Sales. Although we did not directly compete for the same customers, I was well aware of the company and its reputation for customer service.

I'm sure a salesperson of your quality will have no difficulty finding a good position. In fact, we'd be happy to speak with you about an available supervisory job here at Diamond Music Hall.

If you're interested, please get in touch with me soon.

Sincerely,
John Diamond

Accepting resignation without praise

John Block
Smalltown, OH

Dear John:

Your letter resigning your position as advertising director has been received and accepted. It is mutually agreed that it will become effective as of the end of business today.

Sincerely,
John Diamond

Inquiry about benefits

Jennings Bergen, Human Resources Department
Smalltown General Hospital
Smalltown, OH

Re: Morgan Diamond, Employee #xxx-xxxx

Dear Mr. Bergen:

For the past four years, I have worked part-time in the lab department at Smalltown General Hospital while I attended college.

I am now applying to graduate school at Smalltown University and will continue to work part-time at the hospital. I expect to study medical technology, a field related to my current position.

I believe that as a part-time employee of Smalltown General Hospital I am eligible for tuition reimbursement benefits. Please advise me of the benefits available to me and what I must do to take advantage of them.

Sincerely,
Morgan Diamond

Inquiry about accounting for vacation days

Yang John, Administrator
Human Resources Department
Amalgamated Business Software
Smalltown, OH

Re: Michael Diamond, Employee #xxx-xxxx

Dear Mr. John:

I have been employed full-time at Amalgamated Business Software for the past five years, and part-time for three years before that.

I would like to receive an accounting of vacation days I have accrued during that period and those that are available to me now.

Sincerely,
Michael Diamond

Requesting information on vacation-day policy

Sylvia Carroll, Director of Human Resources
Diamond Music Hall
Smalltown, OH

Dear Ms. Carroll:

Please advise me of company policy regarding carryover of unused vacation days from one calendar year to another. I have been working for Diamond Music Hall for six months now and have not taken any vacation time off.

Thank you.

Sincerely,
Chris Blackford

Requesting information on profit-sharing

Howard Canard, Director of Personnel
Amalgamated Business Software
Smalltown, OH

Dear Howard:

My accountant has asked that I provide him with full details on the setup of the company 401(k) retirement account.

Would you please send me the details of the program, along with an accounting of my contributions and the company's matching share for the entire period of my employment at Amalgamated Business Software?

Thank you.

Sincerely,
Michael Diamond

Notification of change of address

Jennings Bergen
Human Resources Department
Smalltown General Hospital
Smalltown, OH

Re: Morgan Diamond, Employee #xxx-xxxx

Dear Mr. Bergen:

Please change my employment and tax records to reflect my new address. Effective May 1, 20xx, my new address is:

Morgan Diamond
999 New Street
Smalltown, OH

Sincerely,
Morgan Diamond

Name change due to marriage

Jennings Bergen
Human Resources Department
Smalltown General Hospital
Smalltown, OH

Re: Morgan Diamond, Employee #xxx-xxxx

Dear Mr. Bergen:

I recently was married and have taken my husband's last name. Please change all records so that they carry my married name: Morgan Diamond Hamilton. Also, please advise me of any forms that need to be filed to update my employment and tax records.

Sincerely,
Morgan Diamond Hamilton

Letter to employee regarding inappropriate dress

Melanie Ashton
Smalltown, OH

Dear Ms. Ashton:

You have been employed at Diamond Music Hall as a sales associate for the past three weeks, and your supervisors have reported favorably on your work. You have a very nice way with customers, and we pride ourselves on our relationships.

However, there is one matter I must bring to your attention. Our company dress code, given to you when you were hired, specifically rules out T-shirts and other articles of clothing with political or suggestive slogans on them. We don't comment one way or another about what they say, but we do believe that they are a distraction in the sales environment.

At work, you represent Diamond Music Hall, and we must ask that you conform to our policies. I would be happy to meet with you to answer any questions you might have about company policy.

Sincerely,
Sylvia Carroll, Director of Human Resources

Warning to employee about chronic tardiness

Bart Smithson
Smalltown, OH

Dear Bart:

It has been brought to my attention that in the last two weeks you have been late for work on six occasions. Since you are the one who opens the store in the morning, this is very significant.

On Wednesday, you did not get to the store until after 10:30 A.M., and two of our best customers were kept waiting outside for more than half an hour.

This situation cannot continue. You have always been very conscientious and punctual and we value you as an employee. If there is a reason why the 10 A.M. time is a problem, please let me know. We will try to work something out.

Sincerely,
Sylvia Carroll, Director of Human Resources

Harassment complaint

CONFIDENTIAL

Jennings Bergen, Human Resources Department
Smalltown General Hospital
Smalltown, OH

Dear Mr. Bergen:

I am writing on behalf of a group of professional women working in the lab at Smalltown General Hospital. This group consists of nurses, technicians, aides, and secretaries.

We want you to be aware of inappropriate and unlawful behavior by a staff member at the hospital, Dr. Peter Gordon.

For some time, many of the female employees in the hospital have been bothered by his offensive language and off-color jokes. He regularly comments about the bodies and private lives of nurses and aides. He has continued to do so even after he was asked to stop by a number of women.

Recently he inappropriately touched some women. We can no longer tolerate his conduct. This letter will serve as notice that unless the hospital succeeds in bringing this unwanted, unprofessional, and offensive conduct to an immediate halt, we will have no other alternative than to consult an attorney, institute sexual harassment charges against Dr. Gordon, and hold the hospital responsible for his behavior.

Sincerely,
Morgan Diamond

Request for maternity leave

Sylvia Carroll, Director of Human Resources
Diamond Music Hall
Smalltown, OH

Dear Ms. Carroll:

I am writing to advise you that I plan to take maternity leave sometime in September. My due date is September 6.

I expect to return to work at the end of my leave. I very much appreciate the generous maternity policies at Diamond Music Hall.

Sincerely,
Abbie Short

Granting maternity leave

Abbie Short
Smalltown, OH

Dear Abbie:

Your request for maternity leave has been approved. We're looking forward to your happy event.

To review, our maternity leave policy is as follows:

- You may take as much as twelve weeks of unpaid leave following the birth of your child.
- During that time, we will continue all medical and insurance benefits at no charge to you.

We will hold your job open during the period of your leave.

Please keep us posted on your situation. We look forward to adding another member to the Diamond Music Hall family.

Sincerely,
Sylvia Carroll, Director of Human Resources
cc: John Diamond

Clarification about casual Friday dress code

Dear Employees:

I'm writing in response to questions from several of you about the exact meaning of "casual Fridays" here at Black & White, Inc.

While we are quite happy to relax our dress code just a bit in the summer, I do want to remind you all that this is a professional services corporation and we expect all employees to be dressed in a way that does not detract from our relations with customers.

In deciding to go with casual Fridays between Memorial Day and Labor Day, we meant that men did not need to wear a jacket and tie and women could substitute an informal outfit for a business suit or dress.

Here's what is *not* permitted: blue jeans, shorts, T-shirts, tank tops, hot pants, sneakers, and any clothing that carries a political or social message. If you have any questions, please ask me or Ms. Bienstock, our office manager. If you have trouble finding me, look for the guy in the Hawaiian shirt and khaki pants.

Thank you.

Howard Black

Announcing new employee benefit

Dear Employees:

This has been a healthy year for Diamond Music Hall. I am not merely speaking of profits, but also the good health of our most important resource, our employees.

To help ensure that this happy situation continues, we have decided to underwrite a discount on membership at Body Basics Gym here in downtown Smalltown.

We will pay 25 percent of the cost of a one-year full-time membership for any employee. Please see Sylvia in Human Resources to find out how to take advantage of this benefit.

I look forward to seeing all of you on the stair stepper after work.

Sincerely,
John Diamond

Letter to employee about advertising suggestion

Alexis Stern, Sales Associate
Diamond Music Hall
Smalltown, OH

Dear Alexis:

Peter Lowe passed along your idea for a new tag line for our advertising and corporate sponsorship. I love it!

Our company has thrived these past sixteen years because of creative people like you.

Please join Peter and me in the corporate boardroom on Friday, September 20, at 2 P.M. for a meeting with our advertising agency to get them involved in promoting our new tag line.

Sincerely,
John Diamond, President
Diamond Music Hall: The Sparkle of Smalltown

Letter to advertising agency about campaign for new slogan

Charles Flannel, President
Grey Flannel Ad Agency
Smalltown, OH

Dear Charlie:

I'd like you to look at the attached materials, prepared by one of our up-and-coming sales associates, for a new advertising campaign based around our new slogan—Diamond Music Hall: The Sparkle of Smalltown.

I plan to join Peter Lowe at your review session next Friday, and I'd like to hear your ideas for a fresh institutional and promotional campaign.

Sincerely,
John Diamond
Diamond Music Hall

Employee award

Alexis Stern, Sales Associate
Diamond Music Hall
Smalltown, OH

Dear Alexis:

It gives me great pleasure to present you with this bonus as Employee of the Month here at Diamond Music Hall.

Your suggestion for a new advertising slogan for the company has been a great hit, and we look forward to getting you more involved in our promotional activities. We recognize talent when we see it.

Sincerely,
John Diamond, President

Congratulations from company president on promotion

Alexis Stern, Advertising Coordinator
Diamond Music Hall
Smalltown, OH

Dear Alexis:

I am so pleased to promote you to advertising coordinator at Diamond Music Hall.

As you know, our advertising agency is off and running with an institutional advertising campaign based on your tag line. We plan to unveil the slogan at the press conference to introduce our sponsorship of the Smalltown Summer Music Festival. I'd like you to join me at the head table; I'll send you details when they are set.

Again, congratulations.

Sincerely,
John Diamond, President

Notice of fire drill

Dear Team Members:

We will conduct a companywide fire and emergency drill sometime on the morning of Wednesday, November 16.

Please take the time before then to familiarize yourself with the evacuation plans listed in the company handbook. I have attached a summary of those instructions for your reference.

Note that we have appointed a male and female warden for each department. They will be responsible for supervising the evacuation and verifying that everyone is accounted for. You'll find the names of the wardens for your department on the attached instructions.

I'm sure you realize the importance of this emergency drill and will participate in it with appropriate behavior.

Thank you.

David Klein, President

57 Employee Suggestions and Awards

Dear Reader:

In the best of companies, the best of ideas come from creative and motivated employees.

A good manager knows the value of encouraging suggestions from the people who know the company from the inside: sales and marketing ideas, operational plans, and benefit programs that help attract, motivate, and keep valued employees.

As a staff member, you should put your ideas in writing to help convey them clearly and to attach your name to them. After all, you want to get the credit, don't you?

Sincerely,
The Authors

Employee suggestion for ad campaign

Peter Lowe, Director of Advertising
Diamond Music Hall
Smalltown, OH

Dear Peter:

I am enjoying my job as a sales associate here at DMH, but as you know my dream is to move up to the advertising department and put my degree in advertising and marketing to work.

I've been working on some ideas for an institutional advertising campaign that could be used as the slogan for some of our community activities, including the summer concert series and our involvement in the downtown revitalization program. I'd very much like to share with you my concepts to promote Diamond Music Hall: The Sparkle of Smalltown.

I've attached some sketches and collateral materials that could be used to develop an advertising campaign around the slogan.

Sincerely,
Alexis Stern, Sales Associate

Announcing employee of the month

Karen Diamond
Fairview, PA

Dear Karen:

It gives me great pleasure to tell you that you have been selected as Employee of the Month at Klein Graphics.

This is the first time that we have ever selected someone who does not work full-time at the Fairview office. Please accept our sincere thanks and the enclosed gift certificate for dinner. And when you do come to the office, you are entitled to park right out front in the Employee of the Month space until November.

Thanks again for your effort and dedication.

Sincerely,
David Klein, President

Congratulations on meeting sales goals

Amelio Rodriguez, Sales Associate
Diamond Music Hall
Smalltown, OH

Dear Amelio:

Congratulations on meeting—and exceeding—our goals for school instrument sales in October. Your work on arranging for a trade-in for a completely new set of instruments for the Nearby Neighbors marching band helped make October a month to remember.

I hope you will put the enclosed bonus check to good use, and continue to bring new ideas to the sales department.

Sincerely,
John Diamond

Suggesting new product to sell

Robert Zimmerman, Regional Manager
Home Station Hardware
Nearby, OH

Dear Mr. Zimmerman:

I am a sales associate in the paint and stain department at the Smalltown Home Station Hardware store.

On my recent vacation, I helped a friend in Halifax, Nova Scotia, work on his deck using a Canadian product called Luxocote, which combines a stain and water seal. I found it to be superior to anything we carry. The quality and ease of application was exceptional.

Every day I deal with people who are looking to make the staining job a little easier. Even at a premium price, I think this product is a better deal for our customers than what we offer now. I would like to suggest that Home Station carry this product.

I've enclosed the Luxocote product label.

Sincerely,
Al Miller

Suggesting instructional day at store

Robert Zimmerman, Regional Manager
Home Station Hardware
Nearby, OH

Dear Mr. Zimmerman:

My customers at the Smalltown Home Station Hardware store are constantly asking me for advice on how to do some of the larger home repair and improvement jobs. All of the sales associates here do as much as possible to help customers decide to do the work themselves, but we also lose quite a few sales to people who lack the confidence to tackle a do-it-yourself job.

I'd like to suggest that Home Station have a day when we can give instruction and demonstrations on doing the most popular do-it-yourself projects. We can have experts take people through jobs like installing a garage door opener, sealing a driveway, installing a faucet, and other common jobs. I'm sure many of our suppliers would be happy to send their own technicians to run the classes, and we can assist them—and sell the hardware and materials.

I would be happy to help set up this program here in Smalltown and in the other stores in the Home Station group.

Sincerely,
Al Miller, Sales Associate
Home Station Hardware
Smalltown, OH

Suggesting frequent buyers club

Robert Zimmerman, Regional Manager
Home Station Hardware
Nearby, OH

Dear Mr. Zimmerman:

Before I came to work at Home Station I worked in customer sales and marketing at a major retail home furnishings chain. While there I participated in the startup of a Frequent Buyers Club. That customer incentive program turned out to be a huge success, responsible for a boost in sales of nearly 10 percent.

I think we could have a similar program for Home Station. With our computerized checkout stations, all we would need to do would be to give our customers a unique customer number and then track purchases made on that account.

We could award special discounts and rebates to members of the club, issue invitations to private sales, and conduct sweepstakes for members.

I would be happy to discuss this idea with the marketing department.

Sincerely,
Al Miller, Sales Associate
Home Station Hardware
Smalltown, OH

Suggesting change in hours of operation

Robert Zimmerman, Regional Manager
Home Station Hardware
Nearby, OH

Dear Mr. Zimmerman:

I'd like to suggest a slight adjustment in the operating hours at the Smalltown Home Station Hardware store.

Although we open to the public at 9:30 A.M., we receive almost no visitors before 10 A.M. during the week. Also, we see a pickup in customers right after 5 P.M. from people on their way home from work.

I think we could better serve our customers, without additional cost, by changing our weekday hours of operation to 10 A.M. to 6 P.M.

We should continue to operate our pickup counter for contractors, open at the loading dock beginning at 7:30 A.M. each day. How about adding a free coffeepot there? We'd be heroes to some of our best commercial customers.

Sincerely,
Al Miller, Sales Associate
Home Station
Smalltown, OH

Suggesting sponsorship of movie series

David Klein, President
Klein Graphics
Fairview, PA

Dear Dave:

The Fairview Multiplex is having a special series on Japanese animation December 4 through 6.

I think it would be an excellent event for Klein Graphics to sponsor. I know we have been looking for the appropriate vehicle to showcase some of our work, and a tie-in with some of the Miyazaki masterpieces would be a perfect fit.

We expect many of the attendees at this festival are among our best customers.

I'd be happy to get involved in setting this up.

Sincerely,
Karen Diamond

Suggesting recycling to save money

Walter Ballou, Administrator
Smalltown General Hospital
Smalltown, OH

Dear Wally:

I'd like to suggest that we look into recycling our laser cartridges instead of throwing them away each time they are empty. We're currently paying about $90 for each cartridge. Several of our suppliers have offered to buy them back from us for $10 apiece and refill them for $50.

There are ten printers in my department alone, and the cartridges are replaced every two weeks or so. We'd save about $30 on each cartridge, for an annual savings of more than $7,000 per year just in the lab.

I'd be happy to help set this up.

Sincerely,
Morgan Hamilton

Suggesting saving money through equipment change

Walter Ballou, Administrator
Smalltown General Hospital
Smalltown, OH

Dear Wally:

As you know, we've been experiencing repeated failures of our printers in the physical therapy department as well as others throughout the building.

I believe the problem is that about five years ago the hospital chose to install many lower-capacity, less-expensive printers on desktops and at workstations. Although that was done for a good reason—to make it more convenient for workers—we ended up with machines that are not suited for the present high level of volume.

I would suggest that we consider installing large, high-capacity printers to serve clusters of eight to ten networked computers. This should reduce the failure rate, and in the end save money. Although one high-end printer may cost about five times as much as a desktop unit, it can replace as many as ten of the lower-cost machines.

I would be happy to assist in a more detailed study of this idea.

Sincerely,
Roger Hamilton, Director of Physical Therapy

58 Office Social Events

Dear Reader:

We know that somewhere, sometime, there is work to be done. Sometimes, though, it seems as if the office parties, football pools, bowling team, and family day events fairly squeeze out productivity.

If you're the boss, you pretty much can set the schedule as you please. If you are an employee, though, be sure you understand company policy about organizing social events at work, and about the use of company resources such as computers, bulletin boards, and copying machines.

Best of luck,
The Authors

Announcement of company picnic

Dear Employees:

Summer has arrived, and our thoughts are drifting to holiday traditions. No, not the Christmas in July sale (although that is on the way). I'm talking about the annual company picnic.

We've decided to add some real thrills to our annual get-together. We have decided to hold our picnic this year at the Whoopee World Amusement Park in nearby Lansingtown, on Sunday, July 23.

All employees of Diamond Music Hall, full-time or part-time, are invited to bring their families for a day of great food and excitement. We have reserved a lawn area in the park for a catered barbecue with all the fixings from noon to 5 P.M. We will provide passes to the park, good until closing at 10 P.M.

Please see Sylvia in Human Resources to obtain passes.

I look forward to seeing you there.

Sincerely,
John Diamond

Suggestion for surprise party for intern

Phil Carr, Assistant Department Head
Political Science Department
Smalltown Community College
Smalltown, OH

Dear Phil:

Friday is the last day of Jessica Nolan's internship in the department. I think we would all agree that she has been a tremendous help to us all. I hope she will consider applying for a position here after graduate school.

I think it would be nice to give her a small surprise party to show our appreciation for her work. We can use the conference room adjacent to my office and have some finger sandwiches, dips, and soda. I'd be glad to handle the details; we have some money in the petty cash budget to cover the expense.

Let me know what you think.

Laura

Follow-up on response to surprise party

Phil Carr, Assistant Department Head
Political Science Department
Smalltown Community College
Smalltown, OH

Dear Phil:

Thanks for getting the ball rolling on the surprise party for Jessica Nolan. All of the party details are under way.

The idea of buying a piece of luggage for her sounds very appropriate. I'm sure she'll be happy to have a new suitcase when she heads off for her semester in London in a few weeks.

Please let me know how the collection of money for the gift goes. If you come up a bit short, let me know and I will make up the difference.

Laura

Memo to coworkers about surprise party

CONFIDENTIAL

To Political Science Department:

Friday is the last day of work for our wonderful intern, Jessica Nolan.

To show our appreciation we are having a SURPRISE party for her on Friday, December 14, at 4 P.M. in the conference room adjacent to my office.

Remember that this is a surprise party. Please don't post this message on bulletin boards or leave it around on desktops. Let's gather (as inconspicuously as possible) in the conference room a little before the appointed hour. When she comes to say goodbye to me I will bring her in.

Phil is collecting for the purchase of a suitcase for her. Any contributions will be appreciated.

Laura

Invitation to holiday party

Dear Employees:

'Tis the season . . . to gather for our annual Christmas, Hanukkah, Kwanzaa, and New Year's Celebration.

We hope you'll join us on Friday, December 12, at 7:30 P.M. at the Ribeye Steak House in Fairview. (Directions are on the attached map.)

We invite you to bring along a guest for cocktails, dinner, dancing, and well-behaved mayhem.

Please let us know if you will attend, and include the name of your guest.

Sincerely,
David "Santa" Klein

Invitation to department holiday party

To all Political Science Department faculty and staff:

It's time for us to put down our books and step away from the keyboards for a while to celebrate the holiday season with each other.

Please join us on Thursday, December 21, from 3 to 5 P.M. in the Poli Sci conference room for some holiday cheer. Any donations of baked goods will be appreciated.

Laura Diamond, Chairperson

Congratulations to company bowling team

Dear Members of the Tri-City Championship Bowling Team:

Way to go, keglers. Our team was the youngest and least experienced in the league, but you overcame the odds to bowl over all the others and come out on top.

Please join me this Friday at 4 P.M. in the conference room for a celebration.

John Diamond

Invitation to a celebration for company bowling team

Dear Employees:

Please join me this Friday at 4 P.M. in the conference room for a celebration of Diamond Music Hall's championship bowling team.

Our team was the youngest and least experienced in the league, but they overcame the odds to bowl over all the others and come out on top.

John Diamond

59 Letters to Customers

Dear Reader:

A personal letter from a business to a customer cements a critical relationship. Remember to use the active voice: thank you for shopping; we're announcing a new service; please pay your bill promptly.

If you are responding to a customer's inquiry or complaint, make specific reference to the essential elements—date, price, product, and so on. Don't be defensive, and be careful about repeating a customer's words of complaint in your own letter unless you are willing to accept the customer's judgment. In most cases, you are better off apologizing for the fact that a customer was less than satisfied with a product than committing a statement such as "the device was cheaply made and should never have been sold to customers" to print.

Sincerely,
The Authors

Acknowledging receipt of returned item

Dennis Jones
Smalltown, OH

Dear Mr. Jones:

We are in receipt of your Jango Bravehart Banjo, model 1942. We are sorry the product didn't meet your requirements.

We will credit your charge card for the original purchase price, minus the standard 10 percent restocking fee that is applied to the return of all musical instruments. For your information, that fee goes to pay for inspecting, tuning, and repackaging returned items.

We hope you will consider Diamond Music Hall when you purchase musical instruments in the future.

Sincerely,
John Diamond
Diamond Music Hall

Acknowledging receipt of item for repair

Randy Williams
Smalltown, OH

Dear Mr. Williams:

We have received your Spender bass guitar, sent to us for a repair estimate.

Our technician says that the bridge is split and cannot be repaired. It is possible to install a replacement bridge, making the guitar as good as new. But we cannot guarantee that the instrument will sound exactly the same as it did before the damage. It may sound better, or it may sound not quite as good.

The cost of a new bridge is $129, and the repair—including installation, painting to match, and lacquering—will cost $100, for a total of $229. All repairs are backed by a ninety-day unconditional guarantee.

Please let me know if you want us to proceed with the repair.

Sincerely,
John Diamond
Diamond Music Hall

Refusing return of product for health reasons

Jonathan Segal
Smalltown, OH

Dear Mr. Segal:

I am sorry to inform you that we cannot accept the return of the package of saxophone reeds we sent you. We are happy to issue refunds or credits for just about anything in our store, but because of health concerns we are not able to restock reeds and mouthpieces. This policy is indicated on the sales receipt you received.

As a courtesy to a longtime customer, I have authorized a one-time 10 percent discount on your next purchase from us. Just attach this letter with your order or bring it in to the store.

Sincerely,
John Diamond
Diamond Music Hall

Refusing return of product not bought at store

Phyllis Stevens
Smalltown, OH

Dear Ms. Stevens:

We are unable to accept the return of the pair of Audiobox speakers you shipped to us.

We do not carry the Audiobox line at our store and never have. These must have been purchased elsewhere.

To save the cost of shipping them back to you, we would be happy to hold on to them for a short period of time until you can come in to the store to retrieve them.

Sincerely,
John Diamond
Diamond Music Hall

Customer requesting rescheduling of payment

Diamond Music Hall
Smalltown, OH

Dear Mr. Diamond:

Four months ago I purchased a Spender guitar at your store. I was pleased with the excellent service and am happy with the guitar.

At the time of purchase, I agreed to a purchase price of $800, including tax. You were offering an interest-free installment plan, and I signed up to make eight payments of $100 each until the amount was paid in full.

I have had some unexpected medical bills and find that it is difficult for me to make the $100 payment for the next four months. Could my payment plan be restructured so that I can make 8 more payments of $50 each?

I hope you can help me.

Thank you,
Ken Smith

Response to customer requesting rescheduling of payment

Ken Smith
Smalltown, OH

Dear Mr. Smith:

Thank you for your letter requesting rescheduling of payments on the purchase of your guitar.

Although we do not ordinarily extend interest-free payment plans, I will make an exception because of your need to pay medical bills. Please make payments of $50 per month until the account is clear.

I hope the guitar helps you get through a rough patch.

Sincerely,
John Diamond
Diamond Music Hall

Requesting payment for invoice

Mareid O'Connor
Smalltown, OH

Dear Ms. O'Connor:

This is just a friendly reminder that we have not as yet received the monthly payment on your account, which was due by June 30.

If you have overlooked the bill, please send the monthly payment to us as soon as possible. If the payment is already in the mail, please disregard this letter.

Sincerely,
A.J. Little
Accounts Receivable
Diamond Music Hall

Second letter requesting payment

Mareid O'Connor
Smalltown, OH

Dear Ms. O'Connor:

Another month has gone by and we have not heard from you with payment of your outstanding balance.

You have always been one of our most valued and faithful customers. We trust this is merely an oversight.

If you have questions, please contact me directly. Otherwise we will expect payment of the past-due balance of $632.56 as soon as possible.

Sincerely,
A.J. Little
Accounts Receivable
Diamond Music Hall

Third letter requesting payment

Mareid O'Connor
Smalltown, OH

Dear Ms. O'Connor:

It has been more than four months since you have made any payment to your account. We have made repeated attempts to reach you to determine the status of the payments, but have been unable to contact you.

We must insist that you make full payment of the outstanding balance of $632.56 immediately.

When you signed the purchase agreement you agreed to make full payment within thirty days. If we do not hear from you by June 6, we must seek other means of collection.

Sincerely,
A.J. Little
Accounts Receivable
Diamond Music Hall

Account to be turned over to collection agency

Mareid O'Connor
Smalltown, OH

Dear Ms. O'Connor:

In ten days, on June 16, we intend to turn over your unpaid account to the Bigtown Collection Agency.

If you would like to pay your outstanding balance before the collection agency becomes involved, please contact me immediately. If we turn the account over to a lawyer, it may damage your credit record and you may incur responsibility for additional fees and legal costs.

Sincerely,
A.J. Little
Accounts Receivable

Announcing new line of products at store

Dear Customer:

Because you have purchased drum kits from us in the past, we wanted you to know that we now offer the complete line of Ringo Tambourines.

The new instruments include the hot new Electro-rine, which has battery-powered LEDs all around the rim.

Bring in this letter or mention it on the phone to receive a special 10 percent discount on Ringo Tambourines. This discount is offered only to previous customers, and is good through December 12.

Sincerely,
John Diamond
Diamond Music Store

Announcing new service

Dear Customer:

We are pleased to announce that Diamond Music Hall now offers free computerized guitar tuning with all purchases of new strings.

Just bring in your guitar, pick out a set of strings, and allow us to install them and tune the instrument while you wait.

We look forward to seeing you again.

Sincerely,
John Diamond
Diamond Music Store

To newspaper announcing new facilities at store

Business Editor
Smalltown Banner
Smalltown, OH

Dear Editor:

We hope you will let your readers know about some exciting new facilities at Diamond Music Hall in downtown Smalltown.

We are the first music store in the state of Ohio to offer the new Engine Ear guitar tuning system to its customers. This highly sophisticated device "listens" to a guitar and helps a technician tune individual strings and adjust for harmonic distortion between adjacent notes.

Even better, we are offering this service free of charge to any customer who purchases a set of new guitar strings.

We would be happy to demonstrate this new system to a reporter for the Banner, and we hope you will help us let local musicians know about this new service.

Sincerely,
John Diamond
Diamond Music Hall

Dinner invitation to discuss bid specifications

George Baerga, Sales Representative
Gray Brass Instrument Company
Nearby, OH

Dear George:

Thanks for the invitation to dinner on Thursday. I will be glad to meet with you.

As I mentioned earlier, we are about to make a bid to provide a full set of instruments to the Smalltown High School marching band. I'd like to discuss this order with you to try to come up with a winning bid.

One way to cinch the deal might be to boost the trade-in allowance we are able to offer for the band's old instruments. Perhaps you could get in touch with your home office before we meet?

Sincerely,
John Diamond
Diamond Music Hall

Apologizing for mistake in order

Ricky Clapton
Nearby, OH

Dear Mr. Clapton:

Please accept my personal apology for the mix-up on your recent order. You have been a longtime customer of ours, and I hope you understand that we very rarely ship a case of clarinet reeds to someone who has ordered an electric guitar strap.

We will credit your account for the returned merchandise and will reship the correct items. We will also credit your account for all shipping costs associated with the return of the incorrect products.

Sincerely,
C.C. King, Shipping Supervisor
Diamond Music Hall

Thanking customer for large order

Jack Damon, Purchasing Agent
Smalltown School Board
Smalltown, OH

Dear Jack:

I would like to thank the administration and school board of Smalltown Public Schools for giving Diamond Music Hall the order for new instruments for the Smalltown Marching Band.

We pride ourselves on providing quality merchandise at competitive prices, and we also very much want to be good neighbors in our hometown.

We assure you that the instruments will be as specified and delivered before September 1 so that they are ready for the new school year. We will be in touch soon to arrange for collection of the old instruments that are being traded in. We have arranged to give them a new life with the municipal band in a little town in Argentina.

Sincerely,
John Diamond
Diamond Music Hall

Commendation of sales representative

Manny Gray, President
Gray Brass Instrument Company
Nearby, OH

Dear Manny:

We're happy to partner once again with your company on a major order, this time for the Smalltown High School marching band.

I wanted to pass along my appreciation of the fine work done by your regional sales representative, George Baerga. He gave us a very good price on the package of instruments, but his real contribution was in arranging for a very advantageous trade-in allowance for our client. Who could have imagined that the tubas and piccolos of Smalltown, Ohio, will soon be strutted down the main street of a small town in Argentina?

What a world! And what a deal.

Sincerely,
John Diamond
Diamond Music Hall

Letter to newspaper about band instruments

Editor
Smalltown Banner
Smalltown, OH

Dear Editor:

As you have reported, Diamond Music Hall won the contract to supply the Smalltown High School marching band with new instruments for the coming school year. We are happy to help our community in this way.

I thought you might be interested in an unusual news angle about the deal. We arranged for the school district to receive a large discount on the order by trading in the old instruments. In partnership with one of our suppliers, we will ship the former Smalltown band instruments as a donation to the municipal band in Ushuaia, Argentina, which is the southernmost city in the world.

We would be happy to help your staff in covering this story, including putting you in touch with our contacts in Argentina.

Sincerely,
John Diamond
Diamond Music Hall

60 Sponsorship of Community Activities

Dear Reader:

Institutional advertising—whether it be your company's name in a congratulatory message in the high school yearbook or your business's name on the back of every uniform of a Little League team—is a way to proclaim your dedication to being part of the community.

A letter agreeing to sponsor community activities should be direct and very specific, making reference to specifications and requirements from the team or club.

Sincerely,
The Authors

Purchase of ad in high school yearbook

Richard Levine
Yearbook Director
Smalltown High School
Smalltown, OH

Dear Mr. Levine:

Enclosed is our check to purchase a full-page ad in the 20xx Smalltown High School yearbook.

We have attached a sketch of the ad and the copy to include in it. Please send us a proof of the ad for our approval before the yearbook is sent to the printer.

Sincerely,
John Diamond
Diamond Music Hall

Company sponsorship of high school football team

Cliff Webber, President
Smalltown High School Booster Club
Smalltown, OH

Dear Mr. Webber:

Once again, Diamond Music Hall is pleased to contribute to the Booster Club in support of the boys' football team and the girls' lacrosse team. Enclosed please find our check for the transportation fund.

Go Goliaths!

Sincerely,
John Diamond
Diamond Music Hall

Asking for pricing of promotional giveaway item

Transnational Geegaw Company
123 Global Trifle Center
Paris, IL

Dear People:

We are considering a promotional giveaway at an upcoming marching band competition.

In your catalog we see a tuba key ring, model 6SJ7-11, which seems to be most appropriate for our purposes. Can you send us a sample of the key ring, along with a price for the purchase of 2,500 key rings with our company name and logo imprinted on them?

Attached is a copy of our logo to be used for the imprinting.

Sincerely,
John Diamond
Diamond Music Hall

61 Business Services

Dear Reader:

Businesses are consumers, too.

Companies (and organizations) need to buy paper and pens and coffee mugs and raw materials for manufacture. They also need to hire consultants, party planners, and computer programmers.

In this section we include some of the letters a small business might produce.

Thank you for your consideration.

Sincerely,
The Authors

Seeking corporate picnic space

Corporate Pavilion Manager
Whoopee World Amusement Park
Lansingtown, OH

Dear Manager:

We are considering holding our annual corporate picnic at Whoopee World in July.

I would like to receive a price quote that includes use of the picnic area at the park plus group admission passes for 150 to 200 guests. We plan to contract with an outside provider for food.

Our preferred date for the picnic is Sunday, July 23. Please advise.

Sincerely,
Sylvia Carroll, Director of Human Resources
Diamond Music Hall

Agreeing to corporate picnic contract

Robert Staples
Corporate Pavilion Manager
Whoopee World Amusement Park
Lansingtown, OH

Dear Mr. Staples:

Thank you for your prompt response to my inquiry about use of the corporate picnic area at Whoopee World Amusement Park. We would like to schedule our company outing for Sunday, July 23, from noon to 10 P.M.

Based on the terms in your letter, we agree that the cost of the use of the picnic area will be $250, and we will purchase 200 day passes to the park at $22 each. Enclosed is a check in the amount of $4,650, representing the picnic area fee plus the cost of passes. You have agreed to buy back any unused day passes at the purchase price.

We look forward to our day at the park.

Sincerely,
Sylvia Carroll, Director of Human Resources
Diamond Music Hall

Request for long distance service analysis

Geraldine Dodd, New Accounts Manager
Teletalk Communications
Bigtown, NY

Dear Ms. Dodd:

Thank you for your call yesterday offering to analyze the long distance phone bill for Diamond Music Hall to find out whether your company can offer us significant savings. I am enclosing the most recent long distance telephone bill from our current provider.

I look forward to seeing your analysis and other information about the services offered by your company, as well as a full listing of fees.

Sincerely,
John Diamond
President
Diamond Music Hall

Asking for proposal for corporate cell phone account

A.G. Belle, Account Executive
NewtalkDigital Communications
Bigtown, NY

Dear Ms. Belle:

We are considering issuing cellular phones to our sales staff when they are out on the road. I would like to receive a proposal to provide six phones.

We would like to pool all available minutes. I understand that your company's system includes unlimited calls among our group of phones without additional charge.

Please advise about available plans.

Sincerely,
John Diamond
President
Diamond Music Hall

Seeking bid for payroll services

Hugh Flote
Paydirt Payroll Services
Bigtown, NY

Dear Mr. Flote:

I am writing to solicit a bid from your company for payroll services for our retail store. We employ about thirty people, with a biweekly payroll of more than $50,000.

We would like to begin payroll services with checks due Thursday, July 6, 20xx.

Sincerely,
John Diamond
President
Diamond Music Hall

Seeking bids for catering of annual meeting

Janette Jean
Janette's Catering Service
Smalltown, OH

Dear Ms. Jean:

Diamond Music Hall will have its annual meeting on Thursday, January 29. We are presently taking bids for the luncheon, which will be served in our conference room at 12:30 P.M. that day.

We are looking for a buffet meal for fifty guests. We would like hot chicken, fish, and beef dishes, plus three cold salads. There should be two dessert offerings, plus coffee. We will supply cold drinks.

If you are interested in bidding, please provide us with a sample menu and the cost per person.

Sincerely,
Sylvia Carroll, Director of Human Resources
Diamond Music Hall

Accepting bid for catering of annual meeting

Janette Jean
Janette's Catering Service
Smalltown, OH

Dear Ms. Jean:

We would like to engage your company to cater the annual meeting of Diamond Music Hall on Thursday, January 29.

Based on your bid, we will pay $7.75 per person. We have selected three hot dishes, three cold salads, and tiramisu for dessert from your menu; they are circled on the proposed menu, which is attached to this letter.

The conference room will be available for setup at 11:30 A.M. Guests will arrive for lunch at 12:30 P.M. and depart by 1:30 P.M.

Thank you.

Sincerely,
Sylvia Carroll
Director of Human Resources

Asking photographer to take passport photos at senior center

Jason Bradley
Bradley Photographers
Smalltown, OH

Dear Mr. Bradley:

The Smalltown Senior Center is sponsoring a trip to London this fall. We anticipate that about eighty of our members will sign up for the trip, and many of them will need to update their passports.

Would you be able to come to the center to take passport photos sometime in the next two weeks? If so, please give us a per-person price for the photography session.

We look forward to hearing from you soon.

Sincerely,
Harold Diamond

Engaging photographer to take passport photos at senior center

Jason Bradley
Bradley Photographers
Smalltown, OH

Dear Mr. Bradley:

Thank you for your bid for passport photography at the Smalltown Senior Center. We accept your price of $8.50 per person. We estimate that fifty to seventy sittings will be required.

We would like to schedule the photography session for Saturday, June 5, from noon to 5 P.M.

We will reserve the large conference room at the center. Per your needs it includes sufficient electrical power for your equipment and space to set up the camera and posing stool.

We look forward to seeing you then.

Sincerely,
Harold Diamond

Notice to customers of change in address

Dear Customers:

As part of the redevelopment of downtown, the city clerk has changed our mailing address. Please send all payments and other communications to:

Diamond Music Hall
1 Sixth Avenue
Smalltown, OH 45601

Please note that we're still in the same old place: Main Street at Sixth Avenue. We'd love to see our regular customers and new visitors anytime. Bring in this letter and we'll have a special gift for you.

Sincerely,
John Diamond
President
Diamond Music Hall

Notice to suppliers of change in shipping address

Dear Suppliers:

Please update your records for the mailing address for statements, invoices, and other communications:

Diamond Music Hall
1 Sixth Avenue
Smalltown, OH 45601

Our physical address for shipments and sales calls remains unchanged:

Diamond Music Hall
Main Street and Sixth Avenue
Smalltown, OH 45601
Thank you.

John Diamond, President
Diamond Music Hall

62 Family Newsletter

Dear Friends:

The past year has been a very busy and hectic one for the extended Diamond and Miller families.

As always, we have experienced our share of ups and downs in the past twelve months, but in the end we are thankful that we are still together and growing.

Please allow me to share some of our memories.

Morgan, our eldest daughter, became Morgan Diamond Hamilton this past May. Her husband (we're still trying to get used to that concept) is a fine young man. He is the director of the physical therapy department at Smalltown General Hospital. Morgan works part-time in the hospital lab, and she entered graduate school in the fall.

Our eldest son, Michael, moved from Smalltown a hundred miles east to Fairview, Pennsylvania, with his wife, Karen, and our two precious grandchildren, Brian and Hanna. We miss them very much but understand that Michael's new job at Moneysworth Investment Group represents a tremendous opportunity.

Karen has a new job as a designer for Klein Graphics in Fairview, and they have been very good about letting her work from home for part of the week.

Joshua, our younger son, graduated with honors in June from Smalltown University and is now attending Smalltown University School of Law. He has moved into his own apartment. I've promised not to visit too often with care packages of food, and I've learned not to ask about the pizza boxes in the kitchen and what looked like an extra toothbrush in the bathroom.

Joshua had a close call this past spring in a multicar accident, but we are thankful he only suffered minor injuries.

And the last of our college tuition commitments, Heather, graduated in June from Smalltown High School. She has begun her studies at Smalltown University.

I guess that officially leaves us with an empty nest, although we're lucky to see our kids and our grandkids as often as their busy schedules allow.

John, of course, is still happily ensconced as head of the burgeoning empire of Diamond Music Hall on Main Street here in Smalltown. They are outfitting school orchestras and bands, rock and roll groups, and kazoo players all across the Midwest.

I am still at Smalltown Community College, head of the political science department.

John and I somehow found the time to break away from the madness and go on a cruise in August, going transatlantic from Dublin to New York by way of Iceland and Newfoundland. It was wonderful, and I am ready to come over with our photo album on a moment's notice.

John's parents, Harold and Monica, are thriving in their retirement. They seem to have more energy than either of us for their church, senior activities, and cultural pursuits.

My parents, Ron and Emma Miller, made the big step of selling their house and moving into an apartment complex. My mother's spirits are still high, despite a few setbacks that have parked her in a wheelchair. My father is editor of their senior complex's newsletter; I guess you just can't keep an old newspaperman away from the keyboard.

My brother, Al, has made some very positive steps in his life and was just promoted to a marketing position at Home Station Hardware after he made some very much appreciated innovations at the local store.

Most important, we are all together, a bit older but ready to tackle another year with all its challenges.

We wish you all a Merry Christmas, Happy Hanukkah, and extend our best wishes for a healthy, happy, and prosperous new year.

Love,
Laura Diamond

The End

Dear Reader:

Thank you for buying this book. This is the final letter we've written.

We hope we've been of help to you in crafting your own communications, and that along the way you've enjoyed your peek into the world of the Diamonds, Millers, friends, family, and businesspeople of Smalltown and Fairview.

We would be happy to receive comments and suggestions for new letters. If you'd like to write us a letter (what an idea!) please send it to us at:

Corey Sandler and Janice Keefe
Word Association, Inc.
P.O. Box 2779
Nantucket, MA 02584

If you'd like a reply, please include a stamped, self-addressed envelope.

You can also communicate with us via e-mail. To reach us, send messages to:

info@econoguide.com

Our Web site is:

www.econoguide.com

We look forward to hearing from you.

Sincerely,
The Authors

Index

A

D

E

F

J

T

U

V

W